THE GOOD HOUSEKEEPING BOOK OF THE HOME

THE GOOD HOUSEKEEPING BOOK OF THE HOME

Contributors:
Cassandra Kent • Shirley Green • Elizabeth Martyn • Susanna Tee • Sarah Graham

Consultant: Diana Austen

First published in hardback by
Octopus Books Limited
59 Grosvenor Street
London W1X 9DA
and
Ebury Press
National Magazine House
72 Broadwick Street
London W1V 2BP

This edition published in 1985

ISBN 0 86273 236 0

Printed in Hong Kong

PREFACE

The Good Housekeeping Book of the Home is a book for everyone – whether they are buying for the first time, renting or just moving onwards and upwards on the housing spiral. It's full of helpful advice on choosing a place and raising the money for it, gives sound counsel on essentials like rewiring, plumbing, painting, papering and curtain making, and is rich with imaginative and original ideas for decorating. Whether your taste is for a pretty, cottagey effect or for uncluttered high tech, here is information on how to achieve it, backed up by over 200 photographs to give you inspiration.

This is a realistic book. It faces the fact that some people prefer to pay professionals rather than do things themselves. It recognizes that people on tight budgets need greater ingenuity than those with a little extra cash. It guides you in making choices for *your* kind of lifestyle. Do you need a dishwasher? Is an open-plan kitchen better suited to your family and entertaining needs than a formal dining room?

Good Housekeeping experts know that people alter with time. Tastes and incomes may change, so home making needs to be flexible, with scope for improvement and alteration when it's required or can be afforded. Today, the choice of home style, furnishing and decoration is enormous, as the property pages of any newspaper and the proliferation of department stores show. Unless you are lucky enough to know exactly what you want and how to achieve it, you'll welcome help in transforming the bare bones of a dwelling into a home you want to live in. So use *The Good Housekeeping Book of the Home* as a wise friend, generous with ideas and suggestions. Unlike most in this busy world, it will always be at hand when most needed.

CONTENTS

PART I. HOUSE INTO HOME: THE ESSENTIAL GUIDE

CHAPTER 1. CHECKPOINT FOR SURVIVAL

CONTENTS

CONTENTS

CHAPTER 4. ENTERTAINING: HOST AND HOSTESS AT HOME

CONTENTS

PART II. THE GREEN HOUSE: PLANTS INSIDE AND OUT

PART ONE

House Into Home: The Essential Guide

CHAPTER ONE

CHECKPOINT FOR SURVIVAL

ASSESSING YOUR NEEDS

Setting up home for the first time can be a daunting project. Make sure you plan *before* you move.

Most of us take it for granted that we have a roof over our heads – first the parental home, then college or university and, perhaps finally, a rented flat – and don't worry too much about how we would set about buying a home of our own. It sounds easy in theory and, of course, lots of people do it. But when it comes down to the actual practicalities of finding a place, buying it and moving in, you do need to know what you are doing or you could find yourself spending a great deal of money and finishing up with something you don't really like. This book is designed to guide you through the possible pitfalls and to help you end up with a home which represents value for money and reflects your personality.

The most important consideration for your first home is how long you plan to stay there. This will dictate what you buy and what you do to it. If you plan to stay only a short time – perhaps one to three years – it's probably sensible to buy something that's modern, in reasonably good condition so you don't have to spend a lot of money and effort improving it, and in an area where you know prices are rising so that you will have some extra money in hand when it comes to buying your next property.

If you are planning on a medium-term stay of, say, five to eight years, you'll have time to tackle fairly major improvements. You will be able to buy somewhere that needs doing up secure in the knowledge that you can take time over it when energy and finances allow. Most people today tend to move every eight to ten years, as their housing needs change or work dictates. A few people do manage to put down roots and stay in a home for ten, twenty, even thirty years. If you think you're one of these people, it's obviously worth hanging on and finding your dream house first time round. However, remember the search may take you a long time, so it could be worth taking the short-term option of buying a stop-gap that is easy to sell, to give yourself time to find a property that is *exactly* right for your long-term needs.

Bear in mind, too, that to make a real home you need possessions as well as the right structure. Some people go through life buying ever bigger and more expensive houses which they do up and sell at a profit but never have anywhere that looks and feels like a real home when they are in it. Life gets more expensive as time goes by, especially in families with children, so it's a good idea to spend your early home-making days buying beautiful things that will always give you pleasure, whatever setting you put them in. Further on in this book are lots of ideas for both portable and permanent furniture and furnishings.

HOUSE VERSUS FLAT

Deciding whether to buy a house or a flat will be dictated by their availability in your price range and what you want from your new home. Flats are usually easy to resell and may – if they are not on a ground floor – be more secure from break-in than houses. However, flats in purpose-built blocks often carry heavy charges for services such as removal of rubbish and a porter who looks after the entrance hall. Flat owners usually have no control over the size of the service charge and, although it may seem reasonable when you buy, it may increase annually and turn out to be very expensive within three or four years. There is also the question of maintaining the exterior and services of the block, which have to be done at specified intervals. These may occur when you don't have the money. In a house you have no service charge and can yourself decide when to repair the roof or renew the drainpipes.

That said, flats are good places for setting up home for the first time if you want somewhere that is easy to run and doesn't require much maintenance. You won't have a garden of your own, but there may be a communal one which is kept tidy through the service charge. Houses require more maintenance and you will have to do what gardening is necessary.

HOW MUCH SHOULD YOU SPEND?

Unless you are fortunate enough to own a large amount of capital, you are going to have to borrow money to buy your new home. Most people have mortgages through building societies, usually with a society with whom they have been saving money for some time. Mortgages are also increasingly available from banks and, in smaller numbers, from insurance companies and finance houses. You can approach your building society (or societies) and bank yourself to see what sort of a mortgage they are prepared to give you, or you can employ a mortgage broker or insurance broker to find one for you. There are different types of mortgage: with a repayment mortgage you borrow the money you need and every month for the period of the loan you pay the same sum (subject to fluctuations in the interest rate). This means that initially you are paying off the interest and only after a few years do you start to pay off the capital sum, so if you end the mortgage or want to change it after a few

Above: town end of terrace or idyllic country cottage (right) could both be first time buys. Which you choose will depend on the kind of life you lead, where you work and what sort of transport is available.

Above: this terraced cottage is built of granite blocks and fronts directly on to the street. Cheerful blue-painted door and windows and flourishing window boxes make it stand out

years you won't have paid off much of the sum you originally borrowed. However, the interest on a repayment mortgage is tax free up to £30,000, so in the early years when you are paying it off you benefit from this tax relief.

The option repayment mortgage is intended to help people who pay no or little income tax and thus won't benefit from tax relief. It is similar to a standard repayment mortgage except that you pay less in the early years and more later when you have, hopefully, reached a higher tax level.

With an endowment mortgage you pay more each month but the loan is linked to an endowment assurance scheme. When the endowment policy into which you are paying matures, you use the sum you receive to pay off the capital of the loan in a single payment. This is a good scheme for people who pay a lot of tax as all the monthly repayments are either an assurance premium (which, if taken out before 14 March 1984 attracted a reduced rate of tax), or interest, which is subject to full tax relief.

There are various types of endowment mortgage: 'without profits' gives you just the amount of money you need to pay off the money you borrowed to buy your home. A 'with profits' mortgage will give you more than you need, and so leave some capital in hand. With a 'low-cost with profits' endowment mortgage you get a sum of money somewhere between the other two. Because this is all fairly complicated it is sensible to take professional advice from a building society or your bank manager on which would be the most suitable type for you – bearing in mind your particular financial circumstances.

In general, you can obtain a mortgage for two-and-a-half times the main breadwinner's salary plus a proportion of the other partner's salary. This, plus the amount of money you are prepared to put down as a deposit (only in certain circumstances will you be able to obtain a 100 per cent mortgage: 90 or 95 per cent is more usual) gives you an idea of the price you can afford for your property.

However, it may not be sensible to spend up to the maximum if you think that it is going to leave you short of cash each month. You *must* make regular payments of the mortgage, otherwise the organization who has granted it may foreclose on you. Work out, with help if necessary, what your outgoings will be on the sum you think you need to borrow.

Then look at what is left over each month and ask yourself if you will (a) have enough to live on after you have paid up and (b) be able to do any home improvements or decorating that you may want to the new home.

WHERE SHOULD YOU LOOK?

Deciding on the area you want to live in isn't easy. You may be restricted to fairly small areas because of where you work or because of transport, or you may be able to choose over a wide spectrum.

Assuming you have some degree of choice there are a number of points to consider before you start hunting in earnest. Town or country is the first decision and will probably depend on where, and what hours, you work. Towns are busy and noisy but do offer a variety of people within easy reach and usually have lots of cinemas, theatres, galleries, colleges of further education where you can do evening classes, and good shops. The country is quieter and, in many people's eyes, more pleasant. But you may end up either miles from anyone or in a community where there are few people with whom you have anything in common. Going out anywhere can be a major expedition, a family or couple could need two cars for getting around conveniently. So before opting for that sweet country cottage you have always wanted think carefully about what you really need. Is transport to work and other activities easy? You may think that the peace of rural weekends compensates for hours of travelling to and from work, often in wet and wintry conditions and entirely – in fare terms – at the mercy of whatever price rises are decreed. But the reality could mean that you are too tired at weekends to do anything more than sleep off the exhaustion of the week. In that case you might as well live nearer to work and take trips to the country when you have the time and energy to enjoy them.

Friends are important, particularly where one partner eventually stays at home with small children. If you move to an area where you know no one you could find you have chosen somewhere where the community is mainly retired, or consists entirely of families with children and has none of the culture and nightlife you enjoy.

Look at an area's amenities. Do you crave a good library, a superstore, tennis courts or rare films? Find out what is available *before* you buy.

Plans for development

Take particular care to find out if there are any local authority plans to change the area in any way. When buying your property, whoever is conveyancing for you should tell you about any schemes which directly affect it. How would you feel if the house next door was pulled down and a block of flats erected in its place? But they won't tell you that they are putting up a new school only a couple of miles away or running a motorway nearby after five years. These are things you should investigate yourself, since they could well affect your decision to live in a particular place.

Looking around

Get as large-scale a map as you can of the area or areas you are planning to look in and draw a line round the districts you want to look at. Buy the local papers for those areas each week or arrange to have them posted to you on the day they come out. Take national papers which have good property columns. Finally, arrange to have your name and requirements put on the lists of all the estate agents operating in the areas.

Unless you are very specific about what sort of property you want, try not to be too rigid in your thinking. There are plenty of people around who were convinced they wanted to live in a Victorian cottage but who are perfectly happy in a modern house which incorporates all the space and facilities they needed. You may be determined to have two bathrooms, or space you can use as a study. The more flexible you can be, however, the better chance you have of finding something that you really like that is either in good condition or has scope for development.

Estate agents will bombard you with details of properties, some of which may well not be what you are looking for. Go through the descriptions carefully and also study the local papers' property sales advertisements with care. Many of the latter will be private sales so you will need to telephone the owners to arrange to look round their house or flat. With estate agents you will usually be shown round by a member of the agency staff.

Before looking at any property you need to make a list of questions that you will ask either the agent or the owner. Be sure to take something on which you can write down the answers. You will also need a 10-metre steel tape in order to check any measurements in the house that might cause problems with items of furniture you already own. Measure these and write the dimensions in your diary or somewhere handy so that you can check on the spot whether your refectory table or extra wide cooker will fit into the space available.

When you have checked out the measurements sit down with the agent or owner while you are still in the place and ask about running costs. You need to know what the rates are, how much they have spent on heating in the past year (ask to see the bills), what money they have spent on maintenance or upkeep recently, what sort of insulation they have and – in a flat – what the current service charge is and how much it has gone up in the past few years.

Sitting down like this may also give you a chance to find out what they undoubtedly won't tell you, which is whether the noise from the street is bad (heavy lorries, nearby traffic lights, music from a boutique) and whether the neighbours can be heard through the walls. Noise can be one of the hardest things to live with and one of the most difficult to eradicate so the more you can find out about it the better.

Look at the property carefully from the outside as well as inside. Although you will obviously have the place surveyed (see page 16), you can be sure that things like missing roof tiles, damaged gutters and rotting external woodwork will mean trouble and expense at some point. You may not mind this, and it may indeed be a lever you can use to get the price reduced, but it's certainly something to take into account.

Indoors, check the number of power points and find out when the wiring was last checked or renewed. Find out how old the central heating boiler is. Ask as much as you can about the general condition of the place and make notes. If you are looking at a lot of properties it's very easy to get confused; when you are back at base it's difficult to remember what was said at each one. Don't worry about the decoration of a place since this is something that is relatively quick, cheap and easy to alter. And don't, while you are looking round, utter cries of 'We could knock that wall down' or 'We could rip that unit out'. Save that till you get home. People are usually proud of their homes and have put effort into making them the way they like. It's disheartening for them to think that all their hard work is going to be undone by the incoming owner. It could mean they take a dislike to you and prefer another buyer in the instance of receiving two similar, simultaneous offers.

MAKING AN OFFER

Making an offer – although it may feel one of the most momentous decisions of your life – is actually extremely simple. All you do is inform the owner or estate agent how much you are prepared to offer for the property, subject to contract. (This phrase, whether spoken or written, means that, if you have to drop out because you just can't find the money or discover there is something wrong with the place you are not bound by a contract at this stage.) If the owner accepts your offer, you must then tell the estate agent

Above: modern brick terraced house is fully double glazed to cut out traffic noise and is designed to be easily run – ideal for a first home where both partners work. *Below:* an Edwardian terrace offers scope inside for knocking small rooms into larger ones and comes with a lot of original features in the shape of cornices, dadoes and picture rails

or solicitor who will be doing the conveyancing (see below) and put down a small deposit – £50 will usually do – either with the estage agent or with the seller's solicitor. Mark your cheque with the words 'as stakeholder' to ensure that the money is kept separately from the general financial affairs of the solicitor or estate agent.

SURVEYING THE STRUCTURE

The organization from which you are borrowing the money to buy your home will insist that it is surveyed professionally. This is merely to assure themselves that the property is worth the money they are lending, so that – in the event of your not keeping up with the mortgage payments – they have a guarantee that they can sell the place for the amount you have borrowed.

You will, however, need an additional survey to alert you to any defects in the structure which might make you decide either to withdraw from buying it or to persuade the seller to reduce the price because of the work needed on it.

You should always use a surveyor who is qualified and a member either of the Royal Institution of Chartered Surveyors (FRICS or ARICS) or of the Incorporated Society of Valuers and Auctioneers (FIAS or AIAS). The head offices of the organizations will supply a list of their members in your area.

Surveyors' fees are not fixed and will depend on the amount of work involved in inspecting the property and producing a report. On older houses the cost is considerably more than on recently built ones. If you are happy about the property you are buying and don't want a full structural survey, you can use the Society of Valuers and Auctioneers' Home Buyers' Standard Valuation and Survey Report which gives a general description of the condition of the property and pinpoints any major defects and areas which need repair. You can ask whoever is providing your mortgage whether the ISVA Standard Valuation and Survey Report will be acceptable to them. If so, it can save you the cost of their surveyor's report. However, on property where you feel a full survey is necessary, discuss with the surveyor exactly what needs to be done. Be sure to give him/her enough time to inspect the property and produce a report (usually about 10 days). If you are in a contract race with another person it may be difficult to get the survey completed on time.

A full survey will cover all the accessible parts of the building, together with the surveyor's opinion on the parts he can't see – for example, floors covered with fitted carpets. If repair work is needed, a surveyor should be able to give you some idea of how much the repairs will cost so that you can discuss the matter with the seller. The surveyor may well be able to recommend builders and specialist firms which can deal with problems like drainage and woodworm.

MAKING A CONTRACT

The contract is the document which makes the property you are buying yours. You may get a solicitor to draw it up, use a conveyancing shop or do it yourself. Solicitors have, until recently, been the usual people through whom to purchase but legislation now allows for conveyancing organizations to be set up to do the job at less cost. You save still more money if you do it yourself, but to carry out all the searches necessary and to be sure that the final documents you produce are correct takes a lot of time and effort. With most properties – except those hedged about with arcane restrictions and problems – it is possible for a layman to carry out the conveyancing, but for most people the amount of work involved makes it more attractive to pay a professional.

Note that the fee you pay the conveyancer is not the end of the matter. Land Registry fees are due on property on registered land to cover the cost of changing the facts on the Register. The cost of this is usually around ¼ per cent of the price of the property. Stamp duty is a tax on the sale of houses above a certain price. At present it stands at 1 per cent of the purchase price on all houses or flats costing over £30,000.

A solicitor's charge for doing the whole conveyancing job will be based on

Top: double-fronted Victorian house has symmetrical windows and a neat garden front and back.
Above: as a complete contrast to the house above, this modern brick design has a futuristic shape, different-sized windows and is built with living space upstairs and sleeping space down

Right: this modern house disguises its fairly stark appearance with a covering of creeper. All the windows are double glazed and the high brick wall surrounding it ensures privacy in the well-stocked garden

the amount of work involved but should not be more than about 1 per cent of the cost of the property plus VAT. Different solicitors may charge different amounts (there is no fixed scale), so ask for an estimate of the likely charge after you have discussed the work involved.

Once your solicitor and the seller's solicitor have agreed the details of the contracts, these are then exchanged. Both you and the seller receive a copy, which you sign. You then pay a deposit of 10 per cent of the cost of the property, less any stakeholder money you lodged with the estate agent. At this stage you are bound to buy the property or lose your deposit and the seller is bound to sell it to you and not to increase the price.

The final stage in the purchase is completion day, when you get the keys of the house and any documents connected with it. You don't usually see the deeds of the house as these are retained by the organization supplying your mortgage, but it can be seen on request.

The time between exchanging contracts and completion can be fairly short if you have sorted out the availability of the mortgage in advance.

The procedure for buying houses in Scotland differs from that described above, which applies only to buying property in England and Wales; many people think the Scottish system is simpler. It is described in detail in a booklet. *Buying or Selling a House?*, free with SAE to the Law Society of Scotland.

MOVING IN

Once you have completed conveyancing, you can move into the property. If it is your first home you may not have very many possessions – in this case the cheapest solution is to do it yourself with a hired van and some strong friends. If, however, you have a lot of possessions or own items which are heavy, awkwardly-shaped or valuable, it is more sensible to employ a firm of removers experienced at manoeuvring through narrow doors and windows and up flights of stairs.

Use a firm which is a member of the British Association of Removers and get estimates from three different firms as charges vary widely depending on how busy a firm is, how convenient your removal is and whether – with a fairly small number of possessions – yours can be tucked into part of a van which is moving house for someone else. The BAR will supply a list of member firms in your area. One of the best sources of general information on moving is The Good Housekeeping Institute. Their booklets are a mine of constructive advice.

Home Improvements – DIY and Professional

A man's home is his castle. That goes for women too. But sometimes even a castle needs another room.

The cost of moving home is so high nowadays that it's often cheaper – and causes less upheaval – to modify your home and, perhaps, extend it in order to produce the kind of living space you need.

Improving your home will also add to its value, although the more expensive extensions and additions may fail to produce the amount they cost you when it comes to selling.

So think carefully about the improvements you make. If you are in short-term property, go for those which will definitely increase the sale value of your home. If you plan to stay for many years, carry out those improvements which will add to the quality of your life in the property and don't worry too much about whether you will get your full money back on them.

THINGS WORTH DOING

Central heating and good insulation are always worth installing. People like to be warm but don't want to spend more than they need on doing so. A well-designed central heating system will run economically and good basic insulation will prevent the heat it generates from being lost or wasted (see also page 44).

Putting the basic fabric of a place into good condition is an important improvement and one that should be done

Above: a fully fitted kitchen will add to the value of your home. For this one, an extension has been built which links it with the dining area (*right*) which, in its turn, looks out on to a pretty walled garden and has a skylight ceiling to let in maximum light and sunshine. The neutral colours of this kitchen/diner can be used to set off flowers and foliage and acts as an uncompetitive setting for a variety of china and glass. Foldaway chairs round the table can be stacked away and the table itself pushed against the wall when not in use

before you start decorating or you could find you damage your work and have to do it again. Get rid of woodworm, dry rot and damp as soon as possible. Most reputable firms will give long guarantees – often 20 years – on their work and will allow you to transfer the guarantee to the next owner when you move. Check this before you use a particular firm.

Rewiring is a sensible safety precaution and designing the wiring system yourself means that you can site socket outlets where you want them and make sure that you have plenty in the kitchen and living room. Don't install it unless you are competent – use a qualified electrician. If you are not sure about the condition of the wiring in your new home, it's worth paying for an inspection. You can arrange this through your local Electricity Board. It's worth asking the inspector if it's possible for you to put in more sockets if needed, and how much this will cost. It's fairly simple and cheap to turn single socket outlets into double ones. This gives you a lot more flexibility with lighting and using electrical appliances.

Above and right: another kitchen/diner, this time in a Victorian house where the original double doors between the two rooms have been removed. The retention of the original wooden fireplace and mirror above it play down the utilitarian aspect of the rooms and give them a warm, lived-in atmosphere. Strategically hung prints decorate the U-shaped cooking area

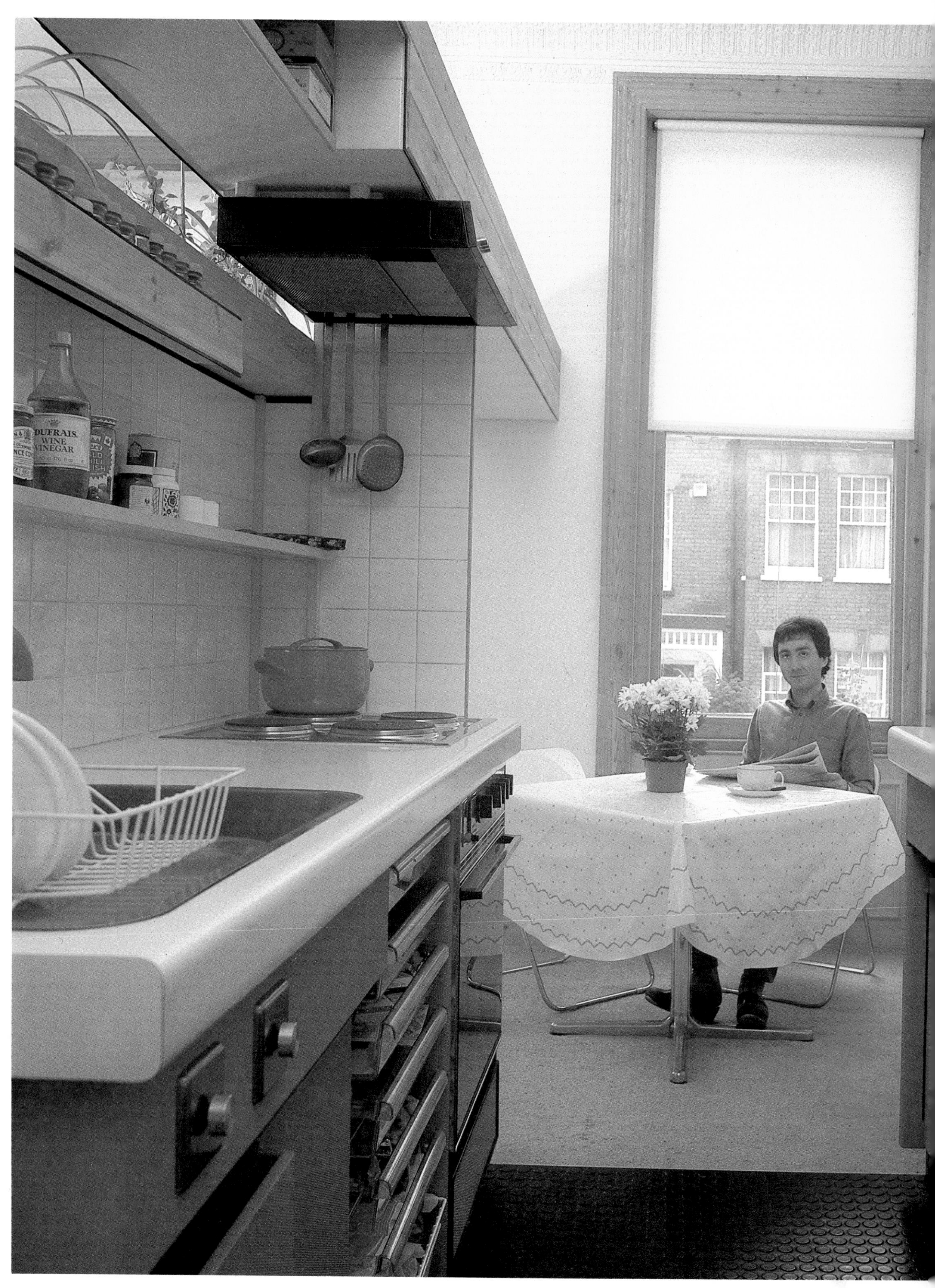
DUFRAIS
WINE
VINEGAR

Top: neat loft conversion has a bedroom in the lower half with wooden open steps up to a galleried half area
Above: a compact bathroom fits into the sloping roof area and is giving a feeling of space by the large skylight/window and diagonal tongue-and-groove boarding in red and blue

Left: here a kitchen has been constructed at the end of a large room by putting up a false wall. This finishes below ceiling height to leave the magnificent cornice both intact and visible

When selling a place, first impressions often stick in the mind, so get the front of your property into good order with a well-painted front door with attractive door furniture, a clean undamaged doorstep and path and, where there is one, a neat front garden. You probably don't think much about the front of your house as you walk through the door, but would-be purchasers will be put off by peeling paint and fifty milk bottles on the step.

Doing up the kitchen and bathroom is a good selling point but expensive. If you can't afford to do this really well it's probably better to live with what is there and let your purchasers spend the money.

Put down good flooring in fairly neutral colours (see Chapter 2). Flooring is an expensive item and if you can include well laid, easy to clean carpet, wood, cork or other flooring, your buyers will feel they are getting a bargain.

THINGS NOT WORTH DOING

Double glazing takes a long time to pay for itself – the Department of Energy reckons around 25 years. Do-it-yourself double glazing is cheap and efficient but doesn't always look good. Only install professional double glazing if you have to replace rotting windows anyway (the difference between single and double glazing in this instance isn't that great), if the property is so exposed that you are losing a lot of heat through glass, or if you are on a busy main road that is noisy.

Fixtures and fittings have to be left when you sell a place. Things like kitchen units, built-in cupboards, a built-on greenhouse or sun room may not raise the value of your home enough to justify their installation. Think carefully about spending money on them in short-term accommodation; you might do better buying things you can take with you when you move on.

THINKING AHEAD

Buying to sell within a few years is a perfectly sensible way of moving yourself up the home buyers' ladder until you reach the kind of place you want to remain in. Be careful, though, not to get so carried away by the idea of doing up tatty properties and selling for a huge profit that you improve them beyond their locality. While some areas change their ownership profile fairly quickly others can take years to gain a new image – indeed, they may never do so. If you are in a first home the chances are that you will expect to sell it to another first time buyer who won't be able to afford what you are asking or who may prefer to look for a more basic house in a better area for the same price. Keep your home improvements to a level which sit comfortably in the area and save your fantasies about whirlpool baths and snooker room extensions until you get into an area where they fit.

MAJOR IMPROVEMENTS

Altering the structure of your home is an excellent idea if you plan to stay there long enough to enjoy it. In most homes there is quite a lot of scope for changing things and this section suggests some of the most common. The first thing is to think flexibly about the way you live in the place. Conventional wisdom has it that in two- or more storey houses you live at the bottom and sleep at the top. This may mean that you don't get the best from the size of the rooms and the light. For example, it makes far more sense to sleep in a darkish basement since you are only there at night and to site living rooms and kitchen somewhere where you will benefit from natural daylight and perhaps a view. If you have got huge bedrooms but only one bathroom, consider taking a corner of a bedroom and installing an en suite shower and loo. If the plumbing permits you can site a bath in a bedroom without putting any walls or partitions round it.

Extra loos can often be tucked into spaces like cupboards under stairs, and roof space can be used for all sorts of things from a study to a model railway room.

Knocking through

Where rooms are small and you want more space it is usually possible to knock down a wall between two rooms and create a larger one. Don't do this without taking advice from an architect or surveyor unless you are very confident of your structural knowledge. Where a wall is load bearing – *i.e.* holds up part of the rest of the house – you will need to install a special beam to perform its function in its absence. Even where a wall is not load bearing, its removal may affect the surrounding rooms and some form of reinforcement may need to be put in.

Splitting up

In converse cases, where rooms are large and you want to divide them, you must put up some form of partition. This can be done in a number of ways. If you are merely putting in a unit to separate a kitchen from a dining area or a study from a living area this is fairly straightforward and certainly something you can do yourself if you want to.

If you are in fact creating two proper rooms out of one, you will have to comply with the Building Regulations which dictate what is needed in the way of opening windows and ventilation. You will probably lose quite a lot of space in creating access to the two rooms. If you are, for example, putting a child's bedroom next to a living room, make sure that the partition is sufficiently thick to provide good sound insulation.

Loft conversions

Lofts may seem quite small as you creep around, taking care not to put your foot through the space between the joists. But they can provide quite large rooms when converted. However, it is vital to take professional advice on whether your loft is suitable for conversion, what sort of conversion you should have and what it will cost. No loft conversion is cheap but it does have the advantage of giving you extra space without affecting the rest of the house apart from the spot on the floor below where the staircase giving access to the conversion will be sited.

There are a number of firms who provide a kind of 'kit' loft conversion. They will come and discuss the job with you, draw up the plans and submit them to the local authority and then deal with all the work. Provided your loft and the conversion you require are reasonably conventional, there is no reason why you shouldn't use one of these firms. Go for one with a good track record that has been around for some time. There are plenty of cowboys in the loft conversion business who either fail to complete the job properly or are not in business any more when any problems arise. When getting quotes, ask the firms if you can see an example of their work. Get two or three estimates, as these can vary considerably, and check exactly what each covers, looking especially carefully at the clauses about insurance. In general, specialist loft conversion firms will complete the work quite quickly since, unlike ordinary builders, this is the only type of job they do and the more conversions they complete, the more money they make.

Agree everything with them in writing, including the size and frequency of the stage payments you will have to make. Withhold a few hundred pounds when the job is completed and pay it when, after a period of six weeks or so, you are satisfied that the work has been done to your satisfaction.

If you are going to organize the loft conversion yourself – and even *do* it yourself – you must take advice from an architect, surveyor or structural engineer. You will have to submit plans to the local authority and these must be properly drawn, usually a job for an expert. The work will have to comply with the Building Regulations and it is possible in certain circumstances that you will need planning

permission. A professional will be able to advise you about this.

Access and ventilation are two important things to consider with a loft conversion. There are strict regulations about how high the roof, or part of it, must be. In England and Wales the Building Regulations insist that at least half the floor area of the conversion has a ceiling of more than 2.3 metres (7 ft 6 in) from the finished floor level and there are similar regulations in Scotland.

Left: glass extension to living becomes almost part of the tree-lined garden. White storage units keep it light and bright

Below: view of the extension from the original small living room

Because you are adding another storey to your home there are Fire Regulations to which you must adhere. This may mean installing fire doors and fitting self-closing hinges to existing doors in your home, and the building inspector who will look at the work while it is in progress will insist that all the precautions are taken.

Unless you have the time and knowledge to supervise the work yourself it is probably best to ask an architect, surveyor or structural engineer to do this for you. They will work either on an agreed fee or on a percentage of the total cost of the work. But for most people this is money well spent.

On a conversion where you are subcontracting work to a number of different firms – builders, plumbers, electricians and decorators – it can be difficult to co-ordinate their activities and ensure that the work progresses smoothly. Paying someone to do this for you is a sensible idea and should mean that the job doesn't involve endless delays, leaving you with rubble in the garden, newspaper over the lower reaches of the house and only polythene between you and the elements when the roof is opened up and taken off.

Work out the services you will need in your loft conversion. Electricity is obviously necessary for light but it wouldn't be worth taking gas up, even if you plan a cooking facility in it. Think carefully about how you will heat it; if it's not in regular use but is a spare bedroom or hobbies area, it's probably cheaper to install some form of electric spot heating rather than extend your central heating system.

If you are putting in a bathroom or toilet you will need to site these as directly above the plumbing on the floor below as possible.

HOME EXTENSIONS

Pushing out the boundaries of your home at ground level can produce either a full-size new room or an extension to an existing one. You may merely want to glass in your porch to give better heat insulation in your hall and provide somewhere to keep wellingtons and umbrellas, or you may fancy a full-scale conservatory leading off the patio doors at the back of the house. As with loft conversions you can in many instances buy a kit or arrange to have it built, or build it yourself from scratch.

Kit extensions

Prefabricated extension kits vary enormously. You can buy them for porches, sun rooms, conservatories and even solid-wall habitable rooms. They can be limiting in that they come in a set of standard designs which may or may not blend in with the existing fabric of your house. Their advantage is that you get all the parts needed to produce the end result – which you can either build yourself, pay a jobbing builder to do or pay the kit manufacturer's recommended agent to do.

With porches, sun rooms and conservatories, you will probably save money by using a kit rather than designing from scratch, but with solid-wall extensions you might well find it's cheaper to get one designed specifically for the kind of extension you want. Take advice from several kit firms and look through their brochures carefully. Ask if you can see a copy of the building instructions if you plan to do this yourself. As with so many self-assembly items, some come with excellent comprehensive instructions for the whole job while others are inadequate or baffling. Note that if you want a solid-wall extension you can only get kits for a single storey extension. If you want a two-storey one – and if you can afford it it's a good idea to do as much extending as you can in one fell swoop – you need to design it from scratch.

Built-on extensions

As with loft conversions it really *is* best to take some expert advice. When planning a major extension, there is a number of factors to take into account which a layman is likely to overlook.

If you are enlarging your home by more than 50 cubic metres – or 10 per cent of the cubic area up to a maximum of 115 cubic metres – you will need planning permission. You are not allowed to enlarge your home so that anything extends beyond the existing front, nor can you build anything higher than the existing roof without permission. Something like a kitchen extension with a roof garden on top may not entail application to the planning authority, but you would be well advised to visit your local authority planning office and discuss what you propose with the planning officer. He or she will be able to advise you on which regulations you need to observe and what you are likely to be permitted to do in the way of extension.

You next need – usually in conjunction with an architect or surveyor – to prepare detailed drawings of the planned extension and submit them to the council for consideration on planning permission and building regulations. You usually need to submit three copies, one of which is put on display in the public register for anyone to look at who thinks they might wish to lodge an objection. Some local authorities also publish details of proposed extensions in the local newspaper to alert people to proposals which the authorities think might affect them.

After this your plans will be considered by the council and, provided that the planning committee is happy with them and they are clearly and comprehensively set out, you should then receive permission to build. If a modification is required you will need to redraw or amend the plans and resubmit them to the next meeting of the council. This can all take time. There is little point in obtaining tenders from builders until the plans are finalized as modifications could affect the price. On *no* account begin work before the application has been accepted, or the local authority will have the right to insist that you put your property back into its original state.

Ask for quotations from three builders. If they vary widely, ask your architect or surveyor to check them over to see if there are major differences in what they are planning to do. Spending more money can sometimes save a lot of trouble and frustration. A builder who gives a very low quotation may decide halfway through building your extension that he must finish off one or two other jobs before completing yours. Accepting a higher quotation which carries a guarantee that work will be completed within a specified time may make your life a lot easier. Ensure that you ask for, and are given, a *quotation*, not just an estimate, before a builder begins work. An estimate is an approximate guide to what you can expect to pay, whereas once he has given you a quotation for the work, the builder is obliged to keep to the quote.

When you have picked a builder for the job and he has agreed, check his insurance. Then set out the ground rules in writing and insist that he provides a written agreement. *Omit this stage at your peril.* It's easy to think that a builder who says he has a team that can start next Monday but won't otherwise be free for three months is one you should seize, but if you have not got a written contractual agreement you could end up being sorry.

Ensure that the contract states when stage payments should be made – after specified parts of the work are completed – and insist that all the materials which the builder purchases for your job (and for which you will probably have to advance cash) are stored on your site and that you have receipts for them. This will prevent him using your money to buy materials for other jobs on which his firm is working.

GETTING GRANTS

There are a number of local authority grants available for certain home improvements. These include money for putting in a damp proof course, extending a tiny bathroom or kitchen and modernizing the electrical circuit. You can get some money towards repairs if your home was built before 1919 and requires substantial structural work. If the place has no fixed bath or shower, wash hand basin, sink or is lacking a hot and cold water supply to any of these you may also be eligible for a grant.

Apply to your local authority grants section for any money you think you may be eligible for and be prepared to spend a fair amount of time waiting for the wheels of bureaucracy to turn. After you have applied, someone from the council will come to inspect your property and will let you know what work you will have to do to be eligible for a grant. This may be rather more than you had originally imagined. If you need to draw up plans, you will have to pay for these yourself – and you may not get a grant in the end.

If you are successful, you can then get builders' estimates (you may need to contact a number of approved local builders) and only then, with full council approval, can you start the work involved.

RAISING CASH

If you are not eligible for a grant, or want to do more work than would be covered by one, you will probably need to borrow money. The building society with whom you have a mortgage may be prepared to top it up with a loan to cover your improvements, provided it is satisfied that they add value to the property. If your mortgage is with a bank it too may be prepared to top it up; if not, it may allow you a separate home improvement loan for a period of ten years or so. This will be a secured loan which means that your house or some major asset is used as collateral. Because this is a legal transaction, you will have to pay a charge for arranging it.

If you have no joy with either building society or bank, consider a finance house loan. Whichever option you choose for raising cash, go into it carefully. You don't want to find that you have cut down on happiness by extending your debts, as well as your house.

Right: bricks and mortar are a sound investment. Don't rush into home improvements without considering whether you are doing the best by your home and your finances.

DECORATING AND FURNISHING

Home decorating is an area where you really can save money and, with practice, achieve excellent results.

Advice on decorating techniques and on useful tools abound in books, magazines and decorating shops. Hardware shops, DIY superstores and builders' merchants are full, not just of equipment and materials, but a staff of people who can advise on what product is best for your needs. As with all manual skills, practice makes perfect and decorating is no exception. If you are a complete novice who has never so much as emulsioned a wall, *don't* start by tackling somewhere like the living room, where any mistakes or crookedly hung paper will stare back at you every time you enter. A small room, like a loo, or a little-used one, like a spare room, are the best places to get the feel of decorating and discover for yourself why the rules suggested later on in this section really are worth following.

PREPARING THE SURFACES

Preparation is the dull part of decorating. It must be done properly if you are to get good results, but it does take time and makes you feel you are getting nowhere when you are burning to start painting with that marvellous colour you have chosen or begin hanging the paper.

Even if the whole place needs redecorating, tackle just one room at a time. Preparation is messy and can be tiring. You need to know that there is somewhere you can sit down or sleep in comfort, somewhere you can cook and somewhere you can wash. If your whole home is a dusty morass of bare plaster and semi-stripped woodwork, you will never feel rested because you can't escape from it. If something urgent crops up at work, or you have family problems which mean you can't get on with your decorating, you could be living in bleak house for a long time. So, prepare one room, then decorate it and *finish* it before moving on to the next. If you don't make the effort to finish a room at the time you are doing the bulk of decorating, you could find you get used to its unfinished condition. You could live for years with no door handle or with masking tape round the edge of the window frame.

You need special tools for particular decorating jobs but, generally speaking, whatever work you are doing you will need protective clothing for yourself and something stable to stand on for getting to the areas you can't reach from the floor. Decorating may make you wet, sticky, dusty or paint-splashed depending on what you are doing. It also makes you hot. Either set aside an old T-shirt or two and some jeans that you don't care about and wear them, or invest in a coverall like a boiler suit which protects body, arms and legs. These are usually available from shops selling decorating materials.

For jobs like sanding and stripping you may want to protect your eyes and nose. Lightweight plastic goggles and face masks are available from DIY shops and could make the job more comfortable.

Don't tackle out of reach areas by perching a kitchen stool on a bed. If you are going to be doing a lot of decorating, you will need a sturdy step ladder which will also be useful for such things as getting into the loft space, dusting picture rails and changing light bulbs. For decorating purposes it's best to buy one with a platform on which you can balance paint tins, roller trays and other paraphernalia.

For less elevated jobs like painting picture rails, or wallpapering in a fairly low room, you can stand on a well-made step stool or a folding workbench. When painting ceilings, you will cover ground more quickly if you have two step ladders (this may entail borrowing one). Put a strong board across them so that you can move in a horizontal plane. This does tend to bounce a little and some people find it disconcerting but, if you get used to the motion, it will save time and can also be helpful when hanging wall coverings.

Right: this bedroom is given emphasis by the use of borders. Strawberry wallpaper sets off green dressing table and armchair.

If you are tackling a one-off area like a particularly high stairwell, you will find it most comfortable and secure to work from a scaffolding tower. These can usually be hired for as long or short a period as you require. This will be cheaper than buying one and also removes the need for storing it when not in use. For hiring these – and any other items, like blow lamps, that you don't use frequently – look under 'Hire' in the Yellow Pages directory.

Other tools you will need for preparing surfaces include a brush, bucket, sponge, detergent, clean cloths, scraper, shave hook, stripping knife, filling knife, trowel, wet and dry abrasive paper and a sanding block.

When preparing walls and ceiling – provided the plasterwork and old paintwork are in reasonable condition – all you will need to do is wash it down. Start at the bottom and work upwards. Use either sugar soap or a special paint cleaner, diluted according to the instructions given. Rinse with clean water to remove all traces of cleaner which could affect the new paint, working from the top to the bottom of the wall.

Where the old paint is cracking or blistered, you need to remove as much as possible. Use a scraper and then sand down the surface with glasspaper until it is smooth. Level off with a filler and rub down to a smooth finish.

If walls have a wall covering in good condition, it is sometimes possible to emulsion over it without first stripping it. It must, however, be stuck down very firmly, particularly along the seams. It's advisable to use a small unseen patch as a check area. There are some papers which can't be painted over, as colour bleeds through or the surface becomes damaged. If you can paint over the wallpaper, first wipe it over with a damp cloth, taking care not to wet the paper so that it comes away from the wall.

If you need to strip wallpaper, you will require a paint brush for wetting it and a stripping knife or scraper. For washable wall covering that has been painted over you will need a wire brush for scoring the top coating so that water can penetrate to the paper backing below.

Wet the paper thoroughly and allow time for the water to soak in and loosen the adhesive. Then take the scraper or stripping knife and peel off the wall covering. Obstinate bits and pieces will need further wetting. After that, wash the walls as for painting preparation.

It is also possible to hire steam wallpaper strippers which can be very time- and energy-saving if you have a large area to strip.

Cracks and holes in the plaster must be filled before you paint or paper over

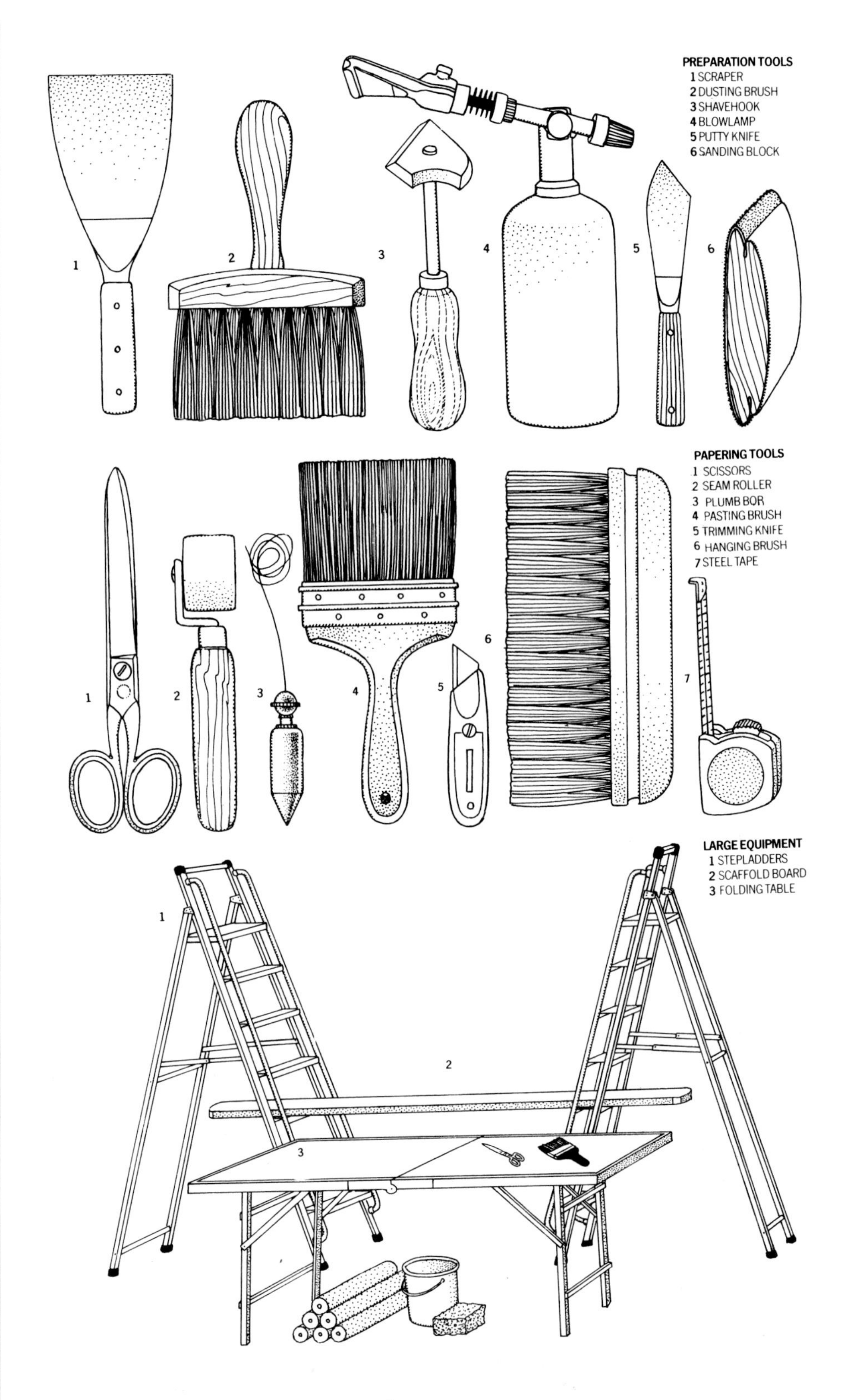

them, or they will show up when decorating is completed. Use the scraper to make the crack wide enough and deep enough for the filler to have something to stick to. With a wire brush, dust out as much loose plaster as you can and either mix your own filler or use a ready-mixed variety. Push the filler into the crack or hole and smooth it off with the trowel or knife. For large holes you may need two applications of filler to seal them up completely. When the filler has set, rub it down with wet abrasive paper so that it is level with the surrounding plaster. Using an orbital sander for this is quiet and easy.

Damp patches on walls may occur because of leaking gutters or a bridged damp course. Do any repairs that are necessary to prevent the damp recurring and paint the original mark with a thin damp sealer to prevent it coming through the new decoration. Where damp patches have produced mould growth, you should paint the area with a fungicidal solution to kill it and stop it regrowing. Check that the fungicide you use is compatible with the paint or paper you plan to put on top.

To prepare woodwork, you should only need to rub down existing paintwork with fine glasspaper and wash it to remove any dust and grease. However, if it is thickly coated in paint, you may want to strip it back to the bare wood and start again. This can be done either with a chemical stripper, by using a blow torch, or by using a hot-air stripper. If you have a sanding attachment on a power tool, this too can be used – although it does tend to create a lot of dust. Using a blow torch requires practice to prevent you from scorching the wood. Work upwards from the bottom and as the paint softens scrape it off with a scraper. Then prepare the wood by rubbing down and washing. Stripping wood is very time-consuming and, if you want to do doors, it may be less effort to take them off their hinges and send them to a paint stripping firm to be done quickly in a solvent bath.

If the bare wood has knots in it which appear to be oozing fluid, use a product called knotting – a solution of shellac in alcohol – which seals the wood and prevents the resin coming through and damaging the new decorations.

PAINTING

Work out how much paint you will need for a particular area by measuring the areas of ceiling and walls. Don't worry about windows and doors; just treat the wall as a flat area with two dimensions. The chart below provides an approximate guide to paint coverage, but this will vary according to the type of paint you use. Most paint manufacturers give a guide either on their colour charts or on the tins themselves. Note that when painting a light colour over a darker surface, you may require more coats to give a good finish. Allow for this when calculating quantities. Buy all the paint at one time and check that it's from the same batch; colours can vary. If you *do* have to buy an extra tin and find that it's a slightly different colour, either mix it up with what remains from the original batch or – if you've run out completely – start the new tin at the edge of a wall rather than in the middle where a colour variation will be more obvious.

You need to decide what you are going to paint with. Brushes are the traditional choice and you will need some narrow-headed ones even if you decide to use a roller or pads. If you do opt for using only brushes, you have to make a decision between cheap ones – which won't last long and will probably need to be thrown away when you've finished – and expensive ones which will last for many years, provided you care for them correctly. Expensive brushes will work out cheaper in the long run if you have got a lot of decorating to do. You will need three or four sizes, ranging from 12 mm (½ in) for getting into crevices and round fittings, to a 100 mm (4 in) brush for walls and ceilings.

Using a roller is the quickest way of covering a large area quickly, but you will also need small brushes for filling in the parts where the roller can't reach. Cheap rollers are made of foam and tend to splash and drip up your arm. A better buy are nylon or lambswool rollers for painting with emulsion, and mohair for eggshell and sheen finishes. Some mohair rollers are sold as also being suitable for gloss paint, but you are more likely to get a better gloss finish using a brush. A roller is used in a sloping paint tray, which will be easier to clean if you line it with foil.

Paint pads cover more quickly than brushes, but they are not as fast as rollers. You don't need the practice to get a good finish that you require with a roller. Paint pads come in different sizes and don't drip, and are therefore a good choice for beginners. However, they do not give the fine finish of a roller or really expert brush work.

Be sure to clean your chosen paint applicator thoroughly when you have finished for the day, although for short breaks you can just wrap it in clingfilm or foil to prevent it drying out. Some paints can be washed out; for others you need a special paintbrush cleaner. Good-quality brushes should not be left to stand in cleaner as the bristles will bend and break. Drill a hole through the handle if there isn't one already and suspend it in a jar of cleaner using a skewer or nail.

Use a special opener for prising the lids off paint tins. Lever them off gently taking care not to distort the lids so they won't go back on again. You will need a wooden spoon or stick (clean, of course) for stirring the paint, unless it's the gel type that shouldn't be stirred. If you are using brushes, pour the paint into a container so that you can dilute emulsion to the consistency needed.

The first coat

Different types of paint are available for different surfaces, both indoor and out. Bear in mind that paint is not just for decorative purposes; it is also intended to protect the surface it's applied to. On some surfaces you need to apply more than one type of paint to seal the original surface and then add the finish you want.

Primer is applied to bare surfaces to form a seal which prevents subsequent coats from soaking into them. Generally, it is not necessary to apply primer to walls or ceilings unless they are completely bare plaster – use an all-purpose primer if you are going to apply an oil-based top coat. With emulsion, the first coat can be thinned down with water to act as a primer. Buy special primers for wood and metal. Standard wood primer is suitable for softwoods and some hardwoods that are not too resinous, but for woods like oak you need an aluminium primer. On metals use a zinc chromate primer which is both anti-corrosive and heat-resistant. On walls with flaking paint use a stabilizing primer to prevent flakes coming off into the top coat. Scrape off as much as possible first.

Undercoat is not often necessary when applying emulsion paint, unless you are covering a dark colour with a light one. Undercoat paint is matt and contains a lot of pigment to mask out the colour below. Use the recommended undercoat to go with the top coat you intend to apply. It may be oil-based or acrylic.

Top coats

Emulsion paints are the easiest to apply, give a tough finish and are easily cleaned. They can be used in virtually any room on walls and ceilings. Most emulsions have a matt finish although a few have a silk or slightly glossy one. Thixotropic (gel) and hard emulsions don't drip so are particularly good for use on ceilings and on walls in high rooms. Buy the grade of emulsion recommended for the job you are doing and thin it down according to the instructions on the tin.

Gloss paints give a shiny, durable finish and are easily washed down. They are a good choice for woodwork, especially doors and skirting boards, because they are tough enough to resist scuffs and kicks and furniture being pushed against them. Some gloss paints need to be cleaned off brushes with solvent; emulsion paints can be washed off under the tap. You can use gloss on walls and ceilings but, because it's shiny, it reflects a lot and is in any case much harder to apply than emulsion and costs more to buy.

Eggshell paint has a slight sheen and gives a good tough finish without the high shine of gloss.

Outdoor paints come in different formulations for different surfaces such as concrete, brick work or stone. Ask in the shop for what you require.

Use lead-free paint when painting in a child's room, especially on things like cots and playpens which tend to get chewed.

If you want to paint radiators white, you must use a special radiator paint,

DECORATING TECHNIQUES – PAINTING

1. Clear the room, lift floor covering if possible, move heavy furniture to centre of room and cover with dust sheet

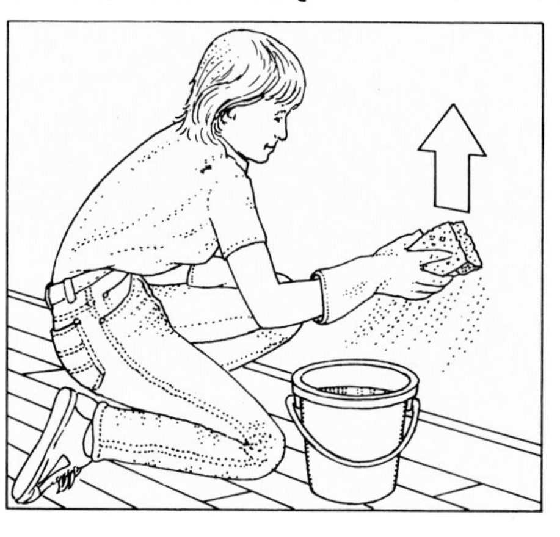

2. Wash the walls down with a sponge and detergent solution. Work from bottom of wall upwards to avoid streaks down wall

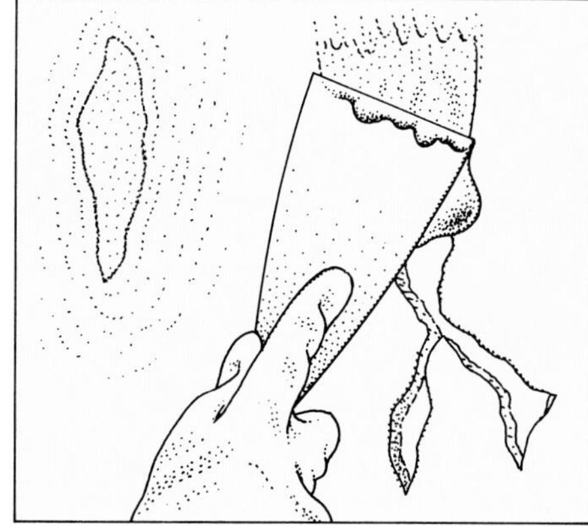

3. Fill cracks with proprietary brand filler using a wide blade filling knife. Allow to dry and smooth off with glass paper

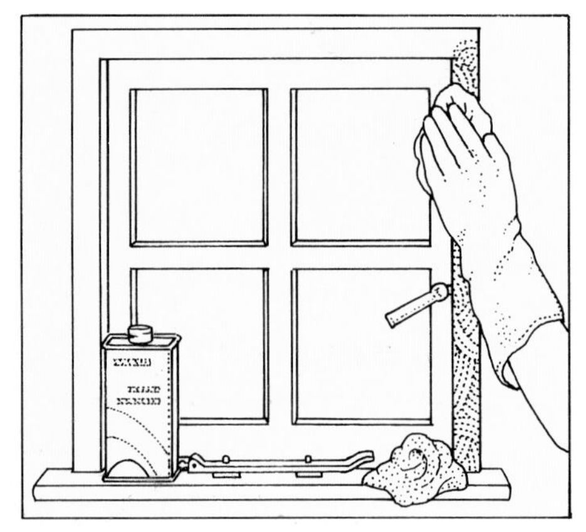

4. Paintwork needs rubbing down before painting. The job can be made easier using a liquid abrasive product on a sponge

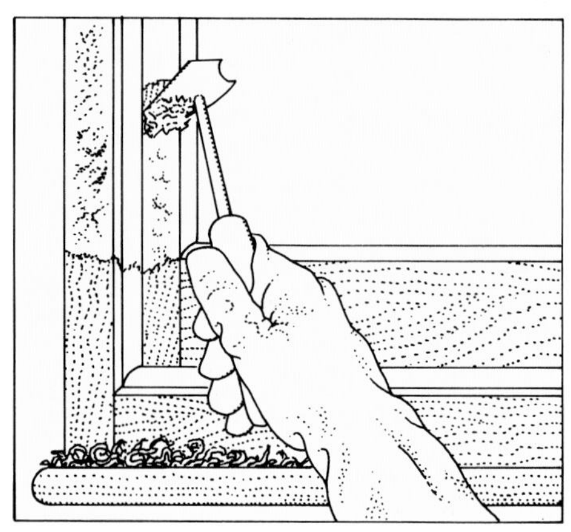

5. Where paintwork is in bad condition, i.e. blistered and chipped, it's best to remove it. A liquid paint remover is ideal on window frames

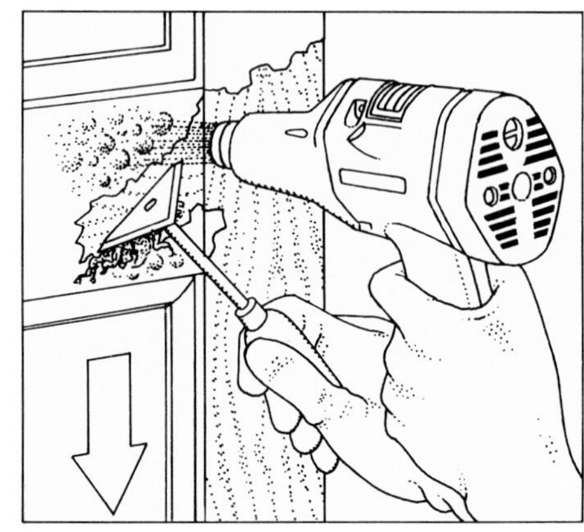

6. On large areas such as doors, a hot air paint stripper is easy to use. Use with care especially near flammable material

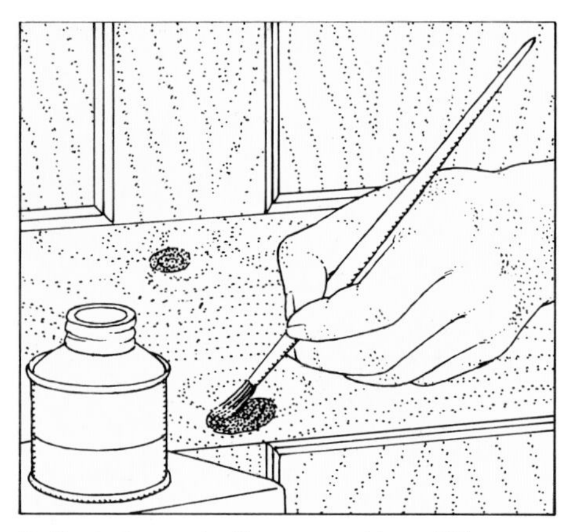

7. Knots in wood will cause problems if they are not sealed. Use knotting applied with a small brush, making sure you cover the knot completely

8. A paint kettle is much easier to hold than a large paint tin. They are available in metal or plastic in various sizes

9. A paint roller speeds up the job of painting ceilings and large areas of walls. Use a brush to paint around edges before starting with roller

which is more expensive than ordinary paint but won't yellow with the heat.

Painting sequence

For best results always paint a room in the correct sequence. Begin with the ceiling, followed by the walls, then the woodwork in the following order – door, window frames, picture rail, dado and skirting board. If possible, always paint in daylight – it's easier to see what you are doing and means you can switch off the electricity at the mains. In any case watch out for water-based emulsion seeping behind light fittings, as this could fuse the supply when you switch on again.

Tackle a ceiling by starting at the window wall and working backwards into the room. A roller is the quickest method and you will also need a 5 cm (2 in) brush for working round the edges and corners and light fittings which you should adjust. Wear an old bath cap to prevent drips falling on your head.

DECORATING TECHNIQUES – PAINTING

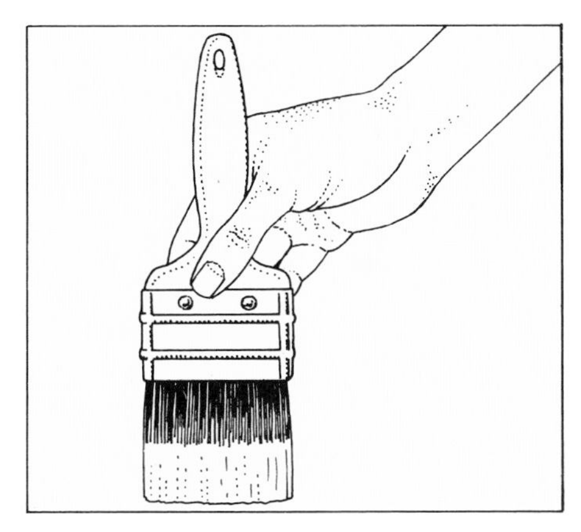

10. You'll find a large brush easier to manipulate if you hold it by the stock like this. Don't dip the brush too deeply into the paint or you'll find the paint dribbles out on to your hand

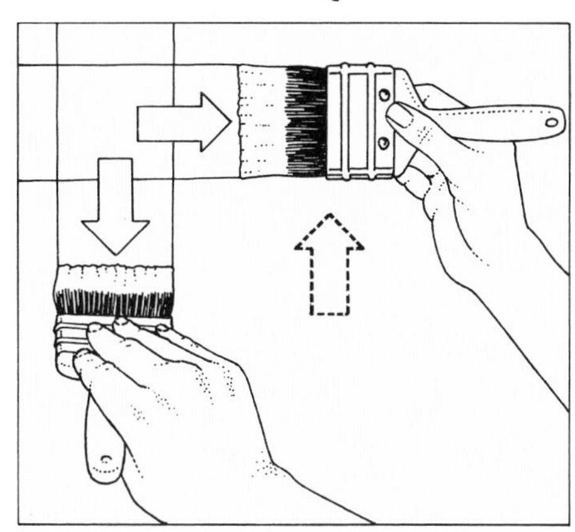

11. To get an even layer of gloss paint and avoid brush marks, "brush out" the paint with horizontal strokes after you've applied it with vertical ones. Finish each section with light upward strokes

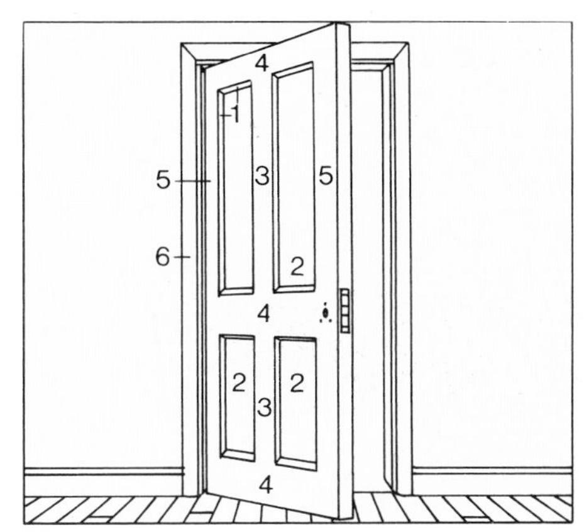

12. Sequence for painting a panelled door. For a flush door, do an eighth of the area at a time, starting at the top. Apply with vertical strokes, brush out with horizontal. Finish with light upward ones

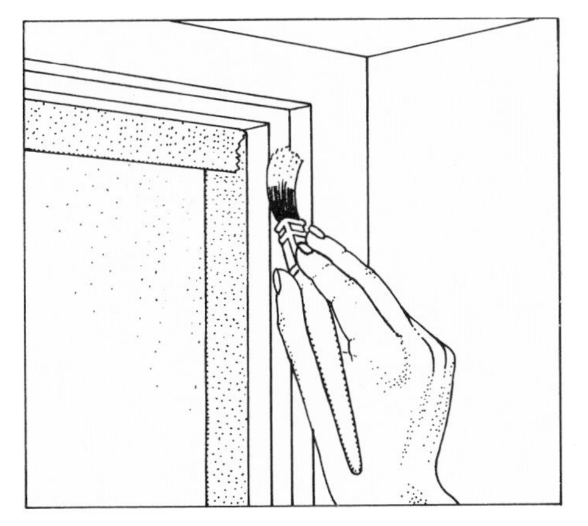

13. Hold a small brush like a pencil. Use masking tape to prevent paint getting on to the glass. Peel the tape off as soon as the paint is dry – otherwise it is difficult to remove

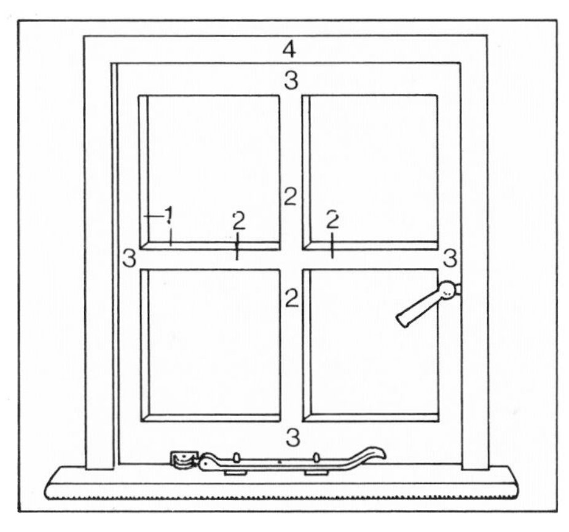

14. Paint the mouldings in a casement window first, then the crossbars. Next paint the top, bottom and side crossrails with the window open. Finally paint the window frame and outer frame

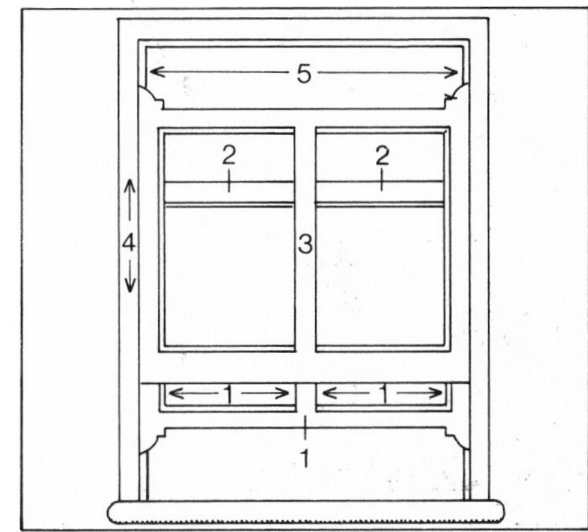

15. With a sash window, reverse window positions. Paint as much as possible of the top window. Reverse again and paint the rest of the top. Then paint the bottom, window frame and runners

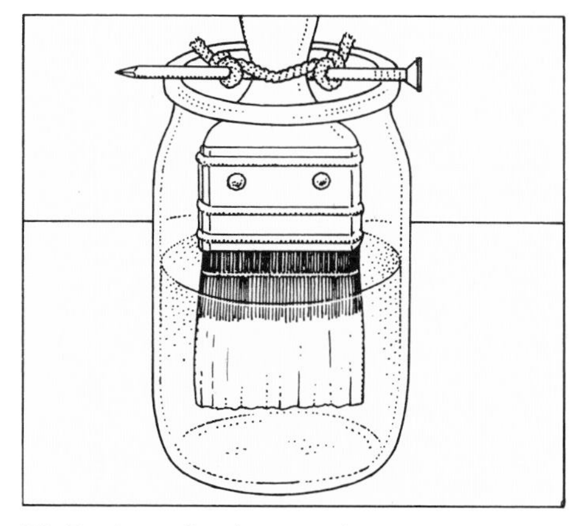

16. To clean a brush suspend it in a jar using a piece of string and a long nail. Alternatively, drill a hole through the stock of the brush and push the nail through it

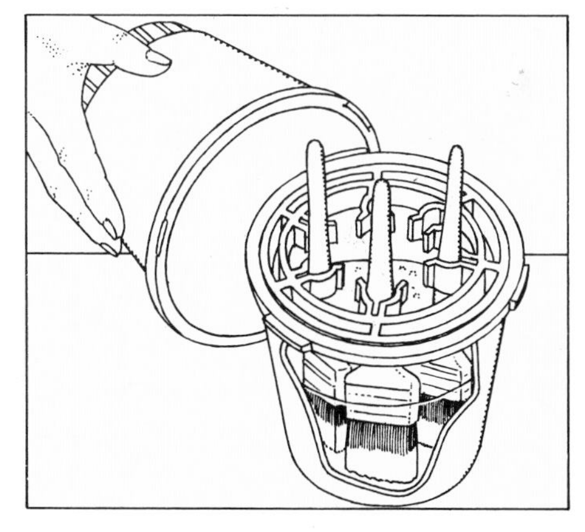

17. Hardware stores and DIY shops stock various brush cleaning appliances that hold brushes clear of the bottom so that the bristles don't get damaged. Change the cleaning solution regularly

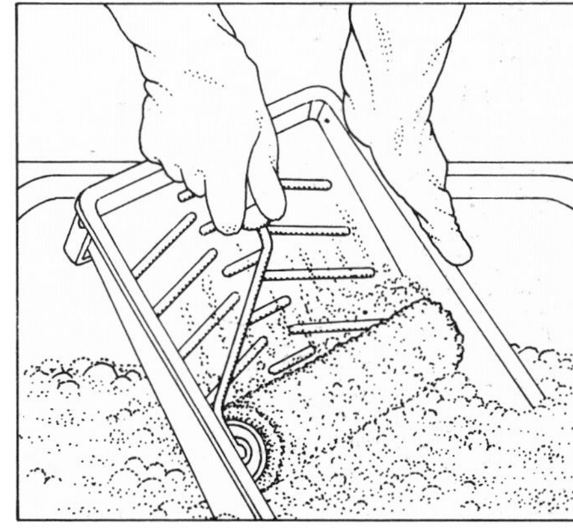

18. When using emulsion or water-based paints, roll your roller up and down on an old newspaper to remove surplus paint. Use detergent solution to clean it and the tray

If you are emulsioning walls start at the top right-hand corner (left-hand one if you are left-handed) and work across in horizontal strips. Be sure to complete a wall before taking a break. Take great care around light switches. For best results switch off the electricity at the mains and cover the edges of the surface plates with masking tape so you don't get paint on them.

For painting behind radiators you will need a specially-angled brush or a paint pad which will cover up as far as you are likely to see. Perfectionists can drain down the system and get a plumber to remove the radiator but it's not really necessary. If you are installing central heating before you decorate, it's possible to have radiators fitted which swing out from the wall so you can paint behind them completely.

Flat doors are easily painted according to the rules for emulsion and gloss on walls. Panelled doors are considerably more tricky and should be painted in the specific numerical sequence shown on page 33. With louvre doors, start by painting the outside of the slats. Brush off drips inside. Paint one slat at a time carefully.

Paint windows as early in the day as possible. They should have a good chance to dry before you have to shut them at night for warmth and security. Start with the outer framework and let it dry before you paint the inner one. Put masking tape round the edge of the glass to prevent getting paint marks on to it, but be sure to remove it as soon as you have finished, or you will find that you spend as long removing the tape as you would have done removing the marks. With sash and casement windows you must paint the different sections in the right order, following the numerical order shown in point 12 on page 33.

Specialist painting techniques

There are a number of specialist painting techniques which give unusual effects on walls and woodwork. Although they sound difficult, they are quite simple with a little practice, and because you create the effect yourself you can be sure you have made a one-off design.

Sponge stippling produces a speckled effect. You first apply the base colour all over the area you are going to stipple and allow it to dry. You may need two coats to get the colour and finish you want. Then take a small natural sea sponge, wet it and squeeze it out so that it is evenly damp. In a bowl spread about 1 tbsp of your sponge colour (either your base paint or a different shade) and place the flat side of the sponge into it. Make gentle impressions on a spare piece of wallpaper until the excess colour has come off the sponge and it is leaving a truly speckled mark. Press this over the area to be stippled, refilling the sponge and removing the excess as necessary. Don't worry if you are trying to achieve a two-tone effect and the colours seem very similar. Paint gets darker as it dries.

When you have sponged over the whole area allow it to dry completely. If desired repeat the sponging using yet another colour or a second application of the first sponge colour. If you make a mistake and apply the sponge when it's too full don't worry. Wait for it to dry and then sponge some of the base coat over it to create the speckles in a different way.

Bag graining produces a broken effect which will be more or less obvious depending on the colours you use. It's best done with two people; one who paints the surface while the other follows on and grains it before it dries. Start by applying one or two coats of the base colour and allow it to dry thoroughly. Take a plastic freezer bag and half fill it with torn up rags and seal it with a rubber band, twist tie or tape. Mix the second colour with equal parts of water and paint this onto the wall, working in vertical strips about 75 cm wide, starting at the top right-hand corner (left if you are left-handed). The second person should follow as soon as possible pressing the plastic bag neatly and evenly over the surface. Lift it off carefully between each 'press' so you don't get skid marks. Overlap the impressions slightly so that the whole area is covered. Work quickly so that lines don't form between the vertical strips and don't stop until you've completed a whole wall.

Rag rolling is done in a similar way but using a rolled up rag that isn't encased in a plastic bag. You need to work in eggshell paint for best effect and to mix the second colour with one part white spirit. As the rag becomes saturated re-roll it to give a clean area and then throw it away and replace it with a rag of the identical material. As with bag graining, you need two people; one to paint and one to rag.

With all these special effects, it's sensible to practise on an old piece of lining paper before tackling the real thing.

WALL COVERINGS

These originally only meant wallpapers but are now made not just from paper but from an astonishing number of other materials. Wall coverings come in a wide choice of patterns and colours and are particularly good at covering up walls which are in bad condition.

Most wall coverings come in rolls which are 10 m (33 ft) long and 250 mm (20½ in) wide and are usually trimmed at the sides ready for hanging. Some special and foreign coverings come untrimmed in

Far left and left: two different decorative treatments of a narrow hall with panelled door show how just a change of paint colours can alter the effect completely

different lengths and widths. When buying these, get the retailer to trim them for you so that there is a good even edge on the seams. You can buy a machine and do this yourself – or even attempt it with scissors – but unless you have endless time, patience and skill, the results are not likely to be very good.

When deciding how much wall covering to buy, beginners often make the mistake of working out the quantity of paper without allowing for the pattern drop when matching it up on the wall, or for the excess which must be trimmed off at top and bottom when hanging. It's best to take the measurements of your room to the shop and have it worked out for you. The chart on page 220 shows roughly how much plain paper you need for the size of your room.

When measuring up the room, you need to know the length and height of the walls, plus any projections like chimney breasts. Check that the batch numbers are the same on all the rolls you buy, as slight differences in colour will stand out when wall paper is hung. You will need one or two specialist tools for hanging wall coverings. A pasting table or its equivalent is important to prevent tearing long lengths of paper as you paste them. It's impossible to do the job on a carpet, and on hard floors you run the risk of making the front of the paper dirty. If you don't want to buy a pasting table, make do with a piece of chipboard over a smaller table. You will also need a rule or steel tape measure, long-bladed scissors or a DIY knife, a pasting brush (unless the covering is ready pasted), a seam roller for getting the covering to butt up well and a handleless paper-hanger's brush, which should be of good quality. You will need a bucket for the paste, a brush to spread it with, a cloth for mopping up splashes of paste and a plumb line for hanging the wallpaper straight. The latter need not be the real thing – make your own by tying a small weight (such as a pair of pliers) to the end of a length of string.

Types of paper

Choose carefully among the various types of covering. Delicate ones, and those like grasscloth which are difficult to clean, shouldn't be hung where sticky fingers will mark them. Kitchens and bathrooms need coverings which will resist steam.

Lining papers are off-white, plain papers and come in light, medium or heavy weights. They are used for cross-lining before hanging the final wall covering to give an even surface and hung vertically to provide a good surface for emulsion paint. Use medium-weight paper if you have never hung lining paper before; the light-weight ones stretch and tear easily when pasted. The heaviest weight can be hung instead of ordinary wallpaper to give a good surface for emulsion paint.

Relief papers are white papers, embossed with a pattern, which are designed to be painted. Once painted over, they are tough and suitable for halls and stairwells, and can be sponged clean. Some are vinyl-coated and can be scrubbed clean. Relief papers are quite difficult to strip once painted, and need heavy scoring first.

Woodchip papers are off-white, pulpy papers with chips of wood bonded in. They come in light, medium and heavy grades. They need painting over and are fairly durable once this has been done. They are not washable (bad marks will need painting over) but provide a quick, cheap way of covering bad wall surfaces. They are extremely difficult to strip cleanly because the chips of wood stay stuck to the wall.

Ordinary wallpapers come in different weights and in a vast selection of patterns. Use medium weight if you are new to paper hanging, as the lighter ones stretch and tear easily when pasted, and are not durable enough for heavy traffic areas.

Washable papers have a surface coated with clear plastic to make them water resistant – some grades are spongeable, some scrubbable. These

Top: the shutters have been stripped down to bare wood and the stencilled cushions are what bring the room to life *Above:* the kitchen units have a hand painted two-tone dragged finish. A touch of culinary realism is supplied by the *trompe l'oeil* still life painted on the wall behind the hob

papers are a good choice for halls, stairwells and children's rooms, and the ready-pasted ones are very easy to hang. Some are peelable (when you want to strip the paper off, to put up another wall covering, you are able to peel off the vinyl coating, leaving the backing paper stuck to the wall to act as a new lining paper) or dry strippable. This rarely works as well as it should, but it's certainly easier than removing washable papers that aren't dry strippable.

Vinyls have a paper backing and may be smooth or embossed. The heaviest grades are those patterned and embossed to look like tiling. They are easily cleaned and very durable; they aren't damaged by steam or condensation, but you should use the heaviest grades next to the bath as lighter ones will lift if water creeps underneath. All vinyls are dry strippable and some are ready-pasted.

Polyethylene wall coverings feel and look like smooth fabric. The only one on the market at present is ICI's Novamura which is hung by pasting the wall, not the paper. It's very lightweight (so suitable for use on ceilings) and dry strippable.

Foils are more difficult to hang than other wall coverings because they crease very easily. You must be very careful with the paste, as it discolours the metallized pattern if it gets on the front. Never tuck it behind the covers of light fittings, switches or wall sockets and don't use in steamy rooms as it will discolour.

Other wall coverings include paper-backed fabrics, grasscloths, hessians and cork veneers. These are much more expensive than other wall coverings and are often sold in wider strips. Hanging is

Right: shutters stencilled with floral swags give this rather plain room an air of elegance and frame the large 12-pane window effectively.

DECORATING TECHNIQUES – WALLPAPERING

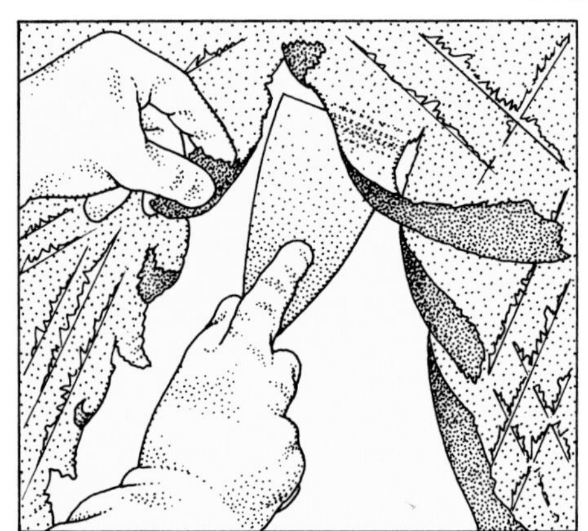

1. Turn off the electricity then soak the wallpaper with warm water using a sponge. When the water has loosened the paste, scrape off the wallcovering

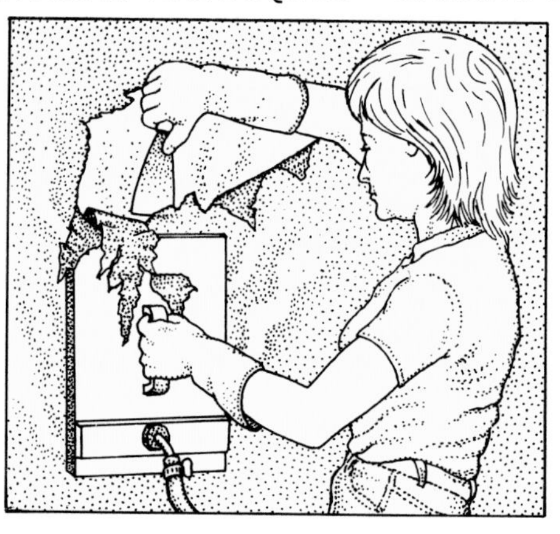

2. It's worth hiring a steam stripper for large expanses of wall. Next, size the walls with paste to avoid air bubbles behind the paper and make it easier to slide the paper to match patterns

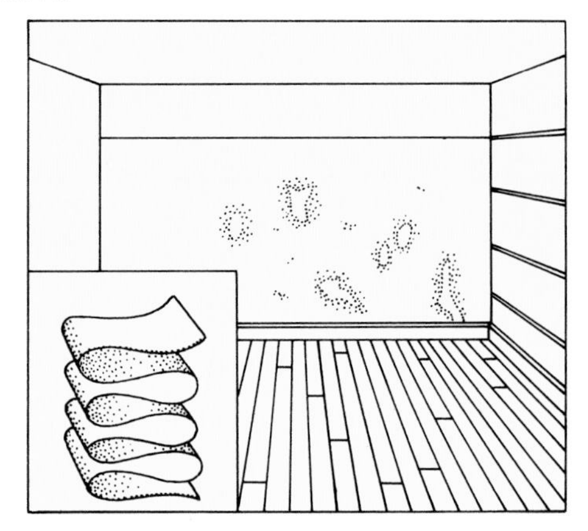

3. Lining paper improves the finish by concealing minor imperfections. Concertina the paper after pasting. Start at the top of the wall; don't overlap the joins

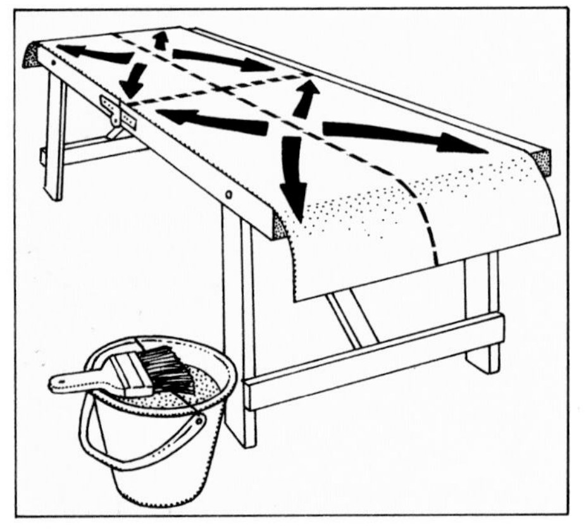

4. Brush paste on in sections, brushing out to the edges. Be careful not to get any on the front of the paper. Use the paste recommended on the roll label

5. Fold the ends of the pasted paper to the middle of the length, and pick up. With extra-long lengths, fold over about 300mm at the top, the rest from the bottom

6. Ready-pasted wallcoverings come with a trough which holds water – you just pull the cut length through it

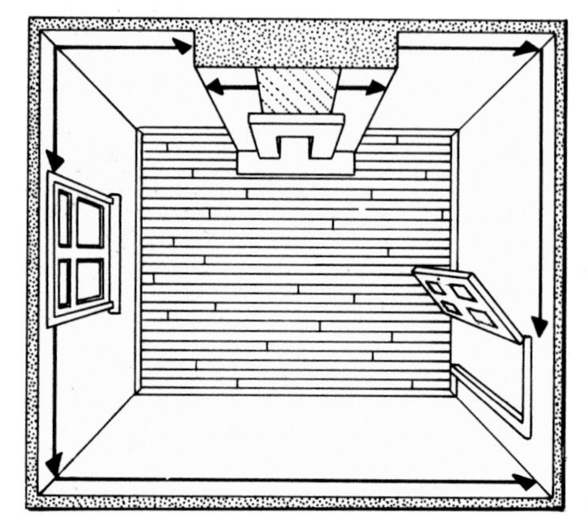

7. In most cases, start hanging the paper on the wall by the window and work towards the door. For a bold pattern, centre it on the part of the room you want to feature and work towards the door

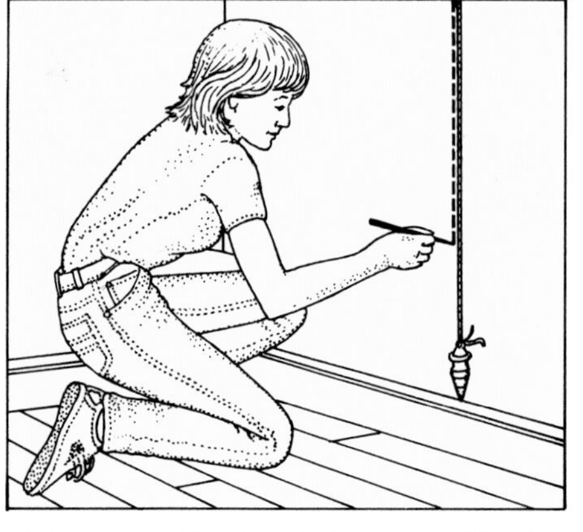

8. Use a plumbline to get a true vertical line to start from. Pin the string to the top of the wall and let it hang freely. Mark the line with a pencil

9. With straight patterns, 100mm waste is usually enough to match repeats. With drop pattern repeats, always check the match before you finally cut the length

more difficult as you usually need to overlap the seams, then cut through with a knife along a straight edge. Unless you are a confident and experienced decorator, we recommend that you get a professional to hang them rather than risk a very expensive mistake which you are forced either to change or live with.

Colour matching

Some shops keep an open roll of the designs they stock and will cut you a sample to take home, so that you can make absolutely sure that the pattern fits in with your room. Few wallpaper shops will let you borrow pattern books, so take snippets from fabric and furnishings in your home when you go to the shop. If you can't do this, mix colours from a paintbox on a piece of paper until you get the right colour, and take that along.

Pasting

You won't get the best results unless you use the paste the manufacturer

DECORATING TECHNIQUES – WALLPAPERING

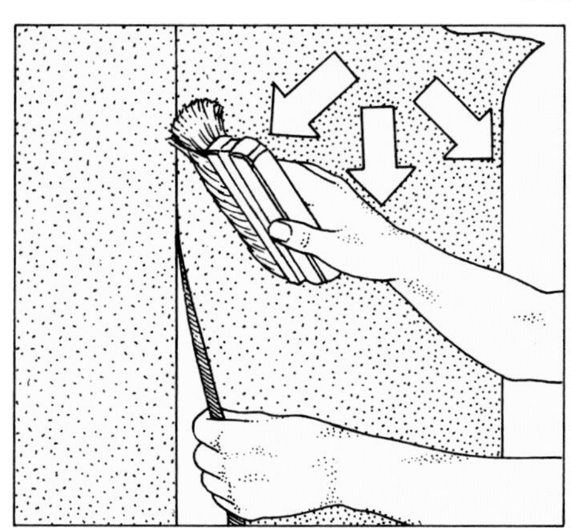

10. Brush down the paper, starting at the top and holding the paper underneath slightly away from the wall until you reach it with the brush. Buy a good wallpaper brush with an all-wood stock

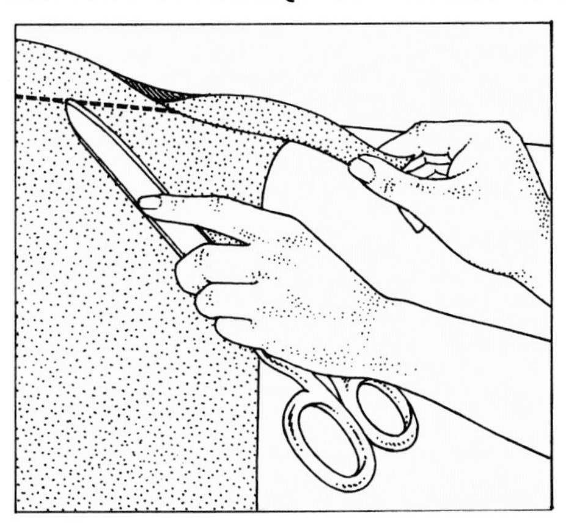

11. Mark the paper with the tips of the scissors, then peel it back until you can cut along the fold. Prick air bubbles with a needle then brush them down with the wallpaper brush

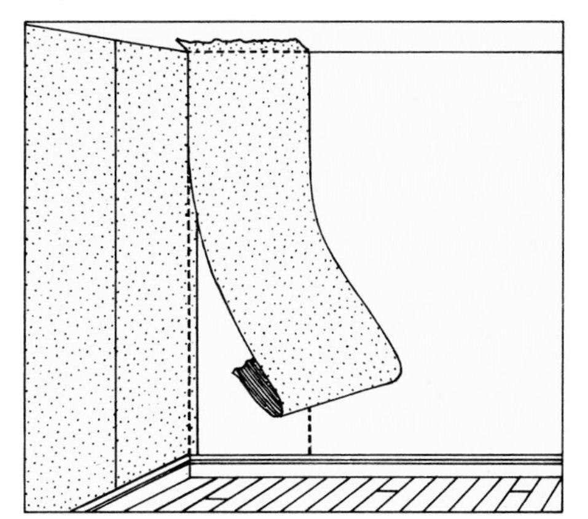

12. Take the wallpaper round an internal corner by about 2cm. If the corner is true, butt the next length up to the edge of the paper. If it isn't true overlap the next length up to a true vertical

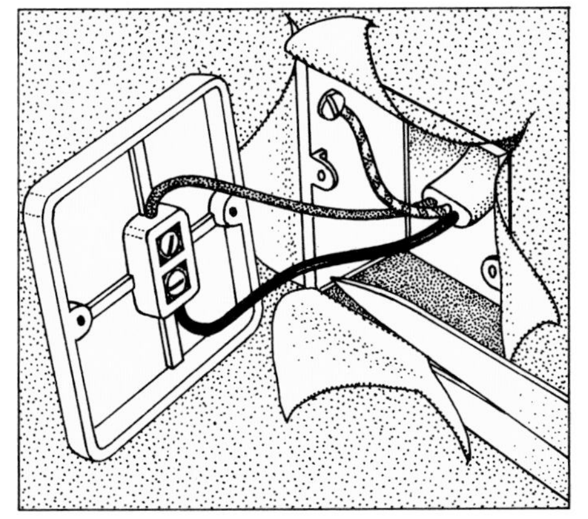

13. Always turn off the electricity before removing light or power fittings. Trim, then tuck, the spare 2 or 3mm of wallpaper inside. Don't *ever* do this with metallised paper

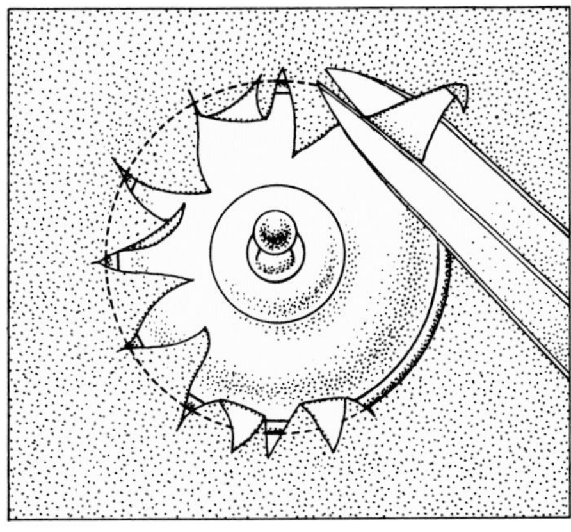

14. When you can't remove a cover, hang the paper over the fitting and pierce it at the centre. Cut slashes outwards to the edge, brush the paper down. Trim off excess

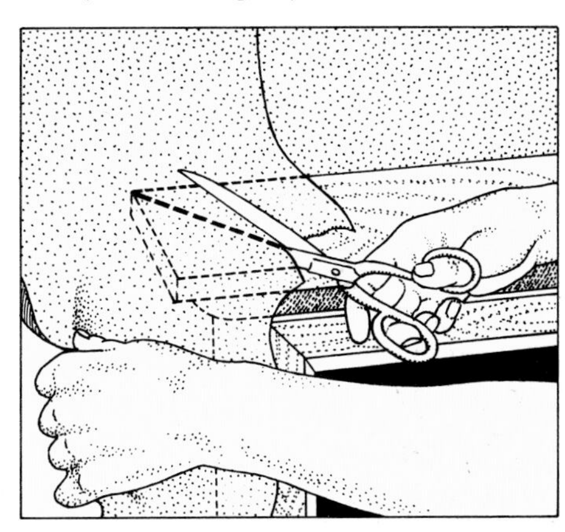

15. When papering round the fireplace, hang the length of paper over the edge. Cut the paper diagonally into the corner, brush the paper down to the top and side, then trim

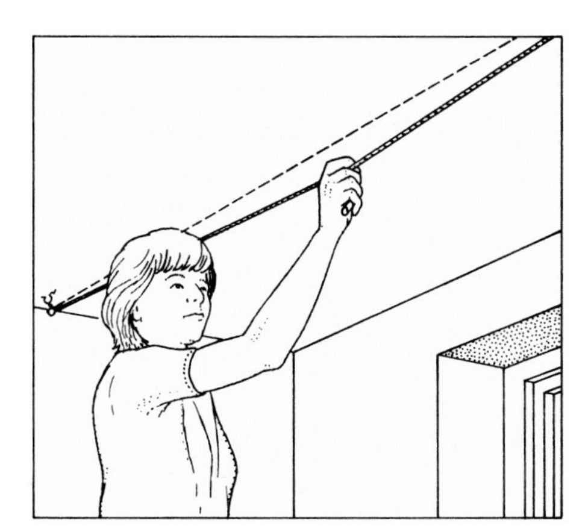

16. Papering a ceiling is tricky. Mark a guideline on the ceiling with a chalked string and paper to this. If the walls are to be prepared too, allow the paper to hang down the wall by a centimetre

17. Rig up a platform to work from. You should have about 25cm headroom. Start papering at the edge of the ceiling nearest the window and work back into the room

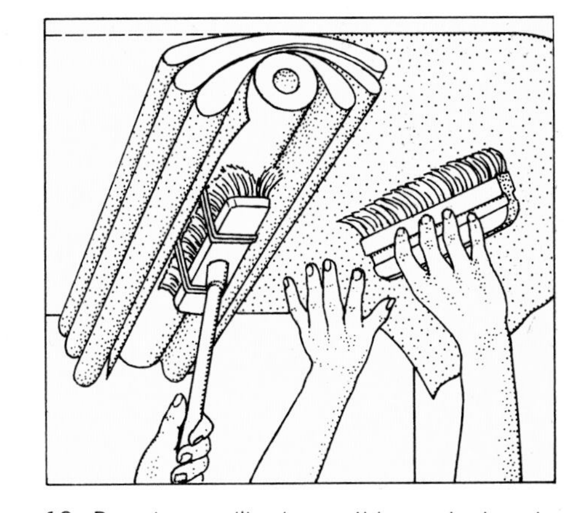

18. Papering a ceiling is very tiring, so try to get someone to lend a helping hand by holding the paper for you and, if possible, changing over

recommends. Use the wrong one and you will find that the paper dries before you have got it from the pasting table to the wall or that the paste just isn't strong enough to stick the wall covering to the wall. Washable coverings usually need a paste containing a fungicide; as moisture behind this type of wall covering can take time to evaporate, you need this to prevent mould growing. You should follow the pasting instructions carefully – some papers need to be left for a while so the paste can soak in and make the paper supple, others should be hung straight away. Always pay attention to the manufacturers' recommended soaking times: oversoaking will weaken the paper – and if you don't soak the paper long enough, air bubbles form under the surface.

If you are starting from scratch you can guarantee a very good match if you go for one of the ranges with co-ordinating fabrics and paint colours matching the colours on the paper.

TILING

Ceramic tiling gives an attractive finish that is easy to clean and is particularly practical in bathrooms and kitchens. You can buy tiles in many styles, ranging from the cheap, plain variety in a fairly standard range of colours, to exotic hand-painted ones which cost considerably more. Make sure that what you buy is suitable for the place where you put it. Tiles which will be wiped down regularly should have a glaze that will withstand this and those which are to be put round a fireplace should be of a special heat-resistant variety which won't crack.

Most tiles are sold in the sizes 108 × 108 × 4 mm (4¼ × 4¼ × 5⁄32 in) or 152 × 152 × 6.5 mm (6 × 6 × ¼ in) although some of the more original ones come in different shapes and non-standard sized squares. When measuring up for tiles, bear in mind that standard tiles have four-squared edges, each with a small lug on the side or angled edges which act as an even spacer between the tiles. With tiles that don't have lugs, you need to put pieces of matchstick-thin card or plastic spacers between the tiles as you hang them in order to keep the spacing even. For the top row or edge row of any group of tiles you need to buy some marked RE which have one rounded side, and possibly some marked REX which have two adjoining rounded sides and are intended for edges and corners.

Any surface on which you are planning to fix tiles should be flat, dry and stable. Don't ever put them onto a surface with a wall covering as it won't be strong enough to take the weight. Painted surfaces should be washed with a detergent solution to remove dirt and grease and newly-plastered walls should be allowed to dry out thoroughly for at least six weeks before they are tiled. If you are putting tiles onto plasterboard, plywood or hardboard, make sure that it is rigid and won't buckle; and apply a coat of primer first. Use a marine grade if the tiles are going in a bathroom, shower or behind a cooker.

It is possible to put new tiles over old ones, but bear in mind that this will marginally reduce the size of the room. You must also be sure that the old tiles, onto which you will be sticking the new ones, are in good condition and provide a flat firm surface. If any are loose, prise them out and refix them. Tell the shop you are tiling over tiles so that you are supplied with the correct adhesive.

You don't need a lot of tools for tiling; just a suitable adhesive – either a standard wall tile one or a water-resistant one if you are tiling in a bathroom. You will also need a tile cutter, a straight edge, battening and a plumb line (see above). Once tiling is completed, you will need grout – a plaster mixture which is spread between the tiles to fill in the gaps. If you are using coloured tiles, it is possible to buy a special powder dye which can be mixed with the grout to match it up with one of the colours on the tiles. Mix sparingly until you achieve the shade you want; by tipping in the whole packet of dye you will get a very dark colour. Some tile adhesives double as grout, which is useful.

To fix tiles to a wall, first decide on the lowest point at which they will be fixed. Then measure one tile's height up from this. Take the batten and, with the help of a spirit level, fix it to the wall with panel pins or nails so that its upper edge is at this height. Fix battening all round the area you are going to tile.

Mark the battening with a pencil in the centre of each wall (or part wall) to be tiled. Then on the wall mark out the position of each tile, including its lugs or matchsticks. You will then discover what size of part-tile you have at each end. If this is very small, and means that you will merely be cutting a sliver to fit in, it's sensible to move all the tiles along a little and have a slightly larger part-tile at one end. Bear in mind that cutting tiles, although fairly straightforward does require confidence and practice. If you are using very expensive tiles, and don't wish to buy spares in case of failure, it's a good idea to buy a few cheap ones of the same thickness and practise cutting when it doesn't matter. To cut a tile, measure and mark the line along which you are going to cut and place the straight edge along it. With the cutter, score along the line several times. Place a matchstick or pencil underneath the line and press down gently but firmly on both sides of the tile. It should break away cleanly. If you are cutting out a shape from the tile, make a cardboard template to score round and use tile nippers or sharp pincers to remove the unwanted pieces.

Left: a small bedroom looks larger with walls and ceilings covered with the same paper. The colour scheme is reflected in the fabric of the eiderdown and tiles of the old washstand
Above: the radiator below the window blends into the wall by being painted the same colour and is virtually hidden by the shelf above it

Use the plumb line to make a vertical line on the wall straight up from where the first tile (usually bottom left-hand) is to go. Mark the line on the wall. Fix a batten along it to make a right angle with the horizontal batten you have already fixed.

Apply the recommended adhesive to the wall with the notched spreader supplied with the adhesive, to comb it into a ridged effect of the right height for the tiles. This provides a good key for the tiles to adhere to. Start by fixing the bottom row of tiles and work upwards, taking care not to spread too much adhesive – otherwise it will dry out before you get to it. Do all the whole tiles first. With cut tiles, apply the adhesive directly to their backs. Check each row with the spirit level to make sure it is horizontal and wipe off with a damp cloth any adhesive that squeezes up between the tiles.

Leave the tile adhesive to set for 24 hours. Then remove the battens and fix the bottom row of tiles and any cut ones that you left out. Leave these to set for a further 24 hours and then make up grout according to the packet instructions and colour it if you want. Apply it with a sponge, pushing well into all the gaps and wiping off the excess with a damp cloth. When you have finished grouting, wipe your index finger gently along the lines to give a smooth finish. Leave it to dry for 24 hours then polish up the tiles with a soft dry, clean cloth.

Cork tiles are sometimes used on walls to give a decorative finish and improve heat and sound insulation. They can also provide a large, useful area of noticeboard. Some cork tiles are fixed with contact adhesive, so they need to be positioned carefully since you have little time to slide them around. If you are going to do a large area, use a slow-drying cork adhesive that allows you to move them around. Tiles are also available in polystyrene (for ceilings), and in metal and plastic. All are fixed in the same way as ceramic tiles – but take advice on what adhesive to use.

MAKING CURTAINS

Curtains – or blinds – add to the decoration of a room, keep heat in, enhance a view and shut out darkness. Both curtains and blinds are easy to make yourself. Doing so can save money over having them done professionally. You may find special offers where curtain making is thrown in 'free' when you buy the fabric – but check that you can't buy the fabric more cheaply anywhere else.

Curtain tracks

Before you make your curtains decide on the type of track you want. Most are made of plastic and are pliable enough to be bent round bays if necessary, but you can also buy brass or wooden poles from which the curtains are suspended on rings.

Modern tracks are unobtrusive but if you don't want them to show, buy the kind over which you can fit a pelmet. When buying, remember that you will want as much daylight as possible when the curtains are not drawn, so allow some width on either side of the window where the curtains can hang during the daytime. You may want to fit a cording set to the track to allow the curtains to be drawn by pulling a cord, thus protecting the fabric from handling. A cord is especially useful with curtains that are light-coloured and get dirty easily, and with fabrics like velvet which tend to show fingermarks.

Curtain headings

The final effect of your curtains will be created by the heading tape you use to gather the fabric. It will also affect the number of widths of fabric you should buy. Basic gathering tape gives a ruched look and requires a minimum of one-and-a-half times the width of the curtain rail for both tape and fabric, plus the amount required (see opposite) for joins, side turnings and curtain overlap, if required. Curtains with gathering tape headings look fuller if you use twice the width of the track.

Pinch-pleat headings are created by using a tape which fans out into a series of two-fold or three-fold French pleats, with spaces of smooth fabric between. The pleats may be deep or shallow. You will need exactly twice the width of the track for both fabric and tape.

Pencil-pleat heading tape produces straight regular pleats in pencil shapes and requires more fabric and tape than any other type – at least two-and-a-quarter times the width of the track. Two-and-a-half times will give a better effect and, when nets and sheers are used to create privacy or hide an unattractive outlook, you will need three times the width. But pencil-pleated curtains are very bulky when pulled back so allow for a good amount of track width at either side of the window. You can use pencil pleat tape either way up, fitting the hooks at the top of tape or lower down so that the track is hidden.

Above: tools of the trade for the home designer. Some samples of carpet, fabric, wallpaper and upholstery webbing

Right: tiled kitchen with pine units has a frieze of red tiles running round the edge of the ceiling. Tongue and grooved ceiling, split-cane blind and wooden table add to the natural feel

Curtain linings

Linings increase the warmth of a curtain, reduce its transparency and give it a better finished appearance. You can either make curtains with sewn-in linings or make the linings separately and just stitch them at intervals to the side of the finished curtains. The advantage of separate linings is that they, and the curtains, can be washed or cleaned separately and any shrinkage which occurs won't cause the curtains to pucker. Linings are usually made of cotton sateen in white or a choice of colours. You can also buy Milium lining – which acts as insulation and reduces the heat loss through the windows – or a special, thick, rubberized lining fabric which not only keeps heat in but also acts as blackout. This is especially useful in bedrooms – particularly children's bedrooms where daylight may cause them to wake up too early.

Curtain fabric

The selection of curtain fabric available is enormous. On small windows you can also use dress fabric, although it isn't as robust and comes in a narrower width. Don't neglect ticking, felt and other unusual fabrics if you want a special effect.

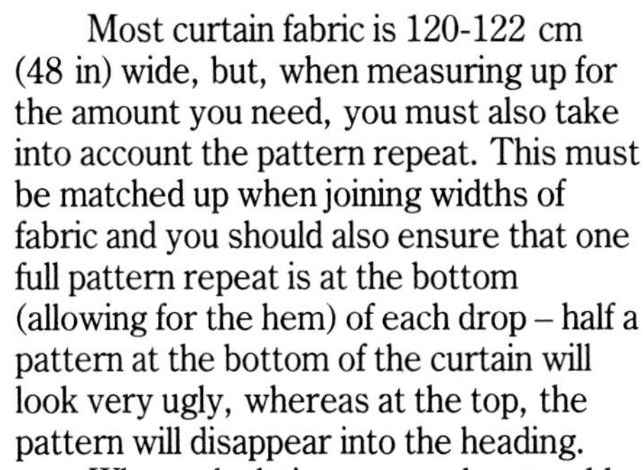

Most curtain fabric is 120-122 cm (48 in) wide, but, when measuring up for the amount you need, you must also take into account the pattern repeat. This must be matched up when joining widths of fabric and you should also ensure that one full pattern repeat is at the bottom (allowing for the hem) of each drop – half a pattern at the bottom of the curtain will look very ugly, whereas at the top, the pattern will disappear into the heading.

When calculating, remember to add 8 cm (3 in) to each width for turnings, plus 8 cm (3 in) on each curtain where you want an overlap.

Work out the length by measuring from the curtain rail to 1 cm (½ in) above the window sill, 15 cm (6 in) below the window sill, 1.5 cm (¾ in) above a radiator or 2.5 cm (1 in) off the floor, depending on where you want the curtains to finish. Add 25 cm (10 in) to each drop to give you a good hem allowance of about 15 cm (6 in) plus the turnover at the top. If you think the fabric is likely to shrink add about 5 cm (2 in) to each length. Wash all washable fabric *before* you make up the curtains, so that shrinkage is completed and the finished curtains will be of the right length before *and* after you wash them.

Join the widths using an open seam and press it carefully. Clip the selvedges diagonally at 8 cm (3 in) intervals to prevent puckering. You must line curtains which have joined widths or light will show through the seams. For sheer curtains, which are unlined, use a flat fell seam.

Make single turns of 4 cm (1½ in) down each edge of the curtains and tack and handstitch them using a herringbone stitch, or use the blind hemming stitch on an automatic sewing machine. If you are putting in a lining, stitch it down the sides and attach it to the main curtain at about 30 cm (1 ft) intervals, using a lock stitch. Thereafter treat the curtain and lining as one when it comes to fixing the heading. Make separate linings in the same way as the curtains, using a special lining tape at the top.

Fit the tape heading according to the manufacturer's instructions and then hang the curtains. Leave them for a week or so, so that the fabric can drop. Then pin up even hems before taking them down to sew them. Mitre the corners but don't cut off excess fabric. You may need to let the hems down if you want to hang them at different windows. With some fabrics you may need to weight the curtains along the hems so that they hang evenly. Weights can be bought from shops which sell heading tape and should be laid along the fold of the hem before you sew it. For very bulky curtains you may need to make tie-backs to hold them away from the window when not drawn.

KEEPING WARM

However you heat your home, it will cost a fair amount of money. Installing the right central heating system helps.

While it is possible to install central heating yourself, it's a time-consuming job and one that requires a fair amount of specialist knowledge and DIY experience. In general, unless you are sure you can cope with the task and the upheaval it involves, it's best to pay a professional to do the work for you.

HEATING OPTIONS

Of course you may not need central heating at all. If you live in a small, well-insulated flat, and spend your days at work and your weekends elsewhere, you could be paying out a lot of money to heat space that you don't occupy very much.

Although most people tend to assume that they need central heating if they can afford it, it's a good idea to think about the alternatives. Do some sums; see whether you'll save money by using on-the-spot space heaters as and when you need the extra warmth.

Space heaters may be gas, electric or paraffin, and you can see a good selection in Electricity and Gas Board showrooms and in department and hardware stores. Some are permanently fixed and may need such features as – in the case of gas – a balanced flue inserted through an outside wall; others are portable and can be moved from room to room as you need heat. *Note*: never move a paraffin heater when it is alight.

Decide whether you want the heat to be radiant – which gives out a warm glow of heat, or convection – which can be natural, rising from the grill of the heater, or which can have hot air blown around by means of a fan. Think too about whether you want the appearance of the heater to be purely functional or decorative as well. Space heaters come in all kinds of styles designed to blend in with various types of home decoration, from high-tech or a chintzy cottage effect right through to the stately home look.

Talk about your heating needs with an expert salesperson. Space heaters provide different amounts of heat output which will also be affected by the size of the rooms they are sited in.

If space heating is your sole form of warmth, consider at least one electric heater. This can be fitted on a time switch so that you can programme it to come on both in the morning before you get up and in the evening to warm the house before you get home from work.

Don't neglect the humble paraffin heater or be put off by the horror stories of houses burning down because one has been knocked over. Modern ones have a fail-safe device which extinguishes the flame the minute they are knocked and are also easier to fill and ignite than older models and look smarter.

Central heating choice

If, however, you opt for full or partial central heating, don't be seduced into employing the first person who pushes a leaflet through your letterbox offering his service. Central heating is a long-term investment and requires careful consideration before you make a decision. If you have a choice of fuel – and it is usually between electricity, gas, oil or solid fuel – try to find out something about running costs as well as the actual cost of the systems themselves. There are other forms of heating system such as solar panels, wood burning stoves, heat pumps and so on, but these tend to be of minority interest and not suitable for all types of home and area.

If you can, ask people in similar places to your own what type of heating they use and how much it costs to run. Get as much literature as you can on the different systems, boilers, radiators and so on and draw up comparative charts. All the four major fuels have central co-ordinating bodies who are happy to supply free leaflets about the various heating options they offer (for addresses see page 214). Remember that electricity operates, in addition to its normal tariff, on a special Economy 7 tariff which can cut your heating costs in some circumstances. It also gives you the benefit of lower running costs on non-heating appliances such as washing machines and dishwashers, if you use them when the low rate tariff applies.

When you have fixed on a fuel and the hardware to go with it, take time and trouble over designing the actual system so that it is as economical as possible to run. Professional advice is helpful at this point. You may want different areas of the house to be kept at different temperatures, in which case you may want to zone the system or to put thermostatic controls on each radiator so that you can adjust each room separately. You need to think about where to site the main thermostat so that it's not affected adversely by draughts or by the constant opening and shutting of the outside doors. You will want to consider radiators whose style blends in with your home. Think, too, about where you site them, so that they give out maximum warmth *and* don't prevent you from arranging major pieces of furniture in the positions you want.

If you inherit an existing central heating system that is unsatisfactory, there are a number of things you can do to improve its efficiency in terms of adding special controls. Discuss this with the original installers or a qualified heating engineer to see what they advise.

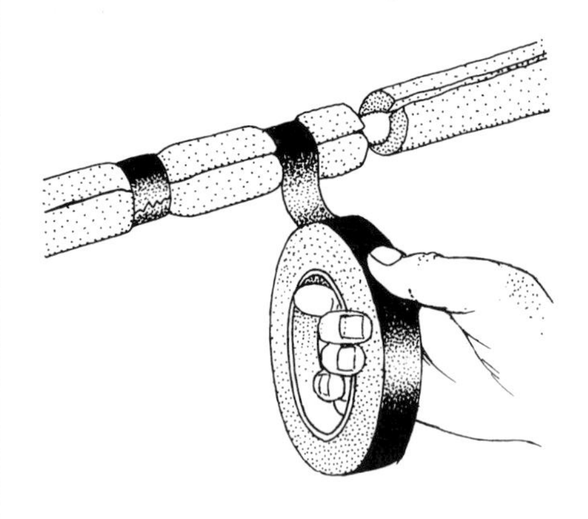

Above: pre-formed pipe insulation is held in position with adhesive tape

INSULATION

Insulation prevents the heat you create within the home from being lost through the roof, walls, windows and doors. Since heating is expensive, however well designed your system is, it's important to insulate your home as well as possible. All forms of insulation pay for themselves in the end in terms of reduced fuel bills, but the time taken to redress the balance will vary. For example, lagging a hot water tank will pay for itself within a matter of weeks, while tailor-made double glazing for an average family home could take up to 25 years to recoup. Insulation will also make your home comfortable to live in and reduce variations in temperature from room to room.

Most insulation can be installed by any amateur DIY person and this will obviously reduce the capital outlay involved. However, some forms – such as cavity wall insulation – have to be put in by professionals.

Tank lagging

Both the cold water tank and the hot water cylinder should be lagged. A cold water tank is susceptible to freezing in cold weather, especially if the floor of the loft has been insulated so that no heat comes up from the house below. Use

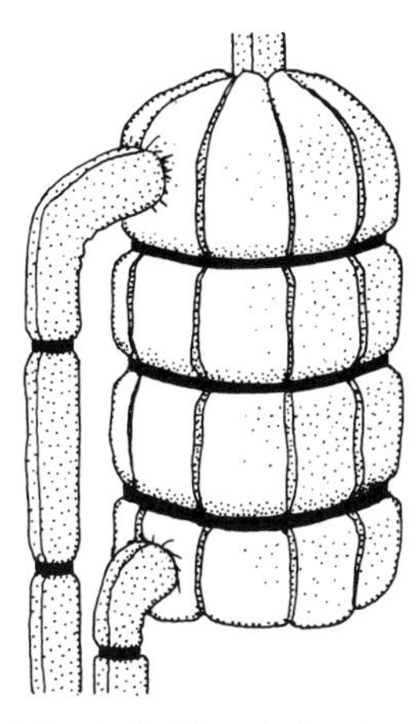

1. An insulating jacket for a hot water cylinder will reduce heat loss. They are available in various sizes and are held in position with tapes

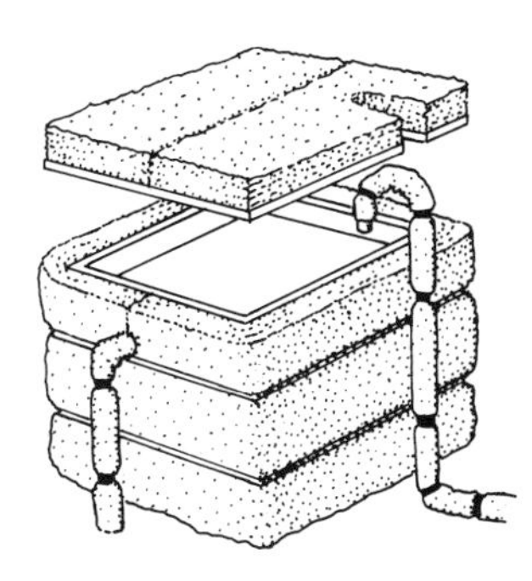

3. A cold water tank can be insulated by using a glass fibre blanket held in position with string. Don't forget to cover the lid as well

mineral wool, glass fibre blanket or insulating board fitted round the side. Also cover the lid or, if there isn't one, make one and insulate that. It is possible to buy tank insulating kits at most DIY shops, but remember to take the measurements of your tank with you when you go to the shop. Do *not* insulate the base of the tank or you will cut it off from the small amount of warmth which comes up from the house below which also helps to prevent freezing. Lagging the hot water cylinder can reduce the cost of your hot water by as much as half. The easiest way to do it is to buy a special lagging jacket and just fit it over the top. Check that the jacket conforms to BS 5615 which means it will be at least 80 mm (3 in) thick.

Lagging the loft

To lag the loft and prevent heat loss through the roof, you need to fill the space between the joists with insulating material. This may be either glass fibre or mineral wool blanket which comes in rolls that are usually 100 mm (4 in) thick. This is just rolled along between the joists and tucked in firmly. Use scissors or a sharp DIY knife to trim it. Alternatively, you can use a loose fill material such as granulated vermiculite or pelletted mineral wool. This can be more effective in homes where the

2. When using loose-fill granules in a loft, level them out using a piece of wood cut to fit between joists

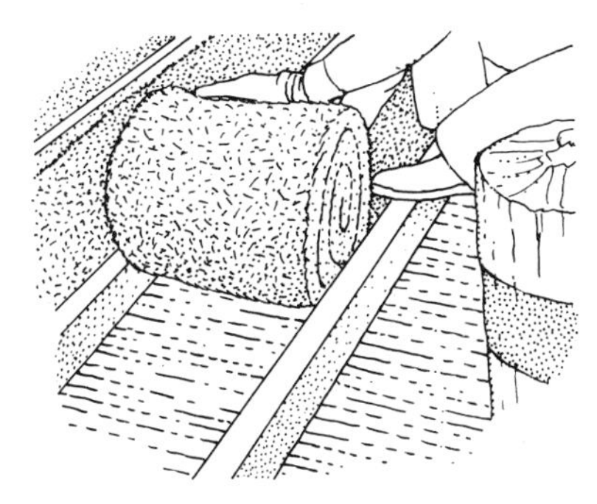

4. Glass fibre blanket is easy to roll out between the joists in the loft. Overlap the section where ends of length join

spaces between the joists are irregular and where there are lots of awkward places to fill.

Be careful when working within the confined space of a loft. Wear protective clothing, goggles and a face mask and put a board across the joists so you don't put your foot down through the ceiling below.

You can get a grant towards the cost

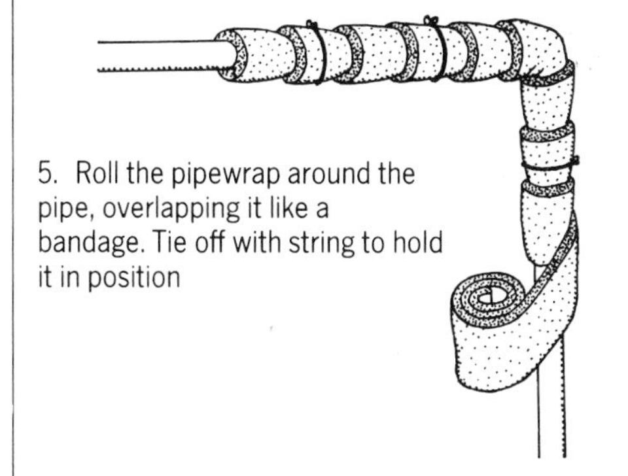

5. Roll the pipewrap around the pipe, overlapping it like a bandage. Tie off with string to hold it in position

of insulating your roof if you have no insulation there and, in some instances, you can get a grant for topping up if the level of insulation is less than 25 mm (1 in). Enquire about this at your local authority and don't start work until the formalities have been completed.

Lagging pipes

You can buy rolls of insulating material which you wrap round and round the pipes like a bandage or pre-formed foam sleeving which you just fit over them. Be careful not to wrap up the pipes so well that you can't get at any vital taps or valves if you need to. Lag cold and hot water pipes to keep the former from freezing up and the latter from losing heat.

Insulating walls

If your home is very exposed, and you lose a lot of heat from the walls, it's probably worth insulating them. Check how cold the external walls are by standing in a corner with one hand on an internal wall and one on an external and feel the difference. If there is an appreciable variation, consider insulating exterior walls.

You can put in internal insulation by lining the walls with aluminium-backed insulation board, but this does reduce the size of the room, which can be a problem if it's small. If you have cavity walls you can call in a firm of professionals and get them to pump treated mineral wool or foam into them to fill the cavity. This treatment is expensive, so get two or three estimates and make sure that the firm you give the job to has a certificate of approval from the British Board of Agrément.

Draughtproofing doors and windows

Any good DIY shop will offer a range of draughtproof materials for doors and windows. All work well but, in general, the more expensive ones look better.

Gaps in floorboards can also produce draughts. Where these are really bad you can either fill with small pieces of wood, or a special filler, or lay treated hardboard over the floor before putting down your chosen floor covering.

Double glazing

Double glazing may take the form of either the sealed unit or the secondary-window type. With the former you usually need to replace the entire window frame and have the new one fitted with a sealed double pane of glass that is factory made. With secondary units you build a separate inner window frame and glaze it. Unless you need, for reasons of rot or other deterioration, to replace your window frames, secondary units are usually cheaper.

Provided you use an installer who is a member of the Glass and Glazing Federation, you have a guarantee. Even if your installer goes bust or fails for some reason to finish the job, the Federation will find another member to complete the work. Get several estimates since they can vary considerably.

Do-it-yourself double glazing is considerably cheaper and also very effective at stopping heat loss through windows and rendering a room with a lot of window space more comfortable in cold weather.

THE WATERWORKS

Major plumbing problems need the attention of a professional unless you are very skilled. But for simple leaks and overflows here is what you should know.

Modern houses have two different types of cistern. One is the cold water cistern for storage and the other is the flushing cistern for toilets. Water flows into both cisterns and is controlled by a valve fixed to a lever and a ball float. As the cistern fills, the float rises; its other end slides along an arm until it presses on a piston which closes the water inlet. If the valve sticks or breaks, flooding is prevented because the water goes out through an overflow pipe fitted inside the tank near the top. This leads to the outside of the house. If, however, a cistern overflows it may be because the float arm is set too high. On modern systems the ballfloat can be adjusted by loosening a nut and lowering it. With older systems, you can bend the arm down, using a pair of pipe grips or an adjustable spanner. Turn off the supply to the cistern first. This cuts off the water at a lower level in the tank. If this doesn't stop the overflow, check if there is water inside the ball; if necessary, unscrew it and replace it with a new one. If you are not confident you can do the job, tie up the float arm to prevent water flowing into the tank. If a plumber can't come at once, operate the arm occasionally to let water into the cistern.

Another reason why a cistern overflows may be because the washer in the inlet valve needs cleaning or replacing. Turn off the water supply to the cistern, remove the split pin and take out the piston and clean it with fine steel wool. Unscrew the end cap of the valve, remove the rubber washer and, if it's worn, fit a new one. Replace the piston, put back the split pin, turn on the water supply and see if the overflow has stopped.

RADIATOR AIRLOCKS

Radiators which don't heat up properly or gurgle alarmingly have probably got an airlock in them. This is most common if the system has been turned off for a period of time. Take the 'key' which should come with the system – or buy one at a hardware shop – and open the vent valve at one end of the radiator, taking care to hold a jug or small bowl underneath to catch the water when it flows. At first you will get a hissing sound as the excess air bleeds out; once the water starts to flow freely, you have cleared the air lock and should tighten the valve again.

PIPE PROBLEMS

You know you have got an airlock in your pipes if, when you turn on a tap, the water trickles out feebly rather than flowing freely. It may even stop completely. This is usually accompanied by a knocking noise in the pipes. You can cure it yourself if you have separate hot and cold taps in the kitchen, but will need the services of a plumber if you have a mixer tap.

Take a piece of hosepipe and two adjustable clips and fit the hose in a U-shape between the hot and cold taps, tightening the clips with a screwdriver. Turn on first the hot and then the cold tap. Let them run for a few minutes so that the mains pressure from the cold tap can force the water and air back through the pipes into the hot water storage tank or

PUTTING ON A NEW WASHER

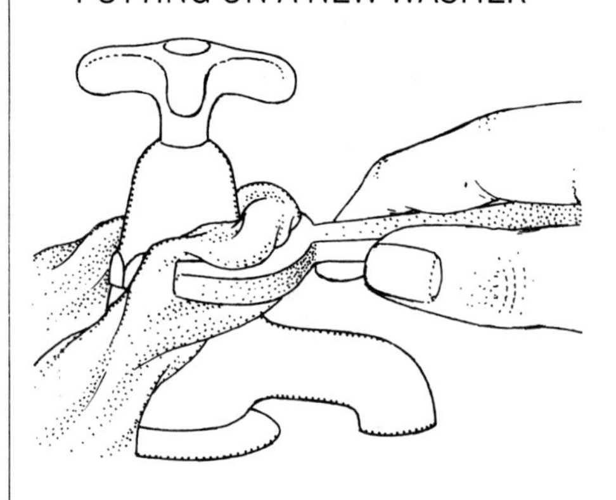

1. Turn off the water supply to the tap. Carefully unscrew the chrome cover, using a piece of cloth under spanner to protect the chrome from damage. Apply pressure slowly

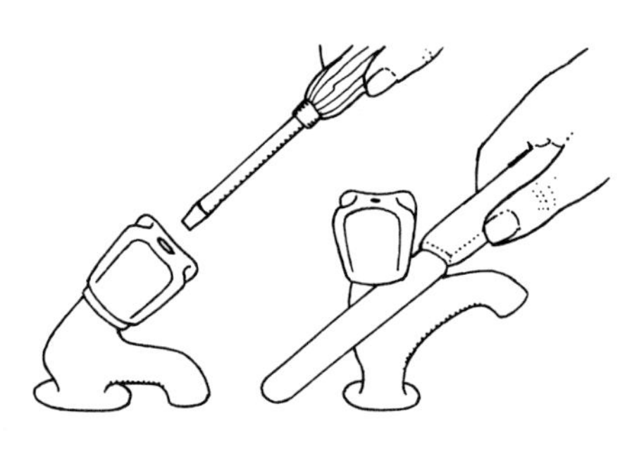

2. Modern taps with plastic tops can be removed by levering out the top disc to unscrew the small retaining screw. If the top won't pull off, carefully lever either side with knive blade

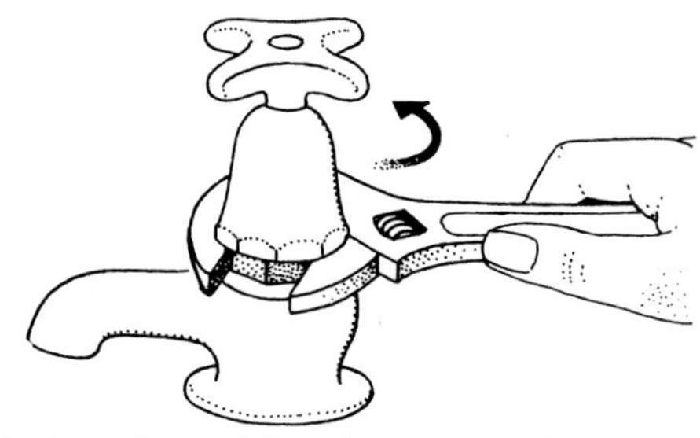

3. Open the tap fully and unscrew the large hexagon nut with adjustable spanner. Lift out the head section from body and remove any loose bits of washer from the inside of the tap

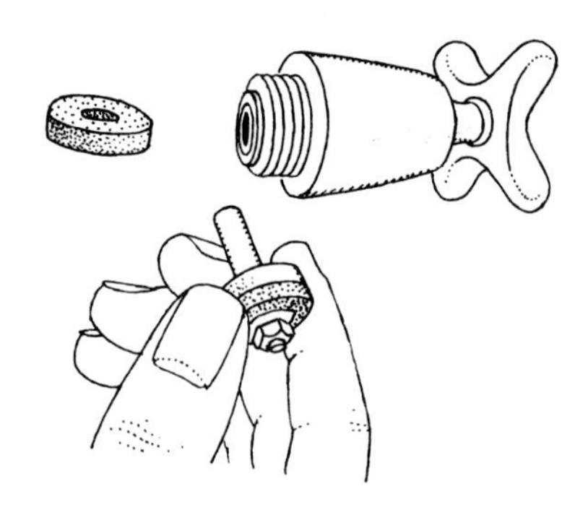

4. Remove the jumper (part that holds the washer) and unscrew the retaining nut with pliers and spanner. Replace washer with a new one of the correct size; refit retaining nut

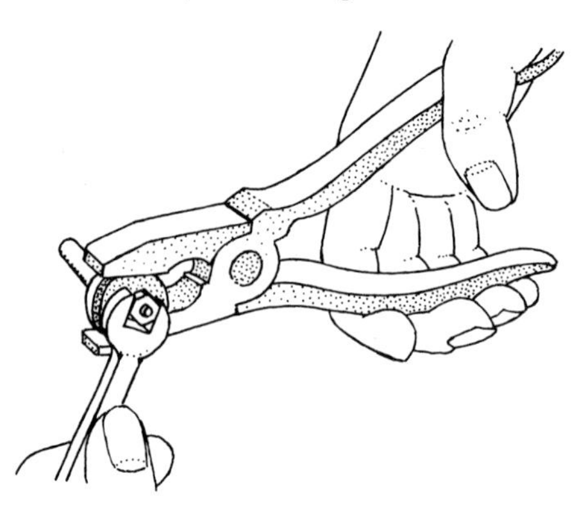

5. Tighten up the nut with the spanner, taking care not to damage washer. Fit jumper back into head section. Reassemble carefully and tighten up head section. Turn on water supply

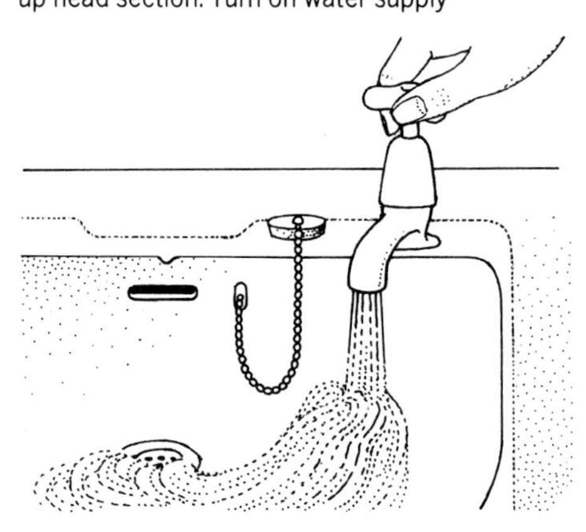

6. Check for drips and leaks around body of tap. Tighten up hexagon nut a bit more if necessary, then screw on chrome cover. Turn on tap to ensure that water is flowing properly

cylinder. This should eliminate the airlock. If it doesn't work after five minutes or so, stop, then try again. After 20 minutes with no success, call a plumber.

Leaking pipes

If a pipe starts to leak near a cold water storage cistern, turn off the stop tap close to the cistern. Otherwise turn off the water supply at the main stopcock. Open all taps and flush the loo to empty the cistern quickly. It is important for every householder to know where the stopcock is and to keep it in a condition where it can be turned reasonably easily without the use of tools. Note that, before turning off the water supply, you should switch off gas- or oil-fired boilers and electric immersion heaters. If your water is heated by solid fuel, shovel as much as you can out of the boiler into a metal bucket to help it cool down quickly.

Copper pipes which fail at compression joints sometimes just need the nuts on either side of the joint to be tightened. If this doesn't work, or if the leak is on the pipe itself, turn the water off and drain the pipe, then make a temporary repair by giving the area a quick coat of epoxy resin adhesive and binding it round first with rags and then with polythene tape. Or keep a special repair kit handy and use this. Leaks in lead pipes usually occur because the pipe has split. Turn off the water supply and tap the split with a hammer to try and close it. Call a plumber quickly.

Frozen pipes

To avoid frozen pipes, take precautions when the temperature starts to drop. Keep plugs in position in baths, sinks and basins to prevent the outlets being blocked by ice. If you have dripping taps that really need new washers (see opposite page), put salt in the waste traps to help prevent freezing.

If pipes do freeze up in spite of this, play a hair dryer along the length of the frozen area starting at the tap end and working back to the tank. If you can't thaw the pipes fairly quickly, call a plumber. In any case, check the joints on copper piping afterwards, as freezing often pushes them out of their compression fittings.

Burst pipes

When a pipe bursts, turn on all the cold water taps in the house and turn off the main stopcock. Wrap old towels or rags around the burst section. If the pipes are part of the hot water system, turn off the boiler or immersion heater. Call a plumber to repair the damage.

BLOCKED SINKS

Sinks which aren't blocked too seriously can usually be cleared by an application of a proprietary drain cleaner, following the manufacturer's instructions, or by putting down a handful of washing soda dissolved in half a litre (one pint) of hot water. Failing this, you will need to use a sink plunger. Block off the overflow and work the plunger up and down. Don't be too vigorous with basins or you may pull them away from the wall.

For really bad blockages, follow the procedure below and, if that does not work, call the plumber.

UNBLOCKING A SINK

1. Blockages (caused by fat, tea-leaves, etc., with other bits of solids) can sometimes be cleared with a proprietary drain cleaner or a handful of washing soda and hot water

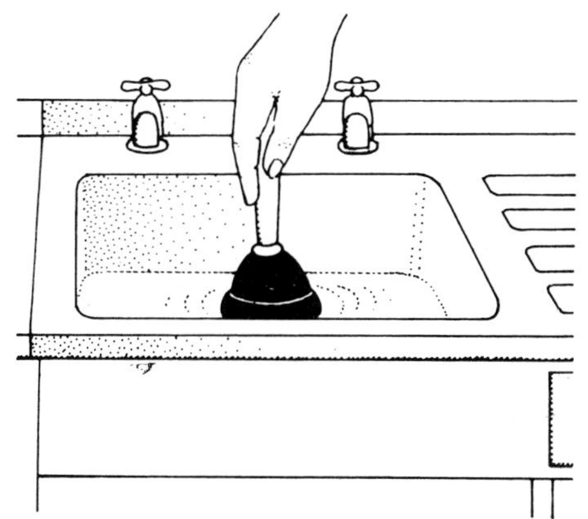

2. Otherwise, use a sink plunger. Block off the sink overflow and work the plunger up and down. With a washbasin, don't be too vigorous – you may loosen the wall brackets

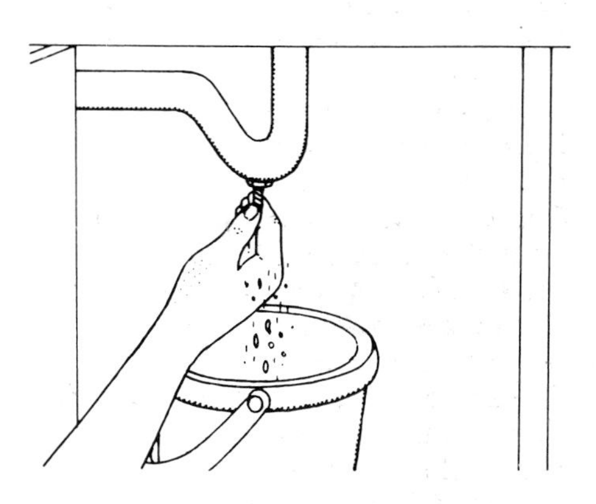

3. If this treatment fails, get to work on the U-bend. First put a bucket underneath it, to protect the floor, and then carefully remove the screw plug at the bottom of the bend

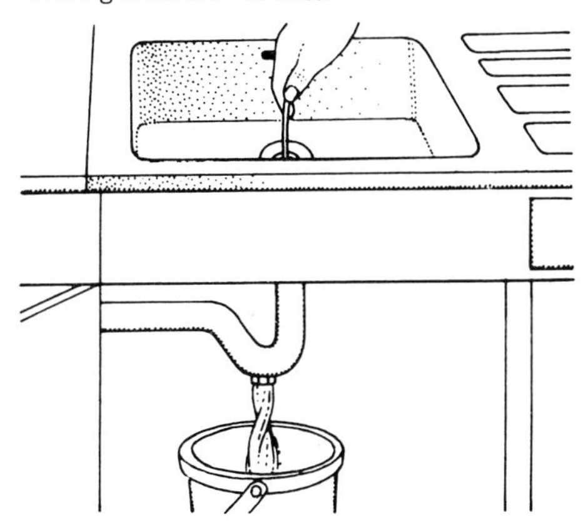

4. Push a piece of flexible wire – a length of curtain wire is ideal – down the sink outlet. Then, using a twisting action, work the wire up and down and try to loosen the blockage

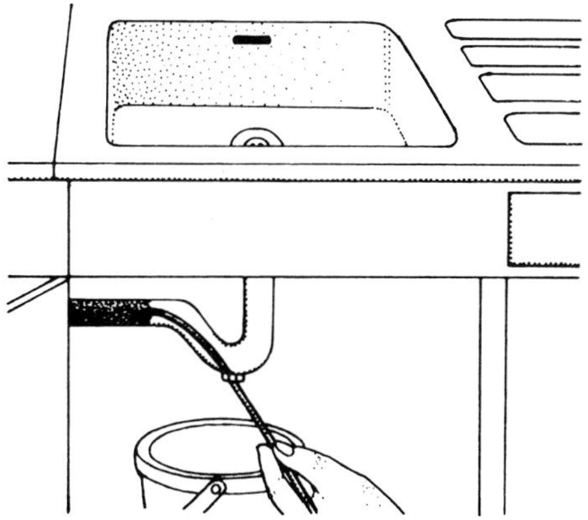

5. If this doesn't clear the obstruction, push the wire into the section of pipe under the sink or washbasin which leads away from the bend, and continue with the twisting motion

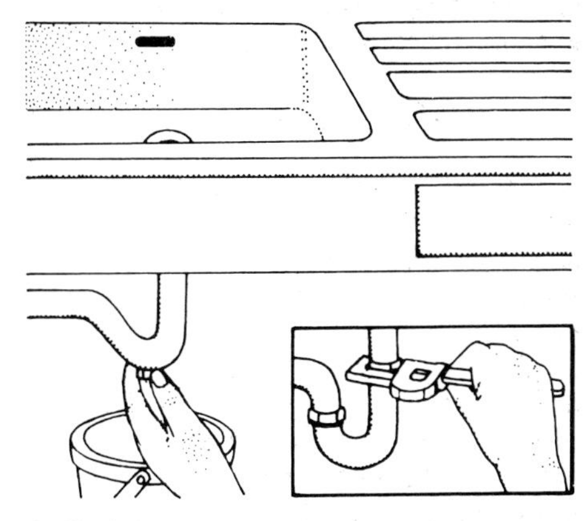

6. Flush through with water; replace screw plug. (If you have a modern trap without a plug, unscrew the trap section; this calls for a large adjustable spanner or a plumber)

Wired Up Safely

Keep a constant check on your electrics. Damaged flexes and incorrectly fused appliances can cause damage.

The first thing to do is to make sure that your wiring is in good order. Unless it's been installed within the last five years, have it checked either by someone from your local Electricity Board or by an approved electrical contractor who is on the Roll of the National Inspection Council for Electrical Installation Contracting (NICEIC). Ask the inspector if the circuit will be able to take the load of any appliance – such as a washing machine, dishwasher or freezer – which hasn't been in the house before. Older circuits can sometimes be altered or extended to cope with this (see also page 20).

PLUGS AND SOCKETS

The most basic parts of your home electrics are the plugs and sockets and you should learn a little about them. Everyone should know how to wire a plug; the information is usually supplied with the instructions accompanying any electrical device you buy.

Britain and many other countries have standard colours for 3-wire flexes on appliances. Brown is for the live wire, usually marked L in the plug; blue is neutral, marked N in the plug; and green and yellow stripes indicate the earth, which is either marked E in the plug or is denoted by a special symbol.

Don't buy cheap plugs from market stalls as these may be imported and have in some instances been found to be lethal. Buy from reputable electrical retailers and check that the plugs conform to BS 1363.

Check all the plugs in the home regularly to ensure that the terminals and cover have not worked loose, that the flex is securely fixed in the flex grip and that there are no bare wires poking through the sides. Replace a plug if it becomes broken or cracked.

For equipment that tends to get rough handling, like vacuum cleaners and electric drills, you can buy smash-proof plugs which are made especially to withstand rough treatment.

FUSE-WISE

It is essential to fit the correct fuse size for the appliance's wattage rating. One higher than that recommended defeats the whole object of a fuse, which is safety. On the other hand, if you use a fuse that is too low it is likely to blow when the appliance is switched on.

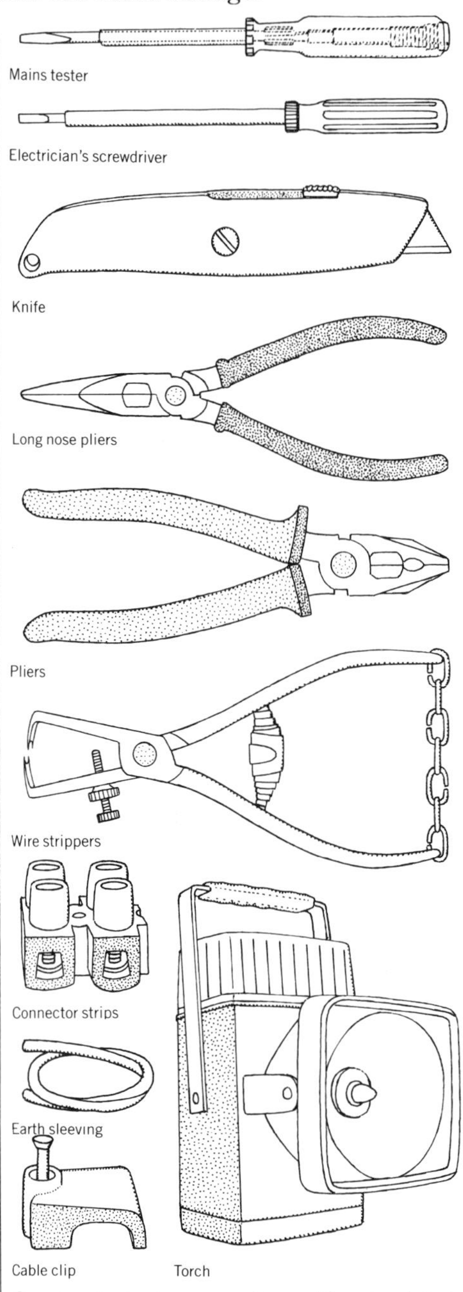

A mains tester is a screwdriver with an insulated shaft and handle. A neon bulb lights up in the handle if power is present. **Electrician's screwdrivers** have insulated handles and long thin shafts to reach into confined spaces. **Pliers** Choose heavy duty combination pliers with wire cutting jaws and insulated handles. Long nosed pliers are useful for manipulating wires. **A sharp knife** is useful for cutting/trimming cable. **A torch** with a swivel head can be stood or hung with the beam directed on the work. **Connector strips** Ready-made insulated connectors for joining lengths of flex and cable sold as a strip to be cut as required. **Earth sleeving** is used to insulate the bare earth wire inside fittings. **Cable clips** are for fixing cable and flex to a wall, skirting or joist. **A wire stripper** can be adjusted to cut through the insulation without damaging the core

In 3-amp and 13-amp plugs, use a cartridge fuse. For appliances rated up to 720 watts you should use a 3-amp fuse and for appliances rated between 720 and 3,000 watts (3kW) use a 13-amp fuse. Keep spare fuses in an accessible place so that you can replace one quickly if it goes.

REWIRING A FUSE

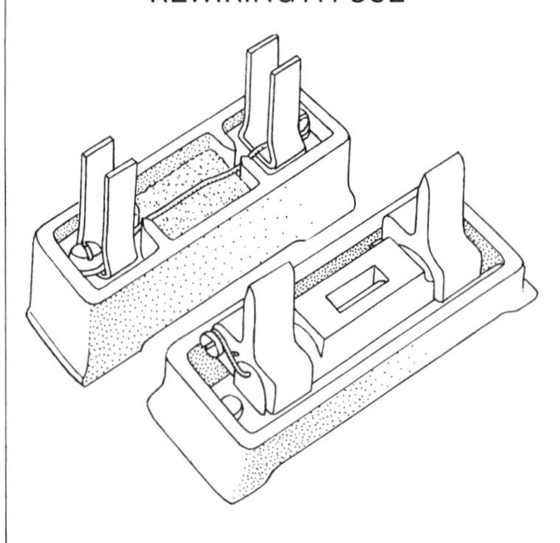

Turn off main switch at consumer unit and inspect each fuse to locate broken wire. Unscrew and remove wire. Insert new wire of correct rating, looping one end round screw and tightening. Run wire across ceramic bridge or through centre insulator and connect to other screw

REPLACING A CARTRIDGE FUSE

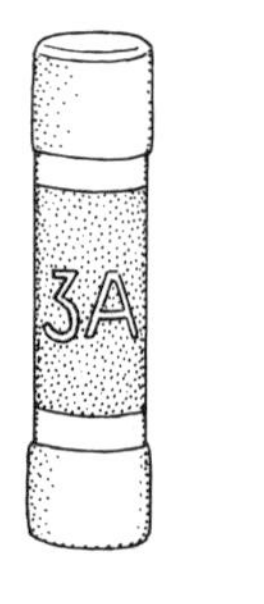

A cartridge fuse is a wire contained in an insulated tube with metal caps. A plug will take a 3-amp fuse (up to 720 watts) or 13-amp (up to 3000 watts). Always use a fuse of the appropriate rating. To replace, lever the old fuse out and clip in a new one. Some consumer units are also fitted with cartridge fuses

WIRING A 13 AMP PLUG

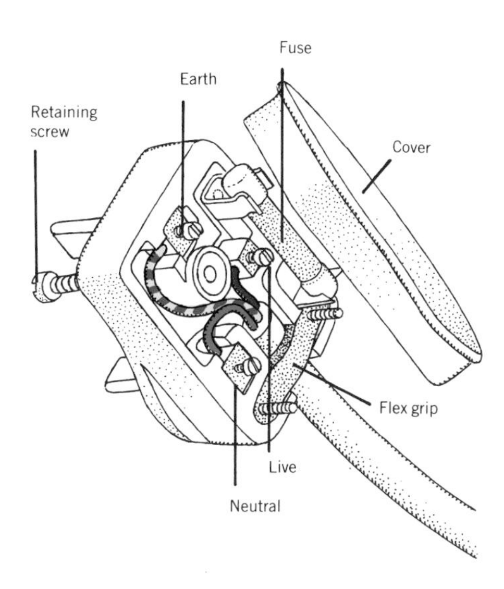

Undo the screw in the centre of the plug to remove the cover. Remove the cartridge fuse and slacken the flex grip. Strip 50mm of sheathing from the flex. Hold in position on the plug to judge required length of core wires and cut them to length. Trim off insulation and fix wires in terminals according to colour code. Live, neutral and earth terminals are always in the same positions. Some flex is only two-core – secure these wires only into live and neutral terminals. Secure the flex with the grips, replace the fuse of correct rating and cover

ADAPT WITH CARE

If you use a lot of multi-adaptors around your home, it indicates that you don't have enough socket outlets; you should consider either turning single sockets into double, adding extra outlets or having the place rewired. Adaptors should not be considered as permanent socket substitutes; they are easy to misuse and can cause problems. If you must use one as a temporary measure, make sure it has its own cartridge fuse and fits firmly into the socket outlet. Don't plug in more than two appliances at one time and always check that their combined ratings don't exceed those of the outlet, which will usually be 13 amp. Check regularly that the adaptor has not worked loose in the socket outlet. If contact points won't meet, that will cause overheating. Too many adaptors in use around a house can mean that the circuit is overloaded – a real fire hazard.

FLEX CARE

Flexes are used to convey the power from the socket outlet to the appliance or light. Check them regularly – especially on things like irons and kitchen appliances, where they can be damaged easily by touching sources of heat. Replace them yourself when they become worn, or have an expert do it. Don't repair them with adhesive or insulating tape except as a temporary measure and don't extend them unless you use a special flex connector; just twisting the wires together and covering them with tape is dangerous. Avoid trailing flexes, especially in areas where people walk since, apart from being easy to trip over, constant walking over a flex will damage its insulation. This may cause overheating and, eventually, fire. Never lay flexes under floor coverings or anywhere they might become damp or wet.

MIND YOUR MACHINES

Use electrical appliances according to the manufacturer's instructions and have them serviced regularly rather than waiting for them to break down. Always switch off at the socket and remove the plug before attempting to check or repair any electrical appliance.

LIGHTING UP

Don't use a lighting circuit for anything over the maximum wattage it is intended to carry and *never* plug an appliance into a lamp holder. Metal light fittings, whether ceiling-fixed or on table lamps, must have the metal parts earthed and should never be used from a 2-pin plug or an unearthed socket outlet.

Check the flexes on hanging lights from time to time, especially if they carry heavy fittings or shades. Find out the maximum recommended wattage of the light bulb for each table lamp and don't exceed it. If it's not indicated on the label, ask in your Electricity Board shop. Bear in mind that potentially dangerous areas of the home like stairs and bathrooms should be well lit so that people can see where they are going.

ELECTRIC HEATERS

Radiant fires must have a permanent safety guard built into them. Don't let them become dusty as this can ignite when they are switched on. Don't use radiant fires or convection heaters within at least a metre (a yard) of furnishings like curtains or loose covers and never hang clothes near them to dry.

REPLACING LIGHT SWITCHES

Turn off electricity at main switch and remove appropriate circuit fuse. Always do this before working on any electrical fittings or wiring. If you are in any doubt, don't take chances. Get an electrician to do the job for you

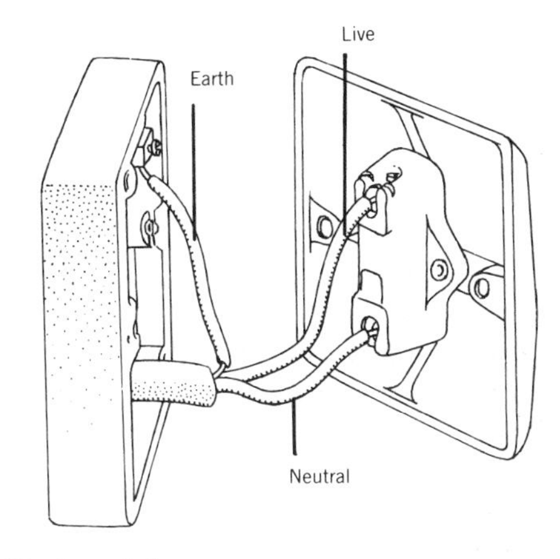

Single switch
To replace a light switch remove two screws holding the cover. Undo terminal screws and remove wires, taking note of where they go. Replace earth wire (green/yellow-sleeved wire) to earth terminal. In older wiring the earth wire will be green sleeved.

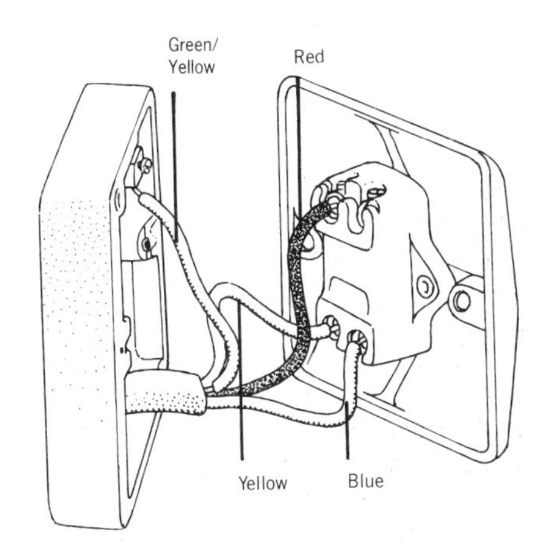

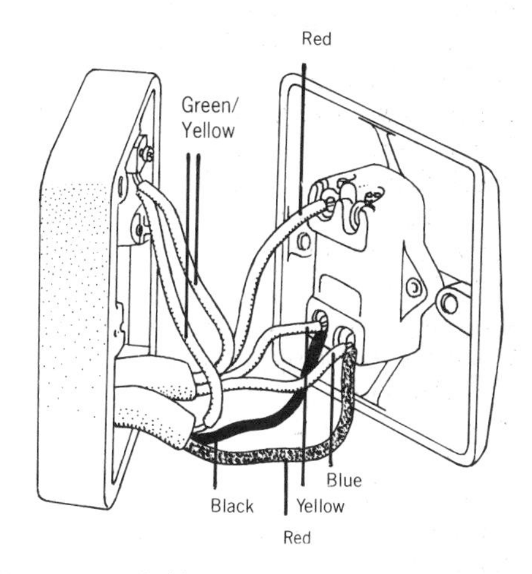

Two way switching
This is a bit more complicated than replacing a single switch, but provided you are replacing the switches with same type it isn't that difficult. Make a drawing showing the colour of wires and where they go before removing from old terminals.
Do one switch at a time. Change the wires one by one and fix them into appropriate new terminals. Two-way switches are completely different from the single type, and you can't change an ordinary circuit into two-way just by replacing the switches.

Making Your Home Safe

Once you have spent money on your home and its contents you want it safe from break-ins. Here is what you should do.

Business is booming for today's burglars. Today they are not necessarily all hard-nosed professionals but frequently children who seize the opportunity presented by an unlocked door or a window left ajar. Home security is thus vitally important if you recall the sobering thought that someone is burgled every 30 seconds.

Some of the things you should do to discourage burglars are pure common sense – such as not leaving a note for the milkman saying 'away till Friday' and not leaving the front door key on a string inside the letter box for your cleaning woman to let herself in. Others are practical, positive measures which you can take to prevent any would-be thief from being successful. While it's true that a determined thief can get in anywhere, he is only likely to persevere if he knows you have got a priceless Old Master on your wall or a cache of fabulous jewels under the mattress. If he is just after cash and valuables that are lying around, he is likely to be deterred by security measures and move on to somewhere that is less well protected.

Different types of home need different protection, and your lifestyle will also determine such facts as whether or not you need a burglar alarm. To find out just what would be best for you, get in touch with the Crime Prevention Officer at your local police station. He will visit your home and explain to you the weak points in your security and what you should do to improve them. You do not pay for this service and it is time well spent.

DOOR AND WINDOW LOCKS

All outside doors should have really strong locks. Even if the existing locks in your new home are satisfactory, it's none the less sensible to change them. You can't be sure how many keys the previous owner had in circulation; fit your own locks and eliminate one possible source of trouble. If the doors themselves are in poor condition or have a lot of glass that, if broken, would allow access, fit new ones.

Each door should be secured with a lock that complies at least with BS 3621 (Specification for Thief-Resistant Locks) and has five levers. These are known as mortise or surface rim locks and should be the deadlock type. They are operated by a key. It is sensible also to have a night latch, which is a rim lock with a spring-operated latch. Some firms will arrange to have your keys registered against your signature so that nobody else can get a set. This means you cannot have new keys cut by anyone other than the manufacturer but is a useful security measure.

On lightweight doors which open outwards it's easy for an intruder to break in on the hinged side, either by using brute force or by knocking out the centre pin of the exposed hinge. Overcome this possibility by fitting hinge bolts at the top and bottom of the door. These will project and lock into the framework when the door is closed so that it can't be forced or lifted off.

French doors are particularly vulnerable and need to be secured with

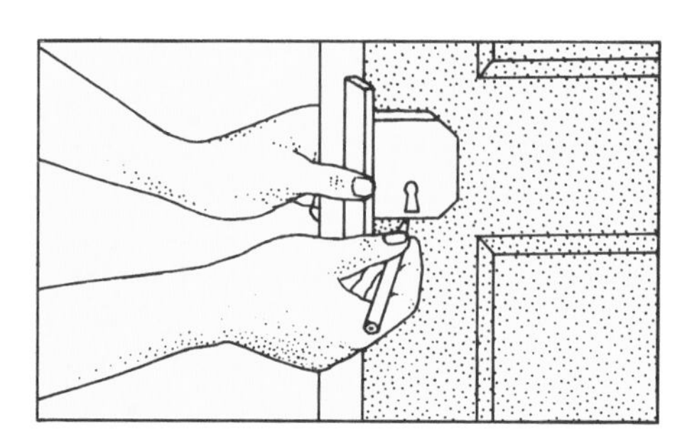

1. Hold the lock against the door stile. With a sharp pencil mark the outline of the lock casing on to the door edge

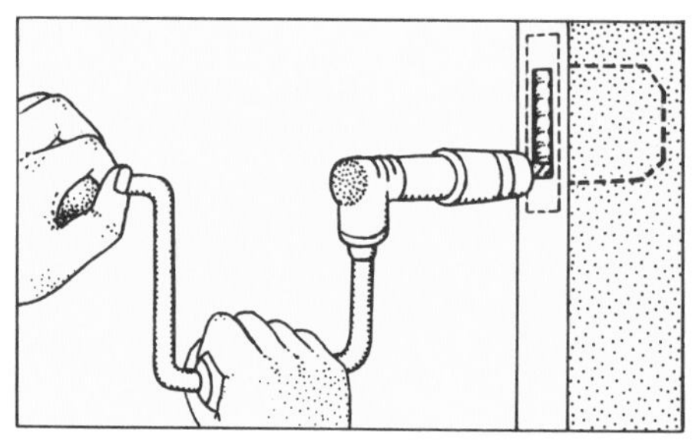

2. Drill a vertical row of holes the same diameter as the lock width and the depth of the casing. Clean out the waste with a wood chisel

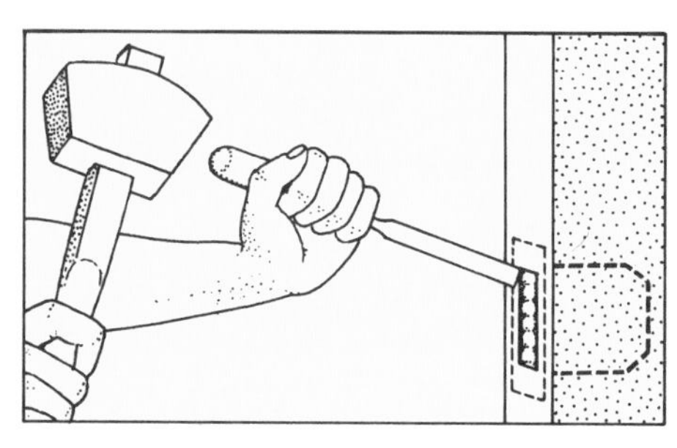

3. Chisel out a shallow recess for the face plate. Hold the lock against the face of the door and mark the position of the keyhole

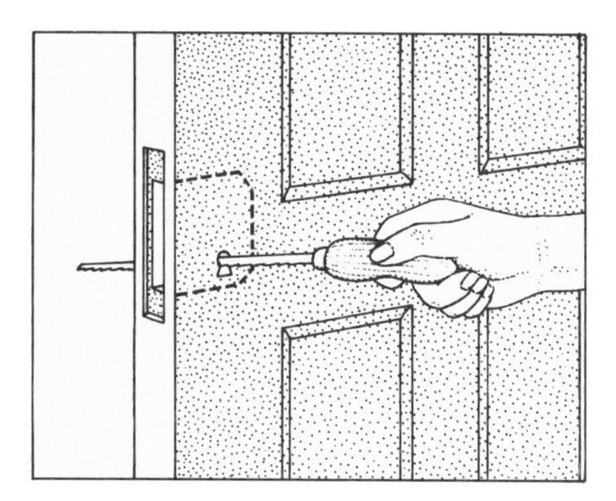

4. Drill a hole to the right diameter and finish it off with a chisel or small padsaw. Make the keyhole slightly larger than the key

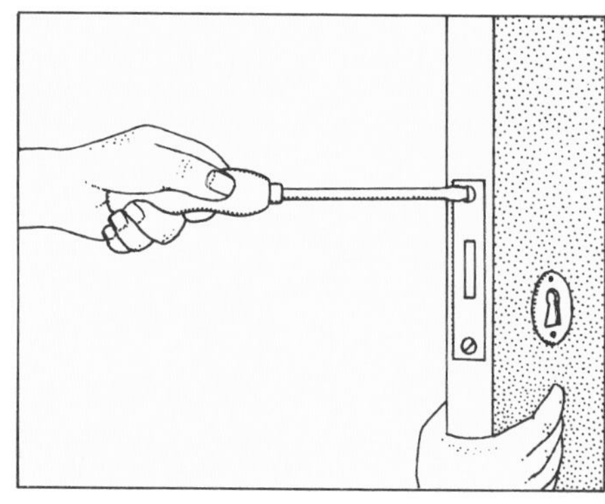

5. Fit the escutcheon plates over keyhole. Fit the lock and test the key in the keyhole Screw the face plate to the door edge

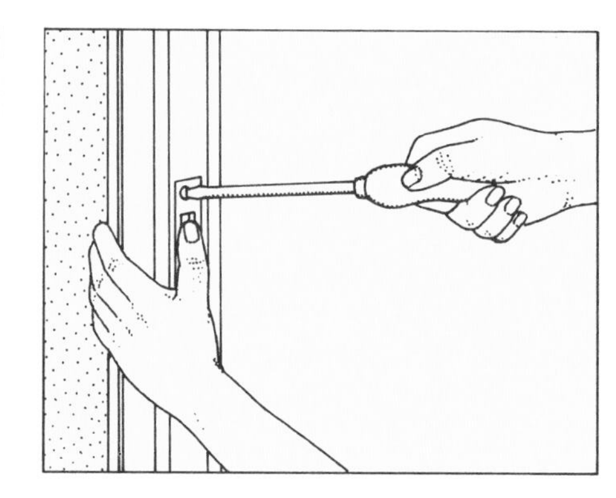

6. Close the door and turn the key. Mark the position of the striker plate on the door jamb. Chisel a recess to fit it. Screw the plate into position

mortise lock and mortise bolts at the top and bottom of the doors. With metal frames you may need to fit lockable surface bolts which will probably have to be installed professionally. With sliding patio doors, fit locks which screw to the frame of the door so that they can't be lifted off their tracks. This is necessary in addition to the locks with which they come fitted, even if they are the high security type.

Front doors should, in addition, be fitted with a chain or bar which allows the door to be opened a few inches so that you can speak with a caller and check who it is. If you don't like opening the door until you know who's there, install a spyhole – there is one on the market that lets you talk to callers as well as see them.

Windows vary from home to home so it's impossible to be specific about what type of lock should be fitted. The Crime Prevention Officer will be able to advise you. Most window locks are sold as being suitable for a particular type of window – be it casement, sash or sliding. Window locks have a key or other opening device which should be kept reasonably near so that they can be opened and shut easily, but out of view of a passing burglar who could break the glass and use the key to open the lock. Louvre windows are easily forced so either glue the glass blades to the end sections, fit bars across the frame or fit a special type of louvre with built-in security fittings.

In high risk areas it may be suggested that you install window grilles or shutters. Make sure that these comply with the fire regulations so that you can escape in an emergency.

BURGLAR ALARMS

Burglar alarms *can* act as a deterrent. It's essential however, that they are properly installed and don't go off unnecessarily, so that your neighbours get used to the sound and take no notice of it. The most expensive types are wired up to the local police station so that when they sound the police are sent to investigate.

You can have your alarm installed professionally or fit a DIY model yourself. It's difficult to assess the cost of a professional installation since the amount of wiring, number of pressure pads and so on will vary according to the size and layout of your home. Do-it-yourself alarm systems are fairly basic and usually include a control unit, alarm, contacts for doors and windows, pressure pads and a panic button which you fit by the bed or the front door.

Whichever type of alarm you install, you must remember to set it when you go out, and have it fused in a position that allows you enough time when you come into the house to switch it off before the alarm sounds.

Don't make it easy for thieves to break in; take steps to protect your home: **1** put lights on a time switch; **2** mark pinchable equipment with a code number; **3** fit a spyhole and **4** a chain to the front door; **5** have a light outside the door; **6** in blocks of flats, use an entryphone; **7** don't leave empty bottles and newspapers outside while you're away; **8** install a burglar alarm and **9** use special paint on drainpipes; **10** install window locks; **11** wire up outside light onto lawn; **12** fasten ladders to walls or put away; **13** engrave car number on each of its windows; **14** keep garage doors locked at all times

SAFELY HIDDEN

Home safes are becoming increasingly popular as places to store valuable items and documents. Apart from being difficult for burglars to break into, they also protect things from flood and fire. While it is possible to install a home safe yourself, it's quite difficult to fix it securely and correctly so it can't be removed lock, stock and barrel. Safes are fitted either into walls or under the floor and most reputable firms have accredited installers.

LOOK AS IF YOU ARE IN

One way of deterring would-be burglars is to make it appear that someone is at home. You can do this by using time switches to activate lights, the radio or television. You can also fit light sensors which switch lights on automatically when it gets dark and turn them off again when it's light. For the very rich there is also the possibility of installing electrically-operated curtains which can be put on a time switch.

KNOW YOUR OWN

It's a help for the police if you can recognize items which have been stolen. After all, one television looks much like another. With small and unusual items it's a good idea to take a photograph and keep it somewhere safe, possibly even in your bank. Large items can be either marked with an anti-theft pen which shows up only under ultra-violet light or be engraved with your name and postcode using a special tool.

BE SENSIBLE

Whatever precautions you take to make your home secure, above all be *sensible*. Lock outside doors even if you are only slipping across the road to post a letter.

Don't leave the back door open on a sunny day if you are going to be upstairs for any length of time. Don't leave cash lying around, or your handbag near a window where it can be seen.

When you go away ask your neighbours to keep an eye on your home and, if possible, to go in every day and remove letters and circulars from your mat so that anyone looking through the letterbox doesn't get a clue that you are away. Never, never leave your house keys under the mat, in a shed or anywhere they could be found. Either give a spare set to whoever needs it or lodge one with a reliable neighbour.

CHAPTER TWO

ROOM BY ROOM

THE KITCHEN

Whether you are cooking in a cupboard or a rambling family room, here is how to make the best of it.

Of all the rooms in the house, the kitchen is the most difficult and nerve-racking to plan, because it doesn't give you a second chance. In the sitting room, dining room and bedroom, for instance, you can shunt around furniture until you have got it right. But you can't juggle creatively with things like cookers, sinks and washing machines. Once they are connected or plumbed in, that is virtually that, so it's worth the effort to get it right first time.

THE SMALL GALLEY KITCHEN

The shape of your kitchen will determine its potential. If it's small, and longer than it's wide, you have no choice but to go for a galley kitchen. In a very narrow room (see the left-hand kitchen over the page), this will mean ranging everything down the length of one wall, although you could – as shown there – continue round the width too, if door and window positions permit it. A less narrow room offers double the scope, because you can range things down the length of both walls. See the black and white kitchen on page 59 for a perfect example. The small galley kitchen is so restricted in area, it's always advisable to install fitted units. This is partly because they use space to maximum advantage, and partly because they give a streamlined appearance – essential in a room that would look claustrophobic if cluttered.

If you can only fit units down the length of one wall, try to exploit it to the full. Choose base cupboards with a width of 600 mm (23½ in) rather than 500 mm (19¾ in). (Width is the measurement front-to-back, not side-to-side.)

Aim to use the wall virtually from floor to ceiling – most manufacturers make tall as well as standard top cupboards, and although their upper regions are not easy to reach, they are useful for seldom-used items. There are also 'midway' units which fit between base and top cupboards.

Two-way stretch

If you are fitting units down the length of two opposite walls, be wary of using every inch of both walls, with a floor-to-ceiling arrangement either side. Although it could work with all-white units in an all-white setting, it often runs the risk of looking 'walled-in' and oppressive. The kitchen on page 59, for instance, uses open ground-level storage with nothing above to balance the 'solid' wall of units opposite. Of course, this is a stylish, high-tech kitchen, but even with a more conventional approach – unless you really need to use every inch – it might be wise to provide a breathing space by confining one wall to just bottom cupboards.

Either way, to fit units along two facing walls, you will need to ensure that there will be a space of about 120 cm (4 ft) between unit fronts to avoid the possibility of cupboard doors colliding. If you have slightly less, there are alternatives. You could choose units with sliding doors, bearing in mind that it only takes a few breadcrumbs to gum up the runners, and when open, you can only see into half the cupboard. Other doors that eat up less space when open include double-doors that open in the middle; doors that fold in the middle; and up-and-over doors. As these tend to be confined to the more expensive ranges, you might simply prefer to go for narrower units. Remember though, that this will mean a narrower work surface.

Even flexible sizing doesn't come cheap, however, so if you are tight for money as well as space, you could consider using top cupboards as bottom cupboards, spanning them with a custom-made counter-top. (Obviously this improvisation could only work in conjunction with a facing run of conventional units, with the width to take equipment and provide a serious work surface.) Alternatively, you could use narrow open shelving opposite conventional units but only if you are a

Right: in this informally elegant kitchen, units with cream-dragged paintwork and tiny-paned glazed wall cupboards provide efficiency in a relaxed and gentle way, and suggest long-established, traditional furniture. The room's light and summery mood is rather Edwardian, and flower-patterned French pottery and Chinese Chippendale-style cane chairs create an easy relationship with the garden outside

really disciplined person, who will keep the contents regimentally neat.

Ideally, all doors into the kitchen should open outwards. If this isn't possible in a small kitchen, switch to bi-fold doors that use half the usual floor-space; or sliding doors or concertina doors, that use up none at all.

THE L-SHAPED KITCHEN

With a larger oblong room, you can create a neat L-shape by filling one long wall and one shorter wall with units – the green kitchen on page 62-63 provides a classic example. This arrangement has the advantage of leaving plenty of floor-area free, and is ideal for people who like room to manoeuvre.

It's a good idea to start from the corner unit and work out from either side. Then any odd gaps at the ends can be filled by work surface with vertically divided tray-space underneath or, better still from a streamlining point of view, with a narrow infill panel. Many unit-manufacturers now make these for a perfect wall-to-wall fit.

THE U-SHAPED KITCHEN

This arrangement uses three out of the kitchen's four walls, and is suitable for square or squarish rooms. Basically this is the shape used in the kitchens on page 58, because although they are open-plan in both cases the peninsular bar, which has units underneath, creates a third 'wall' in working terms.

Whereas in galley kitchens, everything is immediately to hand, in U-shaped and longer L-shaped kitchens, there is inevitably a lot of to-ing and fro-ing between the key areas of cooker, sink and fridge. This is what the experts call 'the work triangle' and, in theory, you should be able to make the entire round trip in about 6 metres (6 yards). The most important distance to watch is between sink and hob, because this is the path that is most frequently trodden. It's up to you, though, how stringently you adhere to this theory.

Above: a wealth of natural material warms this white kitchen. Terracotta quarry tiles cover worktops and floor, unit fronts are trimmed with pale blonde wood, a false ceiling of honey-coloured tongued-and-grooved pine looks mellow – and incorporates recessed downlighters

Left: by sticking to white, this narrow galley kitchen gives the impression of plenty of breathing space. Horizontally-laid ceramic tiles make the floor look wider, and carry up the wall for visual continuity. Inset hob and sink bowls allow the worktop to flow in an unbroken line

OPEN-PLAN KITCHENS

Many of the kitchens on these pages are open-plan, but even so, the actual kitchen areas conform to the three basic shapes, adapted to suit particular requirements. If you look at the example on page 56, it's a conventional galley kitchen, if you look at the main kitchen on page 57, it's basically a conventional U-shape. But think long and hard before opting for an open-plan situation – even a limited one, that combines just dining and cooking areas, without incorporating the living 'room'.

The main thing is to be realistic about your own capabilities. If you are lucky enough to be a relaxed and natural cook, you will enjoy the fact that you can join in the conversation with family and friends while preparing the meals. But less easy-going cooks may prefer peace and privacy to concentrate on the pots and pans – and curse and mutter to themselves with impunity. If you know you prefer privacy, but only have space for the merest sliver of a kitchen, yet hate the idea of being shut in a 'cupboard', one compromise might be to have a simple opening in the wall. Then, although your field of vision would allow you to see nearly all the room beyond, only a small part of the kitchen would be visible from the other room.

Separate tables

When planning a kitchen-cum-dining room where all meals are eaten (not just family snacks and breakfasts), there are essentially two ways of going about it. You can include the table within the kitchen; or divide the room into separate areas, one for cooking and one for eating.

The first approach demands lots of space. You need clearance of at least a metre (a yard) between the edges of work surfaces and the backs of dining chairs to enable people to get up from the table freely. See the farmhouse-style kitchen on page 57 for an idea of the space required.

The second approach requires you to define separate areas while still retaining a relationship between them. The easiest way to do this is with a peninsular unit, which also provides a useful serving area. But if you want a division that provides more privacy, you could use tall, or floor-to-ceiling, free-standing shelves, and fill them with your best-looking casseroles and storage jars, adding a few leafy houseplants to soften the effect. A traditional dresser turned end-on to the wall, with the front and its contents facing the diners, could be an attractive alternative. Whatever approach you finally decide on, try to provide a cooker hood in the kitchen area, so the smell of the first course won't still be lingering by the time diners have reached the pudding stage.

GETTING DOWN TO DETAILS

Once you have decided the basic shape and type of kitchen, you can start on the

Above: two runs of cupboards create an open-plan kitchen where everything – from central heating pipes to factory-style lighting – are meant to be seen in the full glory of their function. Contrasting textures of shiny, gloss-painted surfaces and rough matt flooring, of gleaming steel and natural wood, ensure there's plenty of excitement despite lack of colour

particulars. Aim to create a logical sequence that follows the order in which you do things: getting food out of the fridge, preparing it, cooking it and serving it. A possible arrangement, although it shouldn't be interrupted by full-height units or doors (which ideally should be kept together), could be: work surface with fridge underneath/sink/work surface/ cooker/work surface. Also take into consideration the following points, even if circumstances force you to ignore some of them.

The cooker: avoid siting the cooker in a corner where you won't have any elbow room, or by a door that could crash into you while you are cooking. Avoid placing it under a window, too. This applies even if you have a roller blind rather than dangerously flammable curtains. You could burn yourself reaching over the hob to open the window, and in the case of a gas cooker, draughts could blow out the flames without your noticing. Be sure to provide a work surface alongside the cooker (each side if possible), so that there is somewhere to put down hot pans immediately: in a small kitchen, this could be the stainless steel draining board of a sink on one side. (See Chapter 3 for

Left: in this traditional, farmhouse-style kitchen, table, dresser and fitted units were all custom-built in maple by the same manufacturer. Patterned blue and white wall-tiles, and plenty of blue and white china, bring light relief to the expanses of wood

Below: this superb open-plan kitchen is based around a U-shaped island, which means everything is within easy reach. Far side of the island doubles as a breakfast bar, with stools tucked under the overhung worktop. An inset granite slab for pastry-rolling withstands hot pans too

information on fridges, freezers, washing machines etc.) Try to keep hob and sink within the same run of units, or within the corner formed by two runs, rather than on opposite walls. Then you will not swing across the kitchen to drain boiling water from a pan – a very dangerous move, particularly if there are other people in the kitchen.

The sink: unless you are prepared to pay extra for plumbing, the sink will need to be installed against an outside wall; or at right angles to an outside wall, provided you allow elbow room between it and the sink-bowl. Think twice before siting it under the window. If you spend longer preparing meals than washing up, you may prefer to save the view for the preparation area. As regards materials: stainless steel (although it *will* stain – beware of bleach especially), and vitreous enamel, are by far the most practical surface for sinks. Fireclay will crack and chip, and moulded plastic soon scratches, loses its glossy good looks, and proves very hard to clean once roughened.

If you have space, and don't already have a dishwasher, a double-bowl sink means you can wash up in one bowl and rinse in the other. If you have room only for a single-drainer, the theory is that right-handed people work from right to left, and should have the drainer on the left. Of course, there is no need to have a draining board at all – the bowl can be set straight into the work surface. This certainly looks best in aesthetic terms, and has real advantages in a small kitchen, because it leaves a greater expanse of work surface free. In really tight situations, it also offers the possibility of using a standard oblong bowl from front-to-back, instead of from side-to-side. The disadvantages are that the bowl needs installing with an absolutely watertight seal around its edge, and unless you are draining dishes on a plate rack with a drip-tray, you will need to buy it in conjunction with a specially-shaped work surface, to prevent drained water dripping.

Taps: lever-action taps are marvellous, especially for anyone with arthritic fingers, but not all water authorities permit them. Ordinary swivel-mixers are very good too, preferably wall-fixed so the sink is easier to clean; and preferably with the spout well above the sink, so that glasses don't get smashed against it, and there is enough room to get a bucket underneath. However, mixers restrict attachment adaptors for washing machine or garden hose. If you do decide on wall-fixed taps, make this clear when you are ordering the sink, or it's likely to come complete with tap-holes. One further tap worth noting is a hot, pull-out spray-tap – ideal for rinsing greasy dishes – and almost as useful as a second sink-bowl.

Waste disposal units: although not all local authorities approve them, waste disposers are a wonderful invention, especially if you live in a flat several floors up from the dustbins. There are basically two types on the market: continuous feed, where you keep pushing the rubbish in; and batch feed, where you have to stop and put the plug in place before the grinding mechanism works. The latter is

Left: this character-filled kitchen is a linear symphony, in which the lines complement one another with exceptional skill. The grouting of the brickwork, the beamed ceiling and the vertical stripes of the blinds all work toward a harmonious, clean open look

Below: openess is also the keyword in this small kitchen, where white tiles and white walls create a feeling of roominess. Starkness is avoided by the numerous plants hanging from shelves and dotting the work surfaces

more expensive but safer, particularly if there are children around. As there is only one model that fits an ordinary-sized sink outlet, do specify you want to install a disposal unit when ordering your sink, even if you can't afford to buy the disposer immediately. The extra-large outlet can be fitted with a basket strainer in the meantime.

Other 'waterworks': items like dishwashers and washing machines should be plumbed in near the sink to avoid high installation costs; also because that is where you will need them.

Kitchen units: unless you are having them custom-built, these come in a standard height of 90 cm (35½ in). If you are shorter or taller than average, some units are available with removable plinths, and all units can be raised if you build an extra plinth. Alternatively, wall-hung units can be installed at just the height you need. Always make sure that the sink unit, and any units with work surfaces above them, have a toe recess, so that you can work right up against them comfortably, without having to lean forward at an awkward angle.

If you would like coloured units, but don't want fridge and washing machines to stand out as solid 'blocks' of white, look for a range that offers matching-coloured décor panels. These cover the fronts of below-work-surface equipment making it indistinguishable from neighbouring units.

Work surfaces: incorporate one work surface at least 1 m (3 ft) long to provide uninterrupted space for food preparation, preferably siting it between cooker and sink. (This won't apply, of course, if you have got a kitchen table sturdy enough to meet the same purpose.) Also include a good stretch of work surface for use as a serving area, siting it near the door or serving hatch. If possible, create a slightly lower work surface for arm's-length jobs like rolling out pastry – again, this won't apply if you have a kitchen table.

Plastic laminate is still the most popular work surface, and if you buy a textured surface, it needn't look hard and shiny. Nor need it come in predictable colours. Although unit-manufacturers only offer a restricted range, you don't have to buy their work surface when you buy their units. You can have it made yourself, and then you have a choice of nearly a hundred laminate colours. Although a good quality laminate is very tough, it's still not tough enough to act as a chopping board, and it isn't heat-proof. You can get round the problem with free-standing chopping boards and trivets but, given the choice, set areas of more practical surfaces like teak, slate or stainless steel into the laminate.

Ceramic or quarry tiles make very handsome work surfaces. They are not as hygenic and easy to keep clean as laminate and, unless you use a special epoxy grout that will not stain or get dirty, you will have to scrape the grouting from time to time, and touch it up sometimes to keep it looking good. Tiles are no use, of course for rolling out pastry – or chopping, unless you want to blunt your knives. But they are extremely tough and virtually heat-proof: it would take an exceptionally hot pan to crack a tile.

Slate has all the advantages of tiles, plus the fact that it's smooth and jointless, but it's almost prohibitively expensive. So is marble, although it's not as tough as slate, tends to stain, and may discolour if subjected to hot pans. Wood proves a tough, yet warm and quiet surface, but it's vital to choose a hard and close-grained variety like teak – not something soft like pine, that is porous and stains very easily.

NB. Do remember that ceramic tiles, quarry tiles, slate, etc. are not only much deeper than laminate in themselves, but because they are so heavy, need a much stronger and deeper sub-surface. Take this into account when calculating final heights.

Ideally, the junction of wall and work surface should be curved to avoid a dirt-collecting trap. With a plastic laminate work surface this is simply achieved by buying a post-formed laminate in the first place.

Floors: Chapter 3 deals with flooring in terms of wear and tear, but there are other aspects to be considered. First, comfort. You will be on your feet a lot in the kitchen, so think seriously before you choose one of the hard floors like ceramic or quarry tiles. A cushioned vinyl will prove a great deal kinder, and today's ranges offer designs for every style of kitchen, from crisply graphic grid-patterns, to totally convincing 'slate' or 'brick'.

If you prefer a genuinely natural floor covering, ready-sealed or vinyl-surfaced cork could be the ideal choice, because as

Above: there's not a conventional unit in sight in this stylish high-tech kitchen. The owner built chipboard shelves along the left-hand wall and hung black plastic roller shutters (the kind normally used for office filing cabinets) over them to create a wall of storage. They hide the washing machine and spin-dryer, and a big fridge-freezer, as well as accomodating the oven and ordinary shelving. The worktop running along the right-hand wall was made from blockboard covered with tiny mosaic ceramic tiles. It's supported by wire shelf-units usually used in factories. Cutlery is kept in a filing cabinet – just visible beyond the owner. Black and white ceramic floor tiles clinch a stark approach inspired by the best in industrial design

well as looking mellow, it's soft and warm to walk on, very quiet, hard-wearing and easy to damp-mop clean.

Walls: the vulnerable areas are behind sink, cooker and central heating boiler. Gloss paint is the cheapest and easiest wipe-clean solution, but for a more practical and permanent approach use something like quarry or ceramic tiles: not plastic laminate, because it won't withstand the heat from the hob.

Elsewhere in the kitchen, scrubbable vinyl wall coverings are very practical; washable wallpapers less so, but the next best step. If you prefer paint, avoid gloss unless your walls are in perfect condition, and you have an efficient means of ventilation to obviate ugly condensation runnels. Oil-based eggshell or silthane silk could provide the alternative, because they are washable, and have a softer sheen. More expensive ways of covering walls could be with sealed cork, ceramic tiles, or tongued-and-grooved timber – either sealed and left natural, or painted if you feel that has become a cliché.

Ventilation: this is especially important in small and open-plan kitchens. If your cooker is situated against an outside wall, an extractor fan above it or just to one side, will deal with steam and cooking smells relatively inexpensively – although avoid siting it too near an eye-level grill. If you have a boiler or an Ascot which is not of the balanced flue type, also avoid siting the fan where it could drawer fumes back down the flue: when in doubt, get advice from the manufacturer. Extractor fans needn't look hideous: some are unobtrusive and fit flush to the wall.

Ducted cooker hoods suck steam and smells away to the outside air. The shorter the ducting the greater the efficiency: a run of more than 2 m (6 ft) is not recommended. For cookers too far from an outside wall, recirculating hoods draw air into charcoal filters and return it to the kitchen cleaner and dryer. However, they are not as effective as ducted hoods, and although cheaper to install, filters need replacing every six to nine months according to the amount of cooking you do.

The lower the hood over the hob the better it will work. About 60 cm (24 in) is ideal, but anything up to 80 cm (32 in) will do. Some hoods are not suitable for use above an eye-level grill: indeed, any hood would need to go at least 40 cm (16 in) above one – too high from the hob for real efficiency.

Lighting: all kitchens need good general lighting plus specific task lighting to work by. Fluorescent lighting is extremely efficient because it doesn't throw any shadows and, as manufacturers have discovered how to reduce and bend the tube, it is now available in light-bulb form. However, it gives a colder and less friendly light than tungsten. This coldness may not be a disadvantage if it suits the chosen style of your kitchen – as in the crisp, high-tech example on page 59.

In a very small, or a long galley kitchen, it may be possible to combine general and task lighting. A simple solution could be to run a lighting track down the centre of the ceiling, with several spotlights: some lighting the cooker, sink and work surfaces directly, others bouncing light off the ceiling for more overall illumination.

Larger kitchens: the ideal solution here might be to have ceiling-recessed, semi-recessed or ceiling-mounted downlighters providing both general light and specific light over the cooker and sink; plus strip-lighting fixed to the underside front edge of wall-hung top cupboards to illuminate the work surfaces. (Of course, some kitchen units come with pelmet-concealed strip-lights already fitted – just as many cookers have inbuilt lights in the hoods.)

The important thing about task downlighters is to make sure you install them immediately *above* the area to be illuminated – not behind where you will stand, or you will be working in your own shadow. The main thing about strip-lights is to decide between fluorescent and tungsten tubes. Although tungsten looks warmer, tungsten tubes are really just elongated light-bulbs, and are therefore extremely vulnerable to the slightest knock. Fluorescent tubes are cheaper to buy, much tougher, more economical to run and last much longer than tungsten. Although you can always warm fluorescent lights by adding a prismatic diffuser – possibly incorporating a strip of pale yellow filter – provided the work surface lighting is independently switched (as, indeed, all task lighting should be) – there seems little point to this refinement in a kitchen. If you have no top cupboards to fix strip-lights beneath, you could attach the tubes and pelmet to the front edge of a shelf – or, of course, you could use downlighters.

Open-plan lighting: as well as providing physical barriers to define the separate areas of open-plan kitchens, it's vital to provide psychological barriers too. The easiest way to achieve this is with independently switched lighting. If you add a pendant light fitting or downlighter over the dining-table, it will contain the table-top in an intimate pool of light, allowing the kitchen area, and the shambles of meal-preparation, to recede into shadow once the lights in that area have been switched off.

PS on wiring: set wiring into the wall for safety, and have plenty of socket outlets installed just above work surface height, to avoid unnecessary bending. Never underestimate the number you will need: possibly ten universal 13-amp socket outlets, one 30-amp cooker outlet (two for split-level) and perhaps a 20-amp water heater outlet.

Drawing up the plan

It's best to begin by drawing a scale plan of the room, measuring everything in metrics, as kitchen units and equipment all come in millimetres nowadays. Even if, like many people, you are still thinking in Imperial, don't measure in inches and then start consulting conversion charts – there is far too much scope for arithmetical error. Invest in a steel measure, which will have parallel markings in inches and millimetres, and will be rigid, instead of floppy like a tape measure from the sewing box.

Use graph paper for drawing up your plan, and work to a scale of 1:25 or 1:50. Mark in everything: the position of doors and windows, the height of the sills, the position of electric sockets, gas or electric cooker outlet, water supply and waste. Also mark any wall obstructions like pipes or radiators, and the position of the boiler if there is one. Only then can you start thinking of units and equipment, and the best way to effect an efficient work sequence.

KITCHEN STYLES

Small but perfect

Any small room needs decorating with discipline, but small kitchens, because they are so packed with storage and equipment essentials, demand an even tighter measure of control. Unless you really love a glorious muddle, and find you can work in it efficiently, it's best to go for neatness and restraint.

Below: a simple way of integrating items of dissimilar heights is to run a worktop across them at their highest point. Here, the hob of an old 1930s cooker dictates the level, and cooker, dishwasher and 1930s units are neatly pulled into alignment. A horizontal band of terracotta above the worktop strengthens this alignment further
Below right: this open-plan kitchen and dining room is another example of sophisticated high-tech. Bulk-head lighting with exposed black conduits form an emphatic pattern in the kitchen area, while two 'factory' pendants illuminate the dining table – which was specially made to match the worktops. Continuity of mood between areas is excellent, and is helped by the unbroken flow of the floor-tiles

This doesn't mean being tame or timid. On the contrary, it means being bolder than usual, because you will have to make a very clear and crisp impact. The simplest way to do this is to stick to all-white, which always creates an illusion of space. The galley kitchen on page 54 does this spectacularly, using white ceramic tiles for both walls and floor, to 'stretch' restricted surfaces with visual continuity. The result is humanized with a few softer touches: a natural-reed roller blind, a wicker wine basket, a bowl of fruit, and a flowering houseplant. But these touches are both well chosen and limited: everything else is hidden away in the units.

Such an approach is obviously capable of less extreme interpretation. If you wanted colour, you could introduce a bright, punchy primary – provided you kept it to minor splashes – or you might prefer any light, neutral shade to white. But it would be very difficult to introduce pattern without causing 'busyness' and confusion.

Pattern can succeed in a confined area, but you have to be very sure of what you are doing, and use it as an integral part of your design. It's usually best kept to rigid geometrics, which emphasize the mood of neatness and order.

This has been done in the larger galley kitchen on page 59. Black and white tiles form a chequerboard pattern on the floor – but they only work because they are part of a strong black and white scheme, brightened with the glitter of shiny high-tech metal.

Spend as much as you can

One advantage of small kitchens is that it's easy to justify spending as much as you can possibly afford. There won't be enough wall space for many units, so hopefully, you can concentrate your resources into an expensive few. They won't only look better at such inevitably close quarters, but they will be more flexible and sophisticated in what they offer. So look for interior fittings that exploit your limited space to the full: swivel-out trays to make use of 'dead' corners; pull-out work surfaces to increase your food preparation area; plinths on floor units that double as drawers – useful for things you don't need to get at daily.

As there will be very little floor space to cope with, this is another area where you may feel free to splurge. In any case, something like a cheap vinyl will prove a poor economy, because it will be getting such intensive wear and tear. Whatever type of flooring you choose, be sure to pick a light colour, because dark colours will make the floor area seem smaller. And avoid pattern, other than discreet self-pattern, because this will decrease the apparent floor area too.

One trick that seemingly increases the amount of floor is the use of units with chromed-steel plinths, which reflect the floor so it appears to continue underneath.

Of course, you could genuinely increase the floor area, simply by using wall-hung units.

If possible, be extravagant in the small details as well. You will be working so close to them, you will be aware of their quality. Go for good-looking taps, really stylish lighting, a handsome kettle and a well-designed toaster. Be particular right down to your choice of tea-towels. Little things really mean a lot in a restricted context.

Larger and more versatile

Although small areas cry out for streamlined efficiency, in larger rooms you can afford a more relaxed approach. You can introduce the interest of colour and pattern. You can have open shelves filled with comfortable clutter. You can even reject built-in units altogether, or choose those with a warm and natural wood finish that look as friendly as traditional furniture.

The farmhouse-style kitchen on page 57 uses colour, pattern, natural wood, traditional furniture and plenty of clutter for a mood of total relaxation. It's rather more practical than it appears at first glance, because the hardwood maple table provides a sensible work surface, while the pine floor can easly be damp-mopped clean because it's protected with several coats of clear matt polyurethane varnish. The Aga is in regular use for serious cooking and gets fully exploited. The large maple dresser was made by the same firm that built the kitchen units and, with the open shelves on the opposite wall, provides masses of storage. Of course, everything on display requires dusting and occasionally washing – but it is a labour of love in this kind of kitchen.

No need for clichés

Fortunately, it's no longer a rigid choice between cosy and countrified or bleak and antiseptic. This is largely because most manufacturers have introduced ranges in solid wood or wood-finish with sophisticated rather than rustic styling; there are also laminated ranges softened by natural wood trims that give a friendlier face to built-in efficiency. This in turn has encouraged the realization that natural materials, whether used to cover work surfaces, walls or floors, are intrinsically timeless in appeal. The kitchen on page 55, for instance, is full of warm and sympathetic materials: pine-trimmed white laminate units, a tongued-and-grooved pine ceiling (but note how the grooves run diagonally for an up-dated image), terracotta-coloured quarry tiles on work surfaces and floor – yet its impact remains very simple and modern.

On the other hand, the kitchen on page 58, which already boasts plenty of warmth and texture in the exposed brickwork and original beamed ceiling, can afford to eschew the obviousness of natural wood units, and use red and white plastic laminate with snazzy panache.

Open-plan styling

Open-plan rooms need dividing into separate areas by means of both physical and psychological barriers. Yet at the same time, the different areas need linking with a strongly related sense of style. You can't cut abruptly from a clinical kitchen area to a relaxed and casual dining or dining/living area, so either carry the clinicism over; or move in the other direction, and soften the clinical area.

The open-plan room on page 61 chooses the first option, although the kitchen area can hardly be called clinical. It's high-tech at its sophisticated best, with shiny work surfaces, bulk-head lighting, and exposed black conduit creating a dramatic wall-pattern that contains two highly graphic framed prints. But the high-tech mood continues into the dining area, with black pendant lights hanging over the table, which have an almost 'factory' austerity, and perforated metal dining chairs. Unbroken wall and floor surfaces clinch the visual continuity.

The right-hand room opposite prefers the second option. The living area is traditionally comfortable, with plump crimson-coloured cushions on a cane sofa, and the friendly clutter of houseplants and pictures. So it's this relaxed mood that carries through to the kitchen/dining area, to make it seem conventionally furnished despite the use of built-in kitchen units. A rug shared between floor areas, houseplants, pictures, open shelving crammed to overflowing and, above all, the soft folds of full-length curtains at the window, make the room's 'working parts' look comfortable too. Note the use of a round table, which not only saves space and avoids bruised hips, but introduces curves to offset the angularity of the units. Note also the use of see-through chairs, which avoid creating a solid obstruction in such a busy and crowded situation.

Budget kitchens

If you are starting from scratch on a really rock-bottom budget, essentials can be pared down to a sink, a cooker, a fridge, a work surface and some form of storage. An all-in-one cooker is cheaper than split-level; the separate hob and oven are more expensive to buy and they also demand good-looking housing units.

Self-assembly kitchen units are cheaper than ready-made equivalents, and need no more than a screwdriver or adjustable spanner to assemble – plus a

practical bent of mind. For those who lack the latter, cheaper ready-made units are likely to have doors and drawer fronts finished in a melamine skin – nowhere near as tough as a proper laminate. They also, inevitably, will be more poorly constructed, so check that drawers run smoothly and doors fit and hang level.

Alternatively, forget about units altogether. Cheap second-hand cupboards and chests of drawers can cope with storage perfectly adequately, especially with the addition of open shelving and a second-hand table to provide a work surface. These come cheapest from the less prestigious auction rooms, and can be resold when you have more money, and

Left: this elegant kitchen, at the back of an imposing 18th century town house, was formerly 'country cottage' rustic. Rather than throw out the natural pine units, the present owner painted them a sober and sophisticated green, and then painted the walls to match. By adding textured white floor tiles and a white marble-topped table, they now make a cool and urbane impression

Below: in this open-plan kitchen and dining area, the angularity of built-in units is offset by the use of a circular table. Full-length curtains (far enough from the hob for safety), pictures on the wall, and attractively-laden open shelving, also soften the stark essentials. Furthermore, they establish an easy relationship with the adjacent sitting area

can afford to do the kitchen properly.

The add-on kitchen

If you are short of money but don't want second-best, buy what you can afford of the best now and fill the gaps later. This will demand some forward planning. If you hope to add a washing machine or dishwasher in the future, you will need to leave an appropriate space near the sink, so that plumbing will be a simple matter, and you will not have to re-jig the entire kitchen. Even if you never manage to buy the equipment, the existence of suitable plumbing positions will prove a useful selling factor come the day you decide to put your home on the market.

If you are starting with the minimum of kitchen units but intend to add more as finances permit, do have the whole work surface made at the outset to cover the full length of future acquisitions. Otherwise you will have to make joins in the surface that will look unsightly and act as dirt-traps. The work surface will also have the advantage of making whatever you slot into the gaps beneath – whether open shelving filled with attractive items or just a vegetable rack or rubbish bin – look reasonably integral and intended.

The inherited hotch-potch

If you are not starting from scratch, but are having to make do with a previous occupant's disastrous kitchen, there are one or two cheap and fairly speedy ploys you can use to improve matters visually. One good way of co-ordinating lots of miscellaneous bits and pieces is to pick a strong colour and paint them all to match. But don't stop there if they are really dreadful: paint the walls as well, so they 'disappear' into it, and include anything else that looks unsightly – stray pipes or even an old saucepan rack.

Alternatively, if you can't abide strong colour, you could paint walls and all the bits and pieces white, and then introduce a few brilliantly-coloured extras to draw the eye and hold its attention, like bright primary-coloured vegetable racks and plastic bowls.

Another useful ploy for uniting mismatched items is to establish strict horizontal line-ups. Pick whatever sticks up highest (probably the hob of the cooker) and span the wall with a work surface at that height. Then, however different the heights of cupboards or fridge, they will be contained within the same clear-cut limit, and will give a much more streamlined impression.

THE SITTING ROOM

Your sitting room is the most used – and the most seen – room in the house. It has to be both attractive and comfortable.

Sitting rooms, even if they double as dining rooms, work rooms or guest bedrooms, are, above all, places to relax in. It's important to remember this when choosing a colour scheme. However much you may love strong and vibrant colour, you will want to unwind after a hard day's work – not be forced to live up to stimulating surroundings.

Furthermore, whilst lively and exciting colour schemes work well in places where you spend little time – like the just-passing-through hall, the dining room and the bathroom – they will soon have you climbing the walls with frustration in the rooms where you spend most of your waking hours. In general, therefore, it is always wisest to aim for a restful approach in the sitting room.

CHOOSING A COLOUR SCHEME

An easy way to plan a colour scheme is to pick one patterned item in the colours you like and then keep within its restricted palette. It could be the tiles in a Victorian fireplace; it could be the upholstery fabric on a sofa; it could be the carpet or a rug. Then, as long as you are sure you like it and will go on liking it, all you are left to worry about is using the right 'weight' of related colours and patterns elsewhere. Obviously it makes sense to choose something long-lasting. If you base your scheme around anything short-lived, once it's gone, the whole room will collapse in ruins. If you choose the 'key' item with care, the reverse won't be true; you will be able to ring the changes around it successfully as less durable items need replacing.

The starting point for the room on page 67 was an oriental rug, in creams, terracottas and indigo blue. Its intricate pattern immediately demanded a plain, neutral background – in this case, richly textured coir matting. The disciplined nature of its pattern demanded a similarly disciplined approach in other items. This explains the choice of the ikat-design wallpaper and curtains, because they not only echo the colours of the rug, but echo its mood of order and restraint. They also introduce a repetitive element that is soothing and satisfying without being boring, because it's repeated on a different scale. The sofas are upholstered in a slub-textured neutral cotton, while cushions, covered in hand-blocked Indian fabrics, add richness in a minor way that never threatens to get overbearing.

It's a warm but understated room, where the colour creates pattern; and the pattern, in turn, provides lasting visual interest rather than immediate impact. It's an adaptable room too, because, as the bottom detail shot on page 66 shows, the rug will happily dictate a fresh set of surroundings when you need to decorate again.

It's the same basic story in the room on page 66, except the colour scheme is very different. Everything takes its cue from the dhurrie on the floor. The marbled wallpaper plays up its peach and grey shades with related shades of blue and apricot. The beige and grey find an echo in the curtains and upholstery fabrics, while the cushion covers emphasize the rug's geometric pattern. Another detail shot proves that when the room needs redecorating, there will be no difficulty finding papers and fabrics to form a tightknit, new relationship.

Sticking to neutrals

Using 'non-colours' like white, cream, beige and grey may sound boring – but it's the least boring colour scheme of all. Neutrals are too restful to weary the eye, and properly handled, they are full of sophisticated interest.

There are two essentials when attempting this approach: you must choose good quality furniture and furnishings, because there will be no colour to detract from second-best; and you will need to introduce plenty of different textures, to avoid a flat and anonymous impression. Because you are relying on subtlety for success, every detail must be capable of surviving close scrutiny, and be intrinsically good enough to improve with acquaintance.

Right: although this sitting room looks warm and vibrant, its colour scheme is really neutral. The carpet is mushroom, the walls magnolia, the curtains natural in shade. The only strong colour comes in the sofas, upholstered in a coral fabric that seems extra-brilliant in such muted surroundings. Small touches of more coral, in the lamp-base and the curtain-borders, integrate the colour within the neutrals. But the emphasis could easily be altered if a change of colour scheme is wanted. The ceiling cornice, and beading forming panels on the walls, were once so badly damaged, they needed remoulding. Expensive – but an investment which enhances the room's good proportions

The picture on page 75 is a perfect example of an easy-to-live-in, neutral sitting room. Everything has been designed to look relaxed and calm. The natural-coloured wallpaper tones with the natural wood of the floor and storage; the large grey leather sofas look quiet and unobtrusive (think how they would have dominated the room if they had been in a strong colour); even the picture on the wall is carefully non-colour. But although soothing, there is nothing bland about the result. The rug, the Venetian blinds and the book-filled shelves create pattern in a peaceful way, while all the surfaces provide the intricacy of texture. Even the wallpaper, that at first glance looks plain, has a barely perceptible vellum-effect pattern.

The sitting room looks spacious, but in fact is rather small. This explains the use of clear mirror on the right-hand wall, introduced to 'double' the room's dimensions. But the mirror-trick only works because of the neutral colour scheme. Any less gentle reflection would have jumped out aggressively, and proved very difficult to live with. The advantage of non-colour is that tones flow naturally from one to another without jarring interruptions. In this respect, neutral schemes make all small rooms look larger, regardless of whether or not mirror has been employed.

Splashing out with colour

Boldly-used colour creates immediate impact: it's just that the novelty may soon wear thin. This impact could prove useful if you are furnishing on a tight budget, and want to detract attention from less-than-best contents. And, of course, like using a patterned wallpaper, colour is an ideal way of 'furnishing' a room that is too small to accommodate actual furniture – like a bathroom or a tiny hall.

As all shades of the same colour go together, the easiest approach is to pick a colour you like, and stay with it, simply varying the tones. This has been done in the bottom sitting room on page 72, where pinks range from peach right through to strawberry. The only problem is balancing the different 'weights'. If you are at all apprehensive about getting this right, pick the brains of a professional designer by finding a patterned wallpaper or fabric that confines itself to your chosen colour. Then translate the varying tones to your room in similar proportions, adding some white or neutral for light relief. If you are buying fitted carpet, it's best to make this a neutral area, because it will be too expensive to replace when you want to change the colour scheme.

Be very wary of going for a contrast, because colours react upon one another in extraordinary ways. A pink may look bright in isolation, but if you put it against a brighter orange, it will begin to look washed out and anaemic. Getting the balance of colour-strengths right is very tricky and, again, it's worth analysing a wallpaper or fabric to see how the designer has tackled the problem. As contrasts break up a room instead of uniting its elements, be prepared for them to make your sitting room look smaller.

A smaller splash

The most flexible way of using colour is to add it to a basically neutral scheme. If you avoid strong colour on walls and floor (as in the sitting room on page 65) any colour you add in the form of upholstery, etc. will sing out with an extra intensity. Indeed, just coloured cushions, lampshades and flowers could be enough to make a non-

Below and centre: a grey, peach and beige dhurrie provides the cue for all the other colours in this sitting room. Detail shot shows samples of alternative fabrics and wallpaper. These could be used with equal success, retaining the same dhurrie as the basis. It always makes sense to evolve colour schemes around a constant

Left and opposite: an oriental rug in cream, terracotta and indigo blue forms the basis of this sitting room. Wallpaper and related fabric were chosen for their sympathetic patterns and tones – as was the pale bamboo cotton on the sofas. A rich abundance of Indian cushion-cover fabrics echos the rug's eastern splendour. But still with the oriental rug in mind, see the detail shot of possible alternatives

colour room seem colourful – and be cheap to replace for an instant change.

One final thought on colour schemes: whatever you may decide for the sitting room, unless you live in a very large house that can afford to take the visual interruption, it's best to make one room flow into another, to create a continuity of mood. You could use the same carpet throughout your home – particularly good advice if you live in a flat, because it will make the floor area seem much larger. Alternatively, you could repeat a colour from one room to the next, teaming it with a different colour, and then repeating the second colour in the next room.

FINDING A FOCAL POINT

Even if you have efficient central heating, think twice before doing away with an existing fireplace. This isn't just because open fires are luxurious – with most people out at work all day, and no one left at home to keep the home fires burning, they are likely to be a weekend-only treat anyway. It's also because fireplaces give sitting rooms a focal point: a handsome and logical centre of attraction.

This focal point remains as valid in summer as in winter, because you can fill the empty grate with a large flower arrangement, or a group of green and leafy houseplants that don't mind shade. Indeed, fireplaces can look so attractive in their own right that some people install non-operational versions.

Replacing a fireplace

In an old home, you may be lucky and inherit the original sitting room fireplace. If you are not so lucky, and find yourself faced with a mottle-tiled 1940s specimen, you can either replace it with a period fireplace, or go for a simpler, modern design.

The choice will probably depend on how many other architectural features have survived. If the sitting room still has panelled doors and intricate ceiling roses and cornices, it would be a shame to fight against these decorative details by using anything other than a period style.

Architectural salvage firms are a good, regular source of original period fireplaces, and your local saleroom may occasionally have one. Alternatively, you could buy from a shop that specializes in fireplaces, whether original or faithfully reproduced. The advantage here is that they will have a good range of wooden, cast iron and marble surrounds and – as these shops are usually run by enthusiasts

– advice on which is most suitable for your home. The disadvantage is that they are more expensive. Be prepared for a shock when you get the final price: side slips or tiled inserts could cost as much as the surround – and you will need to buy a grate or fire basket as well.

The hole in the wall

If your sitting room has been denuded of all its character, and you prefer a modern, unfussy approach, it may prove difficult to find a well-designed new fireplace. The easiest way round this sad fact of life is to choose one of the simple, hole-in-the-wall fireplaces, which come with neat, reflective surrounds. These are inserted into the wall above floor level, something that gives you the option of a sunken ash-pit, so you only need to empty it once a week.

But if money is short, there is an even simpler solution. You could remove the existing fireplace completely, making sure you retain the fireproof bricks in the recess: then trim the recess opening with wood or with metal, and plaster right up to it for a professional finish. In a clean-air zone, you will need to add a free-standing fire basket to contain the smokeless fuel and allow a draught beneath it. Logs could sit directly on the fireproof bricks or – if you wanted to raise them to encourage a draught – on a metal grid supported by bricks at the sides.

Not all a rosy glow

Obviously open fires have their snags. They make a lot more work – and a lot more dirt – which means your sitting room will need decorating more often. Solid fuel stoves reduce these problems slightly, and still allow you to glimpse the fire – albeit it via a see-through door. Cast iron reproduction French stoves look best in a period fireplace, but one modern stove, a svelte stainless steel cylinder, looks good in any situation. Alternatively, you could be utterly shameless, and install a 'phoney' gas-log or gas-coal fire. These burn with real, leaping flames and look almost indistinguishable from the genuine thing. Although too expensive to run full-time, for a centrally-heated household out at work all day, such a choice would make a lovely 'open fire' to come home to.

ARRANGING THE FURNITURE

The main thing about a fireplace as a focal point is that it needs to be used to best effect. Don't position a sofa or armchairs directly in front: they will block it off from the rest of the room. If you want the seating to be close to the fireplace, arrange it so it runs at right angles. In the case of period fireplaces especially, treat the adjacent alcoves symmetrically, filling them with items of furniture that have equal visual 'weight'. For instance, a tall and massive bureau-bookcase on one side but a low and fragile table on the other would spoil the scale of the fireplace and minimize its importance.

Settling on the seating

If you don't have a fireplace to provide a focal point, all you have to do is remember that seating is the heart of any sitting room. So, provided you group it around a coffee table – as opposed to ranging it aimlessly around the walls – you will find it forms a satisfying nucleus.

In a small room, where seating has to go against the walls to leave enough floor area free for traffic, it's best to arrange sofas and chairs at right angles in an L-shape. If you need to seat a lot of people, modern seating units prove very flexible in this situation, because they are able to exploit the usually 'dead' corner.

Away from the walls, the most successful approach is to place two matching sofas so they face each other over a coffee table. This creates a logical and self-contained group that looks confident, and full of conviction. Two-seater sofas use space to best advantage, but although no one likes sitting in the middle of three-seater sofas, you may need them if your sitting room is large, in order to establish the right proportions. It's very difficult to make a pleasing arrangement with a three-piece suite, because there is such a difference in scale between sofa and armchairs. Be cautious about buying one; and whatever you buy, remember to take a tape measure with you to ensure new seating will get through your doors.

How to judge comfort

Low and modern squared-off seating, where back and arms are of the same height, don't provide any support for the neck. This won't matter if it is for 'social' seating, because people stay relatively upright when they are talking, but if you need seating that you can really relax in, look for low arms and a high, and preferably sloping, back that will allow you to lean against it fully. Either way, try it out uninhibitedly in the showroom. Unless you can sit right back with your feet still flat on the floor, you will probably start inching forward to relieve the pressure on your legs, until eventually, you have no

support for your back whatsoever.

How to judge quality

Good upholstered seating is very expensive but in this case, price really is the best indication of quality. You can't tell whether the frame has been well constructed and made of a hardwood that has been properly dried, because it's completely hidden beneath the padding. The sales assistant will be able to tell you what the suspension is made of – usually Pirelli webbing, or horizontal lengths of metal springing – but he won't know if they have been spaced at over-wide intervals. Even the cushions can be deceptive, because a feather filling won't last long if the feathers are cheap; and the life expectancy of a foam filling, or foam core wrapped around with a synthetic fibre fleece, depends on the density used. Equally, quality fillings can last for years – even generations.

Above: pictures and books cover the walls of this sitting room as completely as wallpaper. They're solidly arranged to form a definite pattern – not sprinkled around, which would have looked fussy and irritating. By keeping them to the same natural colours as the rest of the room, they become an integral part of a satisfying whole
Far left: unexpected but sensitive mixture of materials surrounds a pink marble fireplace with bronze-tinted sheet mirror, and flanks them with snazzy chrome-steel units
Left: mixing old and new demands a sure eye – and money. It takes good antiques and top modern design to carry off the shock treatment successfully

Still, there are some pointers to look out for. Press the sides and back to find out whether the seating is properly padded, or if you can feel the frame beneath. Look underneath to see how the base cloth has been attached. Most manufacturers use staples nowadays, but if they have been crudely punched in at crazy angles, it could mean the rest of the workmanship is equally shoddy. Check the quality and fixing of the castors. Remove the seat cushions and sit on the base – if you can feel the springing or webbing be very cautious. If the cushions are foam-filled, give them a press and see how quickly they spring back into shape; you can tell a cheap foam because it lacks resilience. Look at the thickness of the cushions, whatever they are made of. They should be fat and bloated – if you can pick up excess fabric there isn't enough filling – and the cover will crease with use and soon look shabby. Finally, ask the sales assistant whether the cushion covers can be removed for cleaning. The fact that there is a zip doesn't mean very much, because machining zips into the final seam is much quicker than finishing the cushion off by hand.

SORTING OUT THE STORAGE

Even a sitting room that is strictly for sitting in is going to need some form of storage. You will want somewhere to keep books, hi-fi equipment and records, drinks, general hobby paraphernalia and ornaments. In a large and traditionally-furnished room, it's safest to go about this the traditional way. In the picture on page 65, for instance, a large Edwardian sideboard houses the hi-fi; a walnut what-not accommodates bits and pieces; and an antique bureau houses writing materials. Old coffers, linen-presses, wardrobes and chests of drawers offer further opportunities for traditional storge.

In a more modern room, where ceilings tend to be lower and you have no decorative architectural features to consider, you will need to decide what type of modern storage suits you. The bedroom section deals with the question of built-in versus free-standing storage; here it's more a matter of being realistic about whether you are truly an 'open' or 'shut' case. You may like the idea of open shelves, and imagine them filled with aesthetically-grouped objects; in practice they may end up as a dumping ground for everything from old papers to bits of string. If you know you are a family that creates masses of junk, you may want to hide everything behind closed doors. The most unobtrusive way to do this is to form a solid 'wall' of storage, as in the dual-purpose dining room on pages 86 and 87.

Above: clever use of storage makes this multi-purpose room possible. Free-standing units take dining essentials etc, and blend well with the wall behind. A vast built-in wardrobe takes clothes and spare bedding: its mirrored sliding doors make the study area seem larger. Light, neutral shades ensure separate areas flow freely

Left: magnificent sitting room in what was formerly a barn retains its original rugged grandeur. Plain white walls, and beams left natural rather than painted black, provide the perfect foil to traditional furnishings

But the ideal compromise is to choose a system that offers both open and closed components, and allows you to combine them in whatever proportions you like.

Add infinitum

Modular systems comprise a series of same-size basic units that you can add to horizontally or vertically as your storage needs increase. Alternatively, you can re-arrange them if your storage needs change. The basic units are merely 'shells', and it's up to you whether you choose to leave them quite open, add open shelves, insert drawers, or front the units with doors. Most modular systems come in white, natural wood or coloured finishes: stick to white – or one of the lighter woods or colours – if your emphasis is on closed rather than open components, to avoid a heavy, overcrowded impression.

Industrial-inspired storage usually comes in natural pine, either sealed or left unsealed for painting. Here, instead of buying basic units, you buy uprights grooved at regular intervals, and then slot in the shelves, drawers and doors. The sitting room on page 75 uses this type of storage, although only shelves have been inserted. Its chief advantage over modular storage is that all the components come in several depths and/or widths, ensuring they will fit any situation. 'Ladder' style storage works in much the same way, but with varying degrees of flexibility.

Storage for all reasons

Obviously storage becomes much more important if you are using the sitting room for more than one purpose. If it's merely doubling as a dining room or study, in a fairly small room that could not cope with more free-standing furniture, choose storage that offers desk inserts or drop-down table-tops. If the room is even more multi-purpose, you will need to design it around the storage because that may be the only way to make the room work.

For an object lesson in doing this, see the L-shaped room on pages 70 and 71, which is for sitting, dining, studying and is also a guest bedroom. A run of free-standing modular units alongside the dining table takes dining essentials, hobby materials and general clutter in an attractive way, with the less good-looking items hidden away behind doors and drawer-fronts. Note how the grey-lacquered units merge into the grey-painted wall, to make them look integral rather than a cumbersome extra.

The desk, made up of a top spanning two pedestal bases, comes from the same grey-lacquered range of storage. This continuity is very important in a room that would soon look overcrowded if it was broken up into separate areas. But the largest item of storage is virtually invisible. It's a vast built-in wardrobe to the left of the desk, big enough to take clothes and empty suitcases as well as spare bedding. It seems to disappear completely, because the tongued-and-grooved pine that clads the wall has been extended to cover the wardrobe's end panel. The sliding doors not only avoid collisions, but because they are mirrored, create an illusion of space in the confined study area.

THE LIGHTING

The principles of lighting are the same throughout the house. It's just that you are likely to need more of it in the sitting room, because different people may be doing different things at the same time.

Although there are thousands of light fittings to choose from, there are really only three types of lighting. General lighting provides overall illumination; task lighting provides specific illumination for jobs like reading or sewing; and effect lighting highlights areas worth featuring, and introduces an element of drama. Ideally, you should use all three to exploit your sitting room to advantage.

Above: this bedsit was designed for an elderly relation, but could suit a teenager with a change of décor. A Sofa-bed solves the sleeping problem. Bi-fold louvre-doored storage contains a shower and wash basin, and the mini-kitchen revealed on the right

Right: peachy-apricot pink on walls and ceiling, and mouldings picked out in contrasting white, ensure architectural details receive full attention

Far right: square and low modern seating and a modern glass and steel coffee table have a simple elegance that's at home in this Georgian country house setting. Because the basics are plain, details need to be perfectionist to withstand the close scrutiny they will receive. Note the coral trim to the oatmeal upholstery; the careful co-ordination of side-lamps and cushions; the immaculate hang of the full-length curtains

If you are lucky enough to be starting from scratch, it's a good idea to have 5-amp sockets installed around the room as part of the lighting circuit. Then, instead of running table lamps and floor lamps off the 13-amp power circuit (which either means groping towards them in the dark, or switching on the central light fitting so you can see what you are doing) you can control them from switches at the door. You can also, of course, use dimmer switches – something not possible on the 13-amp circuit.

General lighting usually comes from the ceiling in the form of a pendant fitting, recessed downlighters, or spotlights – possibly on a ceiling track. Pendant lights are undoubtedly the simplest and cheapest approach, and can look traditional or modern according to the fitting. Recessed downlighters are very expensive to install unless you catch your home at the building stage, or are having a false ceiling put in during conversion works, but they provide a discreet light source that goes with almost any style of room. Because the bulbs are hidden and shine straight down, they offer good illumination without any eye-glare – and lend themselves especially well to use with a dimmer switch. Lighting tracks and/or spotlights are relatively cheap to install, but are difficult to use at ceiling level, because wherever you angle them, they tend to dazzle someone's eyes. Although they look good, they might be best confined to task and effect lighting.

Until recently, if you wanted exciting-looking modern lighting, spotlights were the obvious answer, whether you beamed them directly, or bounced them off the walls or ceiling to provide reflected light. However, with the recent introduction of tungsten halogen to the domestic market (it's been around for years in shops and factories) a whole new field of lighting is opening up.

Halogen gives a very clear and concentrated white light. It's so strong that when used as a floor-standing uplighter (which, with an ordinary tungsten bulb would give you effect lighting), the reflected light from the ceiling can provide general lighting. But it is excellent for effect lighting too, when a tiny bulb, no bigger than a thumb-nail, can pick out a feature and highlight it intensely. Halogen, like all tungsten lighting, can be used with dimmer switches. Unfortunately, however, it can't be used with ordinary fittings. Although Italian halogen fittings have been on sale for some time, they have been very expensive. Now, British designers are producing new, slender halogen floor lights every bit as sleek, but a fraction of the price.

Above: a beautifully-proportioned 18th-century sitting room receives a suitably symmetrical treatment. Antiqued mirrors in the alcoves give a gentle and easy-to-live-with reflection
Right: large mirror-tiles cover the right-hand wall of this sitting room to make it seem double its actual size. Pattern is restrained and colours kept natural, to ensure a reflection that's restful to look at. Visual textures amply compensate

Task lighting works best if it shines directly over a person's shoulder onto the work in hand or – in the case of spotlights, where the light may be too harsh – onto the wall so that reflected light bounces back over the shoulder. Unless a work area is permanent, always aim for flexible lighting that can move around the room to wherever it is needed. A floor lamp is an obvious answer, but for sheer versatility, clip-on spotlights are hard to beat.

Effect lighting can make a routine interior look interesting, whereas the lack of it can make an interesting interior look dull. It can also 'change' the shape of a room. If you want to make your sitting room look larger, consider downlighters that wash the walls with light. If you want to make it seem lower and more intimate, consider using table lamps. If you would like to inject a touch of drama, use uplighters to pick out anything worthwhile – perhaps a large-scale flower arrangement or a trough of plants. It's vital to vary the intensity of light and shade in a room, because a flat, even light irons everything out.

Running costs

Apart from sodium lighting, which is only suitable for outdoor use, fluorescent lighting is the cheapest. It no longer comes only in strip form, but also as a conventional light-bulb, shaped either rather like a jam jar or like a double-D. These fluorescent bulbs burn a fifth the electricity of a tungsten bulb and last over six times as long so, although they cost up to twenty times as much, they are still economical in the long run. One or two of the bulbs can be used with ordinary fittings, but most either need a special adaptor or a completely new fitting: and all are heavier than tungsten bulbs because they incorporate a starter mechanism and choke. This means if you are able to use an existing fitting, you need to make sure it can take the additional weight.

Fluorescent tubes, even in bulb-form, have major drawbacks when considered for a sitting room. They give a cold and shadow-free light, and although it might be possible to warm this with a coloured shade, it would never be possible to control, because you can't use a dimmer switch from fluorescents. Perhaps a better money-saving solution in a sitting room would be to look for some of the new breed of mini-spotlights. These

use small 40-watt silvered reflector bulbs, which give about 30 per cent more light than an ordinary 40-watt bulb.

For good overall economy, it's well worth considering a dimmer switch – provided you buy the right type. Not all dimmer switches are energy saving, so make sure you choose one that reduces the level of light by converting the wattage. Quite apart from any saving on running costs, dimmer switches, which are inexpensive to buy, provide a cheap way of changing the mood of a room when you cannot afford a variety of fittings.

STYLES OF FURNISHING

Style is whatever you can pull off confidently. You can use antiques in a new house, modern furniture in an old one, or mix the two as the inspiration takes you. In the detail shot of a Victorian sitting room on page 69, a huge abstract painting and modern lighting feel completely at home with an antique side table. And on page 68, another Victorian sitting room flanks a period, marble fireplace with cool chrome-steel shelving. This kind of approach demands a very sure eye – and really top quality items that can retain their integrity despite the shock treatment.

If you suspect you lack both the panache and the cash, you are probably best to play it safe, and let the style of your home dictate its furnishing.

The cottage sitting room

Aim for simplicity in a country cottage, because it was probably built for a humble farm-labourer, and needs to respect its modest origins. This is more a matter of following the spirit of the place than the letter – of choosing natural rather than synthetic materials; of preferring peaceful, plain designs or tiny designs to loud, flamboyant patterns; of providing plenty of interesting texture; and keeping items of furniture on the small side.

Walls and ceiling: most cottage rooms look best just painted white. If they need replastering first, ask the workman to use a softer plaster-mix; to follow the undulations of the wall surface; and to blunt the corners slightly and let them drift. This way the walls won't look new and anonymous; they will still have individuality and character.

If the walls are in poor condition and you want to hide them behind a patterned wallpaper, use an overall, small-scale pattern, that looks almost like a textured 'plain' from a distance. Be wary of exposing stone walls or brickwork, because traditionally they would always have been plastered – just as tongued-and-grooved pine would always have been painted. Exposed wall surfaces can work in converted barns – but only because barns were never meant to be lived in: elsewhere they tend to look self-consciously 'primitive'. If you do expose walls, don't pick out stone or brickwork with raised or contrasting-coloured pointing, because this really will look cheap and vulgar. Use a toning colour and recess the pointing, if possible brushing it just before it sets to give a slightly roughened texture.

Low ceilings are best painted white to make the most of the light. If you paint the ceiling beams black, be prepared for them to create a very dominant pattern, and make the ceiling seem darker and lower. It is probably best to leave beams natural, but for a fresh and naïve look, you could paint them white. Matt white, in any case, is the wisest solution for replacement beams, because they are too new to be singled out for scrutiny.

Floors: if you are lucky enough to have a brick, stone, slate, quarry tile or timber floor, do retain it if it's in reasonable condition. If not, pick a plain but textured floor covering like rush matting, natural sisal or a twist-pile or long-pile wool carpet – not a smooth Wilton and not a synthetic. Once you have your neutral and textured basis, you can add a few rugs for pattern and comfort.

Doors: flush doors will look hideous in a cottage. Replace them if they are already there, first making sure they really are flush – not originals with sheets of removable hardboard tacked over. This needn't be too expensive if you are reasonably handy. The kind of cottage door that opens with a latch only consists of vertical boards of wood nailed together with three horizontal boards. Alternatively, you could fit panelled doors, adding plain round brass or white china knobs.

Windows: cottage windows tend to be small, so don't swamp them with generous drapes and pelmets It's advisable to hang curtains as simply as possible, choosing a pretty and unpretentious cotton in preference to an elegant silk or rich velvet. Or perhaps forget curtains altogether, and opt for roller blinds or interior shutters, that leave the window quite uncluttered.

Furniture: avoid anything massive like three-seater sofas or some of the heavier Victorian furniture – it will dwarf the proportions of the room. Avoid, also, any of the grander upholstery fabrics: think in terms of cotton reps, linen unions, nubbly tweeds and corduroys – or real leather if the budget can stand it.

Don't feel obliged to furnish with antiques – although if you do, the safest way to get the look right is to stick to country oak or pine. In an old and simple setting, with plenty of textural interest, cool and sleek modern furniture can look stunningly effective – as can a mixture of old and new. Lighting is best kept neat and functional – a modern approach works better than fake-candle wall fittings.

The 18th-century sitting room

Aim for a mood of restraint and formality in a Georgian house. Forget ruggedness and go for urbane smoothness; use colour, but in a quiet and civilized way. Above all, establish a sense of symmetry and order.

Walls and ceiling: 18th-century rooms tend to be on the generous side, so there are often large expanses of wall to cover. The cheapest way to do this is with emulsion paint – but choose muted colours, like sage green, putty, grey-blue or milky coffee. If you suspect a shade is going to be too bright, provided you buy the same type of emulsion and mix well before using, you can add a dash of grey to the can of colour, to sober it down.

Wallpaper was very expensive in the 18th century, so craftsmen developed painting techniques to make the walls look less bare and boring – like stippling, glazing, ragging and dragging. Since these skills are relatively easy to acquire, they could be well worth using for an authentic look. In any case, they provide a sensitive background to furniture and pictures – and are good at disguising uneven surfaces.

Alternatively, you could create the same effects with wallpaper. Dragged, stippled, rag-rolled and marbled designs have swung back into fashion, and come in suitably subtle colours. It's possible to buy richly-patterned wallpapers reproduced from 18th-century originals, but they are often overpowering and difficult to handle. Perhaps keep them for larger and relatively little-used sitting rooms.

If your room still has its original cornices, you could paint the ceiling in a lighter shade than your wall colour, and

pick out the architectural details in white. If not, you might want to reinstate them with reproductions, making sure you keep them in scale with the room. These are either made traditionally in fibrous plaster; or moulded in rigid polystyrene – which may sound revolting but looks convincing once painted. The advantage of the former is that they are craftsman-installed, so you can have existing cornices matched if they are only partially missing. The advantage of the latter is that you can fit them yourself, and save on installation. Of course you could simply paint the ceiling white: you may prefer to if there are no decorative elements worth featuring.

Floors: the Georgians loved all things oriental, so if you have a good wooden floor, just add Persian rugs or Indian dhurries. They introduce pattern and colour in a disciplined way, and they needn't be as expensive as they sound. Although antique Persian rugs are collectors' items, rugs that are merely old can be surprisingly cheap, especially if you buy them in a saleroom – as opposed to 'special' warehouse or carpet-wharf sales, where prices are often higher than in the most expensive shops. New all-wool Indian dhurries can be fairly expensive, but cotton dhurries are a great deal cheaper, look almost as good, and are thick – not irritatingly flimsy.

If your floor needs covering, other good backgrounds for rugs could be a plain woven haircord; although you might prefer the comfort of a close-pile conventional fitted carpet. The main thing is to keep the basic floor covering plain and confine it to discreet and quietly muted colours.

Doors: doors should always be panelled. If you can't afford to replace flush doors with traditional-style new ones, consider adding wooden beading to create false panels. Jettison any plastic knobs or handles: reproduction period door-furniture is well worth the money in a sitting room, where every detail is eventually noticed.

Windows and details: these are extremely important to the room's proportions, and lend it a sense of elegance and balance. If you have the good fortune to have the original internal shutters, try to make them operational. Then, unless you are overlooked, they may be all you need in the way of

Top left: Victorian-style furnishings needn't look heavy. Here, a trellis-patterned wallpaper and matching curtains look light and airy as well as authentic. Flowery chintz sofas add comfort and colour
Top: in this alternative version of the same sitting room, a 'typically' Victorian wallpaper makes a really strong design statement, echoed by the green-painted fireplace and shutters. Neutral carpet and white lace curtains lift the result
Above: if you don't want to obscure the shape of a bay window with curtains, but want something softer than Venetian or roller blinds, Roman blinds can provide a sympathetic answer. In this Edwardian sitting room, the chosen fabric has been quilted to give a richer impression

Above: in this Georgian sitting room, walls are painted an authentic milky brown. Traditional curtains and modern rug share a chevron motif, while matching upholstery links dissimilar seating *Left:* the same room given a different but still Georgian treatment

'curtains'. Otherwise, consider Roman blinds that will leave the basic shape of the windows free from obstruction. Alternatively, use full-length curtains in a simple way: lavish swags would look blowzy in these surroundings.

If someone has replaced the original skirting boards and architraves you may need to replace their misguided improvements; a 4-in high modern skirting board with a plain convex moulding will

look skimpy and mean in a spacious 18th-century room, as will flimsy modern architrave. Most large timber merchants stock Georgian-style skirtings and mouldings, and they are vital to establishing harmonious proportions.

Furniture: for comfort, you will need modern but traditional-style sofas – 18th-century seating was meant for polite, upright sitting. If you want a patterned upholstery fabric, several manufacturers produce designs closely based on originals. If they seem too strong, a quieter Indian ikat would look appropriate, because most 18th-century fabics were inspired by Indian designs. Furniture doesn't have to be Georgian – although it does have to be elegant, light and formal. Designs overlapped into the Victorian era; Edwardian furniture often looks right.

One solution to the lighting problem is to use the plainest possible brass-finish standard lamp plus strategically-placed table lamps: here ginger-jar-shaped bases prove the most sympathetic. But you could invest in one of the new halogen uplighters on a stand. They come in such pure and sculptural shapes, they would look at home in any simple and elegant setting.

The Victorian sitting room

The Victorian ideal was more relaxed, a reaction against 18th-century formality. Although this sometimes led to claustrophobic cosiness, the aim was to create a casual, 'lived-in' atmosphere.

Walls and ceiling: play up the room's architectural features, because they are the only way to make sense of those high walls and lofty ceilings. The Victorians often divided their walls into horizontal strips with skirting board, dado rail, picture rail and cornice. If you still have them, don't only pick them out with paint; emphasize them further by using different but related wallpaper designs above and below the dado rail; or different shades of paint if you prefer emulsion. If the architectural features have been taken out at some stage, you can restore them as suggested for a Georgian sitting room. Victorian-style cornices and skirting boards will tend to be larger and more ornate, but there is no need to be too slavishly faithful: just the appropriate skirting board and a picture rail can be enough to break up those blank expanses.

The easiest way to make a strong 19th-century design statement is to use an obviously Victorian-style wallpaper: most manufacturers include Victorian-inspired designs among their ranges and also on the market, at a price, are authentic designs from original wood-blocks. The majority of these papers have busy, large-scale patterns; if you don't feel you could live with them, look for wallpapers with tiny, light, 'spriggy' patterns.

Alternatively, you could confine pattern to a 19th-century design wallpaper border, running it around the room at picture-rail height. This could be the ideal solution for people who like plain walls, but still want to introduce a typically Victorian element; it's also a good way of 'replacing' a missing picture rail if you can't afford the real thing.

Floors: there is nothing anachronistic about fitted carpet because the Victorians loved their wall-to-wall comfort. Often they went for large-scale patterns that most of us would find overpowering today, although if you feel you could cope with them, some manufacturers offer original designs. But they also liked trellis patterns, which by their very nature leave lots of 'breathing space'. If you prefer plain floors with Persian rugs, so did many Victorians – and if your budget won't stretch to Persian rugs there are many pretty alternatives which would provide the right 'feel' in a Victorian-style drawing room.

Windows: you can be flexible in your approach, because although most mid-Victorians smothered everything in drapes, earlier and later Victorians responded to the invention of plate glass by letting as much light in as possible, sometimes through tinted panels.

This means if you have internal shutters for night-time privacy, you could just hang lace curtains for an airy but authentic effect. But the lace must be cotton as opposed to Terylene, and hung from a traditional curtain pole with rings, rather than a modern plastic track.

At the other extreme, you could have generously swagged curtains plus a matching swagged pelmet. Again, choose a traditional-style and non-synthetic fabric, and use it lavishly at the windows. The Victorians never skimped on anything: it's better to have curtains made of lashings of cheap material, than buy too little of an expensive fabric.

Furniture: plump, overstuffed and possibly button-backed Victorian or reproduction seating looks blissfully comfortable – but usually turns out to be firm and unyielding. It may be wisest to effect a compromise. Have the occasional original armchair or chaise-longue, but add modern sofas in a traditional style, either covering them in a Victorian-style fabric, or a plain material relating to a Victorian design elsewhere. If you have original Victorian pieces re-upholstered in velvet, do pick a *cotton* velvet – not a synthetic, which will have an artificial, shiny look.

Scale is all-important in choosing furniture. Large, high Victorian rooms need substantial pieces – and fortunately these are still relatively cheap in the salerooms because they are too big for 20th-century houses. Just one important item can give the room its 'key' – perhaps a breakfront bookcase, a mirror-backed sideboard or, more cheaply, a good wardrobe. Even a large chest of drawers can provide useful storage and look handsome in the sitting room. These tend to be very cheap, because they are unfashionably big for bedroom use. Smaller Victorian pieces are much more expensive, so look also for good quality Edwardian pieces.

Lighting is no problem in Victorian sitting rooms because reproduction fittings are readily available.

THE DINING ROOM

If you have a dining room – or simply a dining area – atmosphere is important. It turns eating from a function into an event.

If you are lucky enough to have a dining room that doesn't have to double for another purpose, you can be really adventurous in your approach. Unlike the sitting room, where you spend much of your time and need a relaxing atmosphere in which to unwind, you are free to create a more exciting and stimulating mood. You may not choose to do so, but the opportunity is there if you want to take it.

Much may depend on the pattern of your eating. If lunches tend to be sketchy affairs, snatched in a hurry, or even eaten in the kitchen, you will want to give priority to how the dining room looks at night-time. You may want to do this in any case, if you give a lot of dinner parties for friends or business contacts.

INTIMATE LIGHTING

The easiest way to establish a sympathetic night-time ambience is to choose a strong, dark colour for the walls. This looks soft and rich by artificial light, and provided the table has overhead lighting, will isolate the table-top in a private pool of illumination. The result will not only create an intimate atmosphere that encourages diners to relax and talk freely, but will cause glasses and silverware to come alive and sparkle. It will also allow any dirty dishes stacked elsewhere in the room to fade discreetly into the shadows, encouraging the illusion that there is no hard work involved.

If you are going to isolate the table-top in this way, it's vital that whatever opaque pendant fitting you choose hangs low enough to contain it tightly, without obscuring the view across the table. Finding the right height is critical, because a position that is slightly too high may cause the light to glare directly into the diners' eyes. If you buy a pendant fitting with a rise and fall mechanism, you will be able to find the ideal level by trial and error – and raise the fitting right up and out of the way when you need to lay or clear the table. Otherwise, choose a pendant with a deep, opaque shade, and if you are still worried about possible eye-glare, choose a light bulb where the lower half has been silvered. This would be a good idea, in any case, if you have preferred a translucent to an opaque shade, with a colour that needs a strong light to show it off.

One further advantage of having a rise and fall mechanism is that if you want to dine solely by candlelight, you can raise the pendant fitting till it's out of eyeshot.

Candles add an instant glamour to mealtimes, and are a good way of disguising less than perfect surroundings. If you choose tall candles, make sure the flames are either above eye-level – which will probably mean teaming them with tall candlesticks or candelabra – or below eye-level. If the flames are on a level with people's sight-lines, they will tend to have a mesmerizing effect. Very low candle-flames, however, have an unflattering effect on diners, because they throw shadows upwards, and make faces look tired. This may not matter amongst a group of young people. Indeed, one of the simplest and cheapest ways of dining by candlelight is to mass groups of tiny night-lights in shiny foil baking trays. They throw out a lovely tinny glitter.

As the table-top is the focal point of any dining room, lighting elsewhere should be confined to where it's needed; perhaps just a light over the sideboard or serving area, that can be switched off independently when no longer required.

Above: in this dining room in an 18th-century house, everything is arranged symmetrically, and use of colour is appropriately restricted to subtle putty. This provides a perfect background for the warm and richly glowing woods. Dried flowers, the rush seats of the chairs, and haircord carpet, unexpectedly introduce rugged texture
Right: spectacular stained glass art nouveau doors provide much interest in this dining room. Wisely, the approach elsewhere is simple. Caned chairs quietly suggest the mood of a conservatory, while the bare wooden floor, plain curtains and tabletop, sympathetically offer natural texture

THE DINING TABLE

Dining rooms demand very little in the way of furniture. All you really need is a table, some chairs, and either a sideboard or something to act as a sideboard. The choice of period style is vast, and the adventurous can mix and match.

Unless your room is so narrow that a circular shape would look hemmed in, consider a round table. It encourages a fuller flow of conversation, because people can talk around or across it, which isn't the case with a rectangular table. Circular tables can also seat more people, because the place settings run continuously round the circumference, without any corners going to waste. In addition, the middle is within everyone's reach, instead of requiring a central reservation that extends right down the length of the table. On the other hand, the attraction of the more formal rectangle is eternal. Its clean, uncompromising lines – echoed by rows of gleaming cutlery and porcelain – presents a picture of elegance no other table shape can match.

Ideally, you should allow 66 cm (2 ft 2 in) for each place setting, or 71 cm (2 ft 4 in) if you are using dining chairs with arms. This means a circular table with a 120 cm (4 ft) diameter will seat six people at a pinch; while a 140 cm (4 ft 6 in) diameter table will seat them more than amply. Similarly, a table with a 150 cm (5 ft) diameter will seat eight people at a pinch; while a 170 cm (5 ft 6 in) diameter will seat them more comfortably. Each extra 30 or 40 cm (or an extra foot) in diameter seats two more people comfortably, whereas the same amount on the end of a rectangular table does little to ease the seating problem.

Some circular tables come with an extension leaf which turns them into an oval shape: however, unlike the leaves of many square or rectangular tables, which slide under the main table-top when not in use, they have to be stored somewhere separately. If your dining room is fairly small, but you still like the idea of an oval shape for entertaining, you could look for an old gateleg table with semi-circular leaves. Another alternative is a traditional Pembroke table. Then, when the table is not in use, you can drop down the semi-circular leaves at both ends, leaving you with a slender rectangle.

One advantage of square or rectangular tables is that they lend themselves to being pushed against a wall, leaving plenty of floor area free in smaller dining rooms. You can always pull them out into the room when guests are coming. If people are going to sit on both sides of a rectangular table, the table needs to be at least 75 cm (2 ft 6 in) wide.

PRACTICAL TABLE-TOPS

Many people choose mahogany or rosewood for a formal dining room, and are immediately faced with a dilemma. To protect the table-top from hot plates, they either have to hide the beautiful polished surface under a cloth over an undercloth of felt, or use individual table mats. The snag here is that simple and unfussy mats are hard to find. It's easy if you have a modern table, and can choose something innocuous like natural rush, but once it comes to anything more formal, the choice is not very wide. If you can't find any table mats that look attractive, it could be worth making rectangular or oval place mats (depending on the shape of your table) that are big enough to take an entire place setting. Cover layers of washable Terylene wadding with a washable fabric that matches or relates to a fabric in the room, give a criss-cross of quilting to hold the wadding firm, bind the edges – and you have solved the problem in a handsome way. Perhaps, for an altogether simpler solution (although it could turn out to be rather expensive), buy a set of large and really good-looking silver-plated or pewter plates, to act as underplates that stay *in situ* throughout the serving of the hot courses.

Above: antique chairs of different styles and periods mix inspirationally in this modern setting
Opposite: brave use of colour and space and bold teaming of old and new produce an exciting room. Architectural details are free to be seen

Whether or not you use a tablecloth may depend on the amount of rich wood in the room. If your mahogany or rosewood table has matching chairs and a matching sideboard, you may find you want to cover it up, to create a softer and lighter effect.

The only wooden table that is impervious to both heat and spills is one that is made of oiled teak – as opposed to the polished teak that most dining room furniture comes in. If you can't find one (and it would be very expensive), you could have just a rectangular table-top made, and rest it across chrome-steel trestle legs. Otherwise, woods like pine or oak will be marked by hot plates once they are polished or varnished; and if they are not treated, will be marked by spills.

Other surfaces that can withstand both spills and hot plates include plastic laminate (which always looks good in white), and glass and marble. A melamine surface won't be able to take really hot plates, and you will need to mop up wine-spills with great alacrity.

If you are working to a really tight budget, you could buy an ugly old table in a junk shop and hide it under a floor-length cloth. In fact, as floor-length cloths hide a multitude of sins, you could get a piece of chipboard cut to the size you want, and fix it to any base you can find – it could be an upturned oil drum for all anyone will know. Alternatively, buy a pair of trestle legs, and either span them with a laminate table-top or with an old flush door rescued from a builder's skip. This could either be covered with a floor-length cloth again, or something lightweight but spill-proof like sealed cork tiles.

DINING CHAIRS

Dining chairs take up a lot of space – something to bear in mind when you are choosing a table – you may find you have to settle for a smaller size than anticipated.

This is because, although chairs usually tuck tidily under the table when not in use, once people sit in them, they project at least 50 cm (20 in) from the table, and project at least another 30 cm (or foot) more when people push them back to get up.

Chairs with arms cost more than armless versions, and unless the arms are low enough to go under the table when not in use, they are going to take up much more space depthways, as well as more space widthways. If you want a set of antique captain's chairs, for instance, you will need a rather large dining room, because the chairs will always stand completely proud of the table.

Dining tables with matching chairs are expensive, and often rather staid and predictable too. You may want them in a very formal and traditional dining room, although even here, if you have the patience to hunt around antique shops and auction rooms, you will find it's much cheaper to buy chairs individually than buy a ready-matched set of six. Some 18th-

and 19th-century dining chairs were made to a similar pattern in vast numbers, and it really is worth the effort of tracking them down yourself, since a chair that costs £20 on its own will probably cost £80 rather than £40 as a pair, and so on – right up to a set of six at £600-plus, instead of the £120 you may be able to manage.

But in less stringently formal surroundings, it can be exciting to mix antique chairs of different shapes, as in the dining room on page 83, because they will all share a similar mellow mood. And it can be even more exciting to mix styles and periods. You could marry elegant Regency chairs with a cool modern glass or white melamine-topped table – not a modern, wooden-topped table, where the woods would live uneasily together, and you would lose the surprise of contrasting materials. Or you could team brightly-coloured plastic chairs with an antique dark oak table. Provided you effect the contrasts with conviction and get the proportions right, the results can look better than uniform perfection.

If you are short of money, elegant bentwood chairs are still plentiful and ridiculously cheap. Furthermore, as the bentwood itself provides a unifying element, you don't even need to assemble a matching set. Alternatively, you could buy up ill-assorted junk shop chairs and unify them with a matching coat of paint, perhaps tying on matching cushions to complete the effect.

SIDEBOARDS

Conventional modern sideboards take up a lot of room in relation to the amount of storage they provide. If there isn't much space or you simply don't like them, you might prefer to fix a serving shelf to the wall. This should be at least 40 cm (15 in) deep and, ideally, the wall behind it should be protected with a glass splashback. However, if you are mixing periods or have a traditional dining room, there are several furnishing options open. You could buy a mirror-backed Victorian chiffonier, using the top for serving food (although it would need protecting with a mat) and using the cupboards below to store glass and china. You could buy a marble or

Right: a cool, translucent treatment for a period dining room – modern design at its elegant best. The floor is covered in blue-grey studded rubber. The vast Italian table seats eight comfortably, but with its sleek metal legs and reeded glass top, it doesn't run the risk of swamping the room. New highlights the old. The marble fireplace is flanked by a halogen lamp and a canvas chair, while Hockney's Celia gazes down aloofly

David Hockney · Prints and Drawings of Celia 1970-1980
Petersburg Press at the Chicago Art Fair
Rainbow

ceramic-tile-topped Edwardian washstand, which would provide a practical serving surface as well as storage. You could buy an old dresser base that has lost its top. You could even buy a low, old chest of drawers, which would provide excellent storage for cutlery and table-linen.

Obviously, if you have a serving hatch, the serving area will prove most useful if it's nearby or immediately beneath it. If you don't have a hatch, think twice before creating one. They are only worth having if they incorporate a ledge deep enough for plenty of dishes to stand on; or if there's a willing helper on the other side, to ferry food to the table.

THE TINY DINING ROOM

Benches can seat more people in a row than an equivalent-length row of dining chairs. Provided you team them with a suitable table, they take up less depth when people are sitting on them, as well as tucking right under the table when not in use. Look for a table with a central support, rather than one that has legs at the corners: refectory-style tables with cross-over legs, or the classic pedestal table. These will enable people to sit on the end of the benches and slide themselves along to the middle, as well as enabling the benches to fit under the table-top after mealtimes.

If you don't like the idea of benches because there is nothing to lean back against, you could butt one bench up against a wall, and use chairs for the other side of the table. You could even build the wall-bench in, upholstering the seat and adding a padded back-panel; then make cushions for the chairs in a matching fabric. Indeed, in a minute room where you need to seat a lot of people, you could build upholstered wall-benches into three of the walls, with the table in the middle, rather like the pine eating 'stalls' in some bistros. The size of table-top would be critical though: too near and you wouldn't have room for manoeuvre; too far and you'd be stretching forward to eat at arm's length. If you are considering built-in seating, be sure to allow enough knee-room between the top of the seat cushions and the underside of the table-top. The recommended distance is about 35 cm (14 in). The other space-saving alternative for tiny dining rooms is to team a drop-leaf table or wall-hinged table-top with folding or stacking chairs.

THE FLOOR

Although carpets are quiet and luxurious in a dining room, muffling the scraping back of chairs and all the to-ing and fro-ing from the kitchen, they are very impractical, even if you don't have young children – food inevitably gets dropped at some point. But if you are determined to take the risk, it's advisable to go for a close-pile carpet, rather than anything that will impede the movement of chair-legs. It's probably also wisest to go for a medium colour – although as this is a room where little time is spent, you might consider a patterned carpet to help disguise marks. If you are worried about making the room look smaller, you could perhaps pick a small-scale geometric pattern. This would look particularly good with modern furniture although it would complement simple 18th-century furniture, which would share its disciplined restraint.

But almost any of the practical floor coverings make sense in a dining room: polished wood floors, sealed cork tiles and, unless you are afraid of breakages, ceramic or quarry tiles. Lino and vinyl can look handsome too – it's certainly a mistake to view them only in a kitchen context. If you team black and white vinyl tiles with Regency furniture, for instance, they will appear formal and elegant rather than ordinary and sensible.

THE WALLS

As dining rooms get little wear and tear, yet are very much on show when entertaining, you might consider covering the walls with fabric. This always makes a room feel warm and rich, and prevents voices bouncing loudly off the walls. But it's only a good idea if the room is well ventilated. Otherwise the fabric might retain food smells.

Fabric would be impractical in any dining room where the table is up against the wall, because it would soon get splashed with gravy. The same would be true of a standard wallpaper, though you could give the table area a protective coat of spray-on matt varnish. However, a washable wallpaper would make more sense; and a scrubbable vinyl even better sense. Vinyl wall covering designs and textures have improved out of all recognition in recent years: to give just one example of their sophistication, there is a marvellous moiré-silk design that comes in exquisite shades like silver-grey and oyster. If you used the real thing, you could not expect a more beautiful result.

If you prefer to paint the walls, a sheeny silk vinyl or eggshell looks soft but is practical. Emulsion paint cannot be washed clean very often without creating bald patches, but providing a practical surface may not matter if your table is in the middle of the room, and your sideboard or serving area has some form of splashback for protection.

Top: this small, box-like dining room in a tiny mews house sticks to white and off-white to make it look larger. Circular table, and an open archway instead of a door, create a fluid impression. Open mesh chairs provide stylish seating without causing any visual obstruction

Above and opposite: two views of the same dining room: above, being used as a sewing room; opposite, with all sewing paraphernalia stowed away, and in use as a conventional dining room. It's efficient storage that enables the room to work double-time for its keep. A 'dead end' was filled with 55cm (22in) deep free-standing wardrobe and drawer units, made to look built-in with a fascia board between top and ceiling. Units were painted to match the walls, so they became another 'wall'

THE WINDOWS

As dining rooms have little in the way of furniture, you may want to play up the importance of the windows by giving them a fairly lavish treatment. This could be well worth the effort if you do lots of evening entertaining, when for much of the year the curtains will be drawn and receiving maximum attention.

As a general rule, curtains should either sweep the floor or stop at the sill, because anything else tends to look indecisive. Floor-length curtains always look more opulent – the fashion at the moment is to have them overlength so they actually lie in folds on the floor. But even with a window large enough for this treatment, if a radiator is sited beneath it, you are faced with the problem that once floor-length curtains are drawn over a radiator, they stop the heat from reaching the room. One simple solution is to hang full-length curtains, but drape them to the sides with permanent tie-backs. Then add a sill-height blind to pull down at night. (Of course, if you are leaving the radiator on view, you will need to paint it the same colour as your walls, so it blends imperceptibly into its background.)

If you are lucky enough to have architecturally beautiful windows, and a view that is equally beautiful too, it's a pity to detract from them in any way. If your dining room is not overlooked, and you have preferred a simple look throughout, you may be prepared to leave them quite bare. Otherwise you could give them a simple treatment, choosing plain curtains in the same tone as the walls, that can be pulled right back off the window frame, so the windows' proportions are not interfered with. Carry the simplicity through by choosing an inconspicuous modern curtain track, and make the curtains up with a crisp, unfussy heading – pencil pleats always look sharp and neat. This treatment is especially useful if other walls in the room are highly decorated.

Accommodating window shapes

It's impossible to play up awkwardly-shaped or mis-matched windows successfully. The best you can hope for is to play them down by making them an integral part of the room. The easiest way of doing this is to cover the walls in a patterned wallpaper, and make up the curtains from a matching fabric. If all that is awkward about the windows is a differing level of sills, you can soften the outline of the sills by using floor-length nets or sheers that stay drawn all the time. By day they will diffuse the incoming light softly, and at night you can draw the floor-length main curtains over them. An alternative for an informal dining room would be to fake equal levels of sill by hanging two rows of café-curtaining, keeping the bottom row permanently closed. This could be a good idea anyway in any town house or cottage directly overlooking a pavement.

A narrow window can easily be made to seem wider, because you can extend the curtain track or pole well beyond the window frame. This way, provided you always keep the curtains sufficiently drawn to cover the sides of the window frame, no one will guess they are only covering wall, and will think there is an expanse of glass behind. This confidence trick works well if you have got two windows of different widths along the same wall. Just give them the same size track or decorative poles and draw the curtains to the sides indentically – something that will be determined by the width of the wider window.

In a period bay window, complete with operational shutters, you will probably want to leave the shutters in simple isolation. But if you feel the room needs a softening touch, you could fix a long curtain pole to the walls on either side of the bay, so the pole goes across the bay in mid-air. Then, you could loop a generous length of lightweight fabric or cotton lace (perhaps as much as 14 metres or yards) up and over the pole to create a loosely swagged pelmet; then up and over the pole again in much deeper, waist-height loops at both sides. This would create the effect of swagging. The ends would hang down straight to floor-length behind the swagged sides. It's a marvellous way of making 'curtains' without having to use scissors or sew a stitch, and as all it does is frame the bay window, it doesn't interfere with the working of the shutters.

Curtains can work wonders for most kinds of windows, and help a room feel warm and friendly, but they have one major disadvantage. They need an enormous amount of fabric. How much will depend on the kind of heading you use, and whether there's a pattern that has to be matched. Remember that when a pattern has a large repeat, matching can entail significant wastage. See page 42 for details of how to make your own curtains.

Unfortunately, nothing looks worse than mean and skimped curtains. If you can't afford enough of an expensive fabric, it's better to buy masses of lightweight cotton, and use it so lavishly it looks rich and luxurious. If you have bought a good quality fabric, however, it will last longer and look better if it's lined and interlined. In chilly rooms, perhaps use one of the new thermal linings for extra insulation.

Window blinds

The cheapest way to cover a window with fabric is to make a blind. You may prefer to anyway, if you find curtains fussy. But remember, blinds are no good for disguising poorly-shaped windows.

The simplest blind to make is a roller blind. Wooden roller kits are fairly inexpensive, but you will need to use a closely-woven cotton or sailcloth, because anything heavier or finer might bunch on the rollers. You can give the fabric a wipeable and dirt-resistant finish by spraying it with a fabric stiffener. If you are trying to fill a big picture window, make two or three blinds rather than one large one, because any seams will look unsightly and will affect the 'hang'. One advantage of making your own blinds is that you can use a fabric that relates to your room. Alternatively, there are firms who will make the blinds up for you if you supply a suitable material.

Although you can add scalloped castellated or lace trims to roller blinds, you may want a softer-looking blind at the windows. Roman blinds concertina upwards in deep, loose folds, and look very good in a formal setting. Ruched festoon blinds are altogether more frivolous, but can look splendidly over-the-top and sumptuous. There are special tapes for making up both these types of blinds, so they are no longer only for the ambitious to tackle.

If you want a crisper and less conventional look, you could buy roller blinds with highly graphic screen-printed designs, rather than the usual plains and florals, or you could paint or stencil on your own designs, using a special fabric

Above: this monastically simple cottage dining room revels in the roughness of the whitewashed walls, and the theatrical contrast of light and shade – but the simplicity is no mere accident. Humble table and chairs are top-quality country antiques, and the artless flower arrangement is calculatedly casual. As for the sparseness of the furniture – knowing what to leave out can be just as important as knowing what to put in

Right: here, an opulent and formal dining room looks its best at night, when the rich wood of the furniture and panelling glow by the light of the period-lamps. Note how sensitively the pictures have been arranged within the panelling. Red-painted walls increase the sense of richness

paint. Alternatively, you could use one of the small, specialist firms who screen-print, air-brush or hand-paint one-off blinds to order.

Venetian blinds always look neat and architectural, and give you complete control over the amount of light you let in. If you like the idea but find them cold and clinical, it's possible to buy Venetian blinds with cedarwood slats. These are extremely handsome, but inevitably, rather more expensive.

Louvre blinds have much wider, vertical slats, and are not worth considering unless your windows are large. This isn't just a matter of visual scale. They are extremely expensive in small sizes, but become proportionately cheaper the larger they get. As the slats can be pushed aside and walked through, they are good for any floor-to-ceiling sliding windows.

Natural woven reed blinds roll up via a cord and pulley, and filter light in a way that suggests tropical sunshine outside. They could work in a dining room with a conservatory-mood, but do tend to evoke images of Somerset Maugham. Cane or split bamboo slatted blinds are cheaper and just as evocative.

If you are working on a very tight budget, pleated paper blinds can be very inexpensive. The cheapest come in a standard 2 metre (6 ft 6 in) drop, so you have to leave the bottom of the blind pleated if your window is shallower. Once paper blinds come treated with a wipable finish, they get more expensive, but still remain relatively cheap overall.

THE BEDROOM

A bedroom is a retreat from the outside world – the one place where you can really please yourself.

Unlike halls and sitting rooms, which are frequently on show, bedrooms are very private places. This means you can take a more personal approach. You can be madly flamboyant if you fancy it, using masses of exotic oriental fabrics to create an Arabian Nights' fantasy. You can be unashamedly 'feminine' and frilly. You can be so cool, the look is almost spartan. Fortunately, in terms of the budget, you can choose less practical floor coverings and wall surfaces.

Bedrooms are the one place where buying a cheaper carpet doesn't prove to be a false economy, because it won't be subject to hard wear and tear. It's also one of the places where you are very unlikely to trample in dirt from the street and garden, so you won't need pattern or dark colours to disguise grubby footmarks. If off-white fitted carpet is your idea of ultimate luxury – this is where you can have it without feeling guilty. And if you want a wallpaper on the walls, there is no need to be sensible and choose a washable version, or a tough vinyl wallcovering that can be scrubbed.

Despite the fact that bedrooms offer so much freedom, no-one's obliged to go to extremes just to use it fully. You may prefer a quiet room to sleep in, in which case, perhaps keep to shades of the same colour, as in the monastically simple grey bedroom on page 99. Or if you want the friendliness of pattern, choose a co-ordinated wallpaper and fabric, so the patterns flow smoothly and serenely, as in the bedroom on pages 100 and 101. Whatever approach you prefer, however, make your major design statement with the bed, because everything will follow from its visual treatment. First though, be sure to pick the right bed.

HOW TO CHOOSE A BED

A good night's sleep is more important than anything for a sense of well-being and an ability to cope with the day. Of course, a comfortable bed isn't going to guarantee you get one – but it will increase your chances enormously – so it really is worth choosing with care, and spending the most you can possibly afford. A good quality bed will last from ten to fifteen years, and can be regarded as a sound investment. If you can't manage the initial financial outlay, rather than buy an inferior conventional divan, it might be best to build your own rigid base, and concentrate your resources into a superior mattress.

Soft versus hard

If a bed is too soft, the heaviest parts of the body sink down into it and only the lighter parts receive support. Conversely, if a bed is too hard, while the heaviest parts receive support, the lighter parts are left unsupported. The ideal is a fairly firm in-between, but if in doubt, always err on the firm side. Hard beds give better support to the spine than soft and overyielding beds which can eventually lead to serious back trouble.

Bed bases

There are two types of conventional divan base: sprung edge and firm edge. With sprung edge, the springs are mounted on top of a wooden base, so the resilience extends right to the edges. With firm edge, the springs are contained within a wooden base-and-sides frame. Sprung edge versions are more expensive, and tend to prolong the life of the mattress. However, in a bed-sitter where the bed gets used for seating, it is best to go for a firm edge base: otherwise the springs will start sagging at the edge. Alternatively, choose a studio-bed where the base comprises wooden drawers: these won't sag and they will provide useful storage for pillows and blankets.

As a good mattress should be enough to provide postural support, it's not essential to have a sprung divan base. Indeed, you may prefer to buy a slatted wood base: some of the latest use springy and flexible slats, so they incorporate a measure of resilience. But except in emergencies, it's not a good idea simply to put the mattress on the floor. When people are asleep, their bodies lose up to 1 litre or 1½ pints of liquid a night, and this moisture must be able to evaporate freely. Some form of wooden base is needed to provide adequate ventilation for the mattress. If you intend to build one yourself, a solid wood base should be drilled with 19 or 20 mm (¾-in) diameter holes at 18 cm (7-in) centres; a slatted wood base should allow spaces about as wide as the slats. The BSI recommend 5 cm (2-in) wide and 20 mm (¾-inch) deep slats, run *across* the bed rather than from top to bottom: in the case of a double bed, you'll need to support the slats lengthways to prevent any sag.

Mattresses

Most sprung mattresses are either pocket-sprung or open-sprung. Pocket springing is much more expensive, because each spring is contained within its own calico pocket, and reacts individually to pressure upon it. In other words, it only gives where give is needed – something that makes it a good choice for double beds, where couples tend to be of differing weights. Open springing, because it is inter-linked, yields less specifically to

pressure, which could mean that with a double bed, the lighter partner ends up on a downhill slope.

But the choice isn't quite as cut and dried as it seems. The quality of both types depends on how many springs have been used, so an open-sprung mattress with a high density of small springs will be better than a pocket-sprung mattress with a low density of large springs. If the retailer can't tell you how many springs there are (a good double bed will boast about 500; the very best about 1,000), you will find price always proves a reliable guide and that well-known makers offer several styles of mattress.

Finally, for any couple with widely differing weights – or widely differing ideas of comfort – it's possible to order matching twin beds with separate mattresses that can be zipped together and linked to form a double bed.

A good foam mattress is as comfortable as an interior sprung version,

Above: if you make a strong design statement with your bed, be bold and follow the statement through to make sure it's fully understood. Here, a stylish but informal bedroom takes its cue from the emphatic bed-linen. An extra sheet has been made up into matching window blinds. A bedside rug has been stitched in needlepoint, using a scaled-up version of the design that plays with its proportions for added interest. The skirting board and architraves have been picked out in a paint that faithfully reflects the bed-linen's main colour, while a stencilled check border echos the accent colour. The result is decorative yet disciplined

Courtenay

doesn't need turning, and doesn't harbour dust – which could be important for anyone with an allergy. But it's a mistake to think it will be any cheaper: it's an alternative rather than a budget substitute. There *are* cheap foam mattresses, but they will probably be shallow (be wary of anything less than 10 cm (4 in) deep); and they will be made of low-density foam, i.e. full of big air bubbles surrounded by thick walls. High-density foam is full of tiny air bubbles surrounded by thin walls and, although your safest guide to quality is price, you will find a good foam mattress feels springy and resilient, whereas a cheap one feels unyielding and hard. Some of the best and most expensive mattresses come in different densities of foam, so they are able to yield more at shoulders and hips where more give is needed.

Sleeping on the cheap

Strictly speaking, second-hand beds are not a good idea because all beds adapt to the shape of their owners – one reason why a new bed never really feels comfortable until it's been slept in for several weeks. But good quality and virtually new beds occasionally turn up at local auction rooms, and often sell at very reasonable prices, thanks to the illogical thinking of people who cheerfully sleep in hotels for a fortnight, but dislike the thought of buying a stranger's bed. If you are equally illogical but still want a bargain, you might be lucky and find a new one in a sale: but do be sure you are getting a

Opposite: soft colours, lacy curtains and a prettily be-ribboned bed make this fresh and charming bedroom a delight. The coverlet and cushions would have been very expensive to buy. Instead, the owner made them cheaply and easily – and was able to choose ribbons in pinks and apricots to clinch the colours used elsewhere
Above: the surest way to a successful bedroom is to use one of the many co-ordinated design ranges available. Here, the duvet cover is made from a fabric that matches the wallpaper; everything else from the trellis-patterned fabric
Left: rich, creamy pinks and lavishly used fabrics add up to an almost edible confection. This approach demands a vast room – and sweeping convictions

genuine reduction as opposed to a 'special purchase' or phoney discount. Your best hope is to look for a slightly shop-soiled mattress or an unpopular ticking cover – neither of which will show once the bed is made up – although always avoid synthetic tickings. These can't 'breathe', an essential for good ventilation. They are also slippery, so bedclothes may develop the infuriating habit of sliding off in the middle of the night.

It's a mistake to economize on size. A bed needs to be at least 15 cm (6 in) longer than the sleeper, and wide enough to allow a person to link hands behind the head without elbows projecting beyond the sides of the bed. As mattresses and sprung bases wear out at the same rate, it's also a mistake to replace just one or the other. In any case, the springing of mattress and base is usually inter-related, so you tamper with this relationship at your peril.

Styles of bed

Basically, most beds are boring rectangles. But given that mundane starting point, you can play them up to provide the room's chief feature; or play them down, to form an integrated part of the whole. The easiest way to lend a bed importance is to give it a really attractive headboard. If you don't want the button-back upholstered kind (which really only makes sense if the fabric relates to your room), there are plenty of alternatives to choose from. Wooden-framed cane headboards always look light and attractive, and can be neat and modern or ornate and traditional, as in the pictures on pages 98 and 101. Traditional carved wood headboards, whether antique or reproduction, will turn the bed into a serious piece of furniture – and needn't be teamed with traditionally pretty florals – see page 91 for a strong and stylish treatment. If you don't want a complete brass bedstead you can buy just a bedhead. But be warned: even with pillows propped up behind you, they are still extremely uncomfortable to lean back against.

Above: crisp cotton hangings and a white crocheted bedspread have the strength to stand up to this sturdy oak half-tester. Dense pink-painted walls and off-white carpet and white fireplace continue the use of bold pink/white contrasts that prevents this pretty room from looking merely pretty-pretty
Left: wall-to-wall storage makes this small double-bedroom workable. Three mirror-fronted doors slide between ceiling and floor tracks (the centre door has been slid to the left) so they can be opened without crashing into the bed. By relecting the room, they seem to double its size – a trick helped by the use of restful colours

You can always improvise a headboard or bedhead. You can use an antique mirror that is as wide as the bed – big overmantel mirrors could well fit a double bed perfectly. You could fix a traditional wooden curtain pole to the wall above the bed, and drape it with a length of white cotton lace to form a swagged pelmet with more swags at the sides. Alternatively, if you wanted a crisper effect, you could make a fitted bedspread with inverted pleats at the corners, and carry the matching fabric flat up the wall to form a panel the same width as the bed.

For an even more visually important bed, if your room is large enough, you could buy a four-poster. You could even make one yourself. All it needs is a frame with a curtain track fitted to the ceiling, and four uprights onto which to tie the curtains. This can look grand or pretty – according to your choice of fabric – but if you want a really imposing effect, you could add a scalloped, castellated or swagged pelmet to the frame. Or you could forget four-posters altogether and give your bed a canopy, with swathes of fabric flowing from a ceiling-fixed corona. Or merely extend the idea of a flat wall-panel of fabric and carry the fabric over the ceiling as far as the foot of the bed: using it either flat, or in a luxurious loop and swag.

For people who prefer something less 'fully-furnished', one of the simplest ways of treating a bed is to give it a no-nonsense duvet with a plain and bright-coloured cover: then integrate the bed within its surroundings by running a shelf at mattress level all along the bed wall. Once the shelf is painted to match the duvet cover, it will provide the eye with an unbroken line of colour, as well as providing the equivalent of bedside tables. You could also contain the bed within a run of storage. One of the neatest ways of doing this is to position wardrobe units, with top cupboards, either side of the bed; then continue the top cupboards across the bed to bridge the gap between them. This has the effect of part-recessing the bed within its own intimate and tailor-made alcove. But do be sure the base has easy-running castors – you will need to pull out the bed to make it properly.

STORAGE FOR THE BEDROOM

Built-in storage looks neat and leaves more floor area free (important considerations in a tiny bedroom that would look overcrowded with free-standing items) but it can't travel with you if you move, and is extremely expensive to have installed. One cheaper solution, that's ideal for an alcove (or wall-to-wall if you need a room-length run of storage), is to fix floor and ceiling tracks and fit sliding doors between. Then you can paint or paper the doors to match your walls and the storage becomes virtually invisible. Alternatively, if you need to create an illusion of space, you can buy mirror-fronted doors as in the bedroom opposite, taking care they reflect a gentle and

'non-jumpy' scene. Either way, allow a front-to-back width of at least 60 cm (2 ft) so clothes hang freely, without rubbing against wall or wardrobe doors.

Another cheap and relatively flexible solution is to buy free-standing units and make them look built-in by adding fascia boards to fill any gaps at top and sides. In the dual-purpose dining room on page 86, a fascia board above standard wardrobe-and-drawer units has created a svelte run of floor-to-ceiling storage. In fact, these units were the cheapest-of-the-cheap, and originally came with a white melamine finish and nasty gilt-finish handles. Handles are the weak point of most low-cost storage, but they are easy to replace with something simpler like D-handles. And if you don't want to retain the white melamine finish that the majority of cheaper units come in (worth keeping, of course, if your walls are white) it's always possible to overpaint it. For professional results, wet the surface first, rubbing it down with a fine, waterproof glasspaper – just enough to provide key without penetrating the melamine – and use a sheeny silk vinyl paint in whatever colour matches your walls.

Even if you have more money to spend and would rather invest in a better quality product, it still makes sense to 'build-in' free-standing units; or buy units from a free-standing range that has been specifically designed to look built-in. This way, if you move, you have the option of leaving 'built-in' storage behind you, or taking it with you if you need it. And because it's free-standing, even if you don't need it in a new bedroom, you can

Above: a svelte and architectural approach to the bedroom. A custom-built drawer-unit along one wall incorporates the bed, so it looks built-in – and provides bedside 'tables' in an unobtrusive way. Carpet, continuing up the sides of the bed and units, ensures clear, unfussy and flowing lines. Mirror-fronted storage fills another wall entirely, and with the mirror above the drawer-units, reflect a crisp and clean-cut scene

separate it into individual units to use elsewhere in the house. After all, wardrobe units are really only cupboards, and will provide useful storage anywhere.

Interior fittings

How much clothing a run of wardrobe units can pack away depends not so much on the length of the run but how big a use is made of its potential. The largest unit, inefficiently planned, can simply mean room for a good old rummage; while a smaller unit can hold just as much and have everything within easy reach. The secret lies in interior fittings: knowing which you need and where to put them.

Most wardrobe units come supplied with a top shelf and hanging rail: more sophisticated fittings are usually an optional extra. Before buying them, analyse the empty space. If you like separates, or prefer to put shirts on hangers instead of folding them away in drawers, you may only need one unit for full-length storage of items like overcoats and dresses. In this case, rather than waste space at the bottom of the other units, you could double their hanging potential by adding another, mid-height rail. If, on the other hand, you need to store a lot of folded clothes like pullovers and underwear, you could add a mid-height shelf with drawers below; even a cheap, old free-standing chest of drawers if it isn't too wide from front-to-back. You could add also hanging wire baskets, or a tiered shoe rack if you are someone who accumulates masses of footwear.

If you are an intrinsically untidy person, who can reduce the orderly contents of a drawer to chaos in the hunt for just one elusive item, either go for shallow drawers – where things can only be stored single-layer – or choose wire baskets or deeper drawers in clear Perspex. The latter will enable you to glimpse what you're looking for in cross-section.

Free-standing storage

Although a run of modern storage can be papered, painted or even panelled to look perfectly at home in a traditional setting, it can prove unsympathetic in a period room, where the original proportions are all-important. And it can prove disastrous in a bedroom with architectural details like picture rails and cornices, which would get hidden by any floor-to-ceiling arrangement.

Free-standing items have two advantages. They make a bedroom feel more friendly and furnished – and they are instantly portable if you have to move house. Indeed, they can provide the perfect solution if you know your present home is so temporary that it's not worth

Above: if you live in a small flat, solve the problem of where to put guests for the night by unzipping a double bed in the sitting room. This unusual sofa bed includes its own bedding – the quilted sofa cover doubles as a washable duvet, and the base opens out to reveal two pillows – and a foldaway shelf that can act as a bedside table. All you need to add are sheets and pillow-cases, which take up minimal storage space

'building-in' free-standing modern units that a subsequent owner may not need. The bedroom on page 98, for instance, was specifically furnished with a future move in mind – even to preferring rugs to fitted carpet. The pine wardrobe (really just a cupboard with a hanging rail added) and the false-fronted pine coffer with a lift-up lid, cope with storage in an attractive way. Yet if any future home already boasted built-in bedroom storage, both the wardrobe and coffer would provide handsome storage in any other area of the house.

GUEST BEDROOMS

Few people can afford to leave a spare bedroom spare between guests. But if you intend to make it double as a study, hobby room, or simply a bolt-hole for people fleeing the television, it makes sense to avoid a 'bedroomy' look. So forget frills and fussiness and soft, pretty pastels and go for simpler outlines and more robust colours and textures. If possible, avoid a conventional bed, because its shape and size will dominate the room, and stamp it as primarily for sleeping purposes.

Sofa-beds offer an ideal alternative, because they provide conventional seating during the day, and only turn into a double bed when the need arises. There are three different kinds worth considering if you are looking for an inexpensive sofa-bed. All-foam versions – where the seat unfolds directly onto the floor – are fine for youthful guests but not for the elderly, who might have difficulty getting down to the low level. Wooden or plywood-framed studio couches – where the back drops down level with the seat – are more comfortable for sleeping on than for sitting, because the cushions have to be firm. Japanese futons – where a mattress of calico-covered layers of cotton on a slatted-wood base forms both seat and back when folded – look the most stylish, are available with brightly coloured cotton covers, and could be slept on permanently by people who like a firm bed.

At the expensive end of the market, interior sprung sofa-beds come with either double-action or folding mechanisms. Double-action mechanisms can offer an extra-thick mattress, because it only needs to be folded once, while the rest tucks into the hollow back of the sofa. Folding mechanisms increase the bulk and weight of the sofa without being able to increase the thickness of the mattress, because it needs to be folded twice.

If a sofa-bed is likely to be used for long periods at a stretch – or permanently in the case of a bed-sit – aim to buy one that provides proper support and at least a 10 cm (4 in) thick mattress.

If you have to make do with a conventional single bed, push it lengthways against the wall and back it with cushions so it looks like a sofa. The most effective way is to make a tailored bedspread with inverted pleats that can fit over the bedclothes, so only the pillows need hiding away in daytime. Then cover square or rectangular cushions with the same fabric, add fabric loops, and hang them from a traditional curtain pole fixed to the wall above the bed.

CHILDREN'S ROOMS

Unlike bedrooms, nurseries need to be extremely practical, because they are going to be subjected to merciless wear and tear. They also need to be very adaptable. Children outgrow furniture nearly as fast as clothes, and their tastes in decoration change very rapidly. So, ideally, create a basic and indestructible 'shell', that can be made to look different as the years go by with minor and inexpensive changes, while the furniture 'grows up' with the room's occupants.

Floors

Flooring needs to be quiet – so you can tip-toe in at night to make sure that all is well; easy-to-clean – so you can wipe off spills and scuff-marks; and hard-wearing – to take the constant punishment that will be meted out to it. This rules out most carpets, although you could risk a non-absorbent and durable nylon carpet, preferably with a rubber backing. At all events avoid a long-pile carpet – not only because it's so impractical, but because it will stop toy trains and cars dead in their tracks. For older children, carpet tiles might make sense, because you can replace individual tiles as they get stained or worn out; but they would be too scratchy on the knees for the toddler-stage, as would handsome and hard-wearing sisal. Sheet lino, cushioned vinyl or vinyl tiles are all tough and very easy to clean, and they needn't look cold and clinical if you introduce plenty of warm colours elsewhere. (If you are tempted to add a rug, however, make sure it's either heavy or fixed, so it won't slip and cause accidents while children are playing.)

But perhaps the most suitable flooring is sealed or vinyl-surfaced cork tiles. This isn't cheap, but it's soft and warm, wipe-clean, very hard-wearing, and so good-looking, even once children have turned into teenagers, they will probably be quite happy to keep it.

Walls

Walls are going to take as much punishment as floors, though you can at least try to forestall some of it by providing an official scribbling area. There is no guarantee your child will stick to it, but it might cut down the ravages elsewhere. You could either screw a blackboard to the wall or, better still, paint part of a wall or door with special blackboard paint. Indeed, there is no reason why you shouldn't paint all the walls with blackboard paint up to a height of about a metre (3 ft 6 in), provided you top it with a bright-coloured frieze to cheer up the result.

Unless you are buying it because it gives you pleasure, don't bother with specific nursery-patterned wallpapers. Babies are unlikely to notice the bunny rabbits on the wall, and once they do, it won't be long before they find them babyish. If you are determined to have a specal children's wallpaper, at least buy a cheap one, on the basis that although it will show every grubby fingermark, by the time it needs replacing, it will have served its visual purpose. This is much better than buying an expensive vinyl wall covering with a pattern of ballerinas or spaceships, that gets outgrown long before it's outworn.

Plain vinyl wall coverings are perfect for nurseries, because they are very tough and literally scrubbable. If you can buy one in a neutral colour with a rough and interesting texture, it might last from the toddler stage right through to teenage, without raising a complaint at any point along the way.

If you prefer to paint the walls,

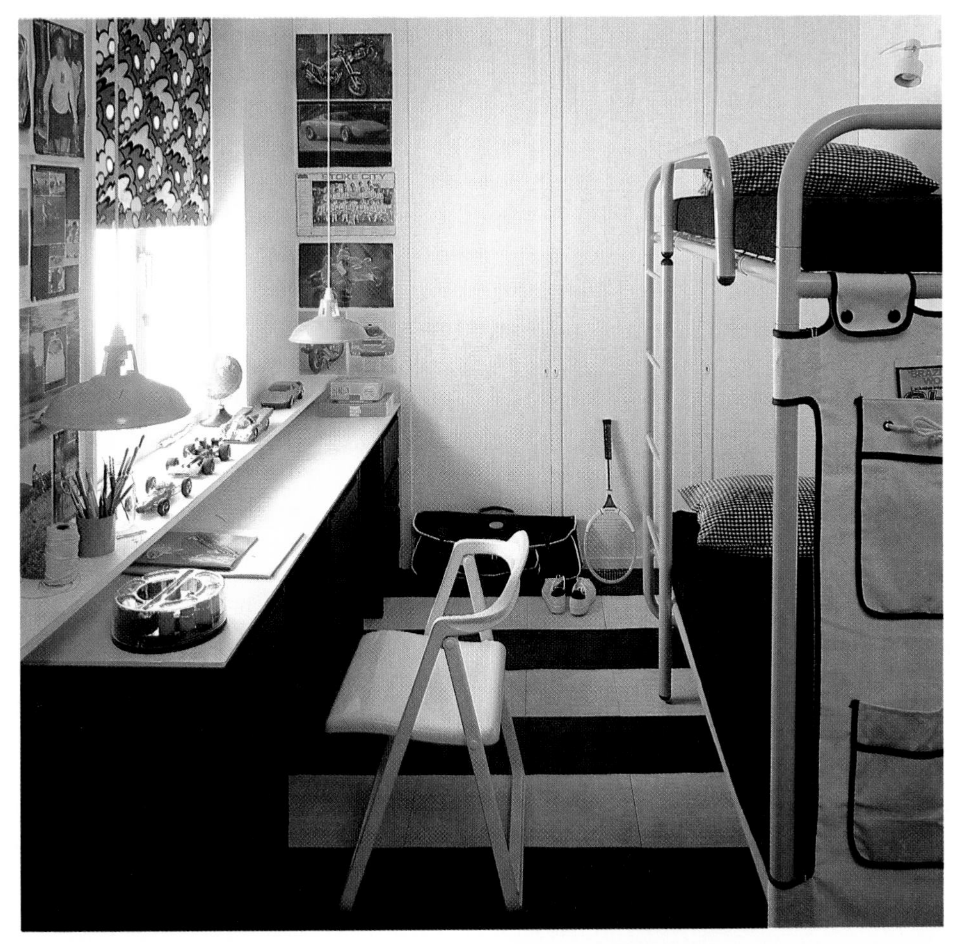

Far left: free-standing furniture and rugs on the floor make this a bedroom that could easily move to a new home. But the ingredients would also look good elsewhere in the house if any future bedroom already had built-ins and fitted carpet
Left: bunk beds, floor-to-ceiling fitted cupboards and two desk units spanned by a laminated chipboard work surface, make maximum use of space in this practical but attractive boys' room
Below: this cool, sparsely furnished bedroom eschews wardrobes. Instead there is a plain hatstand
Bottom: few spare bedrooms can afford to stay spare between guests. This one acts as an all-purpose room – something helped by the use of 'unbedroomy' textures and colours, and the absence of a conventional bed. In its place, a traditional Japanese futon looks stylish as seating and provides firm-based sleeping. The slatted-wood tables become part of the bed-base when the futon needs to sleep two

although gloss will shrug off scuffs and sticky fingermarks, it does look rather cold and unfriendly. It also accentuates any unevenness in the surface. A sheeny silk vinyl or eggshell makes a sensible compromise, because it's hard enough for the walls to be washed, but matt enough to look soft and warm. Emulsion paint is impractical in theory, because it will only survive a delicate sponging; but in practice, it's so easy to apply that many people accept they will need to repaint every few months, and go about it with good grace.

Once you have established the permanent nursery basics, it's easy to introduce small extras within them. All children like bright colours, so you could add a brilliantly-coloured and patterned roller blind; stick vibrant friezes round the walls; introduce bold duvet covers; perhaps paint the furniture yellow (you can paint it white later); fix a piece of pegboard over a desk (so children can hang their treasures from it) and paint it a brilliant colour too. All these bright splashes, plus the muddle of toys on the floor and paintings on the wall, will ensure the room has enough colour and interest.

Furnishing for the future

A be-ribboned bassinet will be totally redundant within three months. It's much wiser to go for a 'Moses' wicker basket, lined against draughts with something like a pretty towelling or cotton gingham. Buy one with a matching stand to avoid possible backache and make sure the wheels won't slide on a lino or vinyl floor. Carry cots are not advisable for times when you are unable to keep an eye on the baby, but they are very useful for general travel. When buying one, avoid a lining of soft plastic that your baby might not be able to breathe against, and look for the Kite Mark and BS 38881.

The next essential is a cot. Here, you can either buy one that is simply a cot, dismantle it when it's outgrown and store it till it's needed again, or buy a cot that converts into a full-size bed. Look for the Kite Mark and BS 1753.

Once a baby can clamber out of its cot, you know it's ready for a proper bed. As children move about in their sleep a lot more than adults, it's worth going straight to the 1 metre (3 ft) wide size. If you have more than one child but only room for one bed, the simplest answer is to buy bunk beds. Some are made so they will split into two single beds (useful if you are hoping to move to a larger house some day); others come with storage drawers below or, in one case, even a spare divan. As there isn't a British Standards specification, check for yourself that the top bunk's safety rail really *is* safe and that the ladder is sturdy and easy to climb. Forget about conventional bedding: although duvets are not safe for babies in cots, they are ideal for children who have graduated to bunks, and can be machine-washed if you choose a man-made fibre filling.

The alternative to bunks is stacking beds, but it's only worth considering the kind that can be stacked ready made-up, if you prefer conventional bedding.

Storage

When they are young, children have masses of toys. When they are older, they have masses of clothes. Either way, they are going to need plenty of storage. Although shops are full of mini-wardrobes and chests-of-drawers, they are a bit gimmicky and soon become obsolete. If you want individual items of furniture, it's probably better to buy full-size versions, taking care to wall-fix anything that might get toppled over – say a wardrobe that a child might climb into to play houses. It could be worth considering old pine furniture, on the basis that bashes and dents just add character: furthermore, it will look grown-up and sophisticated when the kid's room turns into a teenage pad.

Even so, wall-fitted storage, whether built-in or free-standing, provides the most adaptable solution. When interior fittings are flexible (and don't buy any storage system where they are not) you can move up shelves and drawers as the children grow taller. You can also bridge any gap between units with a deep shelf that acts as a desk: this too can go up in the world as the need arises, and with a mirror, can double as a dressing table.

N.B. Make sure any free-standing storage is too stable to be pulled down: otherwise, fix it to the wall. This applies to shelving too – it's a favourite for toddlers to pull themselves up by.

Lighting

Most young children like some kind of night-light. This could be a special low-powered light bulb (enough for a reassuring glow but not enough to keep anyone awake); or just a light left burning on the landing with the nursery door left ajar. Instead, you could add a dimmer switch to the normal lighting. As children graduate to hobbies and homework, be sure to add local lighting above any desk or worktop. If your children sleep in bunk beds, give each of them a wall-fixed light, so one can stay awake reading without disturbing the other; and if the top occupant needs to get up in the night, the ladder can be negotiated in safety.

Right: this period bedroom, full of solid Victorian furniture and busy with pattern, needed plenty of mirror to make it light and airy. Expanses of modern sheet mirror would have looked inappropriate, so individual wooden-framed mirrors were used – some of them taken from cheap old junk shop dressing-tables

The Hall

The hall is the first thing people see when they cross your threshold. First impressions should be good impressions.

Halls get passed through rather than lived in, which is why they are often relegated to the bottom of the list of priorities, and furnished with leftovers from the rest of the house. This is a pity, because they give an initial – and possibly lasting – impression. So it's well worth spending the money and effort to make them warm and welcoming places.

THE ESSENTIALS

Most halls are too small to take much furniture, by the time all the doors have been left unimpeded. If you don't have room for a free-standing cupboard to take coats and macs, and there are no handy alcoves or 'dead ends' for built-in storage, try and hide any line of coat-hooks around a corner. If you must have hanging garments on view, a bentwood hat-stand is an attractive and space-saving way of coping with the outdoor-clothing problem. If you want a more snappy and modern approach, look for one of the enamelled tubular metal versions that come in brilliant primary colours.

If possible, squeeze in some form of hall table, because you will want somewhere to dump shopping as you come in the front door – to say nothing of letters, car-keys, library books and gloves. If you feel your hall is too tiny to take the visual clutter of table legs, perhaps fit a shallow tabletop, or deep shelf on sturdy but good-looking wall brackets. If there isn't even room for this, a long bench can provide a useful dumping ground as well as slim-line seating.

Ideally every hall should include a chair, especially if this is where the telephone is, but it may not be practical in very narrow situations. A wall-hung mirror, however, takes up no space, allows you to check your appearance before dashing off in a hurry, and makes small halls look lighter and larger.

Floors

The hall gets more wear and tear than anywhere else in the house because, as well as coping with incoming traffic, there is constant cross-traffic from the rooms leading off it. It's a good idea to have a generous-sized doormat to cut down the amount of dirt that gets trampled indoors: this will look neatest if it's set into a door-well. In the case of a close-carpeted hall, this will mean you can vacuum right over it without stopping.

A top quality wool carpet is warm, friendly, very hardwearing, and if plain, best chosen in a speckly-textured light colour or a medium colour – although it could be any light colour in a flat, where people have already 'cleaned' their feet on the communal stairs coming up. (A dark plain carpet tends to highlight dirt.) However, top quality carpet is very expensive, and once you have started with it, you are really committed to taking it up the stairs and along the landing. Otherwise the result will look bitty, and will make your hall seem smaller.

If you can't afford an expensive carpet, don't waste your money on a lesser quality that will soon go shabby with the relentless tread of feet. Buy an honest alternative like rubber-backed sisal. This will be able to take all the punishment it gets, and will provide the hall with plenty

Above: in this household with young children, mid-brown carpet – an ideal shade for disguising marks – carries up the stairs for continuity. Lime green paint provides a practical surface for the walls up to the dado rail. Above that, a small-scale leafy wallpaper echos the green. Prints on the wall with turquoise backgrounds, and a turquoise-painted toy basket, sharpen the effect
Left: a beautiful view and a beautiful old stone floor get treated with the utmost simplicity, leaving them free to speak for themselves. A generous arrangement of flowers and greenery establishes a relationship between indoors and out, and softens the hall in a natural way
Right: tucked neatly away, an antique pedestal desk turns a wasted alcove into a study area. Small pictures on the wall are grouped tightly together – vital if they are to make a satisfying impact. Here, they're restricted to the wall-space above the desk. This helps define the work-area as separate, and ensures it looks relaxed as well as efficient

of visual texture. Or buy good quality vinyl tiles or sheet vinyl or lino. Traditional black and white tiles may be obvious, but have never been bettered for good looks.

If you live in the country or want a country look, sisal flooring is always appropriate. If you can't afford it, cheaper rush matting is nearly as attractive, and you can replace individual squares or strips as they get tatty. If mud is likely to get trampled in, it's sensible to go for a durable but really easy-clean flooring like vinyl-surfaced cork or quarry tiles.

If you want carpeting on the stairs, choose a close-pile or a cord (never a sisal, which is hard and slippery – and obviously never a long-pile, which you could catch your toe in); and if possible, have the job done by a professional, because the carpet needs to be really *tightly* fitted. It will save you a lot of dusting and repainting if you have the carpet taken right across the tread of the stairs, rather than using a 68 cm (27 in) wide strip. Of course, buying a wider carpet will be more expensive, and you will probably have to cut it down slightly and waste the surplus.

Walls

Walls need to be tough and practical, because people brush against them when they come through the front door (as do wet dogs and cats), and children skid against them with scooters, etc. What is more, if you keep a pram or pushchair in the hall, it's bound to cause damage.

But wear and tear isn't the only consideration. Halls look best when the wall covering is carried all the way up the stairs and onto the landing – where there are tall expanses of wall to tackle. Whether you employ a costly professional or do it yourself (which will mean balancing ladders on stairs or rigging up platforms on scaffolds), it isn't a job that you are going to want to do often, so it's vital to choose durable decorations. Vinyl wall covering is practically indestructible.

Washable wallpapers are less tough; perhaps buy several extra rolls, so you can re-do the most vulnerable areas, like alongside the front door. If you need to soften a wall with warmth and texture, paper-backed hessian is very long-lasting, the natural colour is dirt disguising, and it camouflages dodgy plasterwork.

If you prefer paint, hard-wearing gloss looks clinical and unfriendly, although you could use it just up to dado height, and then continue in a different finish. Otherwise, eggshell combines a practical finish with sheenier and much softer looks.

Adding pattern

Pattern has two advantages in a hall. It can make a sparsely furnished area feel 'furnished', and it can disguise the ravages of time by blurring the impact of dirt and scuff marks. Whether or not you choose it may simply depend on whether or not you have young children. Be careful if you choose a patterned carpet, because unless you pick a small-scale and repetitive design, it will make the hall seem overcrowded and smaller. It may also make the stairs dangerous to walk down: with any large and rambling pattern, it's difficult to decipher where one tread ends and another begins.

As mixing patterns is a tricky business, it's usually best to team a patterned carpet with plain walls, or walls with a pattern so tiny and overall, it gives the impression of a textured plain surface. If you have used a plain flooring however, the hall is one of the few places where you can risk a bold and flamboyantly patterned wallpaper because you won't be spending much time with it.

Windows and lighting

Theoretically, because halls, stairways and landings are very busy circulation areas, with people continually brushing by the windows, window treatments should be very simple. If you feel conventional curtains would take a battering from your family, think in terms of Roman, roller or Venetian blinds, or wooden shutters. These would be a good idea, in any case, if your windows are so small they would be swamped by drapes. Roller and Roman blinds, made in a fabric that matches your wallpaper, could be a way of integrating awkwardly-shaped windows. Furthermore, as privacy is not a prime consideration, since halls and landing are not actually lived in, you could simply leave the windows bare; or give them just a pretty pelmet; or if you never need to open them, span them with shallow shelves and fill them with houseplants. Green leaves filter light in a most romantic way, and are good at softening ugly outlooks. However, in practice, you may decide that softly-draped curtains are just what you need to compensate for lack of furnishings.

As in so many cases with design, how practical you choose to be may well depend on whether or not you have young children to contend with.

Halls and stairways aren't the place for moody lighting. You need to see where you are going efficiently and clearly. For a good overall light in the hall, ideally use recessed or ceiling-mounted downlighters, or pendant fittings. These will illuminate the traffic areas well – whereas wall brackets, for instance, would mainly illuminate the walls. Once you have established the general lighting, you can always highlight special features with effect lighting.

Provide a really strong light above the stairs, so the treads are picked out emphatically while the risers are left in contrasting shadow. This light will need to be stronger than any light lower down, or it will be balanced out, thus losing the contrast. It's very important to avoid glare: lights should never shine directly into people's eyes. In very tall halls where you need a ladder to reach the light fittings, or on the stairs where it may be awkward to get at them, the less often you have to change the light-bulb the better, so consider paying extra for a fluorescent long-life bulb. As these are far more economical to run than tungsten bulbs (see page 74 for more about them), they would also be good for landing lights that get left on all night, either to reassure very young children, or provide safety for elderly people.

NARROW AND HIGH-CEILINGED HALLS

Installing a false ceiling to lower a dauntingly lofty hall is expensive – but does provide an opportunity for incorporating recessed lighting. In a gloomy hall that needs the help of artificial lighting during the day, you could 'bring down' the ceiling much more cheaply by hanging a low row of pendant light fittings. These would concentrate attention on the

Above: this large hall doubles as a proper dining room, thanks to a 'wall' of storage that keeps outdoor clothing etc. hidden. Free-standing units are 'built-in' with a fascia board between top and ceiling: wallpaper borders, forming a frieze, continue over the board for full integration. Light tones of blonde woods, stencil-style wallpaper and plain, misty grey flooring make the hall still seem spacious despite the full-size table. They also ensure the mirror-fronted units, which 'double' the area's size and light supply, reflect a relaxed and easy scene

Left: rococo shapes of console table and mirror contrast with the straight lines of this period hall

Right: off-white ceramic tiles, laid horizontally to make this narrow hall seem wider, continue through to the kitchen to 'stretch' the floor area. Books add character without causing obstruction

well-lit areas, allowing the shadowy area above to recede into obscurity.

If your hall is too light for this trick to work, lower the ceiling by clever use of colour. Strong colours bring a surface nearer while pale colours make it seem to recede. Don't just paint or paper the ceiling in a colour that is stronger than the walls; bring the ceiling part-way down the walls, finishing it at picture rail height: then make it look really intended by adding an actual picture rail, or running a wallpaper border around.

Alternatively, create the impression of a false ceiling without getting involved in heavy structural work. You could run battens along both walls just above door height, and span them with widely, but regularly-spaced, bamboo rods, that the eye would foreshorten to look more closely spaced. These wouldn't block the light from ceiling fittings, but if the ceiling-fixed light was inadequate anyway, you could add clip-on spotlights to the rods. In fact, just spanning above the doors with bamboo rods would be enough to bring the eye-level down, and then you would have provided accessible 'platforms' that you could use to store light and attractive but little-used items.

Obviously if a tall hall has good architectural features like deep skirtings, dado rail, picture rail and cornice, just emphasizing them will be enough to break up the walls. These in turn, will give the impression that they are lower. If you want pattern, you could use two different but co-ordinated wallpapers, one above the dado rail and the other below. If you prefer plain paint, you could use different shades of the same colour. Or you could use a wallpaper below and a related shade of paint above, linking the two with a related wallpaper border running along the walls just above the dado rail.

In a tall hall that doesn't give you any help, you could either add a real dado rail and decorate accordingly; or simply create interest at dado height – perhaps by running a wallpaper border along the walls, or painting a band of bold, bright

colour. Alternatively, you could hang pictures at eye-level height, letting the largest picture define the outer limits of the band, and grouping the smaller pictures so they're contained within it. The secret is to provide a convincing band that confines attention to a well-defined strip. In a dark hall, instead of hanging pictures, you could hang a collection of old wooden-framed mirrors instead.

Finally, you could concentrate on making the hall look wider, which would automatically make it seem lower. Perhaps buy a carpet with horizontal stripes. Or buy sheet vinyl in two plain colours, get to work with a Stanley knife, and alternate deep expanses of one colour with shallow expanses of the other. This will look more sophisticated than equal-sized stripes. Or create a horizontal pattern with ceramic tiles, and 'stretch' the floor even further sideways by carrying the pattern up the walls to provide a tiled skirting. At least be sure to use a full-width covering: a narrow strip of carpet or a runner will make the floor seem longer and narrower.

Above: dramatic solution to a long narrow hall with a long narrow sitting room leading off was to remove part of the dividing wall, and replace it with floor-to-ceiling 'windows'. Although some solid wall is retained at the front-door-end to ensure privacy, elsewhere floor-to-ceiling Venetian blinds provide no more than a psychological barrier. Whether in the hall or the sitting room, there's a sense of space beyond, and when more physical space is needed, it's an easy matter to raise the blinds.
Above right: an original stained-glass door lends this hall distinction. Pictures and mirrors create eye-level interest on the walls
Right: when a hall has some unusually good architectural feature – like this enchanting Gothic door – always give it a simple, unfussy treatment, so it can make maximum impact

A HALL FULL OF DOORS

Some halls have so many doors leading off them, there is hardly enough wall left even for pictures, so the doors themselves must provide the interest. This might seem difficult if they are flush and faceless but, in fact, if you have used a patterned wallpaper on the walls, it's easy to create door panels with matching wallpaper, and finish the edges with wooden beading. The beading not only adds character to the doors, but protects the edges of the paper. Even if your doors are already panelled, it could still be worth making the panels match the walls, so the doors become an integrated part of the hall.

If you prefer a basically plain hall, and are lucky enough to have traditional doors in good condition, you may simply want to strip them back to the wood – also stripping the architraves and skirting board, which will create the interest of a frieze pattern. For variations on the frieze theme you could cover walls and door panels in something roughly textured like hessian, then pick out the rest of the doors, skirtings and architraves in a punchy-coloured and shiny gloss paint.

If you have flush doors and want to keep them, you could paint a band of strong colour along the top of the skirting and continue it around the architraves, perhaps painting a circle of matching colour around the door knobs.

DUAL-PURPOSE HALLS

Not all halls are small. Some have actually got the space to double as an extra room. In the picture on page 104, for instance, a large hall doubles as a dining room, with the help of floor-to-ceiling storage which keeps hats and coats out of sight, as well as accommodating china and table linen, etc. But even a smaller hall could double for dining if you teamed a narrow table with benches that could tuck under the table when not in use. A drop-leaf table would also make sense, as would folding or stacking chairs.

If you have not already exploited the space under the stairs, it could make an ideal work-study area, because all that is needed is a well-lit desk, a chair and some open shelving.

Alternatively, provided you could organize the plumbing and ventilation, you could use the space for an extra lavatory and wash-basin; or if you organized just the plumbing, a washing machine and tumble dryer. All these possibilities would apply equally well, of course, to any space going spare up on the landing.

The Bathroom

Most bathrooms are small, so you can make a big splash with the minimum of money and effort.

The standard bath is 168 cm (5 ft 6 in) long and 71 cm (2 ft 4 in) wide, but sizes increase and decrease in 10 cm (4 in) measurements. The longest available is 183 cm (6 ft), and will be worth having if you are tall and there is room in your bathroom. The shortest in a conventional shape (see the bathroom on page 113) is only 122 cm (4 ft) long; but the smallest of all is a 91 cm (3 ft) hip bath, where you sit on one level, with your feet lower down. Although hip baths are a good idea for elderly people, who may have difficulty pulling themselves up from a horizontal position even with the aid of hand grips, they are not much use if you like wallowing in water. If you are *that* short of space, you are probably better off thinking in terms of a shower instead. More adventurous corner baths, double-baths and circular baths demand plenty of room, cost a lot more money, and need careful handling if they are not to look mock-Hollywood. If you have the space, but can't afford a spectacular bath, one way of making an ordinary version look important is to place its head against the centre of the wall and use it lengthways, so it projects into the room.

Types of bath

Although porcelain-enamelled cast iron baths are the best-looking and most hard-wearing, they are more expensive and *exceedingly* heavy – any builder will hate you if you want to install one.

Vitreous-enamelled pressed steel baths are half the weight, much cheaper and still very hard-wearing – although like cast iron, the enamel will chip if brutally treated. Quality depends on the thickness of the steel, and shapes and colours are relatively limited.

Acrylic baths are cheaper than cast iron, slightly more expensive than steel, and come with a supporting cradle to keep them rigid. One of their main advantages is that they are very light: a single man can carry a bath on his back like a turtle, which makes acrylic the builder's favourite. They also offer an exciting range of colours, can be moulded to a variety of shapes, and are warm – so they don't steal so much heat from the water. However, they have some serious snags. Although non-chip, they are so easily scratched that they can't be cleaned with an abrasive powder; they melt if they come in contact with a lighted cigarette; and they shift when you get in them, which feels rather disconcerting.

Glass fibre reinforced resin baths are at the luxury end of the market, because they are built up in layers on a mould by hand. They share similar advantages and disadvantages with acrylic, but whereas acrylic baths are coloured throughout their thickness, only the surface of a glass fibre bath is coated with colour, so any deep scratch would show up badly. Their main and really worthwhile advantage is that it's possible to bond a fabric to the surface, producing a bath with a pretty, overall pattern. It's also possible to provide custom-made shapes, specially moulded to suit your situation.

Above: this dark and poky internal lavatory, with nondescript sanitary-ware, could have looked dreary and depressing. Instead, despite a very tight budget, it looks exciting, stylish and full of fun. The witty poster makes immediate impact, while the denim-clad walls continue the blue-jeans joke, cover less-then-perfect plasterwork, and introduce the interest of texture. Downlighters washing both side-walls (only one visible) cleverly make the narrow room seem wider

Right: the most convincing way to create a traditional bathroom is to introduce plenty of rich, mellow woods. Here, a modern bath is panelled-in with dark-stained oak, and a carved oak mirror reflects a mahogany chiffonier. Antique accessories strengthen the period feel of this spacious room

Building in the bath

With the exception of original or reproduction Victorian baths, which come with a handsome rolled top and marvellous ball and claw feet, all types of baths need panelling in. With a few baths, the panels are integral to the design; but usually they have to be added as an extra. The standard panel is made of hardboard, and needs fixing to a specially built wooden frame. It can be painted, covered with a vinyl wallcovering or PVC'd fabric; even covered with a non-absorbent nylon carpet if this is what you have used on the floor. But if you want to tile the sides of the bath, you will need to fix a panel of something firmer, like blockboard, to the wooden frame.

If you want to panel the bath with wood, fixing it direct to the wooden frame, all kinds of possibilities open up. You can used tongued-and-grooved pine horizontally – which can make a narrow bathroom look wider, as on page 113, or if you want a traditional bathroom, you can make a modern bath look mellow and established by adding genuine wood panelling – as in the picture on page 111, opposite. Whatever your approach, however, be sure that the panel is removable for access to plumbing.

Turning to taps

Do specify where you want the taps before buying a bath. They don't have to go at the end above the plug-hole. They can go across the corner, which if a bath is shared, does away with the argument about who gets the tap end. They can be at the side where they are easy to reach, with the spout still located at the plug end. They can be wall-fixed either at the side or the end, leaving the bath-rim clear and easier to clean. This always looks streamlined, but does mean either chasing the plumbing into the plaster, or concealing it behind a duct or false wall.

PICKING THE BASIN

Wall-hung basins, fixed on brackets, are the cheapest and easiest to install, provided you have a solid wall. You can fix them at the height that suits you best: about 80 cm (30 in) is usually recommended. The snag is that unless the plumbing is hidden behind a false wall, you are going to see the hot, cold and waste pipes travelling down to the floor.

Pedestal basins rest on a pedestal as well as being screwed to the wall, so their height is fixed – and the floor space is interrupted. Unfortunately, the pedestal hides only the waste pipe completely; the hot and cold pipes still remain visible, which can look more irritating than obviously exposed plumbing.

Counter-top basins, where the basin is set into a vanity unit, hide the plumbing, provide storage, and give a neat, built-in look. Ready-made vanity units are reasonably cheap – but may not come in the size you need for a wall-to-wall or alcove fit. The counter can be made from any waterproof material, from plastic laminate to ceramic tile, from hardwood to marble. If you are a splash-happy family, consider a basin with an inner lip, to prevent water from slopping onto the counter top. Alternatively, some vanity basins have a front overhang, so there is no need for a waterproof joint at the front, where most of the oversplashing occurs. Whichever inset basin you choose, make sure it has ample toe-space underneath.

Small basins and corner basins are available for separate toilets or mini-bathrooms – see the minuscule wall-hung basin on page 113, that only projects 15 cm (6 in) from the wall. These are only good, of course, for hand-washing facilities. If you want to use the basin for washing your hair or doing light laundry, look for a basin with a relatively flat bottom rather than one that narrows towards the plug-hole – or perhaps, as in the bathroom on page 114, use a kitchen sink instead.

Basin taps don't have to be conventionally placed. They can go across the corner or be wall-fixed; if you tend to wash your hands under running water, you might prefer a mixer tap. Pop-up wastes look tidier than the traditional plug and chain, but they are more expensive, the basin empties more slowly, and the mechanism can go infuriatingly wrong.

Above: this elegant bathroom in an 18th-century house receives a disciplined and symmetrical treatment. A pair of lacquer-red vases above the bath immediately imposes a sense of balance, while muted colours in the wallpaper continue the mood of restraint. Pale blonde wood-panelling surrounds the bath. Also used to build a vanity unit elsewhere, it matches the wooden picture-frame exactly – a telling detail in such a purist setting

Left: internal bathrooms needn't look gloomy. Here, despite lack of an actual window, punchy primary colours and lots of mirror give a bright, open and sunny impression. The room is really very narrow – only 1.65 m (5 ft) across – including the 'wall' of shallow cupboards. Their mirrored bi-fold doors take up little space, but double the room's area and 'sunshine' supply. A ceiling-frieze of mirror tiles adds more brightness

CHOOSING THE LAVATORY

If you buy the lavatory pan and cistern separately, it's still possible to have the old-fashioned arrangement with the cistern high on the wall, and the handle hanging from a chain. Purists might find this worthwhile in a traditional bathroom. Otherwise, today's cisterns are low-level or close-coupled.

The advantage is visual rather than functional. A low-level cistern only needs about a foot of exposed pipe to connect it to the lavatory pan; and the lavatory chain gets replaced by an unobtrusive chrome handle. Close-coupled lavatories look even neater, because the cistern connects directly to the lavatory pan, so there is no exposed pipe left showing at all. As these tend to be lower overall, they could be the answer if you need to fit a lavatory directly underneath a window.

But the neatest of all lavatories is the cantilevered type, where the lavatory pan is fixed to a special bracket, so it appears to hang in mid-air. Here the cistern and plumbing need hiding behind a false wall, with a removable access panel – a good idea for anyone with a traditional bathroom, because it minimises the amount of 'mod con' left visible. If you can't afford to give up much space to a false wall, it's possible to buy slimline plastic cisterns – the slimmest projects no more than 11.4 cm (4½ in). These can be ordered with a top-fixed handle if you want to stop at boxing it in. They are also useful if you want to replace a high-level cistern without having to move the existing pan and plumbing forward.

Seats are usually sold separately, so there is no need to limit yourself to the one displayed with the lavatory in the showroom. Wooden seats are warm and handsome – but not highly hygenic. If you prefer plastic, and are likely to sit or stand on the seat-lid, choose a more expensive, and therefore more rigid, plastic. They come in plain and marbled colours.

Traditionally, British lavatories have always been the wash-down kind, where flushing water roars noisily through the pan. If you are prepared to spend more money, you can buy the siphonic type instead, where a combined flush and suction action empties the pan quietly. In theory this is supposed to be more efficient, but in practice, it's much more prone to blockage.

BIDETS

Basically there are two kinds of bidet. The cheaper type is filled by conventional taps and can be plumbed in relatively simply. The more expensive type is filled by a 'flushing rim' with an ascending spray – and most local water authorities insist that because there is a risk of dirty water siphoning back into the supply pipes, they must have their own independent supplies – which means plumbing in new pipes from the hot water cylinder and cold water tank. Whichever type of bidet you finally decide upon, plumbing costs are likely to remain high unless you can site the bidet near to the lavatory. This is because, for some incomprehensible reason, most local water authorities decree that the waste has to be directed into a soil pipe, rather than be allowed to join the bath or wash-basin waste. If placing it near the lavatory means a really tight fit, it might be best to abandon the idea altogether, because you need plenty of knee room either side of a bidet. If it's the type that butts up close to the wall, make sure there is enough room front-to-back.

SHOWERS

Although few of us would forgo the occasional soak in a hot steamy bath, there are plenty of good reasons for having a shower too. They are more hygenic, better for the skin, safer for young children, and economical – you can have at least five hot showers for the price of one bath. They also take up far less space. Most shower areas are either 81 cm (32 in) or 91 cm (36 in) square; although if the shower is enclosed, you will need to allow as much space again for drying and dressing. However, you also need an accessible water supply and drainage system nearby, unless the plumbing costs are to be astronomical.

Left: in a country cottage, this traditional version of a built-in bathroom minimizes the amount of stark 'mod cons' by hiding unsightly plumbing behind mellow pine panelling
Below: white-painted pine walls and a Victorian wash-basin form the basis of this simple and charming bathroom, where arched mirrors and antique wall brackets receive careful, measured grouping
Right: a three-quarter size bath spans this narrow bathroom entirely. The wash basin projects a mere 15 cm (6 in) and the lavatory has a slim-line cistern – slim enough to box in without losing much space. Tricks to suggest width include the horizontal grooved bath-panel and ceiling, and a mirror-fronted cupboard above the loo

The water supply

If you have a good and adequate supply of hot water from a central heating boiler, immersion heater or water storage unit, you can usually have a shower connected to it. But the water flow and pressure must be correct, otherwise the shower will only manage a dribble of water. To ensure sufficient pressure, the cold water storage tank should be at least 1 m (3 ft) higher than the level of the spray-head. Provided there is enough headroom, a too-low tank can be raised by lifting it onto a wooden platform. If not, you will need to have a small electric pump installed to boost the water flow – something that could be expensive if there is no power supply nearby.

Where there is sufficient water pressure but no adequate supply of hot water, you can heat the water direct from cold by using an independent electric or gas water heater. With the former, water for the shower gets warmed as it circulates around an integral electric element – but because of limitations on the mains electricity supply, the heater can be no larger than 7.2 kW. This means the hotter you want the water the less there will be, so you have to settle for a rather weak jet if you like very hot showers – or merely warm water if you like a powerful spray. All BEAB-approved models on the market have safety cut-outs and come with hose, spray-head, and either an adjustable wall bracket or sliding bar arrangement for fixing the shower-rose. Although they can be installed by a competent handyman, if you are in any doubt at all, it's best to call in a professional.

Instantaneous gas heaters are more expensive to install, because they require an expert to fit them to an outside wall with a flue: but they are cheaper to run and more efficient. If you already have a gas water heater, you may be able to have a shower connected to it.

NB Before fitting any kind of shower, you must check that the installation complies with the local water authority bye-laws: this is usually a routine matter.

Where to put the shower

The simplest way of adding a shower is to introduce one over the bath. Ideally, you should have a wider-than-average bath with a flat, non-slip base at the tap end, for standing on safely. The extra width will prove important if you want a glass or Perspex panel instead of a flexible shower curtain, because otherwise you will be short of elbow room.

All you have to do is replace the ordinary bath taps with bath/shower taps. These are usually supplied with a wall-socket to hold the spray-head, but some have a wall-fitted sliding bar, so the spray-head can be adjusted up and down to accommodate the tall and the small. For a neater result, you can use a more sophisticated version where the control taps and shower-rose are a fixture, either surface mounted or built into the wall. The pipes running to the bath taps still supply the shower, but the shower has a separate control, which works quite independently of the bath taps. These units are also suitable for use in a shower cubicle.

The next simplest way of introducing a shower is to buy a ready-made and self-contained shower cabinet, which just needs connecting to the water supply and waste. This means it could be installed on a landing near a bathroom, or in the corner of a bedroom. Alternatively, it could be installed on the ground floor near the downstairs plumbing. The only snag is that most cabinets are pretty hideous to look at; you will need to hunt carefully for something inoffensive.

If you want to build your own shower cubicle, you have to lay the floor so that it slopes to the drain – something that will involve creating a false floor if you are not starting completely from scratch. This explains why most people buy a ready-made shower tray as a basis. These are available in acrylic or fireclay, but although fireclay is better-looking and stronger, acrylic is cheaper, lighter (which could be good for upstairs), and safer, because the surface is less slippery. However, shower trays create as big a problem as they solve, because it's extremely difficult to achieve a watertight join between the shower tray and the cubicle walls. Your only hope is to use flashing, or continue the waterproof cladding of the walls so it overlaps down into the tray. If you are cladding the cubicle walls with ceramic tiles, be sure to use waterproof adhesive and grouting.

A thermostat control nearly doubles the price of a shower, but could be well worth having in any household where there are elderly people or children to consider. This is because water temperature can change from warm to scalding hot when cold taps are turned on elsewhere in the house, reducing the flow of cold water to the shower. Whether or not this happens depends on your water system: best get it checked in advance before buying anything.

DECORATING THE BATHROOM

Although sanitary ware comes in some beautiful shades, think very hard before committing yourself to colour. You will be restricting yourself to one, or at most two, colour schemes, and you could get thoroughly bored with them as the years go by. A plain white bathroom suite, on the other hand, is endlessly adaptable, because you can ring the changes around it quickly and cheaply. And while it's true that sanitary ware looks sophisticated in 'deep-dyed' colours, these not only highlight tide marks and specks of dust – even splashes of perfectly clean water show up as 'dirty'.

Most bathrooms are small, which has one advantage: you can probably afford to make a big splash without being extravagant. If the floor area only extends to 3 or 4 square metres or yards, you may be able to lash out on ceramic or quarry tiles. For a warmer feel, you could use ready-sealed cork tiles or a non-absorbent nylon carpet with non-rot rubber backing. Otherwise, cushioned sheet vinyl can be practical and handsome.

As there isn't likely to be much wall area either, you may feel justified in buying a really expensive washable wallpaper or vinyl wall covering, since it will only be a matter of one or two rolls. If you fall in love with a standard wallpaper and want to give it a more splash-proof finish, you can spray on a coat of transparent matt varnish; or for a superbly practical alternative, you could cover the walls with a patterned PVC'd fabric. You could also cover the walls with ceramic or cork tiles, or even clad them with wood. Wood is a good way of coping with poor plasterwork – and probably as cheap as getting walls replastered!

Gloss paint looks chilly in a bathroom, encourages condensation runnels, and accentuates imperfections in the wall surface. Emulsion is probably the safest bet, although if ventilation is a problem, there is a special paint that helps prevent condensation forming.

Revamping an old bathroom

Try to retain its basic layout – otherwise plumbing costs could be enormous. Don't be too quick to rip things out. You may hate the pastel sanitary ware, but an unexpected colour scheme can work wonders. Think of subtle mulberry with pastel pink; slate grey with pale blue; and mellow saffron with wishy-washy primrose. If you hate the tiles, they are retrievable too. You can rub down ceramic tiles with fine wet and dry paper, and then give them a couple of coats of a polyurethane paint; or you can stick tiles on top of tiles, if you use the thin, light DIY type; or you can cover them up with 'tiling-on-a-roll' – a heavy tile-patterned vinyl that needs a special adhesive.

If your bathroom is festooned with surface pipes, there are two approaches. Be bold and paint them a strong, defiant colour; or box them in and 'lose' them by decorating the casing to match the room. If you are operating on a rock-bottom budget, one of the cheapest ways of livening up a dreary bathroom is to introduce lots of leafy houseplants. They will thrive in the steamy atmosphere.

Tight situations

Sometimes it's worth sacrificing space to make more of it. Cantilevered lavatories and wash-basins, for instance, although they require false walls that make a room smaller, give a convincing impression of wide open expanses. This is partly because everything looks so streamlined and flowing; partly because the floor area is left unimpeded. Even if you can't afford to give up so many inches, it could be worth boxing in a lavatory cistern, to give the walls a smoother, more svelte look. It could be worth building-in the bathroom entirely, because although this will eat up lots of floor space, it will provide the eye with unbroken lines to follow. (Perhaps look at slim kitchen units – they work well in a bathroom.) Mirrors can add length or breadth to a bathroom. They 'double' the size of the bathroom on page 110, where it was thought well worth sacrificing a little floor space to provide a 'wall' of shallow storage, fronted with bi-fold mirrored doors. If you use mirror, make sure it has a copper backing to protect the silvering from possible moisture. If you are worried about a mirror misting up with condensation, perhaps buy silvered sheet acrilic 'mirror', which is warmer, and looks indistinguishable from the real thing.

If you can't afford mirror, a cheaper way to 'stretch' the floor area is to carry the floor-covering up the side of the bath. It also helps, of course, to use small-scale patterns and light, monochromatic shades. The bathroom on page 113, for instance, keeps to related clays and mushrooms, and sticks to diminutive patterns.

Dark, gloomy bathrooms

Internal bathrooms have no natural light at all; others may only have tiny windows overlooking a neighbour's brick wall. There are two ways of tackling this depressing problem. You can make a virtue of necessity, and aim for a dense and mellow effect, where sunlight would seem a brash intruder. To do this, use lots of dark, rich woods. Perhaps panel the bath in mahogany – stain something cheaper if you can't afford to. Hang a wooden-framed Victorian or Edwardian overmantel mirror on the wall. Paper the

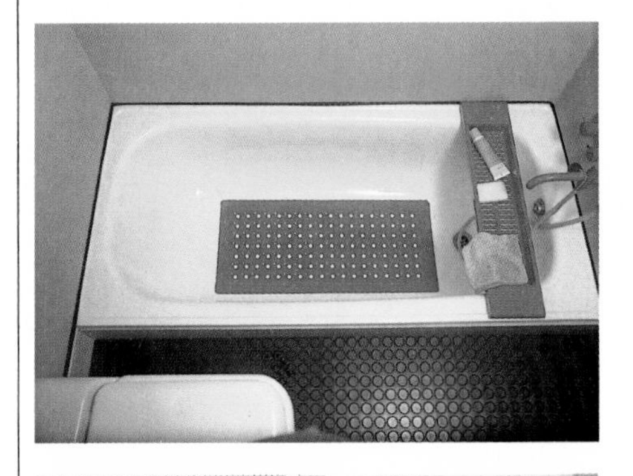

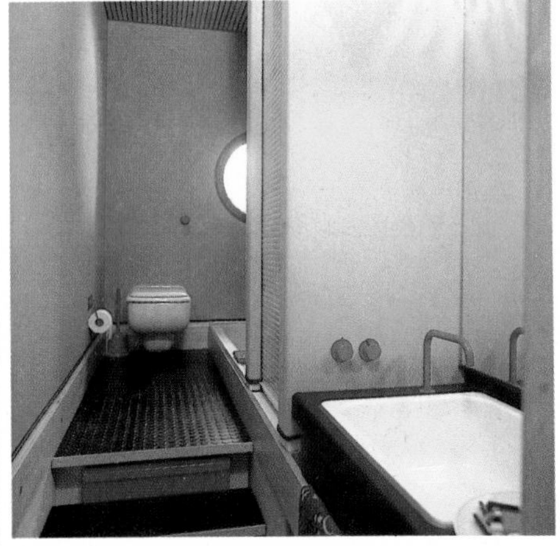

Above: two views of a tiny, split-level bathroom, where a deep kitchen sink, instead of a wash basin, compensates for the small-sized bath beyond
Right: 'theatre dressing room' lighting, built into a mirror-fronted cupboard, adds panache to a truly luxurious bathroom

walls in something warm and tawny: a toffee-coloured stippled design – or just brown wrapping paper with a varnish added. Carpet the floor in terracotta, or use deep honey-coloured cork. Hang wooden-framed pictures on the walls, and instead of flooding the result with artificial light, let traditional brass wall brackets with opaque white globes throw romantic pools of intimate light.

The other way of tackling lack of natural light is to fake it with bright colour and plenty of mirror. One advantage of internal bathrooms is that because they are legally required to be well-ventilated, conventional mirror does not mist up. There is no window at all in the bathroom on page 110, but it could not be further from dull and grey. Sunshine yellow vinyl wall covering and bold primary-coloured accessories inject a mood of zip and energy while a 'wall' of mirror bounces it back. A frieze of mirror tiles adds more verve and sparkle, at the same time seeming to lower the ceiling. Two fluorescent tubes, incorporated into the mirror-fronted bathroom cabinet above the basin, provide shadow-free light.

LIGHTING

Bathrooms need good general lighting: perhaps above the bath in a small bathroom; otherwise in the centre of the ceiling. If you use the bathroom for making up or shaving, you will need specific task lighting for the mirror. Here opt for lights either side, shining onto your face rather than onto the mirror. A light above the mirror throws heavy shadows below the eyes and mouth.

Ideally, you should use Class II fittings in a bathroom, because they are double-insulated and have no touchable metal parts. However, most people use ordinary Class I fittings which need earthing, and these are perfectly safe provided they *are* properly earthed.

It's good practice to use a shade that encloses the bulb entirely – not only because it covers the metal parts, but because tungsten light bulbs get hot, and in a bathroom that suffers from condensation, a drop of cold water could cause them to shatter. It's also good practice to keep light fittings well away from sources of water. You should *never* be able to touch a light fitting while you are standing in – or getting out of – the bath. Although you are unlikely to touch a light fitting above a wash-basin while you still have a hand in the water, again, it's wiser to keep it out of reach.

Strictly speaking, spotlights are not suitable for bathrooms because people may be tempted to adjust them by hand: perhaps keep them high and in a fixed position; or better still, use recessed or ceiling mounted downlighters.

CHAPTER THREE

RUNNING SMOOTHLY: MANAGEMENT MINIMUMS

SHELVING AND STORAGE

Having places to put things away in is vital, whether your home is a studio apartment or a mansion.

Nowadays, even the most modern dwellings lack enough storage space for most people's needs. There are lots of ways to store possessions – ranging from catch-all cupboards and shelves to purpose-built containers with just one use. What you must decide is what best suits *your* needs and your style of living.

The first decision to make is whether you want your storage to be built-in, and thus a permanent part of the fabric of the place, or free-standing so that you can take it with you when you move. Bear in mind that even if you opt for the latter you may find that it is not suited to your next home and stands out like a sore thumb against different-sized rooms, different height ceilings and a different style of decoration. So in general it's sensible to think of basic storage like shelves and cupboards as being part of your current home and furniture storage – chests, chests of drawers and dressers – as movable objects.

CUPBOARD LOVE

If you are blessed with existing built-in cupboards you have already saved yourself money since they are pricey items to install. Don't hesitate to change handles, to paint or wallpaper them to blend in with the rest of the room, or to cover them with mirror to make a small room look larger. If you are starting from scratch, get estimates from carpenters. If these are too high for your budget, consider buying ready-made doors and fitting them yourself (particularly easy in alcoves) or fixing track to floor and ceiling and installing sliding doors to run on it. If you are really thinking short term, consider buying a garment hanging rail of the type used in dress shops or dry cleaners and store your clothes on it behind an attractive curtain or a pull-down blind that matches the wallpaper.

SHELVING PROBLEMS

Open shelving has lots of plus points going for it. You dictate how much you want to spend, choosing between good and seasoned wood at the top of the range and cheaper systems with vertical metal tracking and shelves. The chipboard shelves can vary in thickness, depending on the weight of what is to be stored. While you may prefer a carpenter to fit a system that is designed to be a showpiece, virtually anyone can put up the shelving kits sold in most builders' merchants, department stores and specialist shops. It is, however, vital to think carefully about what you are going to put on a shelf before buying, since the shelf needs to be of a suitable thickness to take it without bowing. Ask for advice when you buy. If you are one of life's less than tidy mortals open shelving may increase rather than reduce the chaos in your life. If so, consider fitting a blind over a set of shelves, or curtains that draw across it. This also has the advantage of keeping dust off the contents – something which can be a real problem, particularly with glass shelves which attract dust.

OLD FURNITURE

Because built-in storage tends to be what people go for, the chests and cabinets of former days are often sold surprisingly

Right: take a narrow room and there is little wall space for shelving without cramping. This living/dining area solves the problem by siting the television plumb in the middle of a purpose-built shelving unit, with some open areas, some closed. It makes a focal point for the living part of the room and is sturdily and robustly built to take the weight of some fairly heavy objects, including the television

Top: mahogany linen press provides elegant storage behind closed doors and blends in harmoniously with the quilted sofa and armchairs and oriental floor rug
Above: neat wooden storage system in light colour incorporates drawers, wine rack, open shelves and a table which extends from within it to give a cohesive and useful area in a fairly small space. Wicker baskets on some of the shelves are used to store things – like sewing gear, which need to be kept together – as is the red plastic vegetable bin on the shelf above the drawers

cheaply in junk and bric-à-brac shops. You have only to look at the price of timber – even in a discount DIY store – to see that something like an Edwardian compactum or Victorian bow-fronted chest of drawers is a real bargain. Country dwellers often fare better than big city folk in this respect, since many of the items can be picked up far more cheaply in areas where there are less people fighting to own them. A point to consider when buying large pieces is whether you will be able to get them through the door of your home and, if necessary, upstairs. These older pieces of furniture were designed for larger homes than those built more recently. Measure before you buy.

ADDING ON

Some storage systems are so designed that you can buy them in sections as and when your cash flow permits. Some consist of cubes which can be stacked to form cupboards and shelves; others offer systems which can be added to sideways. If you are considering this type of storage, check that you are buying a well-established system, sold under a recognized brand name, from a reputable outlet. Otherwise you may find that when you have enough money to add to your existing pieces they are not available.

KITCHEN STORAGE

Kitchen equipment and clutter requires a different type of storage from the rest of the home. However, you don't need to fall for the blandishments of the kitchen furniture manufacturers and opt for fully-fitted units. There is no reason why you shouldn't utilize cheap open shelving or old cupboards and chests of drawers in your kitchen, provided they are practical.

Obviously a fitted kitchen will work efficiently and make your culinary life easier with its run of worktop and specially-designed cupboards. It's certainly something worth aiming for if your kitchen is small as it will make working in it much easier. Note that in cramped areas it's often easier to have sliding rather than opening doors and also consider installing wall units on the floor as base units. It means you have a narrower worktop but it would make extra space for moving around.

Self-assembly kitchen units are easy to put together; provided you take the time and trouble to fit them so that they butt up against each other and have level surfaces, you will end up with a very professional-looking kitchen. Most DIY stores and discount furniture chains offer self-assembly units in many finishes.

Top quality professionally-fitted kitchens usually come with a range of storage extras in the units; things like pull-out extendable worktops, pull-out ironing boards, cantilevered shelves which hold a mixer or food processor, waste bins that fix on to cupboard doors, and revolving trays. You can buy these yourself to fit into your kitchen, although some of the more complicated items will need forward planning when you are installing the units.

PLANNING FOR SENSIBLE STORAGE

Before you buy any item specifically for storage think carefully what you are going to keep in it. Don't fall for that stripped pine dresser or high-tech hi-fi trolley unless you are sure it will fit in with your decoration scheme, really do the storage job and be easy to use and to keep clean.

Bear in mind that as a general rule things should be stored near the place where they are used so that you don't have to carry them further than necessary. Items which are used infrequently – big bowls and plates for parties, spare pillows and so on can be kept in cupboards which are hard to reach.

INGENIOUS IDEAS

There are lots of neat storage ideas which can help you get more space from your cupboards and shelves. Things like shoe racks, tie racks, vertical multi-hangers and wire pull-out drawers can make wardrobe space work better for you. Plastic-covered wire racks of many shapes and styles stack plates, cups and glasses to save shelf space in kitchen or dining room cupboards. Dividing up drawers – by using either a special insert or by making your own divisions with plywood and quadrant beading – makes the storage of cutlery, small kitchen utensils, sewing equipment, etc. much more rational and things are easier to find quickly.

Similarly you can fit extra shelves into cupboards if the distance between the existing shelves is too great to be useful.

It's certainly sensible to have a choice of shelf heights so you don't waste empty space when low items are being stored. Similarly it's a good idea to partition drawers to make it easier to find things and to keep kitchen utensils or cutlery in their appropriate groups.

Take a look round hardware shops, department stores and DIY outlets. Read the small ads in newspapers, since a lot of excellent storage notions are sold by mail. Spend time looking at all types of storage gear available in shops. You may not be able to afford what you want but you could get good ideas which you could adopt and adapt yourself.

Below: built-in shelving on each side of the fireplace in this terracotta sitting room is divided evenly to take books, magazines, ornaments and stereo, functionally yet unobtrusively. Cupboards below the shelves provide further storage for less sightly items

Bottom: green-painted open shelves above the sink unit echo the colour of the kitchen furniture and provide a home for a selection of interesting containers

Cutlery, China And Glass

Your food and drink deserve the best setting you can give them.
Money isn't always the deciding factor.

Large department stores and specialist shops offer such a wonderful selection of cutlery, china and glass that no one could complain that their particular taste isn't catered for. When buying for the first time you must decide whether you will go for something cheap and cheerful to be eventually replaced by a more expensive version or if, from the beginning, you will opt for the very best.

CUTLERY CHOICE

Whether you choose cheap stainless steel or luxurious solid silver cutlery, there are several points you should consider which apply to all cutlery. Always buy from a reputable retailer and look for makes stamped with a well-known brand. Forgery in cutlery is quite common and it could be difficult to match up if you want to add more place settings at a later date. With stainless steel and silver-plated cutlery look for the British Standard Kitemark symbol which means it will meet the standards of quality and durability laid down in BS 5577. Check the pieces for a smooth, blemish-free finish. Satin-finished stainless steel should have a consistent grain. Hold each piece of place setting in your hands to see how comfortable it is and how well balanced. Some cutlery designs look good but are impractical when it comes to eating. Where handles are made from a different material, such as bone or plastic, check that the joins are smooth and well-finished.

Knives should be sharp enough to cut well and 'handle heavy' so that when you put them down on a flat surface the handle keeps the blade clear of it. Press a knife blade to one side to check that it springs back into position.

If you have a dishwasher, ask if the cutlery is dishwasher safe. All metal-handled cutlery is but labels should make this clear anyway. Stainless steel cutlery lasts well, doesn't corrode, keeps its looks and needs no special cleaning. It comes in classic and also more innovative designs. Ordinary washing keeps it clean but an occasional polish with a special stainless-steel cleaner will keep its patina looking its subtle silvery best.

Silver-plated cutlery must be of good quality or constant wear will result in the plating wearing off and showing the metal (usually stainless steel, nickel-silver or brass) underneath. Look for cutlery which conforms to BS 5577. This means it will be plated with at least 20 microns of silver.

Solid silver cutlery should be bought only from the best retailer. It will need regular polishing to keep it looking good. Secondhand silver cutlery can often be found at auctions and in antique shops but you should take a guide to hallmarks and check it before buying to be sure that it is indeed solid silver. Silver isn't as durable as stainless steel but if cared for properly can last for centuries. Knife handles are often made from another material – such as ivory – which may mean they can't be put in a dishwasher.

Chrome-plated cutlery is cheap, not usually very well designed and doesn't last as long as stainless steel or even silver plate. If you are very hard up it could be something to start with and dispose of when you can afford something better.

Gold and bronze cutlery need a lot of cleaning and aren't really suitable for everyday use.

CHINA

China, like cutlery, varies from the cheap to the amazingly expensive and, in general, the price will reflect the shape and decoration. Earthenware is the cheapest type but it does chip easily and tends to come in rather thick designs. Stoneware is stronger and bone china is toughest of all – but it costs correspondingly more.

When choosing china think about how it will look with food on the plates – very busy patterns, may completely overwhelm both the recipe and appetite! Also consider how you will store it. Some ranges are designed to be stackable which can be a help where space is limited.

Cheap china is not necessarily nasty; chain stores produce ranges in all sorts of designs which are very good value indeed. However, they tend to have a fairly short retail life. It's as well to buy as much as you need and a bit over for breakages since you are unlikely to be able to find replacements later on.

If you are buying china that includes ovenware, check whether or not this will go on top of the cooker as well as in the oven. Think about whether you are going to wash in a dishwasher, in which case the china should be dishwasher safe, and whether you will be putting it in a microwave oven in which case it should not have any metallic trim. *Don't* go for very expensive china for everyday use. It's bound to get broken. Have a best set if you want but look for seconds, sale bargains or chain store cheapies to cater for most meals.

GLASSES

Really good quality glass is thin, rings when it's tapped and comes in many beautiful designs. It's also very easy to break. Cheap glass can also be well designed, but is sturdy enough to stand up to being knocked around a bit without chipping.

The crystal glass that is used for most fine glassware is usually hand made and expensive. A British Standard and an EEC directive specify a minimum of 24 per cent lead oxide – the very best lead crystal will contain at least 30 per cent. The more lead that there is in glass (a label should state the quantity) the clearer it will be.

Soda lime glass is what most ordinary tumblers are made from. Silica sand, soda ash and limestone are mixed together in varying amounts to produce different degrees of clarity. These glasses are machine made and come in a good range of designs and shapes.

Above: spread the board with toning greens and cream. Sprays of ivy curled round the candlesticks echo the pattern on the china and are picked up again in the green, leaf-shaped side plate. Restricting table decoration to just two colours sets off food to perfection *Right:* breakfast outdoors on a sunny day well merits this delicately floral-patterned china which fits so well into the garden scene. Note how the soft shapes of the pieces are complemented by the design

Glass oven-to-table ware is made from borosilicate glass which is very strong, dishwasherproof and heat resistant, although it should not be used on a direct heat source unless this is stated on the label. Such glass is sometimes called 'flameproof'.

PLANNING FOR EFFECT

When deciding on cutlery, china and glass it's obviously vitally important to remember that they will all be used simultaneously on the table and should therefore relate to each other. It is pointless to choose a very modern style of cutlery and a traditional dinner service unless you are convinced that the two complement each other. If you already own a dinner service or canteen of cutlery, take a piece along with you when you go to the shop.

Batterie De Cuisine

A sharp eye can be as useful as a sharp knife, when it comes to choosing the best cook's tool.

When choosing equipment for your kitchen it is easy to be dazzled by the range of choice on the market. Not all of it is necessary in every kitchen, though, and it is important to work out initially what you need for your kind of cooking and your lifestyle – not to mention the amount of space you have in your kitchen.

Start by selecting the most important things and add to your equipment over a period of time when you find a need for a new item. There is no point in having kitchen equipment which you do not use; it just gathers dust and wastes storage space. Later in this section is a list of equipment which performs particular tasks: select the basics from it in the sizes you need.

KNOW YOUR KNIVES

If you don't have a good set of kitchen knives your food preparation will take far longer than necessary. Some people find they can manage with just two or three knifes, others like to have several, each designed for a specific task. Knife blades may be stainless steel or carbon steel. Stainless steel is easy to care for and always looks bright and shiny. Carbon steel discolours and needs to be washed and dried immediately after use to prevent rusting. However, it sharpens up to a finer edge than stainless steel, although you need to sharpen it frequently – probably every time you use it.

Serrated blades are usually made of stainless steel and are useful for cutting bread, ham and other cold meats, cheese, grapefruit and tomatoes. They are more difficult to sharpen than straight blades and you need to have this done professionally.

Knife handles are usually wooden or plastic. Wooden handles are traditional but may mean the knives can't be put in a dishwasher. Plastic handles are now required by law in the catering trade (it's more hygienic), so all professional ranges of knives have them. They are often shaped with finger grips and can be put in a dishwasher. Check how a knife feels in your hand before you buy it and look at weight, flexibility and balance.

You will need a knife sharpener to keep your knives at their best. A butcher's steel is the traditional tool for this, but it requires a special technique which some people never succeed in mastering. Most people prefer to use an electric knife sharpener or a small pair of crossed steels which grip the blade at the correct angle for sharpening.

PERFECT PANS

Good saucepans make the world of difference when you are cooking. The range of materials from which they are made allows you to select from a choice of non-stick linings, double handles, thick bases and so on, for different types of food. The materials have different properties as follows:

Aluminium is cheap and, in the thinner grades, of rather poor quality. Medium- to heavy-gauge aluminium is an excellent conductor of heat. Cast aluminium also conducts heat well but is heavy to lift. Enamelled aluminium can hot spot and tends to get food stuck on it.

Cast iron is a great favourite with professional cooks because of the way it retains heat and can cook slowly on a low fire. It is very heavy to lift and tends to rust unless you dry it immediately after washing. Enamelled cast iron doesn't rust but does hot spot and food tends to cling to it.

Copper looks marvellous but needs regular cleaning to maintain its sheen. It is a good heat conductor but should be lined with another metal such as aluminium or tin to prevent the copper producing 'off' tastes in certain foods. The lining will need renewing from time to time.

Stainless steel on its own is not a good conductor of heat, but it looks good and is easy to care for. Choose pans which have a layer of another metal – usually copper or aluminium – sandwiched into the base to improve heat conduction and prevent hot spots.

Vitreous enamel pans come in bright colours and co-ordinating designs but do tend to hot spot. Choose pans with aluminium rather than steel base metal as this conducts heat better. Since enamel can chip, look for pans which have a metal rim round the edge.

Non-stick coatings give quick release of foods which tend to adhere: milk, sauces, fried foods. It is not essential on all pans – for example, those used for cooking vegetables – but manufacturers usually apply it to a whole range regardless. The pans that are most useful with a non-stick lining are the milk pan and the frying pan.

Bear in mind that with saucepans, price is a good indicator of quality. On the whole, the more you pay the better quality you get. However, there is no reason why you shouldn't buy cheap pans – provided you accept that they won't last a lifetime. Whether you are paying a lot or a little, these are points to consider.

The weight of a pan can make it difficult to use. Large ones and those made of cast metal are very heavy and will be heavier still when full of food. If you are going to need to use two hands every time you lift a pan, make sure it has a small supplementary handle opposite the main one to make this easier.

Pan handles should be made of heat-resistant material, comfortable to hold and long enough to prevent your fingers coming into contact with the side of the pan when hot. Good quality pans usually have a guard where the handle meets the pan to prevent burning.

Lift the pan by its handle and simulate a pouring action to check how well balanced it is. Check, too, how the handle is fixed to the pan. Riveted handles will need to be tightened by the manufacturer if they work loose, while those that screw on you can do yourself.

Knobs should also be heat resistant. They should have a guard round the point where they are joined to the lids. You should also be able to lift the knob from the lid of a hot pan without burning your knuckles.

A flat base is essential for good contact with the heat source on a cooker. This is particularly important with ranges, solid electric plates and ceramic hobs. Find a flat surface in the shop and rock the pan on it to see whether it is stable.

Most pans are made with a continuous pouring lip, which means you can pour out from them at any point round the edge. Some have just a spout. If you are left-handed choose pans with continuous pouring lips or those that have a spout on each side.

Pan lids should fit well but have a fraction of movement in them when on the pan so that they can be taken on and off easily, and so that steam can escape. Some pans have special steam vents that you can open and close.

Right: Well-designed kitchen equipment is a pleasure to the eye as well as being essentially functional. No need today for a collection of objects which bear no relation to each other in terms of shape or colour. These basic kitchen items come in compatible wood, steel, chrome and plastic

No pan will last a lifetime if you do not take care of it. When you first buy a pan be sure to follow the manufacturer's instructions for seasoning the surface where necessary. This ensures that all the factory finish is removed and the pan is ready for cooking.

When you have finished using a pan, either soak it so that food does not stick on it or wash and dry it immediately. Never leave food in an aluminium pan or it may cause pitting. Mineral salts present in tap water will cause discoloration of the interior of aluminium pans but this can be removed by boiling up an acid solution such as apple parings or the juice of a lemon in water. Stainless steel tends to watermark, so take care when drying it. Non-stick surfaces should be treated carefully to prevent damage. Use only plastic or wooden utensils on them and watch out that nothing sharp scratches against the surface when on the draining board or in a cupboard.

Pans take up a fair amount of space in a kitchen. Think about your storage space before you buy. Some have rings at the ends of the handles or holes in the handles themselves for hanging up. Others stack on top of each other.

SMALL APPLIANCES

The market for small electric appliances has boomed in recent years. You can now buy from an enormous selection of machines which take the time and effort out of tasks which can be tedious to do by hand. These appliances do take up space in a kitchen, though, especially as to get the best out of them you really need to site them on a counter top at the ready for use.

Most people don't need the entire range of small appliances available. A judiciously chosen selection should cope with the majority of their needs. Think before you buy a new machine: how often are you likely to use it (many of them perform chopping and slicing functions that can be done just as easily with a sharp knife if the quantities aren't too large)? Where will you keep it? How easy is it to clean? Here is a rundown on the various types around.

Multi-cookers (electric frypans) These look like large frying pans and are extremely versatile. They work off a 13-amp socket outlet and can be used to fry, roast, bake, casserole, steam and griddle.

Slow cookers Sometimes called electric casseroles, these run off a 13-amp socket outlet and thus provide controlled gentle cooking at about a third of the cost of heating a large conventional oven. Models with removable pots which can be used to serve at table are easier to clean than those with a fixed pot. Automatic models will turn themselves from the high to the low setting without needing further attention.

Infra-red grills (contact grills) These come with a hinged pair of non-stick heated plates between which you can cook any flat food (chops, burgers, steaks) doing both sides simultaneously. Foil-wrapped vegetables and fish can also be cooked. Some are supplied with a baking tin which increases their versatility by producing a 'mini-oven' between the plates. You can buy a separate tin if yours isn't supplied with one. Infra-red grills run off a 13-amp socket and are cheap to run.

Sandwich toasters are also cheap to run and come in a variety of sizes, some with removable plates for easy cleaning or interchangeable plates for making waffles or grilling burgers. They are very convenient for any household which consumes a lot of toasted sandwiches, though they are confined to fairly thin combinations – cheese & ham, cheese & onion, etc.

Deep-fat fryers offer much the safest method of frying because they are thermostatically controlled, so the risk of over-heating fat and causing a fire is eliminated. Models with filters in their lids will cut down on cooking odours.

Electric woks These offer similar facilities as standard woks, but they can also be used to cook at table. In addition, they can perform many of the functions of a multi-cooker, e.g: stewing, steaming, poaching and simmering. Before buying check that the electric wok heats to a high temperature, otherwise stir-frying might not be as successful as with an ordinary wok on a conventional cooker. Some designs come with several attachments and a lid.

Kettles Electric kettles reduce the time it takes to boil water, and those with automatic cut-out are safer because they will not boil dry. Jug-type kettles are worth consideration if you only need to boil a little water – say one cup – at a time.

Coffee makers Electric coffee makers both boil the water and keep made coffee hot. They come with a variety of refinements such as an insulated jug, a built-in coffee grinder, a clock/alarm and a coffee-strength regulator. Coffee percolators tend to boil the coffee, which purists claim spoils the flavour.

Blenders are marvellous for making batter, mayonnaise, pâté, purée and soup as well as for preparing baby foods. Some cope with dry ingredients, others require liquid before they can operate. Do not be led into buying a blender simply because it has a vast range of speeds. Results are not altered by blending at different speeds and nor does it mean that you can prepare greater quantities or different ingredients.

Food mixers come either as free-standing or hand-held models. If you can afford the attachments and have somewhere to store them, a free-standing mixer becomes a remarkably versatile machine. They work more slowly than food processors, but this can be an advantage in that it reduces the risk of over-processing ingredients. Hand-held mixers are very compact and are a good buy if you have a limited budget or a tiny kitchen. They are also sensible if you do not do enough cooking to justify the purchase of more expensive mechanical help.

Food processors can perform all the functions of blenders and mixers – slice, grate, chop, cream, knead and beat – though not all of them whisk cream or egg whites very well. Some have special whisk attachments. When puréeing ingredients they do not always obtain the same smooth texture as when a blender is used. When making soups or pâtés, it is often worth processing the solid ingredients first (in the case of soup, the vegetables, and in that of pâté, the meat and/or offals) and adding the liquid (cream, stock, brandy, etc), slowly afterwards. Apart from being extremely versatile, their chief advantage is the speed at which they can process ingredients.

Microwave cookers can be used as supplements to conventional cookers or instead of them. They run off a 13-amp socket outlet, can be placed on any flat surface, cook in a quarter to a third of the time required by conventional cooking methods and save energy. Study the manufacturers' brochures and before purchasing think carefully: do you wish to use your microwave cooker merely for defrosting and re-heating or do you plan to do a lot of cooking from scratch? Be prepared for some failures when you start, since the techniques and timing are radically different from those used with a conventional cooker.

Coffee grinders Electric coffee grinders take the hard work out of grinding beans and are usually no more expensive than manual ones. They are noisy but very fast – they will cope with up to 75 g (3 oz) coffee beans in a matter of seconds.

If your favourite coffee shop is not close to home, you can keep beans in the freezer for 4-5 months, and ground coffee for 4-5 weeks.

Coffee machine There are so many coffee-making devices available that it is impossible to recommend just one. Bear in mind that for the best results you need fresh coffee, freshly boiled water and the coffee should not be left to 'stew' for hours, which makes it bitter.

KITCHEN CHECKLIST

Cutting, chopping and opening

- paring knife
- 2–3 cook's knives
- carving knife (plus fork with guard)
- palette knife
- kitchen scissors
- potato peeler
- apple corer
- bean slicer
- knife sharpener/butcher's steel
- wooden chopping board
- can opener
- crown cap opener
- corkscrew
- nut crackers
- cheese mill
- grater with different size holes
- herb chopper/mezzaluna
- lemon zester
- cannelle knife
- mincer

Cooking

- kettle
- milk pan
- frying pan
- 3–4 pans with lids (different sizes)
- omelette pan
- crêpe pan
- double boiler
- pressure cooker
- roasting tin
- chip pan/deep fat fryer
- steamer/steaming attachment for ordinary pan
- pie dishes (different sizes)
- pie funnel
- casseroles
- soufflé dishes (different sizes)
- gratin dishes (different sizes)
- pudding basins (different sizes)
- ramekins

Stirring, whisking and beating

- wooden spoons (lots)
- balloon whisks (different sizes)
- rotary beater
- rubber spatula
- slotted turner/fish slice
- slotted spoon
- ladle
- skimmer
- potato masher

Weighing and measuring

(NB all measures should cope with both imperial and metric scales)

- weighing scales
- measuring jug
- measuring spoons

Checking

- kitchen timer
- cook's thermometer
- meat thermometer
- freezer thermometer
- microwave thermometer

Straining and sieving

- colander
- flour sieve
- wire strainer
- nylon strainer
- conical strainer (for liquids)
- tea strainer
- salad shaker
- flour dredger

Baking

- rolling pin
- pastry board
- pastry brush
- pastry cutter
- baking sheets
- sandwich tins (different sizes)
- cake tins (different sizes)
- flan tins/rings (different sizes)
- bun tins
- bread tins
- biscuit cutters
- cooling racks

Miscellaneous

- mixing bowls
- bulb baster
- citrus squeezer
- jelly moulds
- kitchen jugs
- pestle and mortar
- trussing and larding needles

Seasoning

- salt box/pig
- pepper mill
- salt and pepper dispensers
- herb and spice containers
- spice grinder

Icing and decoration

- icing bags
- assortment of pipes and nozzles
- turntable
- icing rule

Preserving

- preserving pan
- long-handled jam spoon
- jelly bag and stand
- cherry stoner
- jam funnel
- preserving jars and rings
- bottling tongs

Serving

- large dishes
- serving utensils
- bread board
- tongs
- ice cream scoop

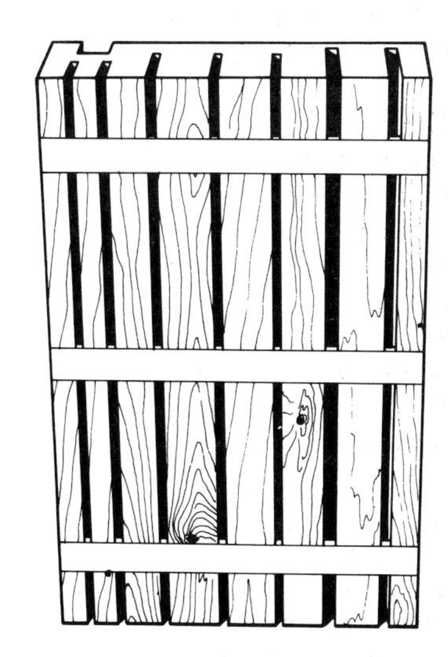

knife storage block

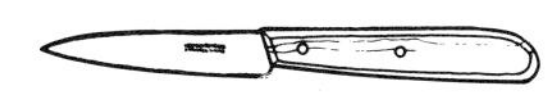

paring knife

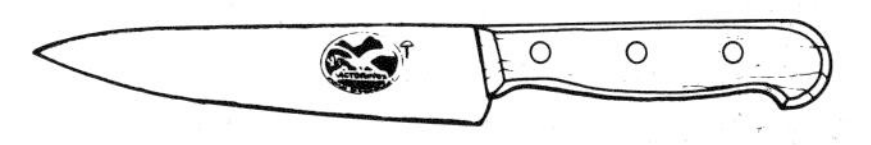

cook's knife

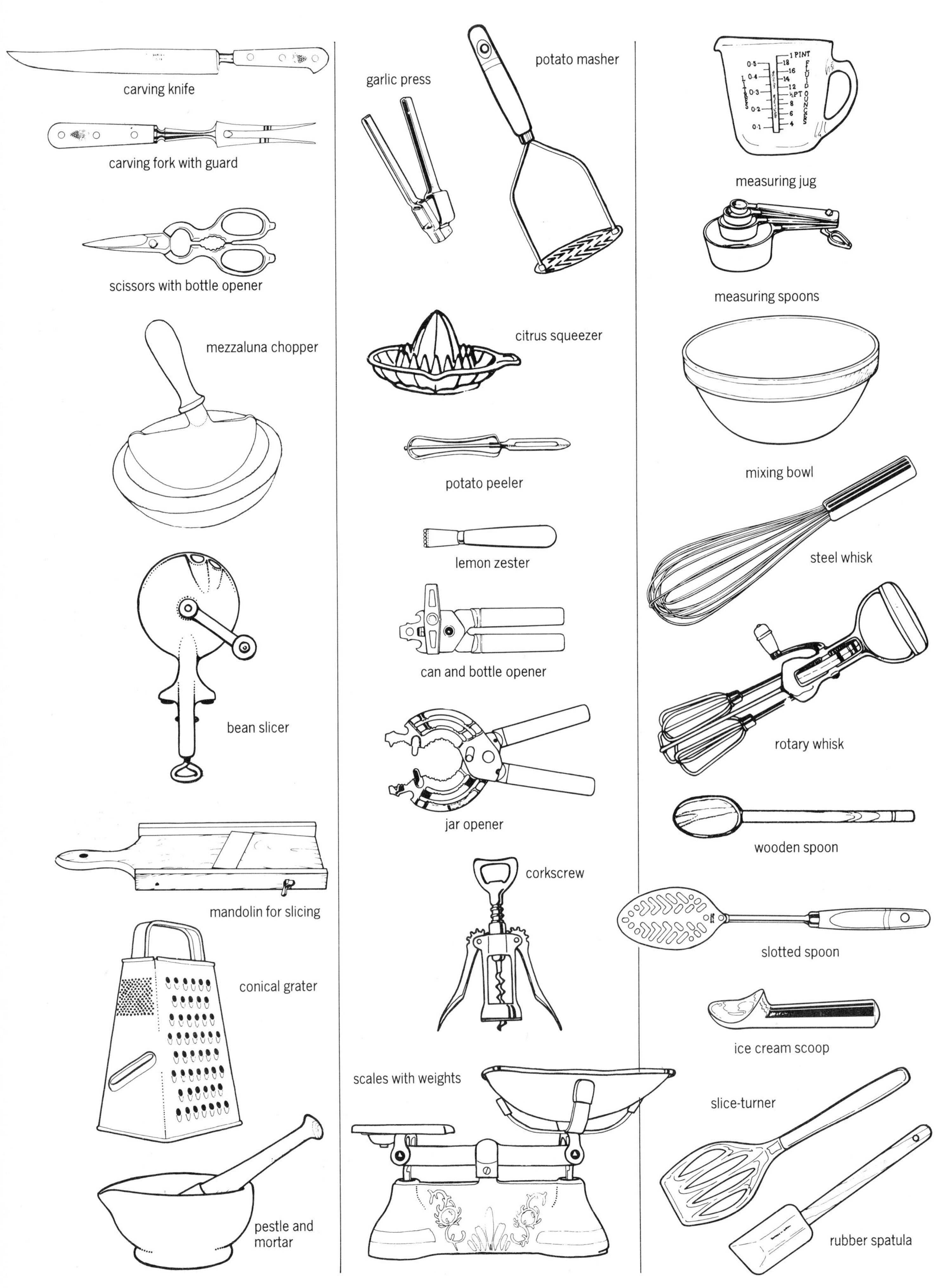
carving knife
carving fork with guard
scissors with bottle opener
mezzaluna chopper
bean slicer
mandolin for slicing
conical grater
pestle and
mortar
garlic press
potato masher
citrus squeezer
potato peeler
lemon zester
can and bottle opener
jar opener
corkscrew
scales with weights
measuring jug
measuring spoons
mixing bowl
steel whisk
rotary whisk
wooden spoon
slotted spoon
ice cream scoop
slice-turner
rubber spatula

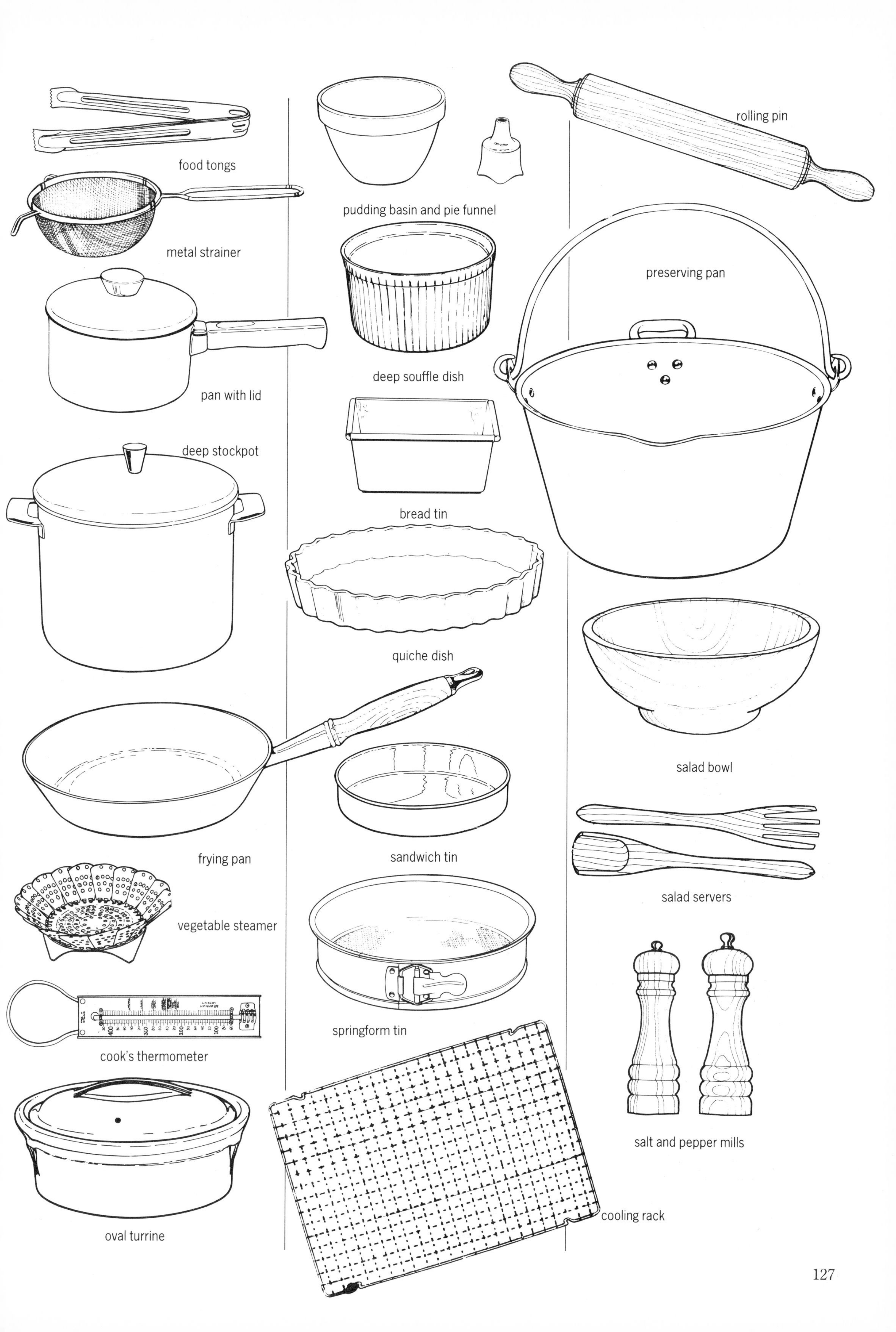
food tongs
metal strainer
pan with lid
deep stockpot
frying pan
vegetable steamer
cook's thermometer
oval turrine
pudding basin and pie funnel
deep souffle dish
bread tin
quiche dish
sandwich tin
springform tin
cooling rack
rolling pin
preserving pan
salad bowl
salad servers
salt and pepper mills

Machine Monopoly

Today, our household machines are our servants. They have given back valuable time – and improved results.

Small appliances (see page 124) add gilt to the gingerbread, but the appliances described here are the ones worth saving up for, buying on hire-purchase or begging relatives for Christmas and birthday contributions towards them.

THE BIG BUYS

Cookers are obviously essential and range from the very basic to computerized complex. Don't be seduced into believing you need a model with expensive extras unless you are sure you will use them. If you are a novice cook or hard up, consider buying secondhand; otherwise look round electricity and gas showrooms and department stores. If you are installing a fitted kitchen you will find that the installer presses you earnestly to buy a particular make which is tied in with his units. If it's not what you want, resist and say that you will supply your own model – even if you do lose an alleged discount.

Basically, cookers come free-standing or split level. Free-standing cookers have hob, grill and oven in one unit while split level separates hob from oven and grill. You can also buy built-under ovens incorporating grills which are sited below separate hobs and slip-in cookers which can be fitted into runs of units or across corners, giving greater flexibility in kitchen design. One advantage of separate hob and oven is that you can mix fuels, although the newer slip-in cookers are available with one part gas and the other electric.

Fridges and freezers should be chosen with size in mind. If you shop infrequently buy big on both; if you shop fairly often but cook in bulk, freeze food from your garden, or buy in bulk, buy a small fridge and large freezer; if you just need a few emergency supplies at hand buy a large fridge and a small freezer. Whether you choose separate appliances or a fridge/freezer is a matter of personal choice and space availability. In general fridges and freezers are reliable machines which don't break down often and have a long life, so choose with long-term use in mind, perhaps larger than you need.

Laundry machines save time-consuming trips to launderettes and mean you can wash and dry clothes and household linens to suit the fabrics they are made from. Washing machines may be automatic or twin-tub. Automatic machines, once set, can be left to run through their cycle but twin-tubs need you to stand over them to adjust temperature and timing of washing, and to control rinsing and spinning. They are, however, cheaper to run. Automatics can be built in – often with a décor panel to match units – but twin-tubs cannot. When choosing, look for choice of wash and spin programmes, for controls that are easy to use. Spin driers aren't necessary if you have a washing machine with a choice of spin speeds, the highest being 800 rpm or more. But they are a boon if you can't afford or don't have space for a washing machine. Tumble driers are expensive to run compared with the humble washing line, but they do get things completely or ironing-level dry – a real advantage if you don't have access to a drying line or have a great deal of washing (nappies, towels) that takes a long time to dry. Most tumble driers can be stacked on top of washing machines of the same make, if you buy a special stacking kit. Washer/drier machines are also available and combine both functions in one machine. This means you can't wash and dry simultaneously (possibly a problem with large families) but does give you two machines which fit into the space of one.

Dishwashers are often thought of as a luxury. But the large amounts of crockery, cutlery and cookware with which they cope and the clean results they produce cost virtually the same as washing up by hand. The outside dimensions of dishwashers vary little from make to make, but there is often a great deal of difference in their capacities, usually expressed as the number of place settings they can hold – 10, 12 or sometimes 14-place services. Consider which machine will best suit the demands you will make on it and look for one where you can rearrange or remove the inner baskets to cope with large pots and pans. If you have an open-plan kitchen, or often eat in the kitchen, try to find a particularly quiet-running machine, as some are surprisingly noisy.

Vacuum cleaners come in various shapes and sizes – see page 130 for details of the different types on the market.

Right: In today's fitted kitchen you can choose whether to have your machines on display or to hide them behind décor panels which match the rest of your kitchen units

Miele

Furniture And Fabric Care

To keep your possessions in good order, they need regular maintenance. This means preventive and corrective care.

Fortunately, modern cleaning aids have transformed housework from the time-consuming chore it used to be. Nowadays it should be possible to keep surfaces free of dust and dirt without too much effort.

Unless you have no soft floor covering at all (see page 138) you will need a vacuum cleaner. There are two main types, upright and cylinder. Upright cleaners work better on carpeted areas because they incorporate a beater bar which raises the dirt to allow it to be sucked up easily. They are less convenient than cylinder cleaners for use on stairs and under furniture. A large upright model will cover big areas more quickly and easily than a cylinder type, but may be very heavy to lift – especially up several flights of stairs. Look for such features as pile adjustment – which means you can move the beater bar up or down to cope efficiently with all types of carpet from shag pile to cord. A light on the front is useful too for picking out bits of fluff under pieces of furniture.

A cylinder vacuum cleaner is lighter and more manoeuvrable on stairs. It is also more effective than an upright model on hard floor surfaces such as wood or vinyl. Most models have suction control and have more powerful attachments than uprights.

Wet and dry vacuum cleaners are intended for use both inside and outside the home and are particularly useful for picking up leaves on patios, wood shavings from garage floors and so on. They are really best kept for outdoor work only as they do not perform very well indoors.

Make full use of the attachments which come with a vacuum cleaner. All dirt picked up through them goes straight into the bag and is not merely shifted – as with a duster – from one surface to another. Vacuum cleaners can be used to collect dust from solid and upholstered furniture, curtains, picture rails, skirting boards and virtually all household surfaces.

FURNITURE CARE

There is a wide choice of home-cleaning products on the shelves of every supermarket and hardware store. Many of them are designed to cope with several surfaces (e.g. wood, plastic, metal), while others are designed for one type only. In general most surfaces only require regular dusting and buffing over with a soft cloth. It is unnecessary to apply polish very often and a complete misapprehension that 'feeding' wood with regular applications of polish will improve patina.

Try not to mix polishes but always to use the same one on a piece of furniture. The different ingredients of different polishes can set up a reaction which affects the furniture adversely. If you want to change to a new brand of polish use turpentine substitute or white spirit on a cloth to remove all traces of the old polish first.

FABRIC CARE

A good iron and ironing board are essential pieces of equipment for anyone who intends to care correctly for fabrics. Irons are sold as dry, steam or shot-of-steam. Dry irons only work well if the fabric is at the correct degree of dampness when you iron it. Steam irons damp the fabric as you iron it but cannot produce sufficient steam to cope with heavier fabrics which also need to be damped manually. Shot-of-steam irons provide a blast of steam on a particular spot at the press of a button and some also incorporate a spray.

The care label on clothes will usually state at what temperature a fabric should be ironed. The one dot setting is suitable for acetate, acrylic, nylon, polyester and triacetate. The two dot setting is used for polyester mixtures and wool, while the three dot setting is for cotton, linen, modified viscose and viscose. Rotary irons are particularly good at ironing large flat items like bed linen and curtains, but require considerably more skill if you are to achieve a good result with shaped garments. They are rather large to store so for most people a standard iron is a better choice. Look for a model which has a comfortable handle and is a comfortable weight. It is not necessary to have a heavy iron to get a good result; the heat will do this for you. Check that the controls are easy to use and that the iron stands up securely on its end.

Ironing boards come in different shapes and with varying heights. Before buying try to stand (or sit, if you sit to iron) at several heights to see how comfortable they are. Ideally the top of the handle of the iron should be about level with your elbow. The more height settings a board has, the better chance you have of finding one to suit you and any other members of the household who iron. A big board makes ironing sheets, curtains and tablecloths easier.

FABRIC LORE

Modern fabrics are infinitely easier to care for than those formerly used for curtains and upholstery. Always check the care label instructions *before* you buy. You may find that large curtains and the removable covers from sofas and armchairs require a trip to the launderette, because when wet they will be too heavy for a domestic washing machine.

If you are making your own curtains, it is a sensible precaution to wash the fabric before you start to sew. This ensures that any shrinkage takes place before rather than after they have been made. The chart below shows the wash programme for different types of fabric.

Examples of application
White cotton and linen articles without special finishes
Cotton, linen or viscose articles without special finishes where colours are fast at 60°C
White nylon; white polyester/cotton mixtures
Coloured nylon; polyester; cotton and viscose articles with special finishes; acrylic/cotton mixtures; coloured polyester/cotton mixtures
Cotton, linen or viscose articles where colours are fast at 40°C, but not at 60°C
Acrylics; acetate and triacetate, including mixtures with wool; polyester/wool blends
Wool, including blankets and wool mixtures with cotton or viscose; silk
Silk and printed acetate fabrics with colours not fast at 40°C
Cotton articles with special finishes capable of being boiled but requiring drip drying
Articles which must not be machine washed. Details will vary because garment manufacturers are free to put their own written instructions on this label
Do not wash

Right: Gleaming wood surfaces don't just look beautiful – care makes furniture last longer. The same applies to fabrics, which should give years of pleasure if cleaned regularly

Always put loose covers back onto furniture while they are still damp and can be stretched to fit properly. They can be ironed *in situ* but take care that the iron is not too hot either for the fabric or for the material (often foam) used to upholster the frame.

Some curtains and upholstery really do need to be cleaned professionally. There are firms which will send someone to your house to do this on the spot or you can take them to be done on other premises. On-the-spot cleaning does have the advantage that you are not without curtains and covers for more than a day or so while they dry. Don't take curtains to a coin-op dry cleaner unless you are absolutely certain that the cleaning solvent is changed regularly. If a lot of very dirty clothing has been cleaned just before you put your curtains in they may come out smelling of perspiration or tobacco, smells which are very difficult to eradicate from large pieces of fabric.

REMOVING STAINS

In all homes things get spilled from time to time and it's important to know how to get the marks out. The increasing number of new fibres and surfaces in today's homes and the use of chemicals in pre-packed foods makes it ever more important to select the right stain removal treatment to avoid damaging the surface or setting the mark in for ever.

There are a few general rules which apply to all stains. Try to mop them up when they occur – a fresh mark is much easier to get out than one which has time to sink in and dry. Use a white absorbent cloth or kitchen paper. Never use anything coloured as the dye may run and cause a worse stain. Test any stain removal treatment you are planning to use on a small patch that won't be seen, such as a dark corner of carpet or the underside of an upholstered chair. When treating a stain work round the edge of it in towards the middle to prevent it spreading. Dab rather than rub. Remember that it is better to use a mild treatment and repeat it if necessary, rather than a drastic one which could be too strong. Where staining is very bad or has occurred on something valuable it is best to have it cleaned professionally. Cleaners of both clothes and furniture have access to solvents which are not on sale on the domestic market and will be able to remove marks you could not get out at home. Make the decision about doing it yourself or paying a professional *before* you tackle a mark yourself; it will be harder for an expert to remove if you have already treated it. Tell them exactly what has been spilled and confess if you have tried to clean it yourself. With absorbed stains like tea, coffee and milk you will usually get the marks out by laundering. Check that the fabric is washable and follow the instructions on the care label. It is possible to sponge these marks off non-washable fabrics using lukewarm water and patting dry immediately with a clean white cloth.

Built-up stains like grease, candlewax and nail varnish leave a deposit on the surface but don't usually penetrate. Remove as much as you can with the back of a knife blade, spoon or paper tissue, and then launder or sponge to remove any remaining marks.

Compound stains are caused by substances like blood and gravy, which are both absorbed into the fabric and leave a deposit on the surface. First scrape off the deposit then launder or sponge to remove the mark.

Several good books on stain removal have been published and it is a wise householder who keeps one handy. Useful items for removing particular stains from particular surfaces include biological washing powder, ammonia, glycerine, proprietary grease solvent, hydrogen peroxide, laundry borax, methylated spirit, white vinegar and pre-wash aerosols. There are also specialist stain removal kits on the market which contain several bottles of different chemicals which you use separately or mix together following the instructions for the appropriate stain.

Above: kitchens, like any other room, need thorough cleaning to keep them spic and span *and* hygienic enough for food preparation. Wipe surfaces between each task and use cutting boards to protect worktops and knife sharpness

Right: soft-toned living room is light and airy but needs to be kept dust free to look good. If you don't have much time for housework, go for this uncluttered effect. It needs little maintenance and will respond to a quick lick and a promise if unexpected visitors appear

BEDDING AND LINEN

Down v. acetate pillow, blankets v. duvet – the choice is enormous. But evaluate your lifestyle before you buy.

Bedding nowadays is considerably easier to care for than the linen sheets and thick wool blankets of yesteryear. To iron or not to iron is the choice of the consumer.

AND SO TO BED

Before it comes to deciding on bedding though, it's obviously important to start with a good bed. Since most people spend about a third of their life in bed it's worth paying out for one that will be comfortable and last a long time. Make no mistake, beds are expensive items but there are often very good bargains in sales, especially if you buy one with an unattractive lurid covering which you need never look at once you have got the bed home and made up. The guidelines to finding a good bed are in Chapter 2, page 90.

PILLOWS

A good pillow can make all the difference to a night's sleep. Check if your existing ones are in good condition by plumping them up then pressing down firmly in the centre. If they go back into shape, they are fine; if not, you need new ones. Only the most expensive down-filled pillows will last a lifetime. Cheaper pillows need replacing every few years.

Natural pillow fillings may be down, feathers or a mixture of the two. Pure down from duck or goose is the most expensive. Down and feather should contain at least 51 per cent down, while feather and down will have more feathers but not less than 15 per cent down. Prices vary according to the type of feathers, with goose and duck more expensive than other forms. Beware of very cheap feather pillows. These are often made from recycled feathers which have lost most of their resilience.

Synthetic-filled pillows are cheaper but don't last as long as natural-filled ones. However, they wash well, which can be helpful with children, and are also good for people who suffer from allergies to feathers or dust.

Left and above: While plain white bedding is always popular, many people prefer to choose from the wide selection of colours and patterns also available. Some bedding is designed to match or tone with wall coverings and/or curtain fabrics for a co-ordinated bedroom look

BLANKETS V. DUVETS

This is a choice you have to make before you buy one or the other since you can't mix the two. Blankets look tidier and can be increased in number and discarded easily as temperatures change. Duvets make bedmaking a lot easier and are less restrictive to sleep under. They also produce the same degree of warmth all year round – unless you buy one of the brands which is in two parts, one of which can be removed in summer and put back in winter.

Blankets may be made of pure wool, synthetic fibres or a mixture. Both types are washable, although a double blanket is very heavy when wet. It is probably best washed at a launderette where the machines are bigger than domestic washing machines.

Cellular blankets have a honeycomb structure which traps warmth between the fibres. They should be used under a solid blanket for best effect.

When it comes to choosing a duvet you need to think carefully about the filling and the size. Somewhat confusingly – since it's the only domestic item the measurement is applied to – the warmth of duvets is measured in TOGs; cool duvets rate about 4·5 or 6 on the TOG scale while the warmest are 13·5. Around 9 to 10·5 TOGs is about right for most people, although if your bedroom is very warm you might be more comfortable with a lower TOG rating.

Duvet fillings are similar to those of pillows. Most expensive are goose and duck down which are both warm and light. Once other waterfowl feathers are mixed in, either as down and feather or feather and down, the duvet becomes heavier and cheaper. Feather-filled duvets cost about the same as synthetic-filled ones.

All natural-filled duvets can be washed but this should be done in a laundrette as when wet they are too heavy for a domestic washing machine.

Some duvets have combed-wool fillings which are very warm although a little heavier than the down-filled type. Wool-filled duvets are the one kind that must never be washed and should be cleaned professionally, *not* in a coin-op machine.

Synthetic-filled duvets are usually cheaper than natural-filled ones and are a particularly good choice for children since they can be washed easily and dry more quickly than down or feathers. They are also essential if you suffer from an allergy or hayfever. Buy one which has a branded filling such as Quallofil, Dacron Hollofil, Dacron Fiberfil 2, Terylene P3 or Terylene Superloft. Cheaper fillings don't mould around the body so well.

Whatever duvet you choose be sure that it's big enough to mould comfortably round the body without letting in draughts at any point. For a single bed the duvet should measure at least 45 cm (18 in) wider than the bed itself; more for a double bed. Length is usually 198 cm or 200 cm (7 ft 6 in) but people who are tall (over about 5 ft 10 in) should buy an extra-long size.

COMFORTERS

An alternative to either blankets or a duvet is the comforter, originally an American invention. This is quilted wadding in a fabric cover – but though it looks rather like a duvet, it is used with sheets like a blanket.

ELECTRIC BLANKETS

Electric blankets come in two different types. Underblankets are used to warm up the bed before you get into it and should be switched off when you go to bed. Overblankets are designed to be left on all night and are usually used over a sheet and under a conventional blanket to trap in the warmth. They have a heat control so that you can vary the temperature. Double overblankets have a control on each side and separate heating circuits, so that the partners' individual requirements for warmth can be set.

SHEETS

Sheets may be made of linen, cotton, polyester, polyester/cotton, flannelette or nylon. Natural fabrics are thought by most people to be more comfortable, especially in hot weather, but the majority opt for a mixture of natural and synthetic fibres which is easier to launder.

Sheets are described as 'flat' or fitted. Flat sheets need to be tucked in while fitted ones have gathered corners which fit tightly over the corners of the mattress. This keeps the sheet in position so that it doesn't get rucked by the sleeper. However, if you like to rotate your sheets, putting the top one on the bottom for a week before laundering it, you will need to buy flat sheets. Having a mixture of flat and fitted means both have to be changed at the same time.

The chart below shows the standard size of beds and the size of sheets and blankets they need. If you have an unusually sized bed that is smaller or larger than the norm you will need to buy different-sized sheets. Work out what the width should be by adding together the width of the mattress, twice its depth and an extra 40 cm (1 ft 6 in) for tucking in. To assess the length add together the mattress length, twice its depth and 25 cm (10 in). Most good department stores stock or can order unusual-sized sheets or you can make your own from sheeting bought by the metre or yard.

Sheets come in a wide choice of colour and design and you can usually buy matching valances to cover the base of the bed. Note that deep-dyed bed linen should be washed separately from other items for the first few times since it tends to shed dye. Include a small piece of old white fabric in the wash with them so that you can tell when the dye bleeding has stopped.

TOWELS

Towels get much harder wear than most people realize so it's important to have plenty so you can rotate them regularly. Ideally a towel should dry you quickly and efficiently but not end up as a sodden rag that looks as if it in turn needs a spell in the tumble drier.

Towels have different finishes. True terry towelling has loops on both sides while Turkish towelling looks similar but feels softer. Friction rub towels feel harsh to sensitive skins as they dry best when rubbed firmly over the body. Jacquard towels have a firm close loop and dry

BEDDING FOR STANDARD-SIZED BEDS

Bed	Sheet size	Blanket size
Single 90 × 190 cm (3 ft × 6 ft 3 in)	180 × 260 cm (70 × 102 in)	180 × 230 cm (70 × 91 in)
Large single 100 × 200 cm (3 ft 3 in × 6 ft 6 in)	180 × 260 cm (70 × 102 in)	200 × 250 cm (78 × 98 in)
Double 137 × 190 cm (4 ft 6 in × 6 ft 3 in)	230 × 260 cm (90 × 102 in)	230 × 250 cm (91 × 98 in)
Large Double (Queen size) 150 × 200 cm (5 ft × 5 ft 6 in)	230 × 260 cm (90 × 102 in)	250 × 260 cm (98 × 102 in)
Kingsize 180 × 200 cm (6 ft × 6 ft 6 in)	275 × 275 cm (108 × 108 in)	250 × 275 cm (98 × 110 in)

These sheet sizes are for man-made and treated cotton and flannelette including poly/cotton

particularly well. Velvet finish towels are soft and should be dabbed rather than rubbed over the body to dry well.

Pure cotton towels last longer than those with some synthetic fibre mixed in, but do tend to shrink when first washed – up to 20 per cent in some cases. So buy the biggest in the range to allow for this.

Check towels before you buy to see that they are well made. Pull on the width to see that the backing is firm and the pile not patchy. Look for good firm selvedges and well turned-in edges. Towels are often good buys in sales, especially if you are not too fussy about design. If they are sold as seconds or substandard ask what the fault is. Even if you decide they are not good enough for bath or hand towels they could be useful for swimming or the beach. You can make your own towels by buying towelling by the metre or yard and machining your own edges. This is considerably cheaper than buying ready-made towels and a particularly good idea for roller towels, as you can select the exact length you want them to be.

Wash coloured towels separately from other items until you are sure that dye bleeding has ceased. Some deep-dyed towels may always need to be washed on their own.

TABLE LINEN

Few people now have the time or inclination to cope with the luxury of pure damask table linen which needs such careful ironing. Polyester/cotton mixtures are the best choice for everyday table cloths and napkins which will need repeated laundering, even if you feel you want to splash out on a natural fabric for use on special occasions.

You can buy cloths to fit virtually any shape of table – rectangular, square, round or oblong or make your own from fabrics which go with your decoration scheme. Many people today do not bother with cloths but use mats of a wipable or washable variety to show off the surface of their table. Some table surfaces are reasonably heat resistant and can just be wiped clean after a meal.

Right: towels for all tastes are available in a wide selection of colours, patterns and finishes. Buy the right size for the purpose. Bath sheets are lovely for wrapping round you, but do tend to look bulky on small towel rails. Hand towels may be too small for family needs. Beware of buying sets of towels unless you have a use for each one. Bargains are to be found in sales where 'seconds' or 'sub-standard' towels may have only miniscule faults. These cut their cost but don't really affect appearance or performance

Carpets And Flooring

Watch where you walk! The floor beneath your feet should be both practical and a decorative asset.

The flooring on the market ranges from cheap, cheerful and fairly shortlived, to types that should last for many years. Even with cheaper flooring your outlay is likely to be fairly high so it's sensible to think carefully about what you want to lay, not just in terms of how it looks, but how easy it is to clean and how hard-wearing.

Some parts of the house take far more traffic than others. These need flooring that will continue to look good in spite of heavy wear and tear. Rooms like bedrooms and bathrooms don't get such heavy use so can be fitted with less robust flooring. Pay special attention to areas which are next to outside doors, as they are likely to have dirt and grit brought in from outside and will present special problems in terms of both wear and cleaning.

CHECK THE SUBFLOOR

Before putting down any form of flooring it is vital to be sure that the subfloor is in good condition. It must be dry, even, level and rigid and, although you may need professional help to achieve this, it's not beyond the ability of anyone who is reasonably handy.

On uneven wooden board you can lay hardboard to create a firm, even base. First punch down any protruding nails and, if the boards are very uneven, you may need to sand off the worst parts that stick up. Condition the sheets of hardboard by brushing about half a litre (a pint) of water on the rough side of each one and stacking them flat for 48 hours. After this they should be laid immediately rough side uppermost and fixed with panel pins or ring nails. The hardboard will tighten up around the nails as it dries.

You can lay a floor covering directly on to a level concrete floor provided it is not damp. Serious damp will require treatment by a professional which may involve alteration to drainage or to the damp course. Minor damp can be treated by painting the surface with a liquid damp proofing solution to render it impervious to water. Note that if you do this it may mean that some flooring adhesives will never dry, so be sure to check with the supplier of the solution which brands of adhesive are likely to be affected.

Cracks and depressions in concrete can be eradicated by applying a ready-mix self-levelling screed over the whole floor.

CARPET CHOICE

The variety of carpets around makes choice hard. Unless you are very sure what you want, it's sensible to take advice from an expert. Bear in mind that, while some carpet salespeople are very good at selling, they don't always know a great deal about their products.

In general, the more you pay the better quality carpet you get, although you don't need top quality carpet throughout the home. Tell the salesperson in which part of the house you will be laying the carpet and how many people (specifying children and pets) are living there.

Take the measurements of the room when you go to discuss the sale, but if you are having a carpet fitted it's vital that a trained operator should do the final measurements before ordering.

Be sure to check what the total final price will be, including underlay and fitting charge. What seems a bargain price for carpet in one retail outlet could actually cost more than in another when all the extras are added in.

If at all possible take a piece of carpet home with you so that you can look at it in both daylight and artificial light and see how it goes with your other decorations. With patterned carpet it's important to look at as large a piece as possible since small areas of pattern are deceptive.

Look at any labels on the carpet to see what information they supply. Most British-made carpets carry standard details specified by the British Standards Institution and these will be marked BS 3655. The information will include the width and, in the case of rugs or squares, the length as well. It will also state the type of construction (Wilton, Axminster), what the carpet is made of (wool, nylon), and any special instructions for cleaning and laying.

The British Carpet Mark also appears on British-made carpets and means the carpet is registered under the British Carpet Classification Scheme. The label gives details of who made the carpet and indicates by a number (see below) what sort of area the carpet is suitable for.

1. Light domestic use, e.g. bedrooms
2. Medium domestic use, e.g. dining rooms
3. General domestic use, e.g. living rooms
4. Heavy domestic use, e.g. stairs and halls and playrooms
5. Heavy contract use, e.g. shops
6. Luxury use, e.g. made for comfort and aesthetic appeal but not necessarily suitable in rooms which get heavy wear

Carpet types

Names like Axminster and Wilton refer to the construction of the carpet and not its content. For example you can get an all-wool Axminster or one that is made of a combination of fibres. These are the types of construction available.

Axminster carpets are woven on looms which simultaneously put the tufts into position and cut them into pile. They always have a cut pile and can be woven either plain or in patterns using a variety of colours. They come in medium to high quality.

Wilton carpets are also woven on looms and the pile is woven at the same time as the backing. They may be plain or multi-coloured in up to five colours. When more than one colour is used some of the pile yarn is carried behind the backing producing extra quality and firmness in the finished carpet. Wilton pile is always cut but may vary in height from thick and luxurious to low and plush. Wiltons may also have embossed (also called sculptured or carved) pile. They are so

Above: rush matting flooring is cheap, hard-wearing and, with its natural finish, an admirable foil for this cork-finished desk set against a painted brick wall. It's loose laid and easy to keep clean by vacuuming

Right: woodblock floor throughout the ground floor of this house gives a gleaming patina and makes narrow passages seem wider. Where warmth is needed the wood will set off handsome floor rugs, although these are best secured with special anti-slip material if people might skid on them

Down East

called when woven with different heights of pile to give a textured effect.

Brussels carpets are made in a similar way to Wilton but have uncut pile.

Tufted carpets are made by needling the pile yarn into a woven backing to form rows of cut or uncut loops. The backing may be foam which doesn't need an underlay, or of non-woven polypropylene or polyester. Pile height is variable and may be sculptured or level, although the tufting process limits the number of coloured patterns that can be produced.

Bonded carpets have pile which is bonded with an adhesive on to a woven backing fabric.

Fibre-bonded carpets consist of fibre webs which are needled together to produce a felt-like floor covering which is backed with a layer of rubber or PVC. Some fibre-bonded carpets are made by the needle punch method, which gives them a raised pile similar to that of woven and tufted carpets.

What are carpets made from?

Originally, carpets were always made of wool, but there is now a wide range of man-made fibres which can be mixed with wool, with each other or used separately to improve dirt resistance and wear, as well as to keep down the cost.

Wool is hard-wearing, resilient and resistant to dirt, but is more expensive than other fibres used in carpets. Most wool carpets are mothproofed and naturally flame-resistant and come in a wide range of colours.

Acrylic is a hard-wearing fibre that looks and feels like wool but is less resilient and cannot be dyed to such subtle colours. It is very easy to clean.

Nylon is very hard-wearing indeed, resistant to abrasion and easy to clean. It lacks the appearance of wool and acrylic but on its own makes a cheap, practical carpet and when mixed with wool increases its wearing properties.

Polypropylene is hard-wearing, easy to clean but lacks resilience and crushes easily. It is mainly used in cord and velour carpets where this does not matter. It has the advantage of being rotproof so is suitable for use in conservatories and kitchens or utility rooms.

Polyester is less hard-wearing than other fibres, but when mixed in with them reduces their cost considerably.

Viscose is also cheap but is not particularly resilient. It is used to bulk wool/nylon blends to keep the price down.

How carpet is sold

Carpet is sold in four standard ways: as broadloom, bodywidth, carpet square and carpet tiles.

Broadloom is made in widths of

1.83 m (6 ft), 2.74 m (9 ft), 3.66 m (12 ft) and 4.57 m (15 ft), while bodywidth is designed for stairs and passages and comes in widths of 69 cm (27 in) and 91 cm (36 in). Carpet squares come in a variety of sizes for loose laying and are not always square. Edges may be bound or fringed and sizes range from 2.74 m × 2.29 m (9 ft × 7 ft 6 in) to 4.57 m × 3.66 m (15 ft × 12 ft). Carpet tiles come as squares measuring 30 cm (12 in), 40 cm (16 in), 45 cm (18 in) and 50 cm (20 in) and are particularly useful in areas which get patchy wear as they can be moved around to even up areas of heavy and light use. They can be particularly good in children's rooms. They are also easy to take up and take with you when you move and are easily laid by an amateur, although the manufacturer's instructions regarding the directions in which they should be laid and the method of fixing them should be followed carefully.

Fitted carpets really are best laid by an expert since it is difficult for an unskilled person to stretch them properly – even if they have access to the professional tools required for the job. You can sometimes save money by using broadloom and bodywidth carpet in one room, thus avoiding waste. Fitted carpets make a room look more spacious and are definitely easier to clean as you can vacuum right up to the edges of the room.

Carpet underlay

A good underlay will make a carpet more comfortable to walk on and also ensure it lasts longer. Never lay new carpet on old underlay, as this will have lost its resilience and may be unevenly worn in patches.

Underlay may be foam rubber, crumb rubber, needlefelt or latex-impregnated felt. Flat foam rubber is hard-wearing and resilient, while ripple foam rubber – although softer and springier to walk on – is more easily compressed. Crumb rubber is much harder and longer-lasting but is less comfortable to walk on. Needlefelt comes in various weights which become less resilient as they get thinner, and latex-impregnated felt is less long-lasting than needlefelt and not as resilient as foam

Far left and left: the effect of a carpet can make a room. Don't just look at colour and pattern – the *texture* of a carpet can enhance furniture, and its appearance can depend on the way the light falls on it. Try to look at carpet samples in the room where you are planning to lay them before choosing

rubber. Take advice from your carpet retailer on the most suitable type of underlay, depending on the amount of use the room gets. Some carpets come with built-in underlay which solves the problem, but these tend to be at the cheaper, less long-lasting end of the market.

Carpet care

Carpets must be kept free of dirt, particularly grit which becomes embedded and cuts the fibres. Vacuum regularly and on long pile carpets (shag) comb from time to time with a carpet rake (available from carpet shops). When carpets are new they will shed fluff for the first few weeks. Brush this up by hand for a week or two then vacuum.

Major cleaning needs to be done only about once a year – or less frequently – depending on how dirty a carpet becomes. Don't leave it until a carpet is really soiled as it is then much more difficult to get it looking clean again. To clean thoroughly you can either shampoo it yourself or get a professional firm to do it for you. Loose-laid rugs and carpet squares can be taken up and sent away for cleaning but you will probably be without them for some time. It is probably less bother to get someone to do the job in your home.

Shampooing carpets yourself is considerably cheaper than paying a professional. However, you must take time to follow manufacturer's instructions and complete the job properly – it's not something you can rush. You can buy a hand or electric shampoo applicator designed for domestic use or hire a deep-clean or hot-water extraction machine. Follow the instructions for use which come with the machine and mix the cleaning solution in the quantities given. Take care *never* to over-wet the carpet and to allow plenty of time to dry. If you are unable to clear the room completely of furniture, place pieces of kitchen foil under feet and legs to prevent them marking the carpet while it is still wet.

OTHER FLOORING

In areas where you don't want to lay carpet there is quite a choice of what is known in the trade as 'hard' floor coverings, even though many are in fact quite soft. Your feet would soon notice the difference between cork and quarry tiles.

Quarry tiles These are the one genuinely hard flooring and always come in shades of brown and terracotta, usually as squares or rectangles although hexagonal and lozenge shapes are also available. Quarry tiles look good and are very hard-wearing, but have the disadvantage of being hard on the feet if you stand on them for a long time – in kitchens, for example – and tend to absorb stains. They also ensure that almost anything – from glass to the hardest enamelled cast iron – breaks.

They are easy to care for; you just need to wash them over with water and a general floor cleaner. If faded, you can restore their colour with a light application of pigmented polish. Newly-laid quarry tiles may throw up white patches for a time as the lime in the mortar used for laying and grouting works through. These patches can be removed by washing over with a solution of one part vinegar to six parts water. Be patient, they will eventually disappear.

Wood floors These are also hard-wearing, look warm and blend in well with any colour scheme. They are not suitable for kitchens and bathrooms because wood absorbs water. You can lay a wooden floor yourself, using tongued-and-grooved hardwood strips or blocks – usually available from good DIY shops. They come sanded and sealed and you must care for them by sweeping or vacuuming regularly and occasionally applying a little liquid or paste wax polish.

If you buy somewhere with wood floors on which there is a heavy build-up of wax or a damaged seal, it is best to sand this off and start again. You can hire a sander from a local hire shop. Reseal the floor with two or three coats of polyurethane varnish.

Vinyl floors Vinyl flooring is a popular choice for bathrooms and kitchens and comes in the form of flexible tiles or sheet vinyl, both of which can be laid easily yourself. Vinyl flooring comes in several thicknesses and the greater the depth, the more comfortable it is to walk on. Cushioned vinyl has a layer of PVC foam between the top layer and the backing which makes it particularly comfortable to stand on; resilient-backed vinyl has a cork, needlefelt or vinyl-foam backing which produces a sound-deadening quality. When choosing vinyl bear in mind that a patterned or broken colour surface is easier to keep clean than a plain colour. Follow the manufacturer's instructions for cleaning which will usually involve damp-mopping and an occasional application of a floor dressing to give a protective finish. Don't dress the floor too often as this produces a build-up which can cause discolouration, a patchy appearance and sometimes slipperiness.

Cork floors Cork, like wood, provides a warm-looking floor but is less hard-wearing. Because cork is porous it must be sealed to prevent it absorbing water and stains, particularly if it is intended for kitchen or bathroom use. It comes in varying thicknesses and you can lay the thinner ones yourself. Most cork tiles come pre-sealed, but check before buying that there is seal on the sides as well as on the top and base. This prevents water being absorbed through the cracks. Because cork tends to dent it's not a suitable floor covering in rooms where there is a lot of heavy furniture.

Vinyl-finished cork can be kept clean by damp-mopping regularly. Sealed cork should be given an infrequent coating of paste wax polish buffed up with a dry mop and then swept regularly. From time to time dust and dirt will build up in the wax around the edges of the room. Remove this with white spirit or cleaner and re-apply the wax.

Whatever type of flooring you choose, care is important. Floors get harder treatment than any other surface in the house and are expensive to replace.

Above: terracotta floor tiles provide the finishing touch for this farmhouse-style kitchen and tone in perfectly with the old pine dresser and table. They are an excellent choice in rooms where people and pets go to and fro from indoors to out, as they can be cleaned with just a damp mop
Right: flooring for this stylish kitchen/diner is vinyl with a blue-grey tile effect. It's warm, soft to the feet and very easy to care for

POUL WEBB
GLYNN BOYD HARTE
Hotpoint

Accounting And Insurance

Root of all evil or not, money is the basis on which you must run a home. Learn to manage it early on.

In order to finance your home-making projects you will need to manage your money carefully. Not overspending in these terms means that you have enough cash to cope with day-to-day living and any emergencies which may arise, as well as putting a bit aside for 'home improvements'. You must also insure your possessions to their proper value so that if there is a flood at your home, for example, or a burglar makes off with things, you will at least be able to claim on your policies.

TAKING ACCOUNT

Most people don't keep accounts because they think it is time consuming and difficult. It need be neither if you take a short time over it each day; it is undoubtedly the best way of keeping track of your expenditure. Everyone can tell you to the penny what the sofa cost but is unlikely to have a very good idea of how much was spent on oddments yesterday. There is no need to wait until January 1 or the beginning of the tax year to start keeping accounts. Tomorrow will do just as well.

Buy a suitable book from a stationer's shop. Most account books come with side headings against which to log your daily expenditure – look at several books to see which one suits you best or buy a blank cash book and write your own. The following headings should cover most people's likely outgoings, although probably everyone will want to strike out some and add others:

Butcher/Fishmonger
Milkman
Greengroceries
Groceries
Pets
Wines/Spirits

Eating Out
Entertainments
Presents
Holidays

Personal – clothes
Personal – cosmetics, hairdressers
Children – clothes
Children – general

Fares
Car/repairs
Repairs and replacements
Wages/extra help
Gas/electricity/solid fuel/oil
Mortgage/rent/rates
Insurance

Miscellaneous

BUDGETING AHEAD

Although accounting will show you where your money has gone it doesn't help you plan your expenditure in advance. This is particularly important when you are starting to build up a home and have to buy things which cost a lot of money. It's sensible to make a budget plan for the year and decide what you are going to buy and what improvements you plan to make to your property and work out when you can afford them.

To budget properly you must first work out just how much money you will get over the period of a year; i.e. after things like income tax and National Insurance have been deducted. Then write down the amounts of all the fixed payments that you know will occur such as mortgage or rent, rates, insurance etc. Draw up a chart listing the twelve months of the year and write these sums down in the months in which you pay them. Deduct them from the total sum of your income.

In a new home it is difficult to work out how much your fuel bills will be, but if you can find out roughly how much they are from the previous occupant or from a neighbour in a similar type of place you will be able to allow for this in your budget plan.

You should have a fairly good idea of how much you spend on transport – which should be taken to include the full cost of running the car (petrol, insurance, servicing and so on), fares to and from work and, where appropriate, the maintenance cost of any bicycles.

Food costs vary so much from person to person that it is difficult to suggest what percentage of income should be spent on them. Try to work out how much you spend each week, taking into account the cost of any meals eaten at work or out. Writing down your expenditure over even so short a period as a week should give you a fairly good idea of this.

Once you have allowed for all the inevitable expenditure that goes with running a home, you will know how much is left over for buying new items, decorating and so on. You will also have a fairly good idea in which months you will be able to afford them.

While you can buy practically everything on credit these days, it is not a good idea to let borrowing money get out of hand. Decide how much you can comfortably afford to repay each month and don't commit yourself beyond this. Obviously, when you are on a tight budget, the only way to buy expensive items is by spreading their cost over a period of time, but it is sensible to make it a rule that you will pay off one item before purchasing the next.

If you have difficulty meeting large bills, it is worth noting that you can buy stamps which can be credited against your fuel bills and television licence. Buy up to the value you can afford each week and stick them on the special card provided.

Don't forget to allow a contingency fund when planning your budget – give yourself some fun and scope for impulse buying. Working to a very rigid plan which allows only for essentials will throw your finances awry if you break out – as you are bound to at some point.

INSURING YOUR HOME

There are two types of insurance you need to have for your home. One is a home buildings policy which covers the actual fabric of the house and the other is a household contents policy which covers what is in it.

Home buildings

A home buildings insurance policy will cover not just the structure of the building but also the permanent fixtures and fittings in it. These include kitchen units and built-in cupboards. In addition it covers outbuildings like sheds and greenhouses and provides limited cover for walls, fences, drives, etc. Most policies cover your home against damage by fire, lightning, explosion, earthquake, thieves, riot and malicious persons, storm and flood, aircraft – things falling from them – subsidence, landslip and heave, falling trees, impact by vehicle or animal, breakage or collapse of radio and TV aerials, escape of water from tanks or pipes and oil escaping from fixed heating installations. The policy should also provide for you to stay in alternative accommodation if your home is so badly damaged that you cannot live in it for a time. It should also cover you against a person being injured while on your property.

Not all home buildings policies are identical – it is important that you are quite sure what you are covered *for*. If you feel it is inadequate in some respect, increase your cover or change to another insurance company. Most people only read insurance policies when they come to claim. The correct time to read them is *before* you sign on with a company. It is your home that is being insured and you must be assured that it is properly covered. The 'sum insured' is the amount of money for which your policy covers your home and is the *maximum* that you will be paid in the event of a disaster such as it being burned to the ground. It is therefore vital that this sum is sufficient to replace your home or to buy an equivalent should you need to do so. The current market value of your home is not a reliable indication of what it will cost to rebuild it and replace all the permanent fixtures. To find this out you should really consult an architect or surveyor who will measure up for you and tell you the true amount for which you should be insured. Bear in mind that building costs tend to rise each year and you will need to increase your sum insured with this in mind. Some insurance companies will index-link your cover so that any increase in building costs is automatically taken care of. With others you will have to review the cost for yourself and adjust the sum insured as appropriate. Note that you should, in addition, inform your insurers if you improve your property by adding permanent features like central heating or double glazing.

Home contents

A home contents insurance policy covers the things in your home that you would take with you if you moved. These include furniture, furnishings, household goods, kitchen equipment and other appliances, food and drink, televisions, radios and similar equipment, clothing, personal effects and valuables such as jewellery and personal money up to stated limits.

Your possessions are usually covered against loss or damage – this includes accidental breakage of mirrors or of glass-fronted bookcases. Things which you take out of your home – like clothes, cameras, jewellery and so on – will need all risks cover to take care of loss or damage while they are outside the home. You will need to specify particular objects which are worth more than a certain amount of money – valuable ornaments, jewellery and pictures are the kind of thing which will fall into this category. The insurance company will probably insist that you have them valued, possibly by someone of their choice, and that you have a certificate stating what their value is.

There are two types of household contents policy and it is important to think carefully about which one you want. If you insure on an 'indemnity' basis, you will be paid for the objects you lose less an amount for wear, tear and depreciation. If you take cover on a replacement-as-new basis, you will be paid the cost of replacing any lost or damaged articles whether you had bought them one or ten years ago. This is obviously a better choice, since with the indemnity type of policy you can end up having to dip into your own pocket in order to replace quite expensive household or personal items. However, as with most favourable options, the premiums cost more.

As with the structure of your home, inflation will affect the value of your possessions and you need to make sure that you keep the sum insured at the correct amount to reimburse yourself properly in the event of loss. Failing to be properly insured can cause problems that are both financial and emotional. It's a subject you should review each year to make sure your policies are keeping up with what you own.

INSURING YOUR HOUSE CONTENTS

1 BEDROOM
Furniture, beds & bedding, carpets, jewellery, clothes curtains, children's toys & computer

2 HALL furniture & carpets, umbrellas, cameras

3 SITTING ROOM
Carpets & curtains, furniture, decorative objects & pictures, books, hi-fi, video & TV

4 CELLAR (OR GARAGE SPACE)
Wine, lawnmowers, freezer & contents, bicycles

5 DINING ROOM
Fine glassware, furniture, silver, lighting fixtures

6 KITCHEN
Cooking utensils, cutlery, china, mixers, washing machine, fridge, cooker

7 BATHROOM & AIRING CUPBOARD
Linens, hairdryers, irons

8 ATTIC/LOFT
Stored items, camping gear & sporting equipment, excess furniture, prams

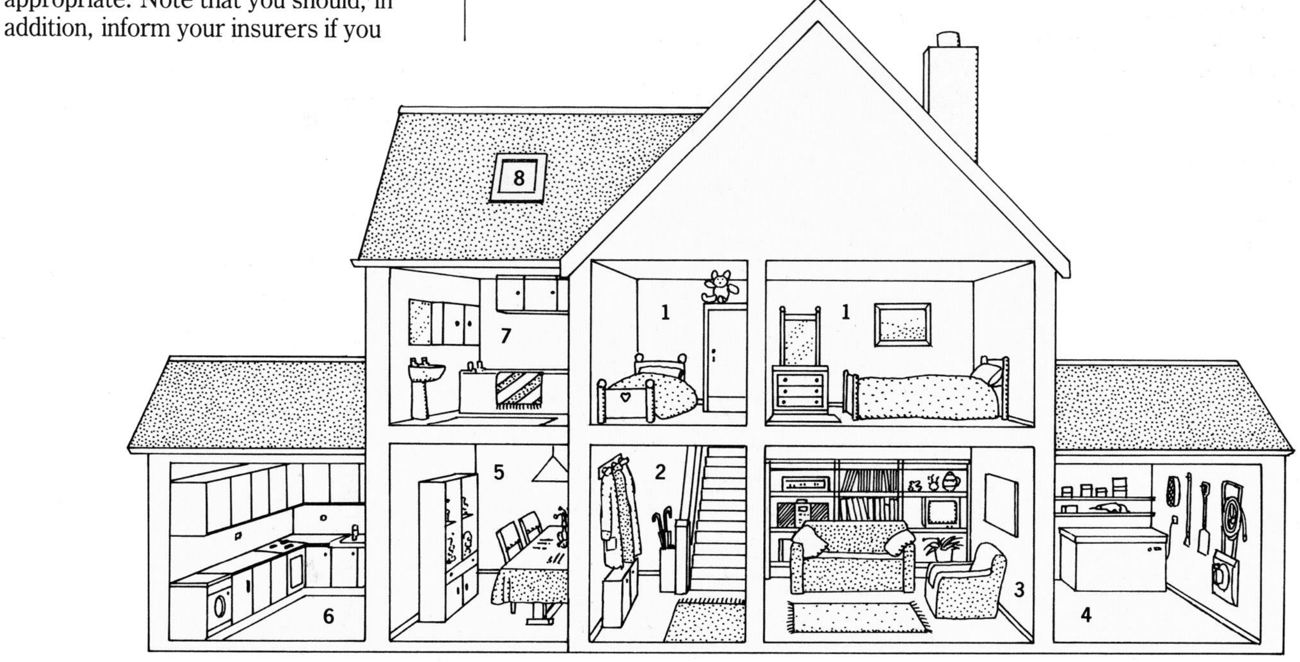

CHAPTER FOUR

THE HOST AND HOSTESS AT HOME

SUMMER LUNCH

Warm weekends mean long, lazy lunches that linger on into the afternoon. Keep the table unfussy, the food simple and light.

Simplicity is the order of the day when you are planning a summer lunch party. Food really *does* taste better eaten out-of-doors, so if you are lucky enough to have a garden, make the most of sunny days whenever you can. And, if you own a light folding table and some collapsible chairs, there is no reason why you can't enjoy an outdoor lunch further afield. The furniture in the picture below right can all be transported easily and it's much nicer to picnic in comfort rather than trying to eat sprawled on the ground.

SETTING THE MOOD

Even if the weather is less than obliging, there is no reason why you can't create a summery mood indoors. Plain white china always looks cool and fresh, complemented with simple stainless steel cutlery (see picture page 149). Beware of overdoing the neutral feel though – low bowls of vivid anemones or other flowers could liven things up. A dish of bright green apples or napkins in a clear, strong colour would also do the trick.

Tablecloths make a great job of disguising an old table – perhaps one that is kept specially for outdoor use – and also form a good basis for an imaginative setting. Don't be afraid to mix primaries and patterns. The brilliant sunshine yellow tablecloth (far right) is very much at home with the charmingly patterned blue-and-white French earthenware. Checked napkins, also in blue and white, add the final embellishment. You don't need any extra table decoration with settings like these – the bold colours and mixture of patterns speak for themselves. Any additional distractions would be overpowering. All that is needed is an appetizing array of food plus uncomplicated glasses and streamlined cutlery.

For a more striking mix of patterns that is very effective, the picture, page 149, marries stripes and spots with happy results. Primary colours and white always make good partners and simple patterns like these look stunning in combination. More colourful accents are added with the red-spotted tumblers, daffodil plates and blue-handled cutlery, in a setting that aims for fun and frivolity, rather than sophistication.

Another way to enhance a summery atmosphere is with pastel shades or white, used in a heavy damask cloth or in pale china with just a rim of colour, echoed by matching napkins or a single-colour flower arrangement. Whichever way you decide to approach them, remember that lunchtimes are relaxed and less formal than dinner, so plan things accordingly.

CHOOSING THE FOOD

With such an abundance of good food in season there should be no problem in selecting a suitable menu. Salads always spring to mind for summer meals – but they do need to be interesting. Experiment with less obvious vegetables – add finely chopped chicory to a green salad, made with crisp Cos or Iceberg lettuce, and look out for the dark red, bitter radicchio which adds colour and flavour to a salad of leaves. Chopped walnuts, crunchy croûtons; crumbled, crisply cooked bacon, chopped fresh herbs – all these can add texture and appeal to salads. Choose your dressing with care and if you make your own use good oil and

Above: a choice of seasonal salads always goes well at a summer lunch
Left: a cool combination of green and white, in which the setting complements the food
Right: sunshine and blue skies set the colour scheme for this cheerful spread

wine vinegar. Again, you can add interest with mustard, garlic or by using a herb-flavoured vinegar.

If your menu is all cold, consider serving homemade mayonnaise as a dressing for the fish or meat, which can be coated with the sauce or served separately. For a simple lunch you may prefer to serve only a main course and pudding, but if you would like starters too, small portions of salad, or bowls of chilled soup are easy and inexpensive ideas.

For a special occasion, you might think it worth tackling a main course that is also a delight to the eye, like the Spinach and Chicken Terrine, or the Poached Trout, shown on page 172.

Just because it's summer, there's no reason to serve only cold food. A light casserole of chicken or lamb, made with fresh tomatoes, would be good, as would fresh fish sautéed in butter and herbs. A dish of new potatoes, cooked in their skins, is always welcome, and slices of warm quiche are guaranteed to go down well. For puddings, there is little more welcome than soft fruits – strawberries, raspberries, blackcurrants – with sugar and cream, in a fruit salad, or made into delectable concoctions with whipped cream and meringue. Homemade ice creams and sorbets are bound to be appreciated. Serve with crisp biscuits.

MOULDED KIPPER AND EGG RING

170 g (6 oz) packet boil-in-the-bag kipper fillets
8 eggs
150 ml (¼ pint) liquid aspic jelly
40 g (1½ oz) butter
40 g (1½ oz) flour
450 ml (¾ pint) milk
5 ml (1 tsp) anchovy essence
150 ml (¼ pint) soured cream
salt, paprika, black pepper
30 ml (2 level tbsp) gelatine
For the salad:
450 g (1 lb) French beans, halved
450 g (1 lb) green eating apples, cored and sliced
50 g (2 oz) walnuts, roughly chopped
French dressing

Cook kippers as directed on the packet. Flake, reserving juices, and cool. Hard-boil seven of the eggs, cool and roughly chop. Set one chopped egg in the aspic in the base of a 1.3 litre (2¼ pint) ring mould.

Make a white sauce in usual way with butter, flour and milk, adding fish juices. Beat in yolk from the uncooked egg. When cool, add anchovy essence, soured cream and seasoning to sauce, then the flaked fish and boiled eggs.

Dissolve gelatine in 120 ml (8 tbsp) water in a small bowl, standing it in a pan of hot water. Stir into mixture. Whisk the egg white until stiff, then fold into mixture. Turn into mould and chill.

Cook beans in boiling water for 5–10 minutes until tender, then cool. Core and slice the apples and mix with the beans and walnuts. Toss in dressing until coated. Turn out mould and pile salad into centre.
Serves 8

SPINACH AND AVOCADO SALAD

350 g (12 oz) spinach
125 g (4 oz) streaky bacon, rinded
125 g (4 oz) Caerphilly cheese
2 medium ripe avocados
50 g (2 oz) spring onions, washed and trimmed
60 ml (4 tbsp) French dressing

Wash the spinach well, remove central stalks and pull into pieces. Grill bacon until crisp and snip into small pieces. Cut cheese into 1 cm (½ inch) chunks. Skin and halve avocados, remove stones and thinly slice. Finely scissor-snip the spring onions. Put all the salad ingredients in a bowl and lightly toss in the dressing.
Serves 4

CHICKEN À LA GRECQUE

1.5 kg (3 lb) oven-ready chicken
25 g (1 oz) butter
200 ml (7 fl oz) chicken stock
75 ml (5 tbsp) vegetable oil
15 ml (1 tbsp) wine vinegar
10 ml (2 level tsp) tomato paste
1 large garlic clove, skinned and crushed
7.5 ml (1½ level tsp) chopped fresh thyme or basil, or 2.5 ml (½ level tsp) dried
salt and pepper
175 g (6 oz) small button onions, skinned
225 g (8 oz) button mushrooms, wiped
5 ml (1 level tsp) caster sugar

Spread butter over the chicken. Place in a small tin and pour in the stock. Roast in the oven at 200°C/400°F (Gas Mark 6) for about 1¼ hours, basting frequently.

Meanwhile, mix 45 ml (3 tbsp) oil with the vinegar, tomato paste, crushed garlic, herbs and seasoning. Blanch the onions for 5 minutes, drain well. Fry in the remaining oil then sprinkle with sugar. Add the halved or quartered mushrooms and toss over a high heat for a few seconds. Tip the contents of the pan into the dressing.

Joint the hot chicken into eight pieces and spoon over vegetables and dressing. Chill before serving with a green salad.
Serves 4

HAM AND TONGUE SLAW

2 × 113 g (4 oz) packets sliced ham
2 × 113 g (4 oz) packets sliced cooked tongue
450 g (1 lb) crisp white cabbage
175 g (6 oz) radishes, trimmed
2 eating apples
150 ml (¼ pint) mayonnaise
45 ml (3 level tbsp) chopped fresh mint
salt and pepper

Cut the ham and tongue into thin strips, about 6.5 cm (2½ in) long. Shred the cabbage finely. Keep a few radishes whole and thinly slice the remainder. Quarter, core and thinly slice the apples.

Mix the meats, cabbage, sliced radishes, apples, mayonnaise and mint together and season well. Cover and chill for 2–3 hours. Spoon into a shallow dish for serving and garnish with radishes.
Serves 6

BRAWN AND COTTAGE CHEESE ROLLS

1 medium cucumber
175 g (6 oz) cottage cheese
salt and pepper
2 × 100 g (3½ oz) packets sliced brawn
450 g (1 lb) tomatoes
45 ml (3 tbsp) vegetable oil
15 ml (1 tbsp) wine vinegar
5 ml (1 level tsp) tomato paste

Peel the cucumber (reserve about one-third of the skin). Cut half the flesh into fine dice, the remainder into fine strips. Shred the reserved skin. Beat the dice into the cottage cheese. Season to taste.

Divide the cheese mixture between the slices of brawn and roll up, cover and chill for about 30 minutes. Place side by side on a flat serving dish. Skin and quarter the tomatoes and remove the seeds. With a knife, shred the flesh.

Whisk the oil, vinegar, tomato paste and seasoning together and pour over the cucumber and tomatoes. Toss together.

Just before serving, pile the salad round the rolls. Garnish with shredded green cucumber skin.
Serves 4

MUSTARD BEEF RING

350 g (12 oz) onion, skinned
225 g (8 oz) sliced salami (not pink)
750 g (1½ lb) lean minced beef
175 g (6 oz) fresh brown breadcrumbs
7.5 ml (1½ level tsp) ground nutmeg
20 ml (4 level tsp) whole grain mustard
2 eggs, beaten
salt and pepper
30 ml (2 tbsp) tomato ketchup and 15 ml (1 tsp) soy sauce to glaze

Grease a 1.1 litre (2 pint) ring mould with a little lard. Mince the onion and salami coarsely. Combine with the remaining ingredients except tomato ketchup and soy sauce, stirring well until evenly blended. Press into the mould and cover with foil. Place on a baking sheet and bake in the oven at 180°C/350°F (Gas Mark 4) for 1¼–1½ hours.

Combine the tomato ketchup with the

soy sauce. Turn out of the tin, cool a little and coat evenly with the sauce mixture. Serve cold, thickly sliced, with a cucumber and tomato garnish.
Serves 8

VEAL AND HAM RAISED PIE

450 g (1 lb) minced veal
125 g (4 oz) minced ham
30 ml (2 level tbsp) chopped fresh parsley
2.5 ml (½ level tsp) ground mace
1.25 ml (¼ level tsp) ground bay leaves
grated rind of 1 lemon
2 onions, skinned and finely chopped
salt and pepper
125 g (4 oz) lard
350 g (12 oz) wholemeal flour
1 egg yolk
3 eggs, hard boiled

Grease with a little lard and base line a 1.4 litre (2½ pint) loaf tin. Combine the first six ingredients, then add the onion and season well.

Gently melt the lard in 200 ml (7 fl oz) water. Bring to the boil, tip in the flour with 2.5 ml (½ level tsp) salt and beat well. Beat in the egg yolk. Cool, covered, until cool enough to handle.

Pat two-thirds of the pastry into the prepared tin. Press in half the meat mixture and place the shelled eggs down the centre. Fill with the remaining mixture. Cover with the remaining pastry, decorate with trimmings and make 2–3 small holes on top.

Bake in the oven at 180°C/350°F (Gas Mark 4) for 1½ hours; cover towards end of cooking time if necessary. Cool and turn out of tin to serve.
Serves 8–10

CRANBERRY PIES

Bake the Veal and Ham mixture (above) in shortcrust-lined individual soufflé dishes and top with cranberry sauce.

SPINACH AND CHICKEN TERRINE

450 g (1 lb) uncooked chicken breast
200 ml (7 fl oz) double cream
300 ml (½ pint) milk
3 eggs
1 garlic clove, skinned and crushed
salt and pepper
1 kg (2 lb) fresh spinach, washed

Butter a 1.4 litre (2½ pint) loaf tin. In a blender or processor purée together the chicken, cream, milk and eggs until smooth. Stir in the crushed garlic and season well.

Blanch a few spinach leaves until just tender, drain. Use to line the base and sides of the prepared tin.

Cook the remaining spinach with salt but no extra liquid until just tender, drain and finely chop.

Spoon half the chicken mixture into the prepared dish. Carefully place the chopped spinach in a layer over the chicken. Finish with the remaining chicken.

Cover with buttered foil. Place in a roasting tin half filled with water and cook in the oven at 170°C/325°F (Gas Mark 3 for about 1 hour 20 minutes. Turn onto a flat serving plate. With the loaf tin still in place pour off any excess liquid. Remove tin and serve at once, sliced.
Serves 8 as a starter

Top left: mustard beef ring, cranberry pies and veal and ham raised pie would be welcome fare at a racecourse picnic or a poolside party
Below left: this elegant cold salmon trout (recipe page 172) with prawns arranged in a pyramid, would be at home at a summer luncheon or a larger, more festive party
Above, top: Spinach leaves envelop this delicate chicken terrine, and add a flavourful filling
Centre: summer comes indoors in this light and airy setting
Bottom: snazzy stripes and spots go down to the river for a stylish lunch

WINTER GATHERINGS

Beat the cold and come inside to heartwarming food, enjoyed in relaxing and friendly surroundings.

A lunchtime get together, in the deep mid-winter, is just the excuse you need to revive your nursery favourites. Sustaining puddings, pasta and stews can all find a place on the menu.

BALANCING THE MEAL

That said, it's important not to overdo the ballast and leave your guests feeling uncomfortably over-fed. By all means have Steak and Kidney Pudding (below) or apple pie as the main attraction, but make sure the other dishes you choose are lighter. One pastry or pudding-based dish at a meal is enough and if you choose it as a main course, go easy on the potatoes. Serve them – creamed or in their jackets – but also offer a crisply-cooked green vegetable such as leeks or Brussels sprouts and perhaps a creamy carrot or parsnip purée. A main course pasta dish, like Macaroni alla Carbonara (page 152) is best accompanied by an exciting salad, rather than a cooked vegetable. Chicory, frilly green endive, lettuce and thinly sliced green pepper make a good, clean-tasting combination, dressed in a plain or orange vinaigrette. A scattering of garlic-laden croûtons provides more crunch.

If it's a substantial sweet pud you have in mind, then consider a casserole for the main course. Beef in Brandy and Mustard is a good choice (page 152), but there are numerous other possibilities, using every conceivable combination of meat and vegetables.

This is the time of year when the standard winter dishes are always welcome, so think about coq au vin, beef stroganoff, roast pork or perhaps a glazed gammon joint. Moussaka or chilli con carne are always a good bet – as is lasagne. If your guests are not keen on meat, an aromatic vegetable dish, like Bean and Aubergine Curry (page 152) is worth thinking about. Serve it with almond rice and an imaginative selection of curry side dishes. Fish is another useful standby – not in light, summery recipes, but instead served in a potato-topped pie or in a creamy sauce as a filling for scallop shells (page 152).

STARTERS AND PUDDINGS

Starters are not vital at a meal like this, but if you do want to serve them, you can't go far wrong with a homemade vegetable soup. Failing that, little pancakes stuffed with spicy vegetables or meat are delicious, if you can spare the energy to make them. If time is of the essence, whisk up some smoked mackerel pâté and serve with freshly-made hot toast.

Puddings *are* an essential component of successful winter lunches. Try syrup pudding, baked apples, cherry pie, compôte of dried fruit, rice pudding. If those seem too heavy, you could offer a real trifle, or individual chocolate mousses. Steer clear of anything too creamy if the other food on the menu has been served in a rich sauce. Lemon soufflé is another tried and tested favourite, popular at any time of year, or you could even fall back on that much-loved perennial, fresh fruit salad. The addition of a few dried figs, a dollop of whisked cream on top of each portion, and a sprinkling of toasted almonds will help to put it into a class of its own.

PLANNING AHEAD

Plan the menu in advance, bearing in mind how much time you have for shopping and cooking. It makes life a lot easier if at least one course can be prepared ahead, and if you have a freezer this is the time to take full advantage of it. Do remember to remove the dishes out in good time to thaw before you want to reheat them. If you don't have a freezer, you can still prepare things a day or two ahead, especially as foods like casseroles, curries and pâtés most definitely improve with keeping and won't mind at all if the flavours are given a chance to develop in the fridge. Take care when reheating chilled or frozen food, and make sure it is warmed through properly. Don't plan too many dishes that have to be cooked or reheated in the oven, otherwise you may run out of space to warm plates and serving dishes.

SETTING THE SCENE

Warmth and comfort are the key notes for winter lunches. Go for dark, rich colours and striking decorations to enhance the food. The black table (right) makes a superb foil for the sober colours of the earthenware plates and smoky pewter goblets. You could achieve the same effect with a dark-coloured tablecloth (you could even dye an old sheet). Twin bay trees flank the table protectively and the dazzling red of the silk poppies provides the essential note of colour. It's always worth remembering artificial flowers in winter, when fresh blooms are expensive and can't thrive in centrally heated rooms. Many silk flowers are very realistic – and anyway, the aim is to provide colour rather than to fool guests into believing you have bought narcissi in November.

Other ideas? You could try taking a traditionally-embellished set of china, patterned with ivy or other leaves, and echoing the pattern with a vase of the real foliage. A plain white tablecloth would be right with this, with green tablemats and green-tinged glassware. Or, if blue is more to your fancy, a mélange of blue-and-white china can be picked up here and there over the years and will be all the more charming if the pieces *don't* match. Again, a white cloth would work well, as would a plain blue one – or combine the two and try a cheerful gingham. This is an informal look and one that would be very appropriate for our simple lunchtime menu suggestions.

Above: two main course choices for a cold day are mustard beef in brandy and steak and kidney pudding. Recipes are on page 152
Right: a formal study in neutrals given life with one well-placed splash of colour

STEAK AND KIDNEY PUDDING

600 g (1¼ lb) stewing steak, trimmed and cubed

225 g (8 oz) ox kidney, cored and roughly chopped

1 medium onion, skinned and finely chopped

30 ml (2 tbsp) finely chopped fresh parsley

45 ml (3 level tbsp) plain flour

salt and pepper

grated rind of 1 lemon

275 g (10 oz) self-raising flour

150 g (5 oz) shredded suet

butter or margarine

Place the steak, kidney, onion and parsley in a bowl. Sprinkle with flour, salt, pepper and lemon rind.

Mix the self-raising flour, suet and a good pinch of salt. Stir in about 200 ml (7 fl oz) water to form a soft, but manageable, dough. Knead lightly and roll out, on a lightly floured surface, to a round about 35 cm (14 in) in diameter. Cut out one quarter of dough for the lid.

Grease a 1.7 litre (3 pint) pudding basin. Dust the dough with flour and fold in half, then half again. Lift the dough into the basin, unfold, press into the base and up the sides, sealing the join well.

Spoon the meat mixture into the basin and add about 120 ml (8 tbsp) water or until two-thirds full.

Roll out the remaining dough to a round 2.5 cm (1 in) larger than the top of the basin. Dampen the edges and cover with the pastry lid, sealing well.

Cover with greased greaseproof paper and foil. Steam for about 5 hours. Top up with boiling water as necessary and do not allow water to go off the boil. To serve, uncover and turn out onto a warm serving dish. Garnish with a sprig of parsley.
Serves 6

BEEF IN BRANDY AND MUSTARD

1.25 kg (2½ lb) chuck steak in a piece

1 medium onion, skinned and sliced

30 ml (2 tbsp) vegetable oil

50 g (2 oz) butter

60 ml (4 tbsp) brandy

1 garlic clove, skinned and crushed

15 ml (1 level tbsp) whole grain mustard

300 ml (½ pint) beef stock

salt and pepper

225 g (8 oz) tender crisp celery, trimmed

50 g (2 oz) walnut halves

75 ml (5 tbsp) single cream

Cut the chuck steak into thin strips, discarding excess fat. Heat the oil together with 25 g (1 oz) butter in a medium-sized flameproof casserole and brown the meat well, a little at a time; take out and drain. Add the onion to the reheated pan juices and fry until golden. Return the meat to the casserole and flame with the brandy. Stir in the garlic with the mustard, stock and seasoning and bring to the boil. Cover the dish tightly and cook in the oven at 150°C/300°F (Gas Mark 2), for about 1½ hours until meat is tender.

Meanwhile, cut the celery into fine strips and, just before serving time, sauté with the walnuts in the remaining butter until golden. Add the cream and heat gently. Sprinkle on top of the meat and serve at once.
Serves 6

BEAN AND AUBERGINE CURRY

225 g (8 oz) blackeye beans, soaked overnight

225 g (8 oz) aubergine

salt

2 medium onions, skinned and sliced

25 g (1 oz) butter

2.5 ml (½ level tsp) ground ginger

2.5 ml (½ level tsp) turmeric

2.5 ml (½ level tsp) ground coriander

30 ml (2 level tbsp) curry paste

15 ml (1 level tbsp) flour

300 ml (½ pint) stock or water

Drain beans and cook in boiling, salted water for about 50 minutes or until almost tender. Or, pressure cook at HIGH (15 lb) pressure for about 15 minutes. Drain.

Trim and slice the aubergine, spread slices on a plate and sprinkle with salt; leave to stand for 30 minutes. Wash in cold water and dry thoroughly.

Cook the onions in the butter for 5 minutes, until soft. Add the spices and curry paste. Cook gently, stirring, for 5 minutes.

Stir in the flour, then gradually add the stock. Bring to the boil, then add the beans and aubergine. Cover and simmer very gently for 15–20 minutes until the aubergine is tender. Adjust seasoning and serve with almond-flecked rice.
Serves 4

MACARONI ALLA CARBONARA

175 g (6 oz) short-cut macaroni

100 g (3½ oz) packet sliced German salami

3 eggs, size 2

30 ml (2 tbsp) single cream

salt and pepper

30 ml (2 tbsp) chopped fresh parsley

25 g (1 oz) butter or margarine

mixed salad to serve (see below)

Cook the macaroni in boiling salted water, drain well. Slice the salami into thin strips. Whisk the eggs with cream, seasoning and parsley, until well mixed.

Heat the butter in a medium-sized frying pan and toss the salami and freshly cooked pasta over a gentle heat until thoroughly heated through. Pour the egg mixture into the pan and stir all the time until the eggs just set through the pasta and salami.

Serve at once – before the eggs have time to overset and become rubbery – with a tossed salad.
Serves 2

For the salad: pull apart half an endive, wash well. Trim and slice a head of chicory. Seed and finely slice a small green pepper. Toss together in a well-seasoned French dressing. Top with fried garlic croûtons.

SCALLOPED FISH WITH CHEESE

450 g (1 lb) potatoes, peeled

salt and pepper

50 g (2 oz) butter

1 egg, beaten

450 g (1 lb) cod or other white fish fillet, washed

1 bay leaf

25 g (1 oz) flour

60 ml (4 tbsp) milk

50 g (2 oz) mature Cheddar cheese, grated

15 ml (1 tbsp) lemon juice

parsley sprigs and lemon wedges to garnish

Boil the potatoes in a saucepan of salted water until tender. Drain and mash. Add 25 g (1 oz) butter and the egg.

Poach the fish with the bay leaf in sufficient water to cover for about 10 minutes. When tender, strain off and reserve the cooking liquid. Discard the bay leaf and any bones and skin and flake the fish.

Melt the remaining butter in a saucepan, stir in the flour and cook for

1 minute. Remove from the heat and gradually stir in the milk and 150 ml (¼ pint) of the reserved cooking liquid. Return the pan to the heat and bring to the boil, stirring. Add the cheese, lemon juice, and season to taste.

Spoon the potato into a piping bag fitted with a large vegetable nozzle. Butter 6 large natural scallop shells and pipe potato round the outside edge of each.

Divide the fish between the shells and spoon over the sauce. Stand the shells on a baking tray and bake in the oven at 200°C/400°F (Gas Mark 6) for about 30 minutes until the sauce is bubbling and the potato golden. Garnish with parsley and lemon.

Serves 6 as a starter

Left: an updated version of macaroni alla carbonara uses salami in place of bacon
Above: bean and aubergine curry shows the Portuguese/Indian influence of Goa in its subtle spiceness
Below: a light, bright setting owes its charm to the uncluttered combination of pine, brick and an oriental rug

Teatime Spreads

That most civilized and soothing of meals, tea, whether taken by a roaring fire or under a shady tree, is one of life's simple pleasures.

Tea is exactly what you want to make it, a meal that is entirely adaptable according to your wish and appetite. From a quick cup of tea and a biscuit, to a table groaning with cold meats, fruit, bread-and-butter-and-jam and cakes, tea can cover all the variations in between. Bone china cups and cucumber sandwiches; scones and cream; toasted crumpets dripping with butter; poached eggs on toast; walnut cake, chocolate gateau – they all come under the heading 'tea'.

BAKING

If you have time on your hands and the mood takes you, there is nothing so satisfying as an hour or two spent baking in the kitchen. And if the mood takes you when time is harder to come by, you can still turn out a batch of biscuits or one of the quicker, no-yeast, breads.

Bread making is a skill, of that there is no doubt, but it *is* one that can be learnt. Start off with simple loaves, and you will soon progress to plaits, twists, cottages and other appealing shapes. Remember to measure quantities carefully, work in a warm room if you can and allow enough time for dough to rise. The delicious aromas wafting from the kitchen and the richly glazed, golden brown results will soon fill you with the enthusiasm to go on experimenting.

Once you have mastered bread, move on to other goodies, like muffins and crumpets. They are fairly easy to produce and, like so many things, do taste better when home-made. You will find some recipes on page 156-157, to get you going.

SPREADING THE BREAD

Bread is usually eaten at teatime – sliced thinly, buttered and spread with jam. Real enthusiasts can make their own jams, a process which again requires care and attention for success, but is an excellent way of using up a glut of fruit. An easier option is lemon curd, which has a depth of flavour and creaminess when home made that puts it poles apart from its manufactured cousin. It doesn't keep as well as jam, but you should have no trouble persuading guests to eat it.

Tea is really a meal designed for people with a sweet tooth, but there are some delicious savoury teatime treats. Try spreading toast with Gentleman's Relish, a delectably salty anchovy concoction. Lightly toasted cheese, or even a proper Welsh Rarebit, are other pleasing teatime ideas that contrast well with the array of sweetness all around.

CAKES

A well-equipped tea table needs at least two decent-sized cakes to adorn it properly. Go for different types – a light delicate sponge sandwich, filled with cream or flavoured icing, coupled with a more down-to-earth fruit bread which can be eaten on its own or sliced and buttered; or a superbly squidgy Rich Chocolate Ring (below) partnered with a plainer cherry cake with a frosted topping. A glazed fruit flan is by no means out of place at teatime, especially if the fruit in question is strawberries.

As well as cakes of the cut-and-come-again variety, it's as well to have a selection of smaller ones. If you are feeling creative, have a go at Danish Pastries (page 156). They take a long time to make, but the wondrously light and sticky results are well worth the effort. On a simpler note, jam tarts are always acceptable and look very pretty arranged on a plate together, especially when filled with different coloured jams. Little Bakewell tarts are another favourite, or you could tempt your guests with chocolate brownies, butterfly cakes or, for a very special occasion, mille feuille or chocolate eclairs.

HIGH TEA

This is a marvellously generous, full-scale meal, for which you will need to provide a cooked dish. Anything eggy would be on the right lines and will usually need to be served with toast. Cheese-filled jacket potatoes are comforting, and smoked fish – kippers, bloaters, haddock – served with melted butter and thinly sliced brown bread, make another traditional and filling high tea treat.

In the summer go for a light salad, featuring eggs, cheese, cold meat or even veal and ham pie. Mayonnaise is essential with these and cold meats will be greatly improved with a selection of pickles. For something more elaborate, take a trip to the delicatessen and lay on a selection of meats and salads – a sort of teatime hors d'oeuvre. With all these meals you should also serve the usual range of bread, jam and cakes.

TURNING TO TEA

There is only one possible drink at teatime, but the question is, which type? Look beyond everyday teabags and consider one of the aromatic teas like Earl Grey, Darjeeling, Orange Pekoe or Lapsang Souchong. They all have very distinctive personalities, are usually better without milk (try lemon), and are well worth investigating.

LAYING THE TABLE

The setting you choose depends entirely on the scale of the meal you plan to serve. Delicate teas with small sandwiches, tiny cakes and little else, deserve lace tablecloths and the finest china and cutlery you can run to. A more robust meal would be at home on the setting shown on page 157. The soft, friendly colours of the tableware with its delightful sampler design are matched in the tablecloth and mat, which have complementary patterns.

Top: Yummy, scrummy Danish pastries can form the focus of a 'continental' tea, together with a tempter like the irresistable chocolate ring (*above*). The recipes for both are on page 156
Right: a traditional teatime spread with all the ingredients – a mouthwateringly pretty pink tablecloth, sprigged china topped by strawberries, and sponge cake, bathed in the afternoon sun

WHEATMEAL FLOWERPOTS

450 g (1 lb) wheatmeal flour or 225 g (8 oz) each brown and white plain flours

30 ml (2 level tsp) salt

30 ml (2 level tsp) sugar

knob of lard

15 g (½ oz) fresh yeast or 7.5 ml (1½ tsp) dried yeast and a pinch of sugar

300 ml (½ pint) warm water

milk to glaze

cracked wheat

Grease two clean clay 10–12 cm (4–5 in) flowerpots well before using them for the first time, and bake in a hot oven for about 30 minutes. This will prevent the loaves sticking and the flowerpots cracking.

Mix the flours, salt and sugar in a bowl, rub in the lard. If using dried yeast, sprinkle it into the water with the pinch of sugar and leave in a warm place for 15 minutes until frothy. Blend the fresh yeast with the water. Add the yeast liquid to the flour, mixing to a soft dough that leaves the bowl clean. Knead the dough thoroughly on a floured surface for about 10 minutes and divide between the two greased flowerpots. Cover with a clean tea towel and leave to rise until doubled in size. Brush the tops lightly with milk and sprinkle with cracked wheat. Bake in the oven at 230°C/450°F (Gas Mark 8) for 30–40 minutes. Turn out and cool.

POPPY SEED PLAIT

450 g (1 lb) strong plain flour

15 g (½ oz) fresh yeast or 7.5 ml (1½ tsp) dried yeast and a pinch of sugar

225 ml (8 fl oz) tepid milk

5 ml (1 level tsp) salt

50 g (2 oz) butter or block margarine

1 egg, beaten

beaten egg to glaze

poppy seeds

Lightly grease a baking sheet. Put 150 g (5 oz) of the flour into a large bowl and blend with the yeast, sugar and milk. Set aside in a warm place for about 20 minutes until frothy. Mix the remaining flour with the salt and rub in the fat. Add the egg and the flour mixture to the yeast batter and mix well to give a fairly soft dough that will leave the sides of the bowl clean. Turn the dough onto a lightly floured surface and knead for about 10 minutes until smooth and no longer sticky. (No extra flour should be necessary.) Place in a bowl, cover with a clean tea towel and leave to rise until doubled in size. Knead the dough again lightly on a floured working surface.

Roll the dough into an oblong shape and cut it lengthways into three strips. Plait the strips, pinching the dough together at the top before you start. Dampen the ends and seal together. Place on the lightly greased baking sheet. Brush with the egg and sprinkle with poppy seeds. Leave to rise until doubled in size. Bake in the oven at 190°C/375°F (Gas Mark 5), for 50 minutes. Cool on a rack.

CHEESE PULL-APARTS

225 g (8 oz) strong plain flour

2.5 ml (½ level tsp) salt

5 ml (1 level tsp) dry mustard

50 g (2 oz) Cheddar cheese, grated

25 g (1 oz) butter or block margarine

50 g (2 oz) celery or onion, finely chopped

15 g (½ oz) fresh yeast or 7.5 ml (1½ level tsp) dried yeast and a pinch of sugar

150 ml (¼ pint) milk

beaten egg to glaze

Grease a tin 18 × 24 × 4.5 cm (7 × 9 × 1¾ in). Mix together the flour, salt, mustard and cheese. Heat the fat and sauté the celery or onion gently until soft. Add to the dry ingredients. If using dried yeast, sprinkle it into the milk and sugar and leave in a warm place for 15 minutes until frothy. Blend the fresh yeast with the milk. Add the yeast liquid to the dry ingredients and work to a firm dough. Knead for 10 minutes. Place in a bowl, cover with a clean tea towel and leave to rise until doubled in size. Turn out and knead again.

Divide into eight and shape into finger-shaped pieces. Cut down the length of each with a sharp knife to a depth of about 5 mm (¼ in). Place side by side in the tin, not quite touching. Cover with a clean tea towel and leave to rise in a warm place for about 45 minutes until doubled in size. Brush with beaten egg and bake in the oven at 190°C/375°F (Gas Mark 5), for about 25 minutes. Cool on a wire rack. Break apart and serve buttered.

CRUMPETS

350 g (12 oz) strong plain flour

15 g (½ oz) fresh yeast or 7.5 ml (1½ tsp) dried yeast and a pinch of sugar

300 ml (½ pint) warm water

about 200 ml (7 fl oz) milk

2.5 ml (½ level tsp) bicarbonate soda

5 ml (1 level tsp) salt

oil or lard for greasing

Place half the flour in a bowl with the yeast, sugar and warm water. Blend until smooth, cover and leave for about 20 minutes until frothy. Gradually stir in the remaining ingredients, beating until smooth. Add more milk if necessary to make a pouring batter. Grease a griddle or heavy shallow frying pan, and about six crumpet rings or metal cutters, 7.5 cm (3 in) in diameter. Heat thoroughly. Pour about 30 ml (2 tbsp) of the batter into the rings on the hot griddle. Cook until set and holes have formed then remove rings and turn crumpets over to brown lightly the other side. Cool on a wire rack. Toast lightly on both sides and serve hot and buttered.
Makes about 16

RICH CHOCOLATE RING

125 g (4½ oz) butter

150 g (5 oz) caster sugar

5 eggs, separated

225 g (8 oz) plain chocolate

75 g (3 oz) ground hazelnuts, toasted

60 ml (4 level tbsp) dried brown breadcrumbs

40 g (1 oz) plain flour

50 g (2 oz) milk chocolate

Grease a 1.7 litre (3 pint) ring mould with melted lard. When set, dust the tin with flour.

Beat together 100 g (3½ oz) butter with the caster sugar until light and fluffy. Gradually beat in the egg yolks.

Melt 75 g (3½ oz) plain chocolate in a small bowl or a pan of hot water, cool until tepid and beat into the egg mixture. Gently stir in the hazelnuts, breadcrumbs and flour.

Whisk the egg whites until stiff then fold into the mixture. Turn into the prepared tin and bake in the oven at 200°C/400°F (Gas Mark 6), for 30–35 minutes. Cool on a wire rack.

Melt the remaining plain chocolate with 30 ml (2 tbsp) water and rest of butter. Cool to a thick spreading consistency and spread over the cake.

Melt the milk chocolate, spoon into a paper piping bag (without a nozzle), snip off the tip and drizzle chocolate over cake, so that it drips over the sides.

DANISH PASTRIES

175 g (6 oz) butter at room temperature

175 g (6 oz) lard at room temperature
450 g (1 lb) plain flour
5 ml (1 level tsp) salt
50 g (2 oz) caster sugar
25 g (1 oz) fresh yeast or 15 ml (1 level tbsp) dried yeast and 15 ml (1 level tsp) sugar
about 200 ml (7 fl oz) tepid milk
2 eggs
10 ml (2 level tsp) ground cinnamon
50 g (2 oz) currants
50 g (2 oz) chopped mixed peel

Almond Paste

15 g (½ oz) butter, softened
40 g (1½ oz) caster sugar
40 g (1½ oz) ground almonds
2.5 ml (½ tsp) almond flavouring

Place all the ingredients in a small bowl and heat well together to give a firm paste.

Glacé Icing

225 g (8 oz) icing sugar
30 ml (2 tbsp) lemon juice

Sift the icing sugar into a bowl and stir in the strained lemon juice, adding water to give a thick pouring consistency.

Butter Filling

50 g (2 oz) butter
50 g (2 oz) caster sugar
10 ml (2 level tsp) ground cinnamon

Beat all the ingredients together until well mixed

Place the butter on top of 150 g (5 oz) of the lard, sandwich between sheets of greaseproof paper. Pat and roll out the fat to a 23 cm (9 in) square. Ease off the top sheet of paper and, using a knife, neaten the edges to form a good square.

Sift the flour and salt into a bowl and rub in the remaining lard. Stir in the sugar. If using dried yeast, sprinkle into half the milk with the sugar and leave for about 15 minutes until frothy. Crumble the fresh yeast into a basin and cream with half the milk until quite smooth. Add the yeast liquid to the dry ingredients with the remaining milk and one beaten egg. Mix to a soft dough, adding more milk if necessary. Knead well for about 10 minutes until smooth.

Roll out the dough to a 28–30 cm (11–12 in) square, pulling out the corners gently to square it off. Place the fat on top of the dough, one corner of fat to the centre of each side of the dough square. Fold each triangular corner of exposed

Top: A selection of classic biscuits, homemade or available in supermarkets and specialty shops, are never out of place at teatime
Centre: wheatmeal flowerpots, poppy seed plaits and cheese pull-aparts are three wholesome teatime treats to team with butter and homemade jam
Above: a charming naive design on the china works well with the restrained pattern of cloth and tablemat

dough over the fat to form an envelope with no fat visible. Press the joins to seal.

Turn the dough through 45° so that it lies squarely in front of you. Press lightly and roll out to an oblong; fold the top third down and the bottom third up, brush off excess flour. Turn the dough through 90°, repeat rolling and folding. Place on a floured plate, cover and chill for 15 minutes.

To shape the envelopes, roll one quarter of the dough out to a 23 cm (9 in) square. Trim off the edges with a sharp knife to neaten and divide into four squares. Fold the corners of each square to the centre and press down firmly. Place a small ball of almond paste over the join. Lift carefully onto a greased baking sheet. Leave space to rise.

To shape the pinwheels, take another quarter of the dough. Roll out and cut into squares as for the envelopes. Cut through each square from each corner to within 1 cm (½ in) of the centre. Fold alternative points to the centre, pressing down firmly, and place a small piece of almond paste over the join. Place well apart on a greased baking sheet.

To shape the twirls, roll out rest of dough into two oblongs 30 × 20 cm (12 × 8 in), trim edges. Spread the butter filling to within 5 mm (¼ in) of the edge, sprinkle with fruit. Roll up from narrow edge, cut each roll into four. Place on greased baking sheets. Make two slashes through each piece, open up and overlap the slices. Press down lightly.

Cover each baking sheet loosely with oiled clingfilm and leave to rise in a warm place for about 20 minutes or until doubled in size. Glaze with beaten egg and bake in the oven at 220°C/425°F (Gas Mark 7), for about 10 minutes or until golden brown. Place on wire racks and, while still warm, brush a little glacé icing over each one.
Makes 16

BARBECUE PARTIES

Nothing sharpens the appetite quite like the tantalizing aroma of charcoal-grilled food, wafting through the evening air.

Barbecues are a great way of entertaining informally, as you take advantage of warm summer nights. You can either be in charge of the cooking yourself, or let your guests loose with skewers of meat and vegetables and get them to cook for themselves.

SETTING UP THE BARBECUE

Always make sure a charcoal barbecue has adequate ventilation. Never be tempted to set one up in the garage, porch or tent if the weather looks doubtful. The fumes given off are harmful, so position the barbecue where air can circulate freely around it, away from the house and any dry vegetation. Never leave the fire unattended.

Choose compressed charcoal briquettes rather than the cheaper charcoal chips, which burn away more quickly. The briquettes give a longer-lasting fire with less smoke, and so are more suitable for party catering. When you start the fire, use enough charcoal to last all through cooking, as adding extra later on will lower the temperature. Pile the charcoal into a pyramid and light with a proprietary lighter. Do not be tempted to use paraffin, petrol or methylated spirits – be patient and persevere if the charcoal refuses to light at the first attempt. The coals will need around 40 minutes to get hot enough to cook over, so light the fire in good time. When the charcoal pile is flaring strongly, spread the briquettes into a layer, so that you end up with evenly-distributed embers. Wait until the charcoal becomes a pile of glowing embers, then place the grid over the fire to get hot a few minutes before you begin to barbecue.

Left: a brick-built barbeque in the garden is ideal, although you can manage on a smaller, bought model
Above: fresh, ripe cherries and strawberries partner a plate of creamy sheep and goat's cheeses. Simple puddings like these form the best ending to an outdoor meal

For a higher temperature during cooking, position the grid nearer the embers, or rake them together into a heap. Move the grid away, or spread the coals out if the food begins to burn.

During cooking, tilt the grid from time to time, so that fat runs off at the edge of the fire rather than dripping into it, which can cause flaring.

CHOOSING THE FOOD

If money is no object, then steaks and chops are the obvious choice, and very good they are too, gorgeously brown on the outside, juicy and pink inside. It is possible to barbecue cheaper cuts successfully, but this is really too quick a method of cooking to allow time for tough meat to tenderize. That said, you can achieve a fair amount with marinades and meat tenderizers, but in general it pays off to buy the best meat you can afford.

Marinades have an important role to play in barbecues – they add flavour as well as helping to tenderize the meat. The acid ingredients (wine, lemon juice or vinegar) do the tenderizing, while the oily ones (melted butter or oil) help to keep lean meats moist and succulent as they cook. Marinading is a simple process that just needs a little forward planning. Place the meat in a container, pour the marinade over and chill for several hours, turning the meat from time to time to let the flavour soak in thoroughly. An hour or so before cooking, drain off the marinade, which can be used to baste the meat when grilling, and let the meat come to room temperature.

Another easy way of adding moisture, this time to the cooked food, is with savoury butters. Garlic, herbs, lemon juice or soft blue cheese can all be beaten into softened butter, which should be chilled until just before it is wanted, then allowed to melt mouthwateringly over the cooked meat.

If you want to use a mixture of meats and vegetables, the most convenient way to cook them is on skewers, as kebabs (page 160). Choose flat-bladed skewers that are long enough to handle easily when they are on the barbecue. Run the skewer through a piece of fat before you thread on the ingredients, so that they slide off more easily. Cubes of beef, pork, lamb or chicken, rolled bacon rashers, chunks of sausage, can all be skewered and alternated with tomato, mushrooms, baby onions, squares of green pepper, chunks of pineapple, olives – the list is as long as you care to make it.

Don't forget about fish when planning a barbecue – most types grill well and oily ones, like mackerel (page 161), will come up with a particularly good flavour.

The extras are an important part of a good barbecue. A nicely piquant, spicy barbecue sauce will be popular, and you will also need easy vegetables like salads (page 161) and jacket potatoes (simpler to cheat and cook them in the oven as timing is tricky in the ashes). Lay on plenty of pitta bread or French bread and butter, plus some good cheese and fresh fruit for pudding. Eating out-of-doors always seems to make people thirsty, so you might decide to offer chilled beer, lager or cider as well as, or even instead of, a choice of red or white wines.

CHICKEN AND PRUNE KEBABS

4 chicken breast portions

1 × 440 g (15½ oz) can prunes

90 g (3½ oz) blanched almonds

15 ml (1 tbsp) Worcestershire sauce

15 ml (1 tbsp) vegetable oil

15 ml (1 tbsp) cider vinegar

salt and pepper

chopped fresh parsley to garnish

Remove any skin and bone from the chicken and bat out each portion thinly between sheets of non-stick paper. Cut each one into three and roll up.

Drain the prunes, reserving the juice. Make a slit in each prune, remove the stone and stuff with the almonds.

Thread the chicken rolls and prunes on to four skewers. Stir the Worcestershire sauce, oil, vinegar and seasonings into the reserved juice. Spoon over the kebabs. Leave to marinate for 2 hours.

Lift the kebabs out of the marinade, place on the barbecue and grill for 15–20 minutes, basting with the juices and turning several times. Serve the kebabs sprinkled with parsley to garnish.

Serves 4

VEAL AND HAM KEBABS

4 veal escalopes – total weight about 350 g (12 oz)

4 thin slices cooked ham

½ green pepper

45 ml (3 level tsp) French mustard

24 stuffed green olives

150 ml (¼ pint) natural yogurt or soured cream

30 ml (2 tbsp) lemon juice

60 ml (4 tbsp) vegetable oil

salt and pepper

Bat out the escalopes thinly between sheets of non-stick paper and divide each one into four. Cut each slice of ham into four and cut the pepper into eight pieces. Spread the mustard over the pieces of escalope and roll up with a piece of ham inside. Thread the veal rolls, green pepper and olives on to four long skewers.

Mix the yogurt, lemon juice, oil and seasonings together and spoon over the kebabs. Leave to marinate for 2 hours.

Lift the kebabs out of the marinade, place on the barbecue and grill for 15–20 minutes. Turn and baste with the juices.

Serves 4

Top left: veal and ham kebabs ring the changes on the traditional lamb version. An inventive variation, it could do justice to an al fresco birthday celebration
Left: grilled mackerel with cider and rosemary is an exceptionally good way to treat this oily fish. The cider and spice marinade combines with the smoke of the charcoal to produce a delicious flavour
Top: not all barbeques take place conveniently close to the house. Some are held at the back of the garden – and others even farther away, at lakesides, campsites and sports events. So both food and equipment must be easily transportable
Above: tossed Italian salad is a piquant addition to outdoor fare

TOSSED ITALIAN SALAD

2 medium red peppers
2 medium green peppers
450 g (1 lb) courgettes
1 small onion, skinned
4 large firm tomatoes, skinned
salt and pepper
90 ml (6 tbsp) olive oil
45 ml (3 tbsp) garlic vinegar
few fresh chives

Seed and thinly slice the peppers. Top-and-tail and slice the courgettes. Finely chop the onion. Separately blanch these three ingredients in fast-boiling salted water, the peppers for 3 minutes, the courgettes for about 4 minutes until the centres look transparent, and the onion for 1 minute. Drain and cool quickly in cold water. Pat dry on absorbent paper.

Quarter the tomatoes and combine with the blanched vegetables in a serving bowl. Sprinkle well with pepper.

To make the dressing, place the oil, vinegar and seasonings in a bowl or screw-topped jar and whisk or shake together until blended. Add scissor-snipped chives and pour over salad. Toss lightly and chill before serving.
Serves 6

MACKEREL WITH CIDER AND ROSEMARY

4 medium mackerel
150 ml (¼ pint) dry cider
30 ml (2 tbsp) chopped fresh rosemary or 10 ml (2 level tsp) dried
salt and pepper

Clean the mackerel and cut off their heads. Wash well under cold running water and drain in a colander. Make four or five deep diagonal slashes on either side of each fish.

Place the fish side by side in a shallow dish and spoon over the cider. Sprinkle the herbs and seasonings over the top, cover and leave to marinate in a cool place for 2–3 hours turning once.

Arrange the fish on a barbecue and brush with a little of the marinade. Grill for about 8 minutes on each side brushing frequently with the marinade.

Heat the remaining marinade in a small saucepan and spoon over the fish for serving.
Serves 4

Sumptuous Evenings

Winter dinner parties can be luxurious without being expensive. Look for warm, vibrant colours in settings and food to keep the mood of comfort.

Make the table look inviting for a dinner party and you immediately turn the occasion into something special. Guests notice attention to detail and an attractively arranged table will make them feel that you have taken extra care.

START WITH CHINA

Let your china dictate the style of the setting and you will find that the other tableware and decorations fall into line naturally. Be consistent – don't mix earthy pottery with cut glass and lace napkins – and choose a centrepiece that fits in with all the rest. Simple fruit or flowers, chosen to match china or cloth, are always effective, or you could be more opulent and go for a cluster of candles or a huge dish of candied fruit (shown right).

The sugar-encrusted limes, nectarines and apples make a true feast of subtle colour, heaped in their patterned bowl and gently echoing the shades of the oriental cloth. Frosting fruit is very easy – just paint with beaten egg white, sprinkle on caster sugar and shake off excess.

The table setting shown opposite is a perfect example of an idea for cosy winter evenings, where the accessories take their lead from the exotic pattern and rich colours of the china. The cloth is a deep shade of claret, picked out from the china, and reds and purples feature again in the superb harvest of fruit spilling over the centre. Polished red apples, the darkest of grapes and, in bright contrast, a pineapple, are intertwined with greenery to make a scene that is strongly reminiscent of the design on the plates.

Lighting is important for atmosphere. The soft glow of oil lamps or the flicker of candles are more appropriate in settings such as these than harsher lights would be. But don't be too discreet – guests need to see each other as well as what they are eating.

Another setting that is invitingly warm and friendly is shown on page 165. The wealth of lively colour and design comes from the clever use of inexpensive Indian cotton bedspreads made into curtains, pelmet and wall-hangings. The theme is taken up again on the table, which is completely covered with more Indian fabric, this time with a neater, smaller pattern. Yet another pattern appears on the napkins and the cinnamon china, and red wine glasses all contribute to the feeling of density and richness. It's a stunning effect that looks lavishly expensive but could in fact be achieved on a very slender budget.

FOOD – THE FINER POINTS

Most of the lunchtime recipe suggestions on pages 152-153 would be equally suitable for dinner. Some people prefer not to eat too heavy a meal late in the evening, so bear this in mind when planning the menu and deciding on the number of courses. You may want to include one or two more elaborate dishes if the party is to be fairly formal, but on the whole it's better – and much easier on the nerves – to stick to simple things you know you can do well.

Clever presentation makes all the difference between a dish that looks dull and one that looks interesting and appetizing. Simple garnishes and decorations don't take long to organize. Think beyond chopped parsley and strategically-placed swirls of cream – how about buttered crumbs, crumbled chestnuts or chopped hard-boiled egg on green vegetables; a light dusting of paprika or Parmesan on cheesy dishes; prettily-cut tomatoes or mushrooms in salads; single frosted grapes, or even frosted flowers, on desserts; pies richly glazed and intricately decorated with crescents of leftover pastry? None of them takes much effort or costs a fortune, but they will give your food a professional look that is worth cultivating.

Left: a thick crusting of white sugar makes everyday fruit look spectacularly ornamental Wash the fruit and dry carefully. Dip in lightly beaten egg white, toss in caster sugar and leave to dry on a cooling rack
Above: look down on splendour. Strong colours, eye-catching china and a magnificent cascade of fruit pull it all together

THE CHEESEBOARD

You can serve fruit and a cheeseboard *instead* of dessert *before* dessert or *after* dessert, The choice is yours and one of the nicest things about leisurely dinner parties is that your guests can chat idly into the night, nibbling on slivers of cheese, for as long as they can stay awake.

Cheese needs to be served in the peak of condition, so bear this in mind if you shop well in advance of the party. Some soft cheeses like Brie are only at their best for a short time. Always take cheese out of the fridge and unwrap it an hour or more before serving. Chilled cheese loses much of its flavour and needs to be brought to room temperature to be fully appreciated.

A good cheeseboard will have a fair selection of different types of cheese. Choose a strong-flavoured Cheddar to contrast with a milder Caerphilly, add a blue cheese like Stilton, a softer variety such as Camembert and perhaps a cheese with herbs or one made from goat's milk. Serve bread and biscuits, butter, and as an optional extra, a jug of crisp celery, with its green, frilly leaves.

ROGNONS SAUTÉS TURBIGO

15 lambs' kidneys
26 pickling onions
175 g (6 oz) butter
350 g (12 oz) mini pork sausages
350 g (12 oz) button mushrooms, halved
45 ml (3 level tbsp) flour
10–15 ml (2–3 tsp) tomato paste
45 ml (3 tbsp) sherry
600 ml (1 pint) beef stock
2 bay leaves
salt and pepper
6 slices white bread
vegetable oil
chopped fresh parsley to garnish

Skin the kidneys, cut them in half lengthways and remove the cores. Pour boiling water over the onions, leave them 2–3 minutes, then drain and skin them. Heat a large frying pan with 25 g (1 oz) butter. Cook the sausages until they are brown on all sides and remove them from the pan. Wipe the pan clean, add 75 g (3 oz) butter and cook the onions and mushrooms over a brisk heat for 3–4 minutes, shaking the pan. Add to the sausages. Add the remaining butter, and when it is foaming, put in the kidneys and sauté briskly for about 5 minutes until they are evenly coloured. Add them to the sausages. Strain the fat and return it to the pan. Stir the flour, tomato paste, sherry and stock into the juices. Bring to the boil, stirring all the time. Add the bay leaves, seasoning and sausage and kidney mixture. Cover and simmer for 20–25 minutes.

Trim the bread into small triangles. Fry in oil until they are golden brown. Drain well and serve around the kidneys. Garnish with parsley scattered on top. Serves 6

ORANGE SYRUP SPONGE

60 ml (4 tbsp) golden syrup
3 medium oranges
125 g (4 oz) butter or block margarine
125 g (4 oz) caster sugar
2 eggs, beaten
125 g (4 oz) self-raising flour, sifted

Butter a 1.1 litre (2 pint) pudding basin. Spoon the golden syrup into the base.

Grate the rind from 1 orange, squeeze and reserve the juice. Slice the remaining oranges thinly. Press the slices on to the base and sides of the basin.

Cream together the fat and sugar until light and creamy. Add the beaten eggs a little at a time with the rind and juice. Fold in the flour.

Spoon the sponge mixture into the basin. Cover with buttered greaseproof paper. Secure tightly. Steam for about 1½ hours. Unmould and serve with more warm syrup in a sauceboat, if you wish. Serves 6

Top: a plethora of pattern in shades of red and cinnamon, in which the table setting exactly complements the room's décor
Above: nursery puddings like orange syrup sponge find their place at the end of a winter's evening
Opposite: rougnons sautés is a winter dish fit for a king. Rich and warming, it is also elegant enough to serve to company, when graced with croutons

Special Suppers

Summertime and the cooking is easy – it's more a matter of mixing the freshest seasonal treats for a meal that is cool and inviting.

Parties held on summer evenings have a magic all of their own. It's something to do with the gradually fading light and the stillness of the air as the first stars appear. Even on chillier nights it often stays warm long enough at least to enjoy a drink outside before retreating indoors.

Candlelight comes into its own in summer. A romantic dinner for two (right) wouldn't have anything like the same impact without the flattering light of candles. The pink cloth and china are suitably pretty and the Victorian wrought iron chairs add a secondary decorative element.

For a day when it's a bit too cold to venture outside, the setting shown on page 168 finds a way to bring the garden to the table. The delightful flower-painted folding doors lend a summery atmosphere to a plain setting, whatever the time of year. Of course, not every household can run to such exotica, but ideas like this can act as a trigger for more easily achieved effects. Flower-patterned china or tablecloth, individual bowls of tiny blossoms at each place setting, an array of greenery on a nearby side table – any of these would have the effect of bringing summer inside.

FAIR WEATHER FOOD

The suggestions on pages 148–149 could all come into their own for a summer supper party. At this time of year, most fresh food can rely on its own natural good looks to cause a sensation. There is no harm in giving nature a helping hand once in a while though, and the Avocado Starters (page 168) look almost too perfect to be real. A platter of these, decorated with orange or lemon slices, would make a show-stopping centrepiece to a buffet table.

Another idea for a help-yourself supper would be an intriguing selection of seafood starters, like those shown on page 169. Elegant and enticing, you could either make them up in individual small portions as shown, or increase the quantities and serve one or more of them as a light main course.

Salmon steaks or chicken breasts are hot alternatives that would give hungry guests a bit more to get their teeth into. Add salads and hot herb-buttered bread to round out the meal.

When it comes to puddings, look no further than those shown here. Cool, pale, delicately decorated, they make a luscious ending to a meal that uses the best the season has to offer.

DRINKS WITH EVERYTHING

It's a nice idea, although unfortunately a rather expensive one, to offer guests a drink before dinner. However, there is really no need to lay on a vast choice and you can if you prefer simply offer the wine that you plan to drink with the first course. Other possible aperitifs include sherry,

Top: light, frothy concoctions – summer finalés – recipes are on page 168-169
Above: coffee and petit fours to linger over
Right: a table for two in idyllic setting, with more than a slight air of romance

one of the many types of vermouth, or a spirit-based mixture such as gin and tonic or whisky and soda.

If you are in the happy position of having a good selection of drinks on hand, you could try mixing a few cocktails. Don't be *too* generous when measuring out the ingredients though, especially if you are planning to move on to wine later, otherwise guests could find your party memorable for all the wrong reasons.

There is lots of information on buying and storing wines on pages 176–179. When you are faced with choosing wines to go with a particular meal the rule is – forget the old rules. While dry white wines certainly do go well with many starters and fish, there is no reason why you could not drink a young, light red wine instead. And a more full-bodied white wine could equally well be drunk with a sturdy beef casserole as the more usual red. Be guided by your taste and don't forget that some foods are better without wine at all – curries, dishes with a high acid content or very sweet puddings, unless you want to serve a sweet dessert wine or a madeira with the latter.

In most cases it is preferable to serve white and rosé wines chilled and red wine at room temperature, although some young red wines – like Beaujolais Nouveau – are better chilled. To chill a wine, refrigerate the bottle for an hour or two before serving, or immerse in an ice bucket for at least half an hour. Uncork red wines half an hour or more before serving to let them breathe and place them in a warm room to come up to room temperature. If you forget to do this in time, you can get away with warming a decanter thoroughly and pouring the wine into it.

If all this sounds as if it could put an unbearable strain on your budget, cheer yourself up with the thought that an informal supper for friends is not the place for a huge selection of smart drinks. If you can't afford to go the whole hog, opt instead for one white wine – still or sparkling – to go right through the meal. Look for the words *Appellation Controlée* on the label and you shouldn't go far wrong. Straightforward still wines that are dry, French, and suitable for the whole meal include Sauvignon and Muscadet.

After dinner, if resources run to it, you may want to serve a liqueur. Brandy or whisky, on their own or with water, ice or soda are suitable, and you could also provide one or more of the flavoured liqueurs widely available. Among some of the most interesting are kümmel, a caraway derivative said to be good for the digestion, calvados – a fiery, less acid, alternative to brandy, and good, old-fashioned port (see also page 178). Coffee is the other essential (see page 124 for more details).

SEAFOOD STARTERS

Individual starters always please and if they are done in aspic look as if you have taken a great deal of trouble. The subtle flavour of *Seafood Aspics* come from the white wine, herbs and onion in the jelly.

Small pasta shapes – they don't have to be shells – make *Tuna Pasta Hors D'Oeuvre* a slightly more filling starter and by adding a side dish of sliced tomato this would provide a main course.

Smoked Mackerel Pâté is interesting and tasty at the start of a meal or is excellent as a light meal. It is a very straightforward pâté to make. Simply beat together the flesh of 225g (8 oz) smoked mackerel, 10 ml (2 tsp) lemon juice, 1 crushed garlic clove, 225g (8 oz) sieved cottage cheese, 125g (4 oz) softened butter and seasonings. Turn into a serving dish or individual pots, pour 50 g (2 oz) butter over the top and chill before serving.

Another salad starter which is easy to assemble and is cool and refreshing is *Melon Seafood Salad.* It's mixture of crabmeat and flaked skate in a lemon cream dressing, sits on a green island of lightly perfumed melon and makes for a lovely marriage of taste and texture.

A more unusual and quite delicious cold starter is *Marinated Kipper and Avocado.* The kippers are left to marinate, in a well seasoned dressing, overnight. The avocado is sliced in the next day then it's ready to serve.

AVOCADO MOUSSE

3 medium ripe avocados

30 ml (2 tbsp) lemon juice

100g (4 oz) full fat soft cheese

60 ml (4 tbsp) mayonnaise

salt and pepper

half a 411g ($14\frac{1}{2}$ oz) can consommé

orange slices and watercress sprigs to garnish

Cut the avocados in half and remove the stone. Cut a thin slice off 3 of the avocado halves, cut the slices in half and remove peel. Toss these in half the lemon juice and reserve to garnish. Scoop out the flesh of the avocados and place in a blender or food processor. Add the remaining lemon juice, cheese, mayonnaise and seasonings and blend until smooth. Spoon back into the avocado shells and top with the reserved avocado slices. Spoon over the consommé and place in the refrigerator for about 1 hour until set. Garnish with orange slices and watercress sprigs and serve with French bread or hot buttered toast.

Top: flowers, flowers everywhere – climbing up the doors, as well as filling a more predictable bowl on the table
Above: Avocados are synonymous with summer, and avocado starter makes the most of this creamy fruit
Opposite: a selection of salad starters – see this page for ideas

CRUSHED RASPBERRY CREAMS

450g (1 lb) raspberries

60 ml (4 tbsp) icing sugar

60 ml (4 tbsp) orange flavoured liqueur

3 eggs, separated

75g (3 oz) caster sugar

300 ml (10 fl oz) whipping cream

10 ml (2 level tsp) gelatine.

Place the raspberries in a flat dish, reserving six berries for decoration. Sprinkle with the icing sugar and spoon

over the liqueur. Leave to stand for 1 hour. Purée in a blender or food processor then rub through a sieve to remove pips.

Whisk the egg yolks and caster sugar until *really* thick. Gradually whisk in the raspberry purée. Lightly whip the cream and fold a quarter into the raspberry mixture. Whip the remainder to a piping consistency, spoon into a piping bag fitted with a small star vegetable nozzle and refrigerate.

Soak the gelatine in 30 ml (2 tbsp) water in a small bowl. Dissolve by standing the bowl in a pan of gently simmering water. Leave to cool then stir quickly into the raspberry mixture.

When the raspbery mixture begins to set whisk the egg whites until stiff then fold into the mixture. Pour into glasses and refrigerate to set.

Decorate with the remaining whipped cream and whole rapsberries.
Serves 6

RASPBERRY SUMMER SALAD

75g (3 oz) granulated sugar

pared rind and juice of 1 medium orange

225g (8 oz) raspberies

225g (8 oz) green grapes, washed

1 large green eating apple, washed

In a pan, slowly dissolve the sugar with the pared orange rind and juice in 300 ml (½ pint) water. Bring to the boil then bubble till syrupy. Strain and cool. Wash and pick over the raspberries. Halve and seed the grapes.

Just before serving, quarter, core and finely chop the apple. Layer the prepared fruit in four deep glasses. Pour over the cooled syrup. Chill and serve.
Serves 4

RASPBERRY HIGHLAND CREAM

50g (2 oz) medium oatmeal

300 ml (10 fl oz) double cream

60 ml (4 tbsp) clear honey

45 ml (3 tbsp) whisky

350g (12 oz) fresh raspberries

Place the oatmeal in a grill pan (without the rack) and toast until golden brown, turning occasionally. Cool.

Lightly whip the cream then stir in the honey, whisky and cool oatmeal. Pick over the raspberies and reserve a few for decoration. Layer up the raspberries and cream mixture in four glasses, cover and refrigerate.

Allow to come to at room temperature for 30 minutes before serving. Decorate with reserved raspberries.
Serves 4

Big Occasions

Catering for a crowd needn't be nerve-racking. Plan ahead, get as much help as you can, then relax and enjoy yourself.

Once the numbers for a party begin to reach about thirty, it's time to start simplifying. Choose uncomplicated dishes that can be made well ahead and won't mind waiting around in the fridge or freezer. Take stock of your surroundings and decide realistically how many people you can cope with in comfort. Then start borrowing. No one has china, glasses or cutlery on such a scale, so fall back on generous friends, or failing that, consider hiring. Paper plates and plastic cutlery are all very well, but they have neither the ease of use or appearance of the real thing.

Next consider the food. Is it going to be strictly 'nibbles' only, or are you aiming for a full-scale meal? If so, and you can't guarantee a seat for all your guests, choose a dish that is easy to tackle with a fork. Casseroles, rice and pasta dishes, mild curries, all come into this category. Steer clear of sliced cold meats, jacket potatoes, large lettuce leaves and anything else that demands knife and fork to transfer it safely from plate to mouth.

Hot dishes are always popular at large gatherings, but you will almost certainly have to supplement them with one or more cold options, depending on the size of your oven. Choose cold puddings, even in winter, otherwise the serving will get far too complicated. You can certainly go to town decorating the food itself, but keep the table relatively simple – with all those dishes, there is not likely to be much room for lavish decorating anyway.

ORGANIZING THE TABLE

Set up the table carefully and lay it out in such a way that people can progress round it in a logical order, without having to backtrack. If necessary, bring out the desserts after the main dishes have been finished with and cleared away, or have them set out on a separate smaller table. Divide anything that is sliceable – cakes, pâtés, quiches – into portions before putting on the table. It's not mean, it simply makes it easier for people to serve themselves when they are already juggling with plate and glass.

If you decide on finger food rather than a large meal, you will need to recruit a few helpers to hand things round. Borrow some good-sized trays or platters and provide paper napkins if any of the food is inclined to be greasy. Hot nibbles are especially moreish – tiny vol-au-vents, chunks of deep fried scampi or chicken, slivers of pizza – but they do mean that someone has to stay in the kitchen to produce them in relays.

GETTING SET

Finalize the menu well in advance of the big day and start cooking as soon as you can to avoid a last minute panic. A freezer is invaluable for this sort of exercise and if you don't own one it's worth trying to persuade a friend to 'lend' you some freezer space. A food processor is another invaluable ally for chopping, slicing and mixing large amounts of ingredients.

Get the final preparations under way on the day before the party. Most dishes will keep fresh for 24 hours, provided they are well covered with clingfilm. Keep piped cream toppings on desserts below the rim of the dish to make covering easier. Even salads can be assembled in the morning and dressed at the last minute.

Judging quantities is always tricky, especially if you don't usually cater for more than two at a time. Consult a reliable recipe book and if in doubt remember that it's better to have too much food than not enough, so err on the side of generosity. As for drink, ½–¾ bottle of wine per head is about right. You will also need to have soft drinks or fruit juices for those who don't like alcohol. Wine cups and punches are a good way of stretching less wine round a lot of people.

Right: for a really grandiose party, a marquee adds a marvellous sense of occasion. Majestic candlesticks and an impressive flower arrangement all add to the feeling of festivity. Marquees are available in a wide range of sizes, with and without floors. Installation companies can also provide ribbons and swags to give an even grander touch

MUSHROOM SAVOURIES

450 g (1 lb) button mushrooms, wiped

25 g (1 oz) butter

50 g (2 oz) fresh brown breadcrumbs

20 ml (4 level tsp) mango chutney

salt and pepper

seasoned flour

2 eggs, size 2, beaten

grated Parmesan cheese

mayonnaise to serve

Remove the stalks from the mushrooms and chop them finely. Melt the butter in a pan, stir in the chopped stalks and half the breadcrumbs. Sauté for 2–3 minutes. Remove from heat and stir in the chutney (cut up large chunks) and seasonings.

Sandwich two mushroom caps together with a little of the mixture. Roll the mushrooms in seasoned flour, dip in egg and coat with the remaining breadcrumbs mixed with 50 g (2 oz) Parmesan cheese. Chill.

Deep fry for 3–4 minutes until golden brown. Drain well, roll in more Parmesan while hot. Leave to cool completely. Serve on cocktail sticks with mayonnaise.
Makes about 30 stuffed mushrooms

CREAM OF PARSLEY SOUP

450 g (1 lb) parsley

450 g (1 lb) onions, skinned

225 g (8 oz) celery

100 g (4 oz) butter or margarine

90 ml (6 level tbsp) flour

4 litres (7 pints) chicken stock, preferably jellied

salt and pepper

300 ml (½ pint) single cream

Wash the parsley, drain and roughly chop. Slice the onion and celery. Melt the fat in a large saucepan and add the parsley, onion and celery. Cover the pan and cook gently until the vegetables are quite soft. Shake the pan from time to time.

Stir in the flour until smooth then gradually mix in the stock. Season and bring to the boil. Cover the pan and simmer for 25–30 minutes. Cool a little then purée in a blender or food processor. Reheat, adjust seasoning and stir in cream just before serving.
Serves 16

POACHED SALMON TROUT

1 or 2 salmon trout, total weight when cleaned about 1.75 kg (4 lb)

150 ml (¼ pint) medium dry white wine

slices of onion

1 bay leaf

salt and pepper

300 ml (½ pint) liquid aspic jelly

45 ml (3 tbsp) sherry

slices of lemon, cucumber and endive to garnish

Rinse the fish, remove eyes and trim tail and fins. Place in a fish kettle or other deep roasting container. Pour over the wine with sufficient water just to cover the fish. Add the onion and bay leaf with salt and pepper.

Bring slowly to the boil, cover the pan and simmer very gently for about 25 minutes or until the fish begins to ease away from the bone. Lift out of the liquid then ease off the skin. Leave to cool then place the fish on a serving platter.

Make up the aspic as directed on the packet and include the sherry. As the aspic begins to set, brush some over the fish. Leave to set. Coat with several layers of aspic in the same way. Warm the aspic gently if necessary.

Garnish the fish with slices of lemon and cucumber. Brush more aspic on top of the garnish. Arrange endive on the side of the dish and serve with lemon or watercress mayonnaise.
Serves 16 small buffet portions

BRAISED BEEF IN ASPIC

1 kg (2 lb) silverside

225 g (8 oz) carrot, peeled

1 medium onion, skinned

125 g (4 oz) back bacon, rinded

15 g (½ oz) lard

15 ml (1 level tbsp) tomato paste

1.25 ml (¼ level tsp) ground allspice

150 ml (¼ pint) red wine

salt and pepper

2 × 28.3 g (1 oz) packets aspic powder

small gherkins to garnish

Trim the beef. Dice the carrot, onion and bacon. Melt the lard in a deep flameproof casserole. Sauté the vegetables and bacon lightly for 5–7 minutes, stir in the tomato paste and allspice. Place beef on top, pour over wine and season. Bring to the boil, cover tightly and cook in the oven to 160°C/325°F (Gas Mark 3) for 2¾ hours.

Remove beef from casserole and leave to cool completely. Strain off the liquid and reserve. Cool vegetables and bacon. Make reserved juices up to 1.1 litre (2 pints) with water. Chill and skim off the fat. Bring juices to the boil and dissolve the aspic powder in the hot liquid.

Meanwhile, thinly slice the beef. Layer with the vegetables and bacon in a 2 litre (3½ pint) serving dish. Pour over 900 ml (1½ pint) aspic. Chill to set. Garnish with gherkins. Spoon over the remaining aspic.
Serves 8 buffet portions

TURKEY JULIENNE WITH ASPARAGUS

1 kg (2 lb) turkey fillet
chicken stock
30 ml (2 level tbsp) chopped fresh parsley
50 g (2 oz) chopped walnuts
20 ml (4 level tsp) ground ginger
450 ml (¾ pint) garlic vinaigrette
450 g (1 lb) fresh asparagus
salt
celery leaves to garnish

Poach the turkey fillets in well-seasoned chicken stock for about 20 minutes until tender. Leave to cool in the liquid.

Stir the parsley, walnuts and ginger into the vinaigrette. Tie the asparagus in bundles of six to eight stalks. Stand them upright in a pan of boiling salted water and cook for 10–15 minutes until tender. Drain. While still hot stir in half the dressing. Leave to cool.

Cut the turkey into 1 cm (½ in) wide strips. Marinate in the remaining dressing for 2–3 hours. To serve, arrange the turkey strips and asparagus in a serving dish. Garnish with celery leaves.
Serves 16 buffet portions

FRESH CHERRY AND LEMON CHEESECAKE

75 g (3 oz) butter
125 g (5 oz) caster sugar
150 g (5 oz) plain flour
1 egg yolk
225 g (8 oz) full fat soft cheese
225 g (8 oz) cottage cheese, sieved
2 eggs, separated
2 juicy lemons
150 ml (¼ pint) soured cream
300 ml (½ pint) double cream
15 ml (1 level tbsp) gelatine
225 g (8 oz) fresh red cherries, halved and stoned, or 1 × 213 g (7½ oz) can cherries, drained
angelica to decorate

Cream butter with 75 g (3 oz) sugar. Mix to a firm dough with the flour and 1 egg yolk. Roll out half the dough to fit the base of a 20 cm (8 in) spring-release cake tin, and the other half to fit a 20 cm (8 in) flan ring placed on a baking sheet. Bake both in the oven at 180°C/350°F (Gas Mark 4) for about 15 minutes. Cut the flan ring into 10 wedges and cool on a wire rack. Leave other round in tin.

With an electric mixer, beat together the cheeses, 2 egg yolks, finely grated rind of the lemons, 75 ml (5 tbsp) lemon juice, the remaining sugar and soured cream. Stir in half the double cream.

Sprinkle the gelatine in 45 ml (3 tbsp) water in a small bowl. Stand the bowl over a pan of hot water and heat until gelatine is dissolved. Leave to cool then stir into the cheese mixture. Refrigerate until beginning to set.

Whisk the egg whites until stiff. Fold the cherries and egg whites into the cheese mixture, turn into tin and refrigerate. To serve, unmould, place pastry wedges on top and decorate with angelica.
Serves 10

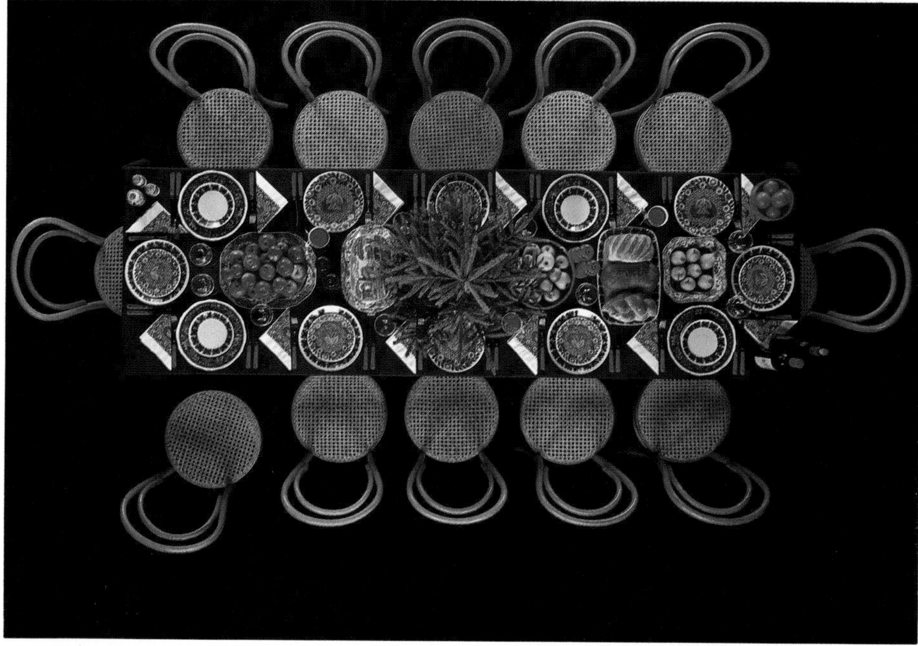

Opposite, top: elegance is often associated with pale colours, but the deep, lacquer reds in this buffet setting give the lie to this concept
Top: not everyone can afford silver candlelabra and crystal. But if you do have them, help your guests to enjoy them by deploying them carefully. Their beauty is timeless and beyond fashion
Above: mixing and matching of plates and patterns, if done with sensitivity and assurance, can actually add to the atmosphere

TIPS TO MAKE A COOK'S LIFE EASIER

Clever shortcuts, simple ways to tackle tricky preparations, money-saving ideas – a round-up of hints to help you entertain effortlessly.

MEAT AND POULTRY

- Although duck makes a delicious dinner party dish, there is a high proportion of bone to meat, especially on birds weighing less than 1.5 kg (3 lb). Allow about 400 g (14 oz) bought weight per person to give good-sized portions.
- Some recipes call for very thinly sliced liver – easier to do if you pour over boiling water, leave for one minute, then drain and slice the liver immediately.
- To be sure of really crunchy crackling on roast pork, make deep cuts across the rind with a very sharp knife then rub in oil and salt before cooking. Roast uncovered.
- Tough steak is a great disappointment, so tenderize it by giving it a good pounding with a steak mallet. Place the steak between sheets of waxed paper to stop it sticking to the mallet.
- Meat for a casserole will brown evenly if you press it down onto the surface of the frying pan with a spatula.
- The easiest way to coat meat or chicken pieces is to place them in a polythene bag with the seasoned flour and shake well.
- To remove fat from the top of a casserole, pass a piece of kitchen paper across the surface. Alternatively, strain off the liquid and add a few ice cubes. The fat will set around them, they can then be removed with a slotted spoon and the de-fatted liquid returned to the pan.
- Don't panic if a curry turns out too hot – cool it down with lemon juice, potato, milk, soured cream or yogurt, whichever is to hand.
- Cream makes simple stews special, it's true, but remember to check the seasoning once the cream has gone in – you will almost certainly need more.
- For quick cocktail nibbles, snip bacon rinds into 2 cm (1 in) lengths and place in a very hot oven until crispy.
- It's preferable to soak bacon or gammon joints overnight to cut down on saltiness, but if you forget, just cover the joint with cold water, bring to the boil, throw away the water then cook as usual, in fresh water.
- Leave a little space between cubes of meat or poultry when making kebabs – helps them cook more evenly on the skewer.

FISH

- Anchovies are a traditional garnish for pizza, but they can be unbearably salty. Soak them in milk for an hour or so before use for a better flavour.
- Skinning fish is an awkward job, made simpler if you use a scallop shell and work in the direction of the head, against the lie of the scales.
- Get to grips with fish when skinning it by dipping your fingers in salt.
- Danish lumpfish roe doesn't cost the earth and makes a very effective garnish for egg mayonnaise.

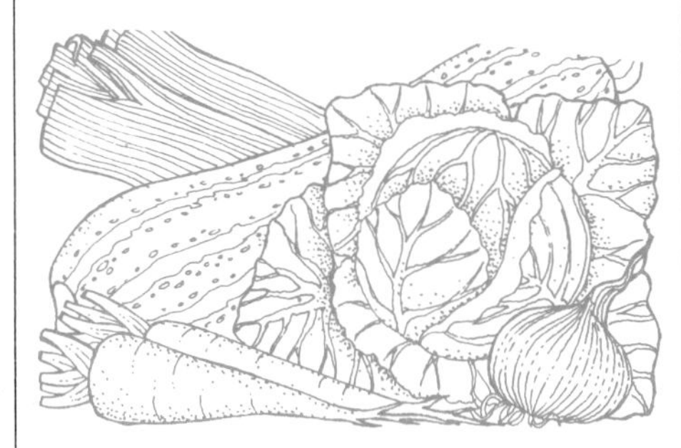

VEGETABLES

- Skin peppers by turning them under a hot grill until the skin blackens and blisters. Place in cold water immediately and the skins will rub off.
- Never buy more new potatoes than you can use in three days. They don't keep well.
- New potatoes are easier to scrape if you soak them in warm water for a few minutes first. It's easier still to cook them in their skins and either peel the skins off when they are done, or eat them with the skins on.
- Roast potatoes should be very crisp and crunchy. Parboil for about 7 minutes, then rough the surface with a fork before adding to very hot fat.
- Jacket potatoes will cook more quickly with a metal skewer pushed through the centre of each one.
- Always dress salads just before serving, and don't overdo the dressing. If you must dress them earlier, invert a saucer in the bottom of the salad bowl, to stop the dressing forming a pool.
- Wooden salad bowls dry out and crack if washed. Just wipe well with kitchen paper after use.
- Salt in the cooking water makes sweetcorn kernels tough, so always cook lightly in unsalted water.
- Onions brown faster if you add a spot of sugar to the pan when frying them.
- Cultivated mushrooms don't need peeling, just thorough wiping.
- Don't cut a chilled lettuce as it will brown and wilt quickly. Instead, break it into pieces.
- Leeks are tricky to clean properly – simpler to slice them first, then wash.
- Dried beans are useful for hearty casseroles, but soaking them is a bother. To shorten the soaking time, bring them to the boil in water, then soak for 1–2 hours off the heat before cooking in fresh water.
- French dressing is best stored in a screw-topped jar somewhere cool, but not in the fridge. Salad oil tastes better if you keep a couple of olives in the bottle.
- Chicory that has green tips will be very bitter.
- You can refresh slightly sad celery by wrapping in newspaper and standing it upright in cold water.
- If fresh French or runner beans start to wilt, chill them in a polythene bag in the fridge to restore crispness.
- Avocados are notorious for discolouring, but you can prevent a mixture from browning by popping the stone in and covering with clingfilm. Remember to remove the stone before serving.
- Asparagus rolls make a lovely buffet snack. Roll the bread with a rolling pin before buttering to make it easier to handle.
- Aubergines can be bitter and need careful preparation. Slice them and sprinkle with salt. Rinse with cold water after 30 minutes then dry well.

FRUIT AND NUTS

- The simplest way to skin peaches or grapes is to place the fruit in boiling water for 15 seconds before peeling.
- No need to fiddle about with a knife when coring pineapple slices – a small round pastry cutter, pressed firmly over the core, does the job more efficiently.

• You will get a better yield of juice from lemons if you warm them slightly before squeezing. Store lemons for up to six weeks in a polythene bag in the fridge.
• If a recipe calls for rind and juice of oranges or lemons, grate the rind before you squeeze the juice. A potato peeler works well as a zester.
• Blanched almonds that have dried up will improve if soaked in hot water for half an hour. Alternatively blanch them when needed by steeping in boiling water for a couple of minutes, then placing in cold. The skins will rub off easily. If you need almond slivers, cut them when still damp after blanching.
• Don't give hazelnuts the boiling water treatment if you want to skin them – instead grill until the skins split, place the nuts in a plastic bag and rub them against each other until the skins come off.
• You can crack walnuts without nutcrackers by squeezing two together in your hand.
• Once you have opened packets of salted nuts, keep them in the fridge. Re-seal the pack with a twist tie or keep in a small airtight box.
• Melons lose their flavour if served icy cold, so don't chill them for too long before you want to eat them.
• Frozen fruit juice is very handy to have in the freezer and can be quickly reconstituted, with the right amount of water, in a blender at low speed.
• Fresh dates can have rather tough skins – simply removed by squeezing the stem end.
• Fresh blackcurrants have a marvellous flavour but can be tricky to prepare. Strip the berries from the stalks with a fork, or open freeze whole and store in a rigid box. When needed, shake the box well before thawing and most of the berries will fall off the stalks.
• Apple sauce is simple to make in the pan. Just use a potato masher to pulp the stewed apples once they are tender.

PASTA AND RICE

A tablespoonful of oil in the water stops pasta boiling over and helps prevent the pieces sticking together. Cook without the lid and make sure the pasta retains some bite.
• Noodles swell by about a quarter when cooked, but spaghetti and macaroni double in size.
• Fresh pasta needs only five minutes' cooking, compared with 10–15 minutes for dried pasta.
• Rice can be cooked in advance and kept, covered, for up to three days in the fridge. Allow 50 g (2 oz) uncooked weight per person. Dot with butter, cover and reheat in a moderate oven. Fork through after 15 minutes.

EGGS, CHEESE, CREAM, BUTTER

• Egg whites will stubbornly refuse to whisk if there is a hint of grease on bowl or whisk. Rubbing a cut lemon round the bowl helps increase the volume and a *small* pinch of salt strengthens the albumen.
• After a meringue-making session, store the yolks, covered with water, for up to five days in the fridge. Use them to replace whole eggs in dishes where the white is not needed to aerate the other ingredients. Two yolks plus 1 tbsp water equals one whole egg.
• You can use frozen cream in hot dishes without thawing first, but don't allow the dish to boil once the cream has been added or it could curdle.
• Chill bowl and whisk before whipping cream. A stiffly whisked egg white folded into whipped cream increases bulk and equal amounts of single and double cream whipped together make a lighter result. You can rescue slightly over-whipped cream by adding a little milk.
• Choose mature cheese for cooking – the stronger flavour means you can use less.
• Always cook cheesy dishes over a gentle heat and never allow them to boil, otherwise the cheese will turn stringy.
• Cheese keeps well closely wrapped in foil or clingfilm in the fridge, but needs to be removed and unwrapped at least an hour before serving to let the flavour come out.
• Butter curls are pretty for dinner parties – make them with a potato peeler, using a block of firm butter.

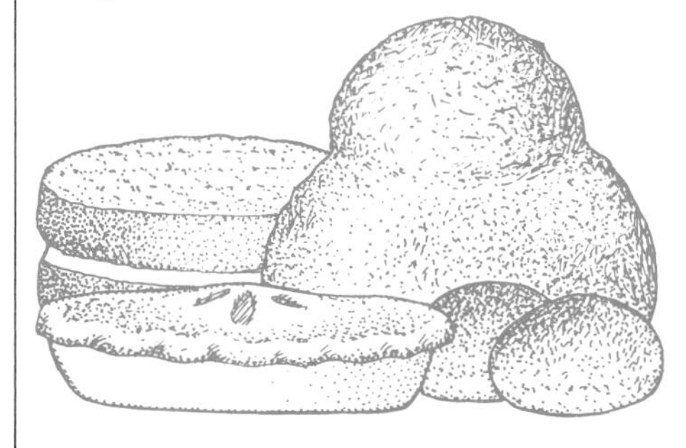

BREAD, BISCUITS, CAKES, PASTRY

• Pastry likes to 'rest' for about half an hour in the fridge before rolling out – makes it easier to handle, as well as shorter.
• Don't overdo the rolling out as the pastry will shrink during cooking if it has been overstretched.
• Neatest way to trim a lined flan ring is to run a rolling pin across the top. Stop the edges from burning by covering them with strips of foil.
• There is nothing worse than a soggy-bottomed flan. You can improve matters by brushing the base with egg white before baking blind, and standing glass and earthenware dishes on a pre-heated metal baking sheet.
• Use vegetable oil to grease baking tins and the finished dish is less likely to stick.
• You can tell if the egg and sugar mixture for a fatless sponge has been whisked enough by lifting the whisk out – it should leave a trail.
• Chill fresh bread in the fridge and it will be easier to slice without crumbling.
• The crusty ends of loaves can be instantly made into crumbs in a blender and frozen – no need to thaw before using.
• One or two sugar lumps in the biscuit tin will keep the contents crisp.
• Crush biscuits for a flan base in a strong polythene bag – bash and roll well with a rolling pin.
• Place flans on an upturned baking tray so you can just slide them off when cooked.

SEASONING AND SAUCES

• Bring the ingredients for mayonnaise to room temperature before you start and the sauce is less likely to curdle. If the worst does happen, whisk the curdled mayonnaise, drop by drop, into another egg yolk.
• Vanilla sugar gives a delightfully subtle flavour to cakes and custards. Place a vanilla pod in 500 g (1 lb) caster sugar in an airtight tin. It takes several weeks for the flavour to reach full strength.
• Salads take on a discreet garlic flavour if the bowl is rubbed over with a cut clove, before putting in the salad.
• Garlic and spices take a bitter flavour if fried for too long.
• Fresh parsley really does take away the smell of day-old garlic from the breath. Eat one or two sprigs.
• Mace and nutmeg are interchangeable as they come from the same plant. Mace is a little stronger.
• Retain as much flavour as possible in herbs by adding them to slow-cooking dishes 10 minutes or so before you want to eat.
• If a sauce insists on staying lumpy, it can be strained, whisked or blended into perfect smoothness.
• Hollandaise is quick to curdle if overheated, but can usually be rescued by placing in a cold bowl and whisking strenuously. Strain it as well, if necessary.
• Cover sauces not needed straight away with a disc of dampened greaseproof paper to stop a skin forming.
• You will get a better flavour if you add seasonings to vegetables *after* they have been cooked. Finely chopped crisply grilled bacon, crumbled chestnuts, browned flaked almonds or grated nutmeg all add flavour and interest to cooked green vegetables.

Buying And Serving Wine And Other Drinks

Good food is only half the key to successful entertaining. Good drink also needs careful attention.

Although they may not think so, people in Britain are fortunate in not living in a wine-producing country, since this means they get a far wider choice of wines. Those who live where there are good local wines tend to stick to them, particularly for everyday drinking, and have a more limited selection. Prices for good drinking wines are also reasonable here.

Sampling different wines and discovering which ones you like can prove a rewarding interest for the novice and there are many good books around which give guidance on different varieties and vintages.

EVERYDAY DRINKING

Wine for immediate drinking can be bought as and when you require it. Supermarket shelves stock a good selection at reasonable prices and by experimenting you will discover the ones you like best. Cheap 'carafe' style wines do not benefit from being kept, so although you will probably want to keep a few bottles in the home at any one time, any suitable storage space you have (see page 178) should be reserved for keeping wines which will improve with age.

If you want advice on everyday drinking you are unlikely to get it in a supermarket. Many chains, however, now give some guidance as to what the wine is likely to taste like, either on the label or on the shelf. Asking for help in an off-licence can be risky. Some managers have a good knowledge of their stock while others have virtually none. Some off-licence chains have adopted a system of numbering which indicates to the prospective buyer where each wine falls on a scale, from sweet to dry.

Don't be put off by specialist wine merchants. They too sell a good choice of wines that are ready for drinking now and will be happy to give advice on what to buy. Provided you can visit their premises you can buy bottles singly if you wish, but if you are having wine delivered it is uneconomic to order less than a case (12 bottles). But there is no reason why this should not be mixed. Special offers in newspapers and magazines are often a good way of sampling a selection of wines at competitive prices.

FINE WINES

However happy you are with your everyday wines there will be occasions, food and people which deserve something better. If you can buy wines at their opening price, when they are still young and not ready to drink, you will end up – after correct storage – with wines at their best but which could be selling in shops and auctions at prices out of your reach.

In general it is worthwhile laying down more red than white wines, since they take longer to mature and tend to increase more in value, but the best white wines are also worth storing. Don't buy more wine than you are able to drink. Once the cellar bug has bitten you it is easy to be seduced into 'bargains' which you may never enjoy. Unless you have the cellars of a stately home it's unlikely that you will be able to store in sufficient quantities to make selling for profit a viable proposition.

Above: an ingenious spot for keeping a few dozen bottles at the ready for everyday drinking is under the sideboard at one end of this kitchen/diner
Right: a more stately solution is to fill up a fireplace with a wine rack. Some firms will custom-make racks in sizes to fit any nook or cranny. Again, this is only a short-term storage solution

DON'T FILL THE CUP

Wine glasses should enable the drinker to enjoy wine in terms both of flavour and smell (known as 'bouquet'). Ideally they should be of clear glass, so that the colour can be appreciated as well. But many people prefer glasses which are cut or engraved. What *is* all important is the shape, which should curve in at the top yet be wide enough to allow the drinker to swirl the wine round the glass to get the effect of the bouquet and appreciate it fully.

Size of glass is less important, although a glass which is too small will make the pourer look mean. Wine should *never* come more than two-thirds of the way up the sides or the drinker will not be able to appreciate it to the full.

This glass lore only applies to fine wines. Everyday *vins de table* will taste the same, whether drunk from your best crystal or from cheap tumblers.

APERITIFS

Though many people like to drink wine as an aperitif, unless you are sure of your friends' tastes you will probably want to keep a basic stock of other drinks too.

Sherry is the classic aperitif and can be deemed to come from Spain unless another country of origin is stated on the label. In general only dry and medium sherries are served as aperitifs; the paler the colour of the sherry the drier it will taste. The driest sherries of all are described as manzanilla, next driest is fino and less dry is amontillado. Oloroso sherries are sweeter but often have an oily finish.

Dry sherries are best served slightly chilled. The correct type of glass in which to serve them is a *copita,* a small, narrow-

Come to a
SUPER
party!

stemmed glass with the rim curved in to leave a relatively small drinking aperture.

Vermouth is a wine-based drink flavoured with the herb wormwood which gives it a slightly aromatic and bitter taste. Vermouths may be white or red and sweet or dry according to taste and are usually served chilled and with ice in a small, straight-sided glass.

Other popular drinks before meals include gin, vodka and whisky for which you will require an appropriate selection of mixers such as tonic, bitter lemon and ginger ale. These are best served in heavy based tumblers with ice.

Aperitifs which are a more acquired taste include bitter drinks like Campari and Punt e Mes, which may be drunk neat or diluted with soda or tonic, and aniseed-flavoured drinks like Pernod and Ricard, which are served diluted with about four parts of water and ice.

BRANDY AND LIQUEURS

The perfect end to a good meal is what the French appropriately call a *fin* – a small quantity of highly alcoholic spirit with a strong flavour.

Brandy is regarded by connoisseurs as *the* spirit to drink after a meal and the choice ranges from young rather fiery marc to the finest old cognac. True cognac comes from grapes produced in a strictly delineated area of western France. After being distilled twice it is blended, then matured in casks, and never exported until it is at least three years old. The most expensive cognac contains the highest proportion of older brandies in the blend.

Armagnac comes from south-western France and may be distilled once or twice. It is left to mature in casks for a minimum of 10 years but even then has a more fiery, raw taste than cognac.

Marc brandy is lower-quality brandy distilled from grape residue pressings. It is cheaper than cognac and armagnac but tastes distinctly raw and has a less subtle flavour.

Liqueurs are made from spirit blended with fruit and/or herbs or other flavourings. There are many to choose from, most of which are made to secret age-old recipes whose exact ingredients are unknown. The best known liqueurs include Bénédictine (brandy-based, flavoured with fruit peel, herbs and edible plants), Cherry brandy (cherries infused in brandy), Cointreau (orange flavoured), Drambuie (whisky-based, flavoured with herbs and honey), Grand Marnier (cognac-based, flavoured with orange), Kirsch (spirit and cherries), Kümmel (spirit and caraway seeds), Sambuca (liquorice-flavoured), and Tia Maria (rum based, flavoured with coffee).

Three wine glasses and sherry glass

White wine glasses

Champagne flutes

Brandy balloons

Red or white wine glasses

Claret glasses

STORING YOUR WINE

If you don't have suitable space for storing wine in your home there is little point in laying down a stock of fine wines. Wines that are maturing gently towards perfect drinking need to be kept somewhere with a cool, even temperature. Obviously an underground cellar is the best place of all, but few homes today come with one and it may be possible to find a spot somewhere that meets all requirements and maintains a temperature of about 10–13°C (50–55°F). Slight fluctuations between winter and summer won't matter since these occur slowly and naturally; what you *must* avoid is a place in which central heating or bright sunlight affects the temperature. This is why wine racks in kitchens or dining rooms – even if they look visually appealing and blend in with the surrounding décor – should only be used for storing wine that is in brief transit between shop or storage and consumption.

Garages and outhouses are not suitable for storing wine, as they could get too cold in winter which adversely affects its condition.

Darkness is important for wine to mature as, if it is left in the light for any length of time, it will start to lose colour and the flavour will deteriorate. Dampness, however, is perfectly acceptable – the only drawback is that it can cause the labels on the bottles to become detached so that you are unable to identify that eagerly-anticipated first growth claret when the time comes to drink it.

Cool cupboards can be turned into good wine stores, but bear in mind that wine doesn't benefit from vibration. If you have a horde of children who thunder up and down stairs incessantly, the cupboard below is no place for your cellar. All wine should be stored horizontally so that the air between the wine and the cork is eliminated. Special racks are the best place to hold bottles securely and it's sensible to position each one with its label uppermost so you can see at a glance what a wine is without disturbing it. If your stock of wine starts running into dozens of bottles it could be easier to keep a cellar book which logs what you have got, when you bought it and what you paid, to save crawling sessions looking for a particular wine.

If you have nowhere to store fine wines but wish to build up a cellar, most wine merchants will, for a fee, keep it for you. But over a period of years this can obviously cost a fair amount.

SERVING WINE

While most people know the general theory that white wines should be served chilled and red wines at room temperature, they are not sure how cold 'chilled' is and what the temperature of the room is meant to be. In general you can chill dry and young white wines either by putting them in the fridge for an hour or so or by placing them in a bucket of ice and cold water for about 10–15 minutes. Ice and water will chill more efficiently and quickly than ice on its own, and there is no need for a special bucket: you can use a kitchen plastic one, provided your guests don't see it. Sweet white dessert wines should be chilled for a little longer and should be opened about half an hour before drinking to allow them to breathe.

Light red wines like Beaujolais and those from the Loire are best served cooled slightly or at a temperature of around 15° (60°F). Red wines with a higher alchohol content should be opened about an hour before you drink them and served at a temperature of 15–20°C (60-68°F). Full-bodied red wines need to be open for longer before drinking, sometimes up to five or six hours depending on type.

Fine wines should not be drunk on the day they have been bought as the journey will have disturbed them. Allow a couple of days, at least, for them to rest in a horizontal position. Then place them in an upright position for a day or two so that the sediment sinks to the bottom of the bottle. The wine should then be decanted into a glass decanter, leaving the sediment in the bottle. To be sure that no sediment seeps into the decanter, shine a torch or light a candle behind the bottle to illuminate the wine as you pour. Always pour gently down the side of the tilted decanter so as not to aerate the wine.

WINE AND FOOD

While there are a number of generally observed guidelines about wine and food, it is important for you to experiment with different combinations and find out what you like. The recommendation that fish should be eaten with white wine, for example, derives from the fact that it makes red wine taste metallic. Other foods have properties which mean they are best not consumed with wine or make the choice of wine very difficult. Some examples are curries – which overpower wine – chocolate, some smoked meat and fish, salad dressings made with vinegar, and fruit salad.

Top right: the drinks tray waits to welcome guests. The soda-siphon is gaining in popularity again, after a domination of several years by bottled soda water

Right: the lower section of a bookshelf acts as a compact, attractive storage space for bottles ready for drinking. A spot such as this, exposed to light and central heating, should never be used for long-term maturation

PART TWO

A GREEN HOUSE: PLANTS INSIDE AND OUT

CHAPTER FIVE

THE INSIDE STORY

TAKING FLOWERS INDOORS

Flowers and pot-plants are not frivolous luxuries. They are one of the cheapest ways of making a home look good.

As well as a link with, or a reminder of the changing seasons, plants and flowers are a vital ingredient of successful interiors, and can play a major role in making them work.

They can clinch a room's colour statement with related colour or introduce the element of surprise with a contrast. They are an instant way of filling a bare corner, or bringing interest to boring areas. They have a softening effect on stiff surroundings. But above all, they introduce a spontaneity and freshness that makes a room come alive. So don't wait for people to give you flowers and pot-plants as presents, or treat them as occasional extras in your home. On the contrary, take advantage of their enormous versatility all year round.

GETTING THE BEST FROM FRESH FLOWERS

Flowers suffer from shock when they are abruptly taken from their natural environment and put in new and artificial surroundings, so aim to make the transition as smooth as possible. They will reward your efforts by living much longer.

When to pick

If you have a garden of your own, take full advantage of having fresh flowers on the doorstep. Cut flowers early in the morning, when they have had a good night's rest to recover from the warmth of the previous day. Failing that, cut them in the evening. At all costs, avoid cutting them while the sun is strong and hot – they will be limp and vulnerable from loss of moisture.

Although everyone talks about 'picking' flowers, with the exceptions of cyclamens and Iris stylosa (where stems need pulling right out) it's absolutely essential that you cut them. Whether you use scissors, secateurs or a knife, it is vital that the cutting tool is sharp, to minimize the risk of bruising.

Always cut flower stems at an angle – this increases the area that can take up water – and if feasible, give them a drink immediately. Ideally, take a bucket of water round the garden with you – preferably water with the chill taken off, rather than icy-cold water straight from the tap.

What to pick

Choose flowers just as they are coming into full bloom. Any earlier, and they will be too immature to develop in water; any later, and they may already be on the downward path. Roses are an obvious example of this truth: young buds shrivel instead of opening up and fully-blown flowers promptly drop their petals. Use stamens as a guide, as well as the state of petals. If they are dusted with pollen, blooms are already past their best. This is particularly useful for judging when to cut daisy-type flowers such as dahlias, marguerites and Michaelmas daisies, where the centres should be firm at the time of picking.

With long spires of flowers – like lupins, foxgloves and delphiniums – cut when the lower flowers are fully open, but there are a few inches of top buds yet to burst. Then you can snip off the lower blooms as they die and the upper blooms will happily take over.

As always, there are a few exceptions. Blossom and daffodils should be picked while still in tight bud, because they will soon burst open in the heat of the house. So also should pussy willow and branches of horse chestnut. Poppies should be picked just as their buds are bursting open; peonies the instant their petals begin unfurling. But chrysanthemums – which last the longest of all cut flowers except orchids – can be cut when the flowers are fully open.

How to condition

All flowers live longer if they are left to stand in a bucketful of water for several hours before being arranged. Put the bucket somewhere cool and dark – or at least away from the glare of the sun.

Right: if you're keeping to all-white, mix different shapes and shades and unlikely blooms to get a rich texture. Here, bluish hosta leaves, lime tobacco plant and vines increase variety

Again, the water should have the chill off, and chrysanthemums and carnations prefer warm water; peonies, dahlias, stocks and some foliage enjoy a long drink of fairly hot water. But first make sure they can absorb the moisture.

Woody-stemmed flowers

Flowering shrubs like rhododendrons, mock-orange (Philadelphus), roses and lilac, and woody-stemmed blooms like wallflowers, should have the last 2 cm (1 in) of their stems crushed. You could lay the stems on a wooden pastry board and crush them with a wooden rolling pin, using a series of small taps rather than one shattering blow, or, if you have only got scissors to hand, you could snip a couple of slits up the stems.

Soft-stemmed flowers

Bulb flowers like hyacinths, daffodils, narcissi and tulips should be re-cut under water once you get indoors, to prevent the possibility of an airlock forming. Cut at an angle in the usual way, making sure to cut back to where the stem is all green, because the white end of the stem is unable to absorb moisture. Some people re-cut all their flowers under water, but this is really a counsel of perfection.

Hollow-stemmed flowers

Lupins, foxgloves and delphiniums – those tall spires that look so triumphant in the garden – often give disappointing results in the house, drooping after only a couple of days. One simple way of making them last up to a couple of weeks is to cut the stems straight rather than at an angle, hold the spires upside down and, using a houseplant watering can (which has a long, narrow spout), fill the stems right up with water. Then plug the end with a dampened twist of cotton wool.

Milky-stemmed flowers

Some flowers 'bleed' after they have been cut and have to be sealed to keep in their sap. These include poppies, dahlias, tulips, Christmas roses and all members of the spurge family. To seal, pat the stem-ends dry with a tissue and hold them over a lighted match for a second or two. Don't be alarmed by the horrid sizzling noise – it's a case of being cruel to be kind. If you find you need different lengths when you come to arrange the flowers, re-cut the stems and seal them again.

If you wish to make your tulips stay upright, instead of swooping at different angles, wrap the stems up to the base of the flowers in a 'chimney' of stiff, non-absorbent paper during their first long drink in deep water. They also benefit from a pin-prick through the top of the stem, just below the base of the flower.

Right: this prolific mixture of pink and mauve flowers, trailing ivy and spilling over its container, suggests it grew there as naturally as the garden beyond, to which it is colour-linked
Below: wild flowers are best 'arranged' just as they were gathered. A loose tangle not only looks fresh and informal – but allows stems, leaves and blooms to form a self-supporting network
Bottom: vibrant red tulips match the intensity of cushions in cyclamen and fuschia pinks. They're a positive part of the room, not a haphazard extra

Drastic measures

Incredible as it may seem, some flowers really benefit from being stood in a little boiling water for a few minutes. These include campanula, Christmas roses, campion, primula and columbine. Place the angle-cut stems in about one inch of boiling water, wrapping newspaper around the rim of the container to prevent steam reaching the actual flowers. This method can often revive any wilting flowers or blossoms – and, once they have wilted, you have nothing to lose by trying it.

Shop-bought flowers

One way to prolong the life of certain florists' flowers is to immerse them, blooms and all, in lukewarm water. This works especially well for roses, camellias, gardenias, pansies and violets, though

handle them very carefully, because they are easily bruised. As for mimosa – that all too short-lived promise of spring that can turn to hard dried-out bobbles within a day of buying – if you place its crushed stems in boiling water for half a minute and, once arranged, spray it regularly with cool water, it should keep its colour and fluffiness for at least a week.

NB. Before finally arranging any flowers, strip all leaves from the lower part of the stems, so that they don't contaminate the water.

Aids to arrangement

Most books on flower arranging (most classes too) will tell you it's almost impossible to get good results unless you anchor flowers firmly by artificial means. This may be true of very elaborate and formal arrangements, but if you prefer flowers to look simple and relaxed, you will find they often fall into graceful shapes naturally. Even with fairly complicated large-scale arrangements, it's frequently possible to create a network of flower-heads and stems that prove mutually supporting.

In general, it's better to manage without aids to arrangement, because they encourage stiff and artificial results. However, if you feel more confident with some help, here is how to use florist-shop 'mechanics' in a sympathetic way:

The most commonly-used aid to arranging flowers is artificial foam, sold in block form under various brand names. This holds flower stems firmly in position – particularly if stems are cut at a very sharp angle, which makes them easier to insert. The foam should be soaked in water before use, when it will retain moisture for up to a week, and more water can be poured on as it dries out.

How big a block of foam you need will depend on the size of the container in which you are arranging the flowers – but beware the mistake of only filling it to the rim. If you do this, the completed arrangement will appear to sit on top of the container, as if it has been dumped there in a solid lump. Instead, use nearly as much foam above the rim of the container as below, so that some flowers can droop downwards over its edge, giving a more casual and free result.

If you are using heavy materials like sprays of leaves that are too weighty to be held by foam alone, you can cover the foam with lightly crumpled medium-gauge chicken wire, pushing it firmly against the sides of the container to ensure a good grip. With this method you get total obedience from your materials – but you rule out the chance of happy accidents.

Pinholders are flat metal discs covered with vertical spikes, but because the spikes are all set at the same angle, they can lead to very hard and rigid arrangements. Indeed, it's so difficult to introduce life and 'movement', pinholders are best avoided except in special situations. They can be useful, for instance, when only a single or a few flowers need supporting – although you could use damp foam or even damp sand for the same purpose. And they are particularly useful if you want to arrange flowers – not in a conventionally deep container, but in something quite shallow or flat like a plate. Then you can use a pinholder as an anchor for some dampened foam, inserting enough flowers and leaves into the foam to render the mechanics invisible.

Other florists' aids include a clay-like material – occasionally useful for fixing pinholders in position, especially where large asymmetrical arrangements are concerned; and florists' wire, for making individual stems behave. As this latter aid is guaranteed to give a stiff result, it's best kept as a last, desperate measure.

A VASE BY ANY OTHER NAME

Gone are the days of the cut-glass vase boasting a few flamboyant spikes of gladioli. Even in the most formal of situations, people tend to think in terms of containers, not just vases, today – and containers can be anything capable of holding flowers to advantage. There are no hard and fast rules on how to choose a suitable container, but as a rough guide, look for clean and simple shapes that will contrast with the intricate complexity of their contents. Look, too, for plain rather than patterned surfaces, which would detract from the natural pattern of the flowers. And unless you are deliberately seeking an effect (say purple and red anemones in a bright red bowl) avoid containers that are strongly coloured. The general aim is to leave the flowers free to speak for themselves.

The kitchen is a rewarding hunting-ground for containers. Think of pottery jugs or stoneware jars – they have a natural tone and friendly texture that is warmly sympathetic to living materials. So has anything made of cane or wicker, whether it's a shopping basket or the bowl you usually serve the bread in. (You will need to insert an inner container to take water, or use a block of dampened foam, but that is a small price to pay for such attractive results.) Think of tureens, casserole dishes and coffee pots.

Right: simple flowers demand simple treatments, that leave them free to speak for themselves. This casual arrangement allows full-blown poppies to express their fragile and fleeting appeal

The rest of the house is worth plundering too. For large-scale arrangements, re-appraise wastepaper baskets. The wicker kind will need an inner container, perhaps an empty paint can washed clean for the purpose. But the cylindrical-shaped white plastic kind is ready for use just as it is, and its straight, uncompromising lines provide the perfect foil to soft and frothy flowers – say clouds of white gypsophila. Clear drinking glasses and tumblers make perfect 'vases' too, as do water jugs and carafes – even perhaps, a redundant fish-tank. Once you have stopped thinking in terms of conventional vases (often with narrow necks, which are the least conducive to successful arrangements), you will find there is no end to the possibilities of the ordinary, everyday objects around you.

HOW TO APPROACH ARRANGING

Arranging flowers is a very personal matter. There are no stringent rules that must be adhered to, although there are several guide-lines that prove generally helpful.

Basically, flowers are meant to look as happy and exuberant as they do when they are growing profusely in a garden, so aim to mass them lavishly together in your container. If you don't have enough flowers for this approach, fill out the arrangement with contrasting foliage, or abandon all thoughts of a full arrangement, and sit the flowers starkly in something like a clear glass tumbler. This 'specimen' treatment works especially well with stylish flowers such as tulips, irises and lilies – where just a single bloom can command attention. Whatever you do, avoid a mid-way arrangement, where the flowers will look thin and miserable.

Florist-bought flowers are the cause of most 'thin' arrangements, partly because they are too expensive to buy in generous quantities and partly because they tend to come with extra-long stems that most people hesitate to cut any shorter. But if stems are left long they demand a large container – and then even a dozen roses or carnations will look mean-spirited, lost and leggy. Far better to cut the stems right down and pack them closely in a smaller container, so the flowers can provide a thick and luxurious impact.

In fact, for anyone nervous about flower arranging, the simplest answer is to shorten stems drastically. Then, provided the lengths have been varied slightly, if you mass them tightly in a bowl, with the tallest stems in the centre and the shortest at the edges, you will automatically create a 'pin-cushion' shape that looks good from whatever angle it's viewed.

There is no such thing as clashing colour where flowers are concerned. A glance at any garden will confirm this readily. But once flowers come inside the house, they need to relate sensitively to their surroundings. In other words, if your sitting room makes a definite colour statement, your flower arrangements should make a deliberate colour statement too. This doesn't necessarily mean complementing what is there – although it's a foolproof formula for success. You can't go wrong if you put white marguerites in a white room, for instance. But if you prefer an element of surprise, you can contrast the flowers with their surroundings completely. Imagine glowing blue cornflowers or fiery orange marigolds in the same white room.

These are extreme examples of complementing and contrasting, but there are much softer variations on the theme. Stick to a single colour but mix different flowers freely – say pink roses, pink peonies and pink carnations. You can keep to a single flower but mix related shades freely – say whites, creams and yellows, or blues, lilacs and mauves. You can mix both flowers and related shades, or even go in for a riot of colour – provided one key colour relates to your room.

Whichever room you intend your flowers for, decide in advance where you are going to put them, because scale of arrangement is all-important. If you need flowers for the dining-table, for instance, avoid a tall and substantial arrangement that is impossible either to see through or talk through. Aim for low arrangements that won't cause obstruction and that are attractive from all angles.

Similarly, if you need flowers for low side tables, it's best to go for low or medium-height arrangements that can be looked down upon and seen in entirety, even when people are sitting on sofas. This is especially important if there are table-lamps on the tables. Unless arrangements are low enough to be contained within the pool of light thrown, they will disappear upwards into meaningless shadow.

Keep tall arrangements for situations where they can be seen as a whole from a distance. This is for practical as well as aesthetic purposes – if they are too close, they run the risk of getting knocked over.

Right: even when flowers are sparse in the garden, there's no need to settle for meagre arrangements. You can team the last, brave blooms with fruits and richly-tinted foliage, and exploit the wealth of autumn's abundance. Here, a cache-pot, decorated with ripe fruits and vine leaves, provides an ideally sympathetic container

Making The Most Of Dried Flowers

Dried flowers have a romantic, ethereal charm that transcends seasonal appeal. Treat them as a decorative feature in their own right.

Forget vases of tired pampas grass, dog-eared Chinese lanterns and those luridly dyed orange and purple teazels, because dried flowers don't have to look stale or artificial. In their own way, they can look as vital as the living thing, because although colours may become muted during the drying process, the shapes always retain their natural vigour.

Dried flowers are the perfect winter solution in centrally heated homes where fresh flowers wither within a day. If you dry them yourself – which isn't difficult – you will be able to create far more satisfying arrangements than the routine and highly-priced florist's offering of a few helichrysums filled out with gypsophila.

FLOWERS TO GROW OR BEG FROM FRIENDS

Some flowers – like helichrysums, rodanthe and acrolium – grow in their dried state quite naturally, as do seed heads like honesty and Chinese lanterns. It makes sense to plant some of each of these in the garden because they will get you off to a foolproof start.

But there are several other flowers which are easy to dry, because they are not very fleshy in the first place. These include sedum, statice, golden rod, cornflowers, achillea, gypsophila, anaphalis, salvias, lupins, sea holly, poppies, echinops, acanthus, hydrangeas and delphiniums.

Fleshier flowers, or flowers with many-petalled blooms, require a little more attention but will still give highly successful results. They are the 'soft' flowers like tulips, roses, clematis, peonies, carnations, calendula, dahlias, ranunculus, liliums, stocks, magnolia, chrysanthemums, marigolds and Christmas roses.

But really, it's worth trying to dry almost anything that blooms. Drying flowers is an art – not an exact science – and it's rewarding to experiment and see what happens.

It's also worth planting far more flowers than you think you will need. Then you can be sure of suitable shapes to choose from, and be covered in case of any failures. You will also have enough to use generously – something you will find is vital to successful dried flower arranging.

When to pick

It's too late to realize you need dried flowers when the evenings have already begun drawing in. You need to gather your harvest from spring through to autumn, although late summer will be your busiest time. You may also need to rise early in the morning, because that is when flowers are at their best for picking – making sure the dew has already dried off them.

As a general rule, choose blooms just before they are fully open, as they will continue to open slightly after picking. But cut helichrysums as soon as their buds start bursting, because they open out vigorously afterwards. Cut all flowers and seed pods that fluff up when mature – such as golden rod and clematis seed – while they are still in early bud or pod form. And cut spiked flowers like delphiniums when their lower flowers are open, but there is about 5 cm (2 in) of bud left at the top of the spike. As for hydrangeas, they are a complete exception, and need picking when they have already begun to change colour, and their petals (or strictly speaking, their bracts) have become papery to the touch.

If any flowers look wilted after they have been gathered, you can revive them by standing them in a little water for an hour or two, provided you cut off the wet part of the stem before dryng.

How to dry

Naturally 'dry' flowers and the less fleshy varieties can simply be hung heads downwards in bundles to dehydrate, a process that should take about three weeks. Strip the leaves off first and – with the exception of large flowers like acanthus and delphinium, which are best hung singly – make up small bundles of no more than six stems, so the air can reach

Right: baskets brimful of dried flowers await arrangement. Generous quantities are needed to cover possible failures and ensure a wide choice of shapes and shades. Flowers include helichrysums, Chinese lanterns, hydrangea, achillea – and in the basket on the right, the round, fluffy heads of gone-to-seed leeks

freely to the centre. You will need to check the bundles occasionally, because the stems may shrink and allow flowers to fall out.

The enemies of successful drying are damp and light – damp because it causes midlew, and light because it bleaches out colour. So you will need somewhere that is cool, dry, fairly dark and well-ventilated – perhaps the loft or a seldom-used guest room. If you have plenty of space, hang the bundles from a series of strings near the ceiling, stretching from side to side of the room. If not, you can suspend wire coat hangers from a single string, and hang several bunches of flowers from each hanger. If you prefer to operate on a much smaller scale, hang bundles from something like a clothes horse.

Although not fleshy, hydrangeas prove an exception again. After hammering the stems, they should be stood loosely in a container with a little water, allowed to drink it up, and then left *in situ* where they will turn a good colour. Delphiniums need special treatment too. When the suspended flowers begin to feel dry, they need standing upright to complete the drying process, when their florets will fall back into their natural position. If you are very careful, you can smooth each petal between finger and thumb, to prevent a slightly crumpled appearance.

THE MORE TRICKY SUBJECTS

It's possible to dry fleshy and many-petalled flowers by hanging, but you can be more confident of good results by using a dessicant like silica gel crystals. This is available from florists' shops and is fairly expensive – but fortunately it can be re-used continually, provided it's dried between operations.

Ideally, for 'round' flowers like roses, use a separate container for each bloom. Plastic freezer boxes are perfect for the job, but anything airtight – say a biscuit tin – will do as well. Cover the bottom of the container with a layer of crystals, bank the crystals round the upright flower to retain its shape, and lift the petals very gently so the crystals work right into the bloom. Finally, cover the flower completely before sealing the container.

For 'flat' flowers like zinnias, cover the bottom of the container with a layer of crystals, and then dry several blooms at a time, laying them face downwards. If the container is deep enough, you can dry at different levels, making sure to separate them with layers of crystal. In both cases, leave stems as long as you can, because although it's always possible to wire them, too many wired stems will lead to stiff arrangements.

Drying time varies according to the thickness of a flower's petals and calyx – a rose might be ready within two days, whereas a magnolia might take anything up to a week. But timing isn't critical, and the flowers come to no harm if you get impatient and take occasional peeps.

FROM FIELDS AND HEDGEROWS

Grasses make a worthwhile contribution, because they are good for filling awkward gaps in dried flower arrangements, and introduce flexible and graceful shapes. Best gather them early in the year while they are still green, and the seed heads have just begun to emerge from the sheath. And gather as many different kinds as you can – it's impossible to calculate in advance just which will work best when it comes to arranging.

All the following grasses will provide rewarding dried material: squirrel's tail grass, Feather grass, *Briza maxima* and *minima*, marram grass, *Lagurus ovatus* (Hare's Tail), and if you have access to pools and marshes, the Bromes and Foxtail grasses that often grow there. If possible, add a few stems of wheat, oats and barley too – if you take from those that have sprung up near the hedgerow, where the combine harvester can't reach, you won't be stealing from a valuable crop.

To dry, hang them head downwards in bunches – making extra efforts to find a dark place, because light will swiftly turn them to hay – and check the bundles carefully, because the stems shrink considerably during drying. If you can find them, dry rushes and sedges the same way. But dry bulrushes (which should be picked at the light brown stage) by standing them upright in a jar. And be prepared for disappointment, because, sadly, the failure rate is high.

PODS AND SEED-HEADS

Although pods and seed-heads will dry naturally *in situ*, they are liable to damage from wind and weather, and because they have been allowed to develop fully, they could disintegrate when handled. If you pick them before they are fully ripe, however, and dry them by the hanging method, they will not only be more likely to stay intact, but you will be able to retain their subtle shades of colour.

Look for the umbrella-shaped clusters of seed-heads like cow parsley, angelica and wild chervil – these sometimes dry to a delicious lime green. Pick tall seed-spires of the ubiquitous dock at varying stages, so they range from pinky-green right through to rust red. Look, too, for natural-coloured teasels and the pretty star-shaped pods of mallow.

Don't forget to have another look round the garden. The following pods are most attractive: clematis, poppy, *Moluccella* (Bells of Ireland), larkspur (but strip off the untidy lateral shoots), mullein (another tall spire like larkspur – usefully impressive for large arrangements), and leeks from the vegetable garden – worth letting go to seed, when they explode into marvellous pink and mauve-tinged balls.

But don't restrict yourself to these obvious examples. Gather anything that looks promising, because virtually all pods and seed-heads dry successfully.

Left: whereas live flowers fall naturally into graceful shapes, the stems of dried flowers are stiff. This arrangement packs in flower-heads densely to disguise the fact by filling all gaps
Below: varied shapes and sizes create intricate texture to compensate for lack of strong colour
Bottom: this 'tree' is just a raffia-wrapped wooden dowel cemented into a terracotta pot, with a lump of florist's foam jammed on top to provide a 'pin-cushion' for sticking in flowers. These need massing tightly to hide the foam, and to form a round and well-balanced shape

LEAVES AND BERRIES

It's impossible to dry by hanging whole sprays or branches of leaves – they require a form of preservation involving the use of glycerine. It isn't difficult and it gives extremely beautiful results. Instead of drying to a sere, papery texture, the leaves will become supple and acquire a lustrous, almost waxy look.

Although some people only think of beech leaves, because they offer such a wonderful range of colours, most other leaves preserve nearly as well and could prove easier to find. Many people use leaf-sprays exclusively for large-scale arrangements – where they make a major and dramatic contribution or perhaps provide their own display in splendid isolation – they can cater, too, for smaller, softening effects. If you preserve big sprays of ivy, for instance, you can break them up into shorter tendrils, to curl prettily through a floral arrangement.

When to pick

Don't wait until the leaves are already changing colour. It's vital to cut them while they are still absorbing moisture through their stems – any time from around the end of July up to September. The earlier you cut the branches, the richer and deeper will be the preserved leaf tones. So vary the timing if you want differing shades.

After cutting the sprays or branches, strip off the lower leaves, and crush or split the ends for about 5 cm (2 in). Stand them in water overnight. If any branches have wilted by the morning, throw them away because it will mean they have already stopped absorbing moisture.

How to preserve

Buy some glycerine from any chemist's shop and, stirring really vigorously, make up a solution of one part glycerine to two parts boiling water. Plunge in the stem-ends of the branches immediately, before the mixture has a chance to cool. As the solution will only need a depth of about 8–10 cm (3–4 in), it's a good idea to make it up in something small like an empty soup can; then stand the can in something large like a bucket, that will support the branches so they can't topple over.

As the glycerine works its way through the leaves, they will take on a glowing, silky sheen, and, if you have varied the time of picking, colours will change to a mellow range of dark browns right up to mid and light tans. This could take anything from a few days to a few weeks. As soon as the undersides of the leaves feel damp to the touch, the process is complete, and you can remove the branches, drying the foliage very gently with a soft cloth.

Hips and haws and holly berries, etc. that soon shrivel up miserably when placed in water, respond well to the glycerine method of preservation – although you may want to clear-varnish them to bring back their shine.

ARRANGING DRIED FLOWERS

Dried flowers are stiff, unyielding – and unhelpful. They haven't enough 'give' to intertwine like fresh flowers, and are always likely to spring out of the container unless they have been anchored by mechanical means. So this is one time when you do need to buy artificial foam and, although there's a special kind for dried flowers, you could use the ordinary kind if you already have it, and just not soak it in water. For large-scale arrangements, incorporating very heavy material, you will probably need to add crumpled chicken wire too.

With fresh flowers you can choose your style of arrangement. You can use them lavishly, massing them together, or you can use them sparsely, for a look of purist perfection. With dried flowers there is little choice in the matter. Because there are no sappy stems to make graceful shapes, you will need to disguise this lack of fluidity by filling out all the available air-space with a rich abundance of tight-packed flower heads.

And there is another reason for taking this 'solid' approach. Because dried flowers often lack strong colours, it's vital to play up their textural interest with a prolific mix of different types and sizes. Always aim for a thick and physical effect, so dense and intricately deep, you'll almost long to dig your fingers in the richness of the completed arrangement.

How you position dried flowers is of real significance. Since they *are* dry, they lack any translucency (unless, like honesty, they are sufficiently see through to be enhanced by back-light), which means it's no good putting them in a window or with a light shining behind them, because all you will get is a flat silhouette. Dried flower arrangements need to be seen in general light, front-on light, or light from above. Then their subtle colours will be enhanced and their varied textures thrown into detailed relief.

Such lighting naturally tends to dictate the style of arranging yet further. If dried flowers are placed in a general light, for instance, they will probably be somewhere where they can be viewed from every angle, and will need therefore arranging 'in-the-round'. Fortunately, this isn't difficult. The mere fact that you are packing the flowers quite tightly into the container will give a full and three-dimensional effect, and provided you pay attention to balance, the 'in-the-round' look will come almost automatically.

Dried flowers have a charm that is

subtle and understated, and choice of container can be critical to sympathetic results. Avoid overwhelming them with anything strongly-coloured or patterned – but also avoid anything cold or unfriendly. Plain white china might seem a very good choice for dried flowers, but in fact, it tends to look chilly and insipid. Glass containers also prove antipathetic – and in any case, you don't want the holding materials to be visible.

Best choose a container in a warm and natural material that has patina, or texture, or possibly both. Look for anything in glowing brass or copper, for instance, or wicker, which comes in soft, honey colours and has the added interest of self-pattern. Try speckly salt-glaze pottery, mellow lustre china – even an ordinary terracotta clay plant pot.

Finally, although dried flowers are everlasting, it's a mistake to make arrangements a permanent fixture. They only get dusty and visually boring. So take them apart in the spring, store them in plastic bags, and then re-assemble them differently in late autumn, replacing anything weary with newly-dried material.

Below: flowers hanging up to dry in this cool, well-ventilated and usually dark potting shed look so attractive in their bundles, you may well want to forget about arrangements, and hang them in the house just as they are

PLANTS FOR ALL PLACES

Houseplants last longer than cut flowers, but they need loving care. Keep them healthy and happy.

Like flowers, unless you are dealing with a specimen plant (say a single tall palm or an aspidistra), houseplants are best used massed together. This way they look lush and luxuriously jungly, whereas dotted around individually, they fail to make an impact. Worse – they can even look self-conscious and silly.

WHAT HOUSEPLANT WHERE?

There is little worse than a Mother-in-Law's Tongue (*Sanseviera*) sticking up rigidly in the middle of a kitchen window sill. In the right situation, of course, it could stand alone – but it would need a very sophisticated, or stark setting, where it could be treated almost as a piece of modern sculpture. In most cases, however, it would look far happier in the company of other, more fluid-looking plants that would soften the stiffness of its outline.

There are various ways of grouping plants. In the case of slow-growers you can plant them in a communal trough (with a layer of broken crocks on the bottom topped up with a good potting compost) taking care to mix different heights, leaf shapes and colours. You should also take care to mix compatible types that share similar light, temperature and water requirements.

As this isn't as easy as it sounds, you may prefer to leave plants in their individual pots, adding moist peat to the trough rather than compost, and then sinking the pots to their rims in the peat. This way, if a particular plant begins to look sickly – or does too well and outgrows the others – you can easily switch it for something else. If you don't want to go to the expense of buying a trough, you can simply group the plants in their free-standing pots on a plastic tray containing pebbles or gravel.

A possible grouping for the Mother-in-Law's Tongue, with its long, spear-like leaves soaring uncompromisingly upwards, could be with the Spider plant (*Chlorophytum*) – because it has a soft, cascading shape like a fountain – and a trailing ivy (*Hedera*), because its movement is graceful and its leaves provide a complete contrast in shape.

If you have no starting point for filling a trough, the best way to achieve a variety of height and form is to mix climbers, trailers and upright plants. Any of the following would grow reasonably compatibly together. For a climber, choose from the Kangaroo Vine (*Cissus antartica*), the Grape Ivy (*Rhoicissus rhomboidea*), and the philodendrons. For a trailer, choose from any of the ivies (*Hedera*), Wandering Jew (*Tradescantia*), and the tiny Creeping Fig (*Ficus pumila*). For an upright, pick from the *Diffenbachia* (Dumb Cane), the colourful crotons – or that trusty old standby, the Spider plant.

Larger plants with differing heights look good grouped together in their pots on the floor. But it's easy to create differing heights where they are uniform by placing the pots at different levels. Some could stand on the floor, some on a low table behind them, perhaps some on a shelf above the table, or in a tall tower pot or jardinière. When banked in this way to use space creatively, even medium-sized plants can give the impression of a dense and impenetrable growth.

If you want to use a plant in isolation, choose one that will be sympathetic to its surroundings. Any 'spiky' plants, like yuccas or most of the bromeliads, will look their best in a coolly modern setting that will play up the purity of their hard, simple outlines. They are stylized plants that demand a highly stylized situation, and can be very difficult to live up to.

Softer-looking plants are far more flexible, because they look good in any style of room. To stand alone, they will need a bushy, spreading shape, that gives a satisfying and self-contained sense of balance. The Figleaf Palm (*Fatsia*) is an excellent example. So too is the lush-leaved aspidistra – ideal proof that 'soft' plants are timeless in appeal, because although the aspidistra is associated with Victorian parlours and today still looks magnificent in traditional settings, it is also splendid in sparse and 'graphic' interiors. For more proof, think of feathery-fronded ferns. These plants look at home in any kind of room, and have beautifully full and balanced forms that are worthy of being singled out for attention.

Right: plants virtually furnish this all-white room, providing interest and colour at every level. They include a weeping fig (*Ficus Benjamina*), an avocado, ferns, and in the foreground, a flourishing screw pine (*Pandanus*). Venetian blinds can be lowered to filter the sun at its strongest

When it comes to really large-scale plants and trees, it's important to choose the right 'weight' of leaf. Anyone with a Swiss Cheese Plant (*Monstera*) that has grown nearly taller than they are will know how threatening it can become. This is because the glossy, dramatically-slashed leaves, which can grow to a terrifying 60 cm (2 ft) wide, prove very dense and overwhelming.

Unless you actually want a larger-than-life impact, it's wiser to choose something less 'solid' and forceful, that will permit more peaceful co-existence. Palm trees are very easy to live with, because however large they grow, they still look light and airy. So do avocado trees, which you can grow from a stone. Other 'airy' trees – or evergreen shrubs that look like trees in a domestic setting – include the Weeping Fig (*Ficus benjamina*), the House Lime (*Sparmannia*) and the Silky Oak (*Grevillea robusta*).

Whatever kind of houseplants you invest in, use them so they become an integral part of your home instead of an unrelated addition. If you buy a climber, for instance, allow it to climb rather than tying it to a cane in the middle of its pot. You can train it to climb round a mirror or a window frame, or even up the banisters of the staircase. Unless plants are allowed to live naturally in your home (give or take the occasional pruning), you can't expect them to make your home look more natural – which is the whole point of introducing them in the first place.

Green, leafy plants prove the most rewarding in interiors, because they can be used as strong and *lasting* elements of design. Flowering plants, on the other hand, often become insignificant once they have flowered. Furthermore, unless you mass together several of the same kind, it's virtually impossible to get a really abundant look, because flowering plants rarely mix well with one another. Azaleas need a great deal of moisture, for instance; cyclamens must have plenty of fresh air; the leaves of the African violet rot or become damaged if they get splashed while you are watering plants alongside them.

It's probably best to use them singly, putting them in the same places where you might otherwise have put a flower arrangement. Indeed, they can be the perfect solution for people who can't bear to amputate garden flowers.

SUNSHINE AND SHADOW

It's a myth that plants love lapping up sunshine. In fact, if you put plants – with the possible exception of pelargoniums, and cacti, which can never have too much sun – on the sill of a south-facing window, the midday sun will bake them to death.

Fortunately, this doesn't mean the windowsill needs to go to waste. There are plants that like sunshine provided it isn't too strong, so as long as you can protect them from the sun at its peak (perhaps by drawing net curtains, lowering a blind, or slipping a temporary screen behind them) they will do very well in the situation.

Most flowering plants are happy to bask in moderate sunshine, because they need plenty of light for the production of florigen, which determines how prolifically they flower. So are most variegated leaf plants. This is because the green parts of the leaves need as much light as possible to make up for the lack of chloroform in the non-green parts.

But neither flowering plants nor variegated plants actually *need* sunshine. What they need is a good light as opposed to being in the shade. So they can live just as well in a north-facing window, or away from the window in an extra-bright room.

THE SHADY CHARACTERS

Plants with all-green rather than variegated leaves are content to live well away from windows. This includes all the ferns, which thrive best in the shade: after all, they are used to growing on the floors of forests and jungles, where they are overshadowed by the trees above. Palms are less particular in their requirements. They accept semi-shade as well as direct light, which makes them very flexible in possible sitings. But green climbers or trailers prefer the shade, and their leaves may turn a sad and sickly yellow if they get too much exposure.

All plants need light, and even these shady characters would die if relegated to a totally dark corner. But there are a few that will survive in gloomy situations. The aspidistra, for instance, has an amazing constitution, and is capable of putting up with very poor light. Several other plants will survive with the help of artificial lighting, though to be on the safe side, stick to ferns, and climbers like the Kangaroo Vine (*Cissus antartica*) and Philodendron scandens.

Although spot-lit plants look very dramatic, the bulbs create a lot of heat, and could cause scorching to the leaves. Best keep them several feet back from your jungle. Even an ordinary light-bulb can do harm if it's very close to the leaves, so if you are hanging a pendant light above a plant or group of plants, keep it at least 60 cm (2 ft) above if you are using a 60-watt bulb; at least 1 m (3 ft) above for a 100-watt bulb. Ideally, it should be switched on for at least twelve hours daily.

GETTING THE WARMTH RIGHT

Once you have decided where to put your plants in terms of light, you must consider the best situation in terms of temperature. Fortunately, most plants will survive a fairly wide range, although none take kindly to sudden changes.

When so many houseplants come from hot climates, you might expect central heating to be a blessing. However, most tropical plants are used to the steamy heat of rain forests, not the dehydrated air that results from central heating. In fact, central heating has probaby killed more plants than unheated homes ever did in the past.

This means that unless you are going to restrict yourself to cacti and succulents, which regard a dry atmosphere as the norm, it's vital to re-introduce humidity. You don't have to buy an expensive humidifier to achieve this end. You can stand pots in a trough or bowl of pebbles, and water the pebbles so that as the water evaporates, it will rise as steam around the plants. (Stand pots directly in water and the roots will rot.) Or you can simply stand a bowl of water near a plant. In addition (though this is less important for groups of plants, because they humidify one another as they transpire), you can spray the leaves with a fine mist of water each day.

Surprisingly, even with central

Above: most plants thrive in the steamy heat of bathrooms, provided the temperature remains fairly constant between baths. In this internal bathroom, which relies on artificial light, shade-tolerant plants have been sensibly preferred
Right: grape ivy (*Rhoicissus rhomboidea*) looks natural rambling across a ceiling beam, instead of being tied stiffly to a stake

heating, it's still possible for plants to suffer from cold, if they are left on the windowsill during winter. This is because – unless the window is double-glazed – when the outside temperature drops, the temperature of the glass drops correspondingly. Any leaves touching it curl up and die. This is rarely enough to kill the plant, but badly browned leaves look very unsightly. So either draw the curtains *behind* the plant, or move the plant right into the room. Whatever you do, don't give plants a 'treat' by standing them on the radiator shelf, because they will get so hot and dry, they will shrivel up. Only if a radiator-shelf is really deep can you risk a plant in this situation.

Cooler customers

Plants to avoid in centrally-heated rooms are the very ones to seek for rooms that lack it.

Most of the ferns, as well as requiring high humidity, prefer a cool temperature during the winter. Of course, cool doesn't mean cold – the majority like a minimum temperature of 10°C (50°F) – including the Ladder Fern (*Nephrolepis exalta*) that most people buy. But Asparagus Fern – the delicate kind used in wedding bouquets – will survive temperatures as low as 4°C (40°F); and Maidenhair Fern (*Adantium*) requires a minimum of 7°C (45°F). One fern worth making a special note of is Holly fern (*Cyrtomium falcatum*). This will put up with temperatures of 4°C (40°F), but more important, because it's such a rare attribute, it will put up with draughty situations too. It could be ideal for halls full of doors that the wind whistles beneath – but don't expect a conventional-looking fern. Although it's as gracefully shaped as its relatives, its non-feathery fronds are made up of pairs of glossy green leaflets, which gives it a more substantial look.

Palms aren't able to tolerate cold and need a minimum temperature of 10°C (50°F), as does the Swiss Cheese Plant (*Monstera*) and the Umbrella Plant (*Cyperus*). But there are several plants which will withstand 7°C (45°F). These

include the climbing Grape Ivy (*Rhoicissus rhomboidea*) and the Spider plant (*Chlorophytum*) – or that is the theory – because in practice, they have been known to survive a slight degree of frost, as has the Wandering Jew (*Tradescantia*). As for the aspidistra and the Rubber Plant (*Ficus elastica*), they are both prepared to put up with 4°C (40°F). The aspidistra will even put up with draughts too.

Without doubt, though, the best plant for very cold situations is the Figleaf Palm (*Fatsia*). This is virtually as hardy as an outdoor plant (indeed, it's sometimes grown outdoors in very sheltered areas) and can survive all but the most prolonged bouts of frost.

Many trees take unkindly to central heating, and would be happier in homes that don't have it. The bay tree (*Laurus nobilis*), for instance, loathes a winter of warmth and dryness, and would much prefer cool or cold surroundings. What it would really like is a temperature of 1–6°C (34–42°F), although it might just survive in the bedroom of a centrally-heated home if the humidity problems were sorted out.

The Silky Oak (*Grevillea robusta*) likes to be cool but not cold during winter. It prefers somewhere between 4–10°C (40–50°F). Despite being greedy for sunshine during the summer, the miniature orange tree (*Calmondin*) demands a cool winter too, with a temperature around 10°C (50°F).

Other trees can survive fairly low temperatures happily. The minimum for both the House Lime (*Sparmannia africana*) and the Weeping Fig (*Ficus benjamina*) is 7°C (45°F).

A common bloomer

Contrary to popular belief, most winter-flowering pot plants dislike a high temperature. This is why so many Christmas presents bite the dust – sometimes as soon as New Year's Day, the poinsettia (*Euphorbia pulcherrima*) has shed all its leaves, so the flower-like bracts sprout forlornly from the top of bare stems.

But at least poinsettia likes a warm temperature – anything between 16–18°C (60–65°F) – provided it's steady and there are no draughts. The African violet (*Saintpaulia ionantha*) prefers a constant 16°C (60°F), though it can survive 13°C (55°F). And the cyclamen, although it will become very miserable if the temperature rises above 18°C (65°F), likes a minimum of about 13°C (55°F).

So don't worry if you can't provide luxury conditions. Some of the most beautiful winter bloomers will bless you for spartan conditions, with a temperature of 7–10°C (45–50°F). These include the azalea, the cineraria (with its masses of colourful daisy-shaped flowers), the Kaffir lily (*Clivia miniata*) and the primula. They will all show their gratitude by flowering more prolificly. And the Busy Lizzie (*Impatiens*) will show its gratitude later, becaue it needs a cool winter temperature to give it a rest from flowering so abundantly throughout the rest of the year.

TENDER LOVING CARE

More pot plants are killed by misguided kindness than by neglect. In summer they get put on window sills when they may cringe from direct sunlight; in winter they get stuck on radiator shelves, where the compost dries out and the roots get roasted. Throughout the year, they will probably get over-watered. This can be disastrous, because roots get their oxygen from tiny pockets of air in the soil, and over-zealous watering washes them away.

When to water depends on various factors: the type of plant, the plant's growth rate, the temperature, the humidity – even the size of pot makes a difference. But although there is no easy theoretical answer, in practice, it's generally just a matter of feeling the surface compost – and if it's dry to the touch – the plant needs watering. In summer, you will find this means watering frequently, perhaps as much as two or three times a week, because the plant will be transpiring in the higher temperatures. But in winter, except in centrally-heated homes which create a 'summer' all year round, you may only need to water once a fortnight – once a month or less in the case of cacti. Always use water at room temperature: ideally rainwater or tap-water that has been boiled to soften it.

It's no good giving a plant a dribble of water. This will only wet the surface of the compost while the rest eventually dries out completely, and starves the roots of the moisture they require. You need to pour on enough water to fill the

Top: a weeping fig tree (*Ficus benjamina*) adds a softening touch to this cool modern room that would have looked cold and clinical without it
Above: this leggy specimen of silky oak (*Grevillea robusta*) has suffered from lack of natural light – but still looks good in a sparse modern setting. Indeed, it's bareness looks intentional
Right: trees always work well with long, low seating: their height introduces a new dimension

gap between the surface of the compost and the rim of the pot. Then, when the surplus water has drained through to the saucer or holder, empty it so the plant doesn't get wet 'feet'. If there is no surplus water, the plant must be thirstier than you realized, and you will need to repeat the watering process.

To feed or not to feed

When you buy a plant from a nursery, do ask about its diet. It will probably have got used to a liquid fertilizer, and will feel very aggrieved if the supply dries up. This doesn't mean it will do anything as drastic as die, but if you want a really healthy-looking plant, it's best to pay attention to its nutrition.

Plants vary considerably in their needs. Some, like the bromeliads and cacti, require next to no food. But most others, if freshly potted in spring, will need feeding once a fortnight between mid-summer and autumn, the period of their most vigorous growth. There is no need to feed plants during the winter while they are resting.

Over-feeding, like over-watering, can kill a plant. Be sure to use liquid fertilizer *only* in the strength and frequency recommended by the manufacturers. Before applying, ensure the compost is moist, as dry roots are very easily damaged.

Potting on

Although wispy roots pushing through the bottom of the pot doesn't necessarily mean a plant needs re-potting, it's usually a fairly good indication. The best time for re-potting is March or April, when the roots are beginning to get active, and will quickly work their way into the new compost you give them. But don't leap the plant straight from a small pot into a big one; work your way up the potting sequence, from a 12 cm (5 in) pot to a 18 cm (7 in) pot, or a 18 cm (7 in) pot to a 25 cm (10 in) pot – after which time it's ready to move into a tub. If you are using a plastic pot, it won't need any help with drainage, because the bottom will be punctured with a number of small holes. But if you are using a traditional clay pot, which has the advantage of looking nicer and staying moist, it's important to cover the single hole in the bottom with a layer of crocks.

Position the plant centrally in its new pot, making sure the surface compost is 1–4 cm (½–1½ in) from its rim, to allow enough space for watering. The depth you allow will depend on the size of the plant and pot. Fill in the sides with good new compost, firming it (but not jamming it) in with your fingers, water it once, and then place it somewhere warm but slightly shaded to recover.

Going on holiday

In summer, if you have a garden, find a shady area and 'plant' your houseplants in the earth while still in their pots, watering them first if the weather is dry. Ideally, dig the holes slightly deeper than the pots

to leave an air space. This will prevent pests and excess moisture entering through the drainage hole.

If you only have a patio or terrace, group the plants together in a shady spot, preferably against a wall or fence, to lessen the chance of their being blown over. In this case, as there is no surrounding soil to keep the pots moist, give the plants a thorough soaking before you put them out, by immersing the entire pot in a bucket of water until bubbles of air stop coming to the surface.

If you have no great outdoors at all however, and no friendly neighbour to come in and look after plants, they can fend for themselves with a few precautions. Move them away from the windowsills, and group them together in the coolest and least sunny room in the house, being sure to draw back the curtains so they get a good light. Leave hall and room doors open so fresh air can circulate. Then water the plants well, and set about evolving a way of watering them in your absence.

Most garden centres sell extra-absorbent matting to stand pots on. It works by capillary action, and allows the roots to draw up water as and when they need it. But if you forget to buy the matting in time, you can create a version of your own by covering the bottom of a washing-up bowl with a dishcloth in 1 cm (¼ in) of water. For longer periods, you can cover the bottom of the bowl with broken crocks instead, and pack crumpled pieces of damp newspaper between the pots. And for even longer periods, you can fill the bowl with water, range the pots around it, and then place one end of a woollen thread or strip of lint through the soil of each individual pot, with the other ends extending into the water.

There is very little you can do for plants that have to be left alone during the winter. They certainly don't need a good water – quite the contrary – because if there's a frost, a wet soil-ball freezes quicker than a dry one. So give them just enough water to moisten the soil, and of course, move them well away from the window. If you are seriously worried about the risk of frost – provided you leave the upper leaves protruding – you can try wrapping the pots in thick newspaper or blankets. When you arrive back home, *do* introduce your plants to increased temperatures gradually – don't rush them into a heated room thinking what they need is a really good warm-up.

Above: this thoughtful grouping of plants and small-scale statuary creates a romantic indoor garden that seems a continuation of the garden outdoors. The mood is temperate rather than lush and tropical, which makes the visual link even more convincing

Left: deep glossy-green and fleshy-leaved plants loom dramatically large in this open-plan room that has the space and character to carry them off. They flourish happily away from direct light, unlike the geraniums (*pelargoniums*) which need to live in the window

CHAPTER SIX

THE OUTSIDE STORY

LIVING OUTSIDE

Patios, terraces and paved back gardens should be treated imaginatively, to form an extra, special outdoor room.

Because these small green havens lead immediately off the house it's a good idea to relate them to it, establishing a link between indoors and outdoors. If one area flows easily into another, it suggests a whole that is much larger than the parts.

At its simplest, this could mean no more than having plenty of green leafy plants in whatever room leads onto the patio, but it could also mean choosing the plants for outside in shades that are sympathetic to the colours inside. If your room is all creams and soft corals, for instance, tubs full of bright red geraniums and blue lobelia will drain it of colour and make it look dreary. Conversely, a room full of punchy primary colours would make delicately beautiful pink and mauve petunias look merely washed out and insipid.

The most convincing way of linking indoors and outdoors is to use materials that are common to both. If your room has quarry tile flooring, for instance, and provided the exterior is very sheltered, you could carry the flooring straight on out; or you could use frostproof engineering bricks for a handsome through-floor. In the kind of basement patio that is partly overhung by a room or verandah on the floor above, it might even be possible to use continuous rush matting. Much smaller touches could help create a relationship: perhaps houseplants grouped together on a tray full of cobblestones, if cobblestones have been featured outdoors. A large mirror could work the trick. Strategically hung on the wall opposite the window, it would reflect a garden 'growing' within the room.

In general, the style of your house will dictate your choice of style of patio, terrace or backyard. If it's older and fairly formal in aspect, you may want to pick traditional paving stones, with antique or reproduction garden furniture, urns instead of chunky tubs, and a layout that is measured and symmetrical. If it's modern, you may prefer coloured concrete slabs, built-in brick benches, and an asymmetrical arrangement. Sometimes contrasts in style work excitingly well, so nobody need feel obliged to play safe.

PAVINGS

Any 'outdoor room' needs a practical 'floor' that is easy to sweep or hose clean, and easy to walk on. York stone looks mellow and instantly established, but it's very expensive and extremely heavy – if you're laying it yourself, you will need someone with a strong back to help you. Concrete slabs are relatively inexpensive, and come in a variety of textures and colours, but it's a mistake to get carried away with the colour potential. Too many colours will look messy and garish: it's best to stick to one, or at most two shades, taking care they echo or blend with the colour of the walls around them. Always wet a piece of the concrete before finalizing your choice. You will be seeing the patio in downpours as well as sunshine, and you may find the 'wet' colour becomes so strong you will prefer to pick a lighter tone.

Bricks are an attractive alternative to paving stones, and they are ideally suited to covering smaller areas because they are small-scale themselves, and will make the ground space seem larger. In a very tiny area, straightforward laying is probably the best: anything more ambitious might look confusing. It's also best in any situation where you need to create an illusion of width or depth, because the coursing provides the eye with clear directional lines to follow. Elsewhere there are marvellous opportunities for interesting arrangements: herringbone pattern; basket-weave pattern (made up of squares of alternately vertical and horizontal bricks); and any pattern you care to build in if you want to use bricks in two different colours.

Sadly, ordinary building bricks are relatively soft, and will tend to flake or crumble during a hard frost. In a sheltered position, you may be prepared to risk this,

Right: old stone paving and a central cherry tree look so right in this elegant setting, to tamper with them would be sacrilege. Regency wrought iron garden furniture is original, and with annual repainting, survives all weathers

Left: modern furniture and a built-in barbecue look at home in this old-fashioned garden because natural materials and colours have been used. The barbecue is built from second-hand bricks, carefully matched to the nearby building. Chairs are teak; umbrella etc, grass-green
Below: red plastic garden furniture and geraniums make this modern-block balcony bright

particularly if you want to use secondhand bricks that will match the house or the walls of the garden. Otherwise use engineering or special paver bricks. Paver bricks (often called stable bricks) are thinner than other types, and come plain, diamond-textured, or panelled like bars of chocolate. If you are worried about slipping – and some new bricks have a very hard smooth surface – paver bricks are the wisest choice.

The smaller the simpler

Cobblestones, set in concrete, are beautiful to look at – but they are agony to walk on, and they don't provide a stable base for chairs and tables. It would be a mistake to use them all over, but in a largish area that can take the busyness of pattern, you could include a few squares by omitting the occasional concrete slab or 'square' of brickwork.

As a rule, the smaller the space to be covered, the plainer and lighter-coloured the approach should be. If you try to visualize the space when it's liberally sprinkled with plants, furniture and people, you will appreciate the need for simplicity. This approach effectively rules out crazy paving in a restricted area. And unless you have plenty of space and money, very expensive slate, which can be used continuously indoors and out, is so dark it would shrink the paved area considerably.

Similarly, although the idea of butting up paving instead of pointing it is very appealing (imagine sweet-smelling herbs growing in the cracks), it would look merely untidy in a tiny setting. You may even want to get rid of any moss or lichen that forms, because although it adds character and looks very romantic, it's dangerously slippery when wet. In a back area, where you don't have to consider the rest of the garden, you can swill the surface over regularly with a solution of one part household bleach to ten parts water. Leave the liquid to stand for about thirty minutes (which will probably entail temporarily blocking the drain), and scrub it with a stiff yard broom before rinsing in clean water. This treatment should be enough to shift most mosses. Otherwise, treat the surface with a bactericide, taking care to localize it to the paving only.

Practical pointers

Whatever kind of paving you choose, do make sure that it's laid to fall away from the house, so that water will drain off it towards the garden – or towards an actual drain in the case of a completely paved area. Also ensure that the hard surface is at least 15 cm (6 in) lower than the damp proof course of the house, and avoid covering over any air bricks. If you need steps from your terrace leading down to the garden, make them from the same material as the terrace, so one area leads naturally into another. However, if your patio is on a level with the garden, and surrounded by lawn, lay the paving 1 cm (½ in) below the level of the grass. You will then be able to mow right to the edges of the lawn, without having to worry about possible damage to the blades.

One good-looking alternative to paving an area – particularly if it's already been concreted or asphalted, and you don't like the utilitarian look of the surface – is to cover it with a platform of slatted wood. A non-porous wood like teak would be prohibitively expensive: but any softer wood could be gloss-painted, stained with a wood preservative, or left natural and sealed with clear varnish – and of course there would be no problems with drainage, provided the original surface was properly drained. However, the wood would need re-treating each autumn.

THE WALLS

The house itself will provide one wall, but in narrow town houses, the garden walls may provide two more, and a back yard will be completely enclosed. In situations where light is restricted, all too frequently the automatic reaction is to slap gallons of whitewash on the walls. But this really can look brash and insensitive. Plants and flowers need a less harsh background: if they work against white in hotter countries, that is because their colours and the sunshine are harsh to match. The British climate demands gentler treatment. For much of the year, you will be seeing your patio, terrace or backyard in a cold, grey light – probably viewing it through a drizzle of rain too, so go for something softer and less stark. Perhaps cream for a simple and straightforward solution, although ochres and browns provide sympathetic backgrounds, and don't show up the splashes of mud that inevitably spatter the walls after heavy rainfalls.

But in a really gloomy basement terrace, particularly where the paved area is overhung, you could create a dense and mysterious arbour-effect by painting the walls in a deep shade of green. With masses of foliage plants in contrasting shades and shapes, climbing the walls and running over the 'ceiling', as well as standing about in tubs, the result would be very lush and romantic.

Whatever colour you paint your walls, however, use a cement paint that will last for several years, rather than something that will need repainting annually. Repainting walls is a tricky task once climbing plants have become established, so the less this chore needs doing the better.

But if your walls are built of mature old bricks, why paint them at all? Mellow brick is beautiful, and provides an ideally muted background that will not only go with plants and flowers, but with the curtains and furnishings in the room that overlooks it.

In a terrace leading onto a garden, it's a good idea to create a low 'wall' to give definition to the different areas, and avoid the exposed feeling that you are actors on a stage. The French café look is a quick and easy way of achieving this: just edge the area with fairly deep troughs holding clipped conifers. In a sunny situation, you could even extend the look by having a shop blind fitted to the back of the house.

ROOF GARDENS

If a roof has been specially constructed to take a conventional garden, it can bear enough soil for a lawn and plants to grow in. However, such roofs are extremely rare. Most are not meant to be used for anything, so if your plans are at all ambitious, it's vital to get advice from a building surveyor or architect. Otherwise, it's largely a matter of common sense. Keep as much weight off the roof as possible, by using wall-hung pots, baskets and troughs. If there are no walls, although you may need planning consent before going ahead, you could build them up from the walls of the house. Alternatively, you could create an evergreen hedge in pots or troughs – making sure to position them over the walls of the house, so they take the weight instead of the roof. Also make sure they are very firmly fixed: rooftops are very windy places, and even a small flower pot falling from a height could kill anyone in the street below. Choose lightweight containers for floor-standing plants – plastic or fibreglass rather than stone or cast iron. And even though they are light, keep them on the small side, because they will become very heavy once they are filled with soil, and even heavier when the soil is watered. (Indeed, it might be better to fill the containers with peat compost, because this is much lighter than ordinary earth.) Ideally, keep the pots near the edges too, because this is where the roof is at its strongest.

Most roofs are covered with a bituminous compound or lead sheeting, both comparatively soft materials, particularly in hot weather. This means they could easily get cut by heavy or sharp containers, which would cause leakage through to the ceiling below. It makes sense, therefore, to spread the load as widely as possible, either by using shallow containers, or resting containers on planks of wood. If you are sure your roof can take the additional weight, you could have it covered with special lightweight outdoor tiles; although asbestos-cement tiles are still manufactured, non-asbestos equivalents are now available.

Disadvantages of rooftops

The snag about creating a lightweight roof garden is that container-grown plants dry out very quickly; peat dries out more rapidly than soil; shallow containers dry out faster than deep ones; and roofs are very exposed to wind, which has a harsher drying effect even than strong sunlight. This means plants may need daily water in summer as well as fairly frequent watering in winter and, as in window boxes, they are going to need feeding. See the window box section on page 211 for information on plant drainage and maintenance.

Furthermore, plants that thrive quite happily at ground level may so dislike the wind and polluted atmosphere that they die on a rooftop. Given that plants will need extra attention to survive, and that everything needed for them – from peat and containers to tools and possibly water – will need lugging up a flight of stairs, there seems little point to creating a roof garden if you have got one below. Even if you don't have any other form of garden, it's vital to be sensible about what you attempt. The average roof is only intended to take the weight of snow, and an occasional repair-man. If, in addition to the weight of pot plants, you add a table and chairs and start inviting friends round for al fresco meals, you are just asking for serious structural problems.

If this is what you want to use a roof garden for, you will need to have an entirely new roof constructed. If, on the other hand, all you want is to potter peacefully on a private island 'walled' with plants and flowers, and have somewhere to sunbathe with a (preferably lightweight) friend, the charm of a roof garden in the middle of a town is such that you won't be put off by the snags. As with all container-grown gardens, you will be able to enjoy one major advantage. You can grow acid lovers and acid haters in pots next to each other: think of azaleas beside pinks, or camellias beside peonies. Another plus factor: you shouldn't have to do much weeding, because you are too high up for most wind-blown seeds, and will only have to bother with those the birds deposit.

THE BALCONY

Most balconies in modern blocks of flats are built to take a lot of weight – but they are so tiny it's difficult to exploit this advantage. You may manage to fit in a small-scale table and chairs, as in the tiny picture opposite; but you may only be able to treat it as an extended window box. Even if this is all you intend, it's possible your landlord or the local authority has placed restrictions on gardening activities, either limiting the number and type of plants you can grow, or banning their presence altogether.

Presuming you are free to do what you like, much will depend on the type of balustrade. If it's a solid wall, you will find yourself restricted by the lack of light below. You could put troughs right along the base of the wall, and grow shade-loving plants like ivies and hostas – perhaps sticking to climbing ivies if your balcony is very shallow, because they won't project and get in the way. You could also try an evergreen honeysuckle, which likes its feet in the shade and its face in the sun, though it will need to be given something to climb up. It would, of course, be a mistake to put window boxes on top of the wall – not only because they would block light to the room beyond, but because they are potentially lethal if they topple onto passers-by below.

If your balcony has an open-railed balustrade, you can fill the troughs with sun-loving flowers, creating the equivalent of a narrow herbaceous border. You can also include some trailers to spill over the edge of the balcony. However, unless the room below is also yours, avoid any really rapid grower like Russian Vine (*Polygonum baldschuanicum*), that would soon obscure other people's view. Ivy geraniums would look superb in summer without going on the rampage.

A bower of flowers

If your balcony is completely enclosed at both ends, you can exploit the end walls fully by creating a series of floor-to-ceiling steps, with a trough of plants upon each one. If this eats up too much floor space, you can simply fix shelves, so the plants rise one above the other. Then, if there is enough headroom, you can hang pots and baskets high up on the wall of the house, where you won't brush past them as you walk. This way you will have plants at every level: at your feet, at waist and eye-level, and above your head.

In the case of a partly-enclosed balcony, where the end walls don't afford complete privacy from your neighbours, you can train climbing plants up the sides and along the top to create a self-contained arbour of greenery. Or more simply, you can stand pot-grown trees or raised shrubs at both ends. For all-year-round privacy choose evergreens. Bay trees, rhododendrons, Portuguese laurels and mahonia japonica will all thrive in containers with relatively little attention.

In older houses, where a balcony may only be the roof of the bay window below, you are safest treating it as a walk-in window box, because it probably won't be strong enough to take much weight. All the advice for a lightweight roof garden holds good here, as does the information in the window box section.

CHOICE OF CONTAINER

At ground level, where weight is not a problem, you can build low retaining walls for permanent flower beds. The plants will enjoy having plenty of root-space and, as there will be enough soil to retain moisture, you will find you don't need to water so often. It's fun to do a little amateur bricklaying – just three or four courses of brickwork will be enough – and it's the ideal way of adding flower beds to an area that has already been paved or concreted over, because you don't have to take up the hard surface.

Otherwise, buy individual containers that will be in scale with the height and breadth of your plants. Low spreading plants will look best in low and shallow containers. Bushy-type plants will look good in the conventional flower-pot shape, because they will have the height as well as width to balance it out. Tall containers will usually look best with a mixed planting, so that some plants grow upright while others spill over the sides. Small trees and shrubs will demand a large container for their roots as much as for a sense of proportion. Aim for something at least 30–40 cm (12–16 in) deep and 30–45 cm (12–18 in) wide and, if you are likely to want to move the containers – perhaps to a more sheltered position in winter, or out of the way if you are trying to sunbathe – sit them on a tailormade platform with castors. In general, choose the containers before worrying about the contents. It's important that they suit the size and type of your house, and whereas you can't adapt them to fit the plants, plants will prove far more obliging and flexible.

Terracotta clay pots, either plain or decorated, look warm and mellow in any setting, but they dry out quickly in exposed conditions. If they are new, always soak them in water for at least a day, or they will steal moisture from the soil and parch the plants.

Cast iron urns and cisterns look magnificent in formal, older gardens, and come in 18th- and 19th-century designs – but make up your mind in advance where you want them. They are far too heavy to move about. The same is true of *stone* pots and sinks. Even *timber* containers, whether in a hardwood like teak and iroko, or in a painted softwood, are fairly weighty to lug around. Square Versailles tubs in painted timber are ideal for larger pot-grown trees, and have a pleasing formality that requires them to be used in strictly symmetrical arrangements. They would be wasted in a grouping with other pots.

With the exception of the conventional terracotta plant pot (a real bargain in the 35 cm (14 in) size), all containers made from traditional materials are frighteningly expensive, so even if you are not worried about weight, you may prefer far cheaper modern alternatives.

Plastic containers come in a wide range of colours and shapes, although natural and some of the brown shades show off plants and flowers most sympathetically. They also come in simulated stone, with elaborately 'sculpted' traditional patterns. Although these look fake on close inspection, given a coat of paint, they pass for painted stone; and given a coat of matt terracotta-coloured paint, they look like genuine clay containers. More expensive *fibreglass* containers come in a very convincing 'lead' finish, and there is a good range of period reproduction designs to choose from. Fibreglass is also used to simulate wood, although it's rather less successful in this application. *Stone composition* containers look good once they have weathered, particularly if they attract moss or lichen. If you live in the country, it's a good idea to mellow them down with a watery solution of cow-dung. *Concrete* containers tend to look municipal, and in any case are probably too big for domestic use, but they do come in very simple shapes, which could be useful in a modern setting.

Improvising containers

Even the cheaper containers are still not cheap, so look around for anything that can hold plants attractively and is capable of having drainage holes drilled. Large tin cans can make handsome cylindrical containers, and can easily be given a coat of paint. A redundant wire vegetable rack, floor-standing or wall-hung, can be filled with plants, including trailers. Old fireclay or stone sinks make marvellous troughs, and the plug-hole provides a ready-made system of drainage. An ancient metal hip bath will make a spectacular container – but perhaps only in a paved backyard – it would look out of place on a modern patio. Tall clay chimney pots can double as

Above: bright orange and yellow nasturtiums contrast boldly with plain black and white
Opposite: two antique wrought-iron chairs and a reproduction cast aluminium seat (much lighter than the cast-iron original), look romantic in this flourishing Central London roof garden

sculpture and plant-holder: they look good grouped together in differing heights, and their simple, cylindrical shapes feel equally at home in modern and traditional situations. On the whole, improvisation works best in a traditional setting, where you can jumble old things together for a pleasing effect, and encourage trailing plants to hide anything that is damaged. Even here, you need to know where to draw the line. A discarded doll's pram, for instance, would look merely ingenious however beautifully it was filled with plants.

FURNISHING THE OUTSIDE

The ideal garden furniture looks good, is comfortable, and can be left out all year round – but unfortunately it doesn't exist. This means you have to decide where your priorities lie. If the all-year-round aspect is important to you, either because your patio or terrace would look bleak without furniture, or because you have nowhere to store it during winter, you will need something that can stand all winds and weathers.

Cast iron needs annual repainting to prevent rust forming, and it's excruciatingly hard to sit on. You may find it such a joy to look at that you are prepared to take cushions with you each time you use it. This would be necessary, because although there are such things as plastic-covered cushions that can be left outdoors, they soon become sticky and uncomfortable to sit on in hot weather.

Cast aluminium is cheaper than cast iron and a great deal lighter – important if you like to move things around. But it looks lighter too: somehow the very beautiful reproductions of Victorian designs lack the guts of the cast iron original. However, it does have one major advantage – it's non-rust, so you only need to repaint it when it's beginning to look shabby. Also available in modern designs, cast aluminium is just as uncomfortable to sit on as cast iron; once again you will need to approach it armed with cushions.

Plastic-covered metal furniture combines strength with a maintenance-free plastic surface. Any seat with a perforated metal or slatted base will have more 'give', and so offer slightly more in

Left: a slightly winding stone path and a raised lily pond provide this basically rectangular walled garden with varied visual contours. Plants spilling over the edges of the path soften the outline.
Top: even the most unpromising places can be turned into gardens. A wooden stairway virtually fills this example widthways, so plants had to be thought of in vertical terms. Climbers ramble up the walls (hiding an ugly drainpipe), and flower-filled tubs sit to the side of the steps, leaving just enough room for people to pass
Above: An old chimney pot and a wooden tub provide friendly and sympathetic materials to warm the coldness of a stone-walled and cemented yard. Ivy, geraniums (pelargoniums) and roses spill colour softly. Wooden trellis has wisely been left natural: it would have looked brash and jarring painted white

the way of comfort and coolness.

Timber furniture always blends in well with its surroundings, but needs cushions for comfort and meticulous maintenance. Although you can leave hardwoods like teak and iroko exposed to the elements (in which case they will weather to a bleached-out finish), they will last much longer and keep their richness of colour if you give them an annual application of oil. Softwoods will need resealing with a clear varnish or repainting each year. Sadly, log furniture should be stripped of its bark: otherwise it will harbour damp and pests.

Softer options

The most comfortable garden furniture is the most impractical, which is why those opulently *upholstered armchairs* with matching *swing seats* come with an optional set of waterproof covers. In theory, you are supposed to shroud them like typewriters each night, because even if it doesn't rain, the morning dew will eventually rot the fabric. But few people can be bothered, and they soon begin to look faded and forlorn, especially once they are covered in bird droppings.

For many people, the simplest solution to garden furniture is to use lightweight items that can be carried out, and carried back in at the first drop of rain. *Cane* furniture is ideal in this respect, because it looks as naturally attractive indoors as out, and can even survive the occasional light shower. Wood and canvas *director's chairs* are just as adaptable, although since they fold away, you could (as with deckchairs) keep them exclusively for the garden, and hang them on a hook in the garage, if you have one.

Even built-in garden furniture, whether made of bricks, paving slabs, timber or concrete, still has the problem of carry-out cushions. But at least a long and uniform run of seating means you can make them from flat squabs of foam, which will stack into a neat pile when not in use.

WINDOW BOXES

Window boxes brighten up the exterior of a house as well as brightening up the view from inside, and create maximum impact from minimum space. They are easiest to install if you have a window ledge, but although this should preferably face south or west, there are plenty of shade-loving plants for other points of the compass.

Any window ledge must be deep enough to take a box safely. The box should be tailored to fit the space as nearly as possible, and if it has drainage holes, it should be raised by short legs, or blocks of wood, so that air can circulate underneath. In this case, there should ideally be room for a fixed drip-tray, so that excess water doesn't splatter people or windows below.

Above all, though, the box should be made absolutely secure, either by means of brackets, a safety rail, cementing to the walls, or a hook and eye arrangement. This is really important even at first floor windows, because a window box can kill or cause injury when falling from a relatively low height.

If your window has no ledge, or the windows open outwards, you can hang the box from the wall below the window – a job best done professionally in view of the safety aspect. Gardening will be easier at the lower height, but it's best to forget about drainage holes because it will be impossible to attach a drip tray. Sadly, if your windows open outwards, it will also be impossible to see the flowers from inside, because you will need to restrict yourself to low-growing plants.

Window boxes are made from various materials, including terracotta clay, concrete, plastic, fibreglass and wood. Designs range from the plain to elaborate 18th- and 19th-century reproductions, but unless your home demands a particular period, or you are limiting yourself to evergreens only, you will find flowers look best in a simple setting. An unobtrusive colour will make life easier too. A brightly-coloured plastic window box, for instance, demands that you make it look intentional by relating it to the colour of flowers, external paintwork and curtains.

If you prefer a wooden window box, it will either need painting inside and out, or treating with a suitable wood preservative – not creosote, which is liable to poison the plants. Some wooden boxes come with inner containers, but these are primarily intended for indoor use, and rule out the possibility of having drainage holes.

Good drainage is essential in window boxes because too much trapped moisture can turn the soil sour. Actual drainage holes are recommended, though not absolutely vital, but whether you have them or not, it *is* important to cover the bottom of the box with a 2.5 cm (1 in) layer of broken flower pots, stones or brick rubble. This should be covered with coarse compost or peat, to retain moisture and prevent fine soil washing through. Only then should you fill the box with the growing soil – not tired old soil dug up from a friend's garden, but soil recommended for your plants by a nursery. If you can, prepare the window box at least a week before planting, to enable it to settle. Plants like to get their roots into something firm, rather than grope around trying to get a grip.

Where there is heavy air pollution,

you may need to renew the soil every year, although a few pieces of charcoal in the compost, peat or soil will absorb harmful gases and keep the earth sweet. You should certainly add charcoal if your box lacks drainage holes, because it will help to alleviate the lack.

Because window boxes – like all plant containers – are too small to accommodate much soil, the plants will soon exhaust the supply of nutrients. It will be necessary to feed them. Bonemeal is a gentle, long-lasting fertilizer and perhaps better suited to the heavy-handed than one of the more powerful liquid feeds. Unless the latter are administered exactly as the instructions stipulate, you will get a short spurt of growth followed by a sorry collapse.

Window boxes are easy to fill with bedding plants during the summer. Petunias, begonias, lobelia, geraniums, marigolds, nasturtiums, fuschia, etc. will provide a profligate riot of colour, and flower for months provided you dead-head them. Indeed, if money is no object, you can leave them in their pots, sink them in moist peat rather than soil, and replace them with new the moment they pass their peak. In winter, the time people really need cheering up, many window boxes get left full of summer's sad corpses – or emptied and left as depressing hulks. The way around this is to provide a basis of evergreens to provide colour during the winter months but form a quiet background to flowers during the summer. (Of course, the same is true of all container-grown gardens, whether at ground, balcony or rooftop level.)

At its simplest, this could be a row of dwarf conifers, underplanted with trailing variegated ivy. Then you could also underplant with spring bulbs, extricating them gently once they have flowered, and filling the gaps with your favourite summer plants. Most herbs need a good supply of sun in order to grow successfully, and a window box on a south-facing ledge might seem an ideal place for these useful plants. Be wary, however, of which herbs you choose. Some, like mint, sage and tarragon take up a lot of root-space – mint in particular should have a container to itself to restrict its roots. As all herbs require a lot of light, it may not be practical to plant them in a window box already inhabited by miniature evergreens, so bear in mind that a herb window box will be depressingly bare during the winter months.

HANGING BASKETS

Hanging baskets are exclusively summertime delights, because they can't hold enough soil to protect roots from the cold. This means they need planting in late spring, and growing along under cover, before finally facing the great outdoors. Although semi-circular baskets are available for hanging flat against a wall, most are meant for seeing from many angles, either hanging in the corners of buildings or hanging from the roof of open porches.

Hanging baskets are usually made of wire, and look most attractive lined with sphagnum moss. The only drawback is that the moss allows the soil to dry out rapidly, and in hot or windy weather, you could find yourself having to water plants twice daily. It will cut down the watering if you give the moss an inner lining of plastic, with a few holes made in it to allow for drainage. In any case, it's a good idea to install a saucer in the bottom, because this retains moisture as well as preventing anti-social dripping. The ideal way to water baskets is to take them down and lower them in water for about twenty minutes. If you have hung yours in a hopelessly inaccessible position, you may find the only solution is to throw in ice.

Planting a hanging basket is a delicate procedure if you want to exploit its potential fully. Half-fill the lined basket with suitable soil and at this stage plant any trailing plants, gently threading the shoots through the linings and wire, while making sure you have left the roots inside. Then fill the basket to within a couple of centimetres (about an inch) of the top, and plant it with the non-trailing varieties. Whereas window boxes and containers often look spectacular with just a single type of flower, these most miniature of miniature gardens usually look their best with a jubilant mixture.

GIVING BARBECUES A GRILLING

The best-looking barbecues are those you build in as an integral part of your patio, backyard or terrace. They are not only more handsome in appearance, but you can build them with as big a cooking area as you need; extend them to include a sensible work surface (something free-standing models conspicuously lack); and you can even extend them to include built-in seating. This could be a good idea in a tiny paved area, where free-standing garden furniture would not only look cluttered but seriously impede people's freedom of movement.

If you don't want to design the barbecue yourself, it's possible to buy kits that include a charcoal grid, cooking grill, supports, and sometimes a battery-operated rotisserie. These come with construction plans and instructions, but you have to supply the bricks and mortar yourself – and of course – the size of cooking surface is pre-determined.

A cooking surface of about 30 × 50 cm (12 × 20 in) is usually enough, although if you intend to give ambitious barbecue parties, it will certainly be well worth making it larger. It will also be worth using fireproof rather than ordinary building bricks.

If you have an old cooker to plunder, it is very easy to brick-build a basic barbecue. Using a rack from the oven as a measure, just build three sides of a rectangle up to stooping height, and lay a tray from the oven over them. Continue building up the sides of the rectangle for about another nine inches, and top it with the oven rack. Unless your barbecue is in a very sheltered position, continue the three walls upward for a few extra courses, to protect the cooking area from draughts. A baking tray from the oven can provide a charcoal grate to slide onto the oven tray at the lower level, while the food for grilling goes on the oven rack at the top. If you want to be able to remove the grilling rack for cleaning, loose-lay the bricks that form the windshield.

If you have not got room for a permanent structure, and either don't like the look of free-standing metal barbecues or don't have anywhere to store them in winter, the Brick Development Council has designed a simple brick-'built' barbecue that only takes 15 minutes to assemble. (The design is free from them on receipt of a stamped addressed envelope.) Bricks are loose-laid in circular courses, because a circular structure is much stronger than a square and can be reasonably stable without the use of mortar. The main advantage is not so much the speed of assembly, or the fact that the barbecue can be dismantled in five minutes, but that the bricks can be stacked neatly and unobtrusively against a wall when not in use.

Choosing a barbecue

The appearance of most free-standing barbecues leaves a lot to be desired, so it's worth researching the market fully before making your choice. It's also worth analysing their capacity carefully: some models are far more sophisticated than others, offering cooking grids that can be raised or lowered; charcoal trays at the back of the cooking area as well as beneath (back-heat is useful during spit-roasting, because it prevents fat dripping onto the coals and smoking); vented lids for cooking larger items quicker and less smokily; separate charcoal grates, which allow air to circulate freely and ashes to drop away, so the charcoal burns more intensely; and warming grids, to keep food hot during serving. You may or may not need these refinements, but if you want a barbecue that includes a rotisserie, it's a good idea to buy a battery-operated version, or one to which a battery-operated spit motor can be attached. Turning the spit by hand gets very monotonous – bearing in mind that a chicken can take up to three hours.

Compromise meaures

If you're only thinking in terms of grilling chops and sausages, table-top grills or Hibachis offer a compact and visually inoffensive way of having a barbecue. They are much neater to look at, easier to store and, of course, you can stow them in the back of the car and drive away for a picnic-barbecue.

Some free-standing barbecues that offer grilling and spit-roasting facilities run off portable gas cylinders. This means they provide instant, smoke-free, adaptable and *reliable* heat. But the food lacks the unique flavour that charcoal imparts, so there seems little point to this form of cheating.

Whatever kind of charcoal-burning barbecue you choose, long-handled utensils are essential to keep you a comfortable distance from the heat and smoke. You will need at least a long-handled fork, tongs, spatula and a brush for basting and, even then, it's advisable to use oven gloves too. You may even want to consider a long-handled and hinged wire basket, especially constructed to take food like hamburgers or fish, which can be turned over as a whole, instead of requiring you to turn over items individually. Finally, you may want a pair of bellows. Charcoal usually takes about forty minutes to heat up, and one of the most exhausting aspects of a barbecue can be trying to huff and puff it into life.

Above: this basement backyard, which receives little sunlight, concentrates on green, leafy plants that don't mind the shade. Flowering pot-plants can easily be added for extra colour in summer, and nothing-but-green looks dense and mysterious in winter

Left: different levels and different materials fill this child-geared and labour-saving garden with interest. Built-in flower beds (solidly green for strong winter colour), built-in sandpit and seating platform, impose the discipline of squares. This is softened by overhanging trees

WHERE TO FIND THEM

Useful general addresses for the home

NB The addresses given in this section are not comprehensive. While every effort has been made to ensure that firms and organisations mentioned are reputable, the publishers can give no guarantee that they will fulfil their obligations under any circumstances. Readers must be prepared to deal with them at their own risk.

Aluminium Window Association, The Building Centre, 26 Store Street, London WC1. A trade association for aluminium framed windows. Send SAE for free literature.
Architectural Association, 34 Bedford Square, London WC1. Will supply list of members willing to undertake domestic work.
Asbestos Information Centre, Sackville House, 40 Piccadilly, London W1. Represents the industry. Advises on safety aspects and supplies free leaflets on request.
Association of Master Upholsterers, 348 Neasden Lane, London NW10. Deals with any complaints arising from members' work. Send SAE for members in your area.
Bituminous Roofing Council, PO Box 125, Haywards Heath, West Sussex. Deals with queries concerning flat roofs.
Brick Development Association, Woodside House, Winkfield, Windsor, Berkshire. Gives advice on most matters concerning bricks and brickwork. The BDA can also be found at the Building Centre, where an enormous range of brick samples can be seen.
British Association of Removers, 279 Grays Inn Road, London WC1. Send a SAE for list of members in your area, and helpful leaflets on moving house.
British Bath Manufacturers' Association, Fleming House, Renfrew Street, Glasgow. Represents manufacturers of cast-iron and steel baths. Will supply a list of members.
British Board of Agrément, PO Box 195, Bucknalls Lane, Garston, Watford, Hertfordshire. The Board assesses building products. If you want to know whether a particular product has been approved, check with their Marketing Department.
British Ceramic Tile Council, Federation House, Station Road, Stoke-on-Trent, Staffordshire. Generally promotes the use of ceramic tiles. Will supply a list of members, and literature on fixing and cleaning tiles.
British Chemical Dampcourse Association, PO Box 105, Reading,. Berkshire. Represents installers of chemical damp-proof courses and manufacturers of chemicals. Send SAE for list of members (all of whom subscribe to a Code of Practice), and details of literature.
British Decorators Association, 6 Haywra Street, Harrogate, North Yorkshire. Will supply list of members in your area, all of whom subscribe to a Code of Practice.
British Electrotechnical Approvals Board, Mark House, The Green, 9-11 Queens Road, Hersham, Walton-on-Thames, Surrey. An independent testing board for most domestic electrical appliances. Those that pass carry the BEAB label.
British Insurance Association, Aldermary House, Queen Street, London EC4. Runs a consumer information service dealing with all aspects of personal insurance, as distinct from life assurance. Free leaflets available.
British Standards Institution. 2 Park Street, London W1. Sets high quality and safety standards for a wide range of products. Those that meet them carry the Kite Mark or Safety Mark. Publishes an annual Buyers' Guide, available at most libraries.
British Wood Preserving Federation, Premier House, 150 Southampton Row, London WC1. Gives independent advice on all aspects of wood preservation. Will supply a list of companies specialising in curative treatment of timbers.
Build Electric Bureau, The Building Centre, 26 Store Street, London WC1. This is the Electricity Council's main advice bureau for domestic electricity. Plentiful supplies of mostly free literature.
Builders' Merchants Federation, 15 Soho Square, London W1. Represents the majority of the trade, and operates Approved Display Centres for kitchens, bathrooms and heating systems. Will supply a list of BMF merchants in your area.
Building Centre, 26 Store Street, London WC1. Virtually everything concerning building and building materials, concentrated under one roof. Permanent displays of products; comprehensive fact sheets, etc; expert advice available if you make an appointment. There are also Building Centres at the following addresses: Colston Avenue, The Centre, Bristol; Green Lane, Durham City; 113-115 Portland Street, Manchester; 3 Claremont Terrace, Glasgow.
The Building Employers Confederation, 82 New Cavendish Street, London W1. The Confederation has members in virtually all the building trades. Affiliated federations include the National Federation of Plastering Contractors; the National Federation of Painting and Decorating; the British Woodworking Federation. A Code of Practice covering members' work on home improvements is currently being negotiated. Write for a list of members in your area.
Building Societies Association, 14 Park Street, London W1. Will help with queries about obtaining a mortgage.
Cavity Foam Bureau, 9-11 The Hayes, Cardiff. Will give advice on cavity foam insulation. Will also supply a list of installers who are members of the British Standards Institution registered-firms scheme.
Cement and Concrete Association, Wexham Springs, Slough, Berkshire. Will supply technical advice: also a free 30-page booklet called 'Concrete Round Your House and Garden'. Write for it to the Publications Distribution Department.
Chambers of Commerce. These exist in all local authorities, and usually have offices in the Town Hall. Mines of information on everything from where to find a local window-cleaner, to when the local sale-room holds its auctions.
Clay Roofing Tile Council, Federation House, Station Road, Stoke on Trent, Staffordshire. Supplies information on products of clay roof tile manufacturers.
Confederation for the Registration of Gas Installers. St Martins House, 140 Tottenham Court Road, London W1. Also regional offices, found in the phone book under CORGI. Will supply list of local and approved installers from their Register of Installers. (Gas showrooms supply similar lists).
Council of British Ceramic Sanitaryware Manufacturers, Federation House, Station Road, Stoke on Trent, Staffordshire. A trade organisation, which will supply all members' literature upon receipt of a very large SAE.
Design Centre, 28 Haymarket, London SW1. A Government-sponsored body. Promotes good design by selecting well-designed products, some of which are always on display; the remainder catalogued. An Information Desk deals with queries: design-books and gift-items are for sale.
Domestic Coal Consumers Council, Gavrelle House, 2 Bunhill Row, London EC1. An independent body dealing with all queries (and complaints) about solid fuel and solid-fuel appliances.
Draughtproofing Advisory Association, PO Box 12, Haslemere, Surrey. Will supply a list of members, who include manufacturers as well as installers of draughtproofing products.
Electrical Association for Women, 25 Fouberts Place, London W1. Gives advice on all aspects of electricity in the home, from how to change a fuse, to using a freezer. Send SAE for list of publications – and details of their one-day courses.
Electricity Consumers' Council, Brook House, 2-16 Torrington Place, London WC1. A government body set up to protect the interests of consumers. Will supply general leaflets on receipt of SAE, but individual queries get referred to local Area Electricity Consultative Councils.
Electrical Contractors Association, 34 Palace Court, London W2. More than 2000 members, all of whom undertake to work to the Institution of Electrical Engineers stringent standards. The Association guarantees both standards and completion of work. List of local members available on request.
External Wall Insulation Association, PO Box 12, Haslemere, Surrey. Will supply a list of members, both manufacturers and contractors, in your area.
Federation of Master Builders, 33 John Street, London WC1. Admits only experienced builders to membership, and offers wide consumer protection, including a 2-year guarantee on completed work. Send SAE for local members.
Glass and Glazing Federation, 6 Mount Row, London W1. Offers advice on double glazing and safety glazing. All members conform to the Federation's Code of Practice. Write for leaflets and list of local members.
Guild of Architectural Ironmongers, 8 Stepney Green, London E1. Send SAE for list of members, who are manufacturers of locks and security devices.
Guild of Master Craftsmen, 170 High Street, Lewes, East Sussex. The Guild keeps a central index of members highly skilled in all trades and crafts. If you specify which skill you require, they will supply relevant addresses. They also sell a comprehensive publication called *Guide to Restorers*.
Heating and Ventilating Contractors Association, 34 Palace Court, London W2. Will supply a list of members who can give impartial advice on the merits of different fuels and systems; will also supply useful (but not free) publications. Installations carried out by members are covered by the Association's Double Guarantee Scheme.
Institute of Plumbing, Scottish Mutual House, North Street, Hornchurch, Essex. A professional body aimed at promoting high standards in the plumbing industry. Write to them for local registered plumbers, and send SAE for their helpful leaflets.
Kitchen Specialists Association, 31 Bois Lane, Chesham Bois, Amersham, Buckinghamshire. Members are kitchen specialists who cover display, design, supply and installation – which rules out many builders merchants, etc. The Association operates a Code of Practice and provides a Consumer Protection Scheme, and will supply a list of members in your area.
Law Society, 113 Chancery Lane, London WC2. For lists of solicitors in your area, broken down into categories of work, ask to see the Solicitors' Regional Directory at your

local library.
Law Society of Scotland, 26 Drumsheugh Gardens, Edinburgh.
National Association of Chimney Sweeps, PO Box 35, Stoke on Trent, Staffordshire. Send SAE for list of members. A Code of Practice is currently being established.
National Association of Loft Insulation Contractors, PO Box 12, Haslemere, Surrey. A trade association: will supply list of members.
National Association of Plumbing, Heating and Mechanical Services Contractors, 6 Gate Street, London WC2. A trade association: will supply list of members.
National Cavity Insulation Association, PO Box 12, Haslemere, Surrey. Operates a Customer Protection Plan, based on British Board of Agrément Certificates and British Standards requirements. Will supply a list of members.
National Fireplace Council, PO Box 35, Stoke on Trent, Staffordshire. Promotes the fireplace surround. Publishes and sells a Book of the Fireplace, showing different styles by different manufacturers.
National Gas Consumers Council, 162-168 Regent Street, London W1. Will supply leaflets, and addresses of the 12 regional councils. These councils will take up individual consumer complaints with British Gas.
National Home Improvement Council, 26 Store Street, WC1. Gives basic advice on home improvement grants, but will refer you to your local authority for anything specific.
National House Building Council, 58 Portland Place, London W1. Inspects, and gives a 10-year warranty on new houses built by registered builders; also a 6-year warranty on old buildings converted into flats or houses by registered builders. The warranties do not cover works of maintenance, as opposed to failure to comply with specifications or structural defects. Write for leaflet and names of registered builders in your area.
National Inspection Council for Electrical Installation Contracting, 237 Kennington Lane, London SE11. Publishes an annual Roll of Approved Contractors, all of whom work to Institution of Electrical Engineers' wiring regulations. The Roll can be inspected at any electricity board showroom.
National Master Tile Fixers Association, Fairfax House, Fulwood Place, London WC1. Members are specialists, able to undertake ambitious projects such as murals. Write for list of local members.
National Society of Master Thatchers, 25 Little Lane, Yardley Hastings, Hampshire. Send SAE for leaflet, and list of members.
Office of Fair Trading, Field House, Bream's Buildings, London EC4. In response to numerous complaints about "cowboys", this Government body, set up to protect both consumers and traders, is currently working on a general Code of Practice for the home-improvements industry. In the meantime (as the list of general addresses shows) they have approved a number of Codes of Practice with individual organisations. Most include some form of guarantee, but as the Codes vary, best check what they offer.
Paintmakers Association of Great Britain, Alembic House, 93 Albert Embankment, London SE1. Where they relate to members' products, will answer queries on the uses and suitability of paints.
Plastics Bath Manufacturers Association, Fleming House, Renfrew Street, Glasgow. Will supply free leaflet on acrylic baths; also list of members, on receipt of SAE.
Plastics Window Association, Elizabeth House, Suffolk Street, Queensway, Birmingham. Members must meet the Association's standard for high performance uPVC window systems. Will supply a list of manufacturers.
Royal Institute of British Architects, 66 Portland Place, London W1. Operates a Clients Advisory Service, to help members of the public choose an architect for specific work: i.e. home extension specialists; conversion specialists, etc.
Royal Institution of Chartered Surveyors, 12 Great George Street, London SW1. Will supply lists of its members. Will also supply an expert to arbitrate between householder and builder: a fee is charged for this service.
Society of Industrial Artists and Designers, 12 Carlton House Terrace, London SW1. Will supply list of interior-designer members from their Designers' Register. Photographic reference of designers' previous work can be seen by appointment.
Solid Fuel Advisory Service, Hobart House, Grosvenor Place, London SW1. Gives advice on solid fuels and related appliances, with regard to water and space heating. As the central service, it may well refer you to your nearest regional office.
Steel Window Association, 26 Store Street, London WC1. Will supply list of manufacturers who comply with the relevant British Standard.
Suspended Ceilings Association, 29 High Street, Hemel Hempstead, Hertfordshire. Answers queries relating to suspended ceilings, and will supply list of members.
UK Fittings Testing Station, Water Research Centre, 660 Ajax Avenue, Slough, Berks. The body that approves all fittings which connect to main water – from taps, showers and bidets to washing machines. Using unapproved fittings could result in heavy fines, so in the case of imported taps and bidets especially, best check with the Station before buying.
Ventilation Advisory Bureau, PO Box 16, Poole, Dorset. Send a SAE plus 25p in stamps for details of members' products.
Wood and Solid Fuel Association of Retailers and Manufacturers. PO Box 35, Stoke on Trent, Staffordshire. Tests wood and solid fuel appliances and promotes them generally. Will supply list of members.

The Kitchen

KITCHEN UNITS

Most manufacturers produce more than one range of units. Particular features available are indicated as follows: SA self-assembly. SD sliding doors. D specially designed for disabled users.

ALLMILMO allmilmö Ltd, Station Rd, Thatcham, Nr Newbury, Berks.
Showroom: at Thatcham. List of UK dealers available. Planning service offered by all appointed dealers. All units custom-built. (D)
ALNO Alno (UK) Ltd. Unit 10. Hampton Farm Industrial Estate, Hampton Rd West, Hanworth, Middx.
Showroom: Alno Information Centres at address above and Unit 5, Ringway Trading Estate, Shadowmoss Rd, Wythenshawe, Manchester. Planning and installation services offered by individual dealers. List supplied on demand.
ANDERIDA The Bunting Woodworking Co Ltd. North Lane, Boughton-under-Blean, Faversham, Kent.
Showroom: The Building Centre, Store St, London WC1. The firm supplies direct. Planning and fittings services. All fitted and free-standing matching furniture is custom-built.
ARCLINEA Arclinea (UK) Ltd, 12 Cheval Place, London SW7.
Showroom: at Cheval Place. Planning service offered here or by individual dealers. List available from firm.
ARCO Arco at Waterford, Industrial Estate, Waterford, Ireland.
Showroom: 34 UK retailers; addresses from firm. Planning service via network.
ARISTON KITCHENS Barget plc, 4 Stepfield Industrial Estate East, Witham, Essex.
Showroom: at above address. Contact firm for a list of stockists. Most offer a planning and installation service.
BAUKNECHT KITCHENS Beekay Kitchen Furniture Ltd, 455 Walton Summit, Bamber Bridge, Preston, Lancs.
Showroom: at above address. List of dealers available from firm. Planning and fitting services through dealers. (SA)
BECKERMANN Beckermann Kitchens UK Ltd, Unit 14, Industrial Estate, Roman Way, Godmanchester, Cambs.
Showroom: list of appointed dealers from above address. Planning service through dealers.
ARTHUR BONNET Cuisines Bonnet UK Ltd, 10-12 Bromley Rd, Beckenham, Kent.
Showroom: at Bromley Rd. List of dealers available from firm. Planning and installation service provided by each.
BOSCH Robert Bosch Ltd, PO Box 98, Broadwater Park, N Orbital Rd, Denham, Uxbridge, Middx.
Showroom: list of Bosch Kitchen Studios available from firm – planning and installation services at each studio.
BRUYNZEEL Bruynzeel Kitchens (UK) Ltd, Barkergate House, Belward St, Nottingham.
Showroom: at Nottingham. List of dealers from firm. All have planning and installation services.
BULTHAUP Bulthaup, 241 High St, Walthamstow, London E17.
Showroom: write or telephone firm for address of your nearest Bulthaup Studio. All operate planning and installation services.
CAMARGUE KITCHENS Camargue Kitchens Ltd, 98 Luton Rd, Harpenden, Herts.
Showroom: at Kitchen Elite; address as above. List of dealers available from the firm. Most offer planning and installation services.
CLARE KITCHENS Bowater Ripper Ltd, Castle Hedingham, Halstead, Essex.
Showroom: at Castle Hedingham and Bowater House, Knightsbridge, London. List of retail outlets from firm. Some provide planning and installation services.
COMMODORE KITCHENS Commodore Kitchens Ltd, 81/83 Orsett Rd, Grays, Essex.
Showroom: at above address. List of dealers available from firm. Planning service offered by the firm or appointed dealers.
CROSBY Crosby Kitchens Ltd, Orgreave Drive, Handsworth, Sheffield.
Showroom: at Orgreave Drive. List of stockists from the firm. Both manufacturer and stockists operate planning services. (SA).
DHI KITCHENS Direct Home Improvements Ltd, Lyon Way, St Albans, Herts.
Showroom: at Lyon Way and elsewhere. Full In-Home planning and ultimate service for complete contract or DIY Kitchen Kit service covers home counties and southern England.
EASTHAM KITCHENS Thomas Eastham & Sons Ltd, Holmes Rd, Thornton, Blackpool, Lancs.
Showroom: stockists list from above address. Planning service offered by the firm and appointed stockists. (SA)
ELIZABETH ANN Elizabeth Ann Woodcraft Ltd, Rhyl, Clwyd, Wales.
Showroom: 3 Portman Square, London W1. List of dealers from firm. Planning service operated by individual dealers.
ELLIS KITCHEN FURNITURE J T Ellis & Co Ltd, Crown Works, Wakefield Rd, Huddersfield, W Yorks.
Showroom: at works. List of retail outlets from firm. Most have planning service; some install.
FLOWLINE Boulton & Paul

(Joinery) Ltd, Riverside Works, Norwich.
Showroom: at 14 Stanhope Gate, London W1. Units through local builders and builders' merchants; addresses from manufacturer. Kitchen advisory service available at Norwich.
FORMAT Format Kitchens Ltd, 5 Fox Lane, Palmers Green, London N13.
Showroom: addresses of local dealers available from firm. All offer a complete planning and installation service. The range for the disabled can be adjusted for use by other members of the family. (D)
FRAMFORD Framford Kitchens Ltd, Sunderland Road, Sandy, Beds.
Showroom: at Sunderland Road and The Building Centre, Store St, London WC1. List of local dealers available. Planning service provided by dealers. (SD)
GEBA Geba UK, Abbey House, Wellington Rd, London Colney, Herts.
Showroom: more than 50 studios throughout UK all offering design and installation services. (SA)
GOLDREIF Goldreif Kitchens UK Ltd, Thames House, 63 Kingston Rd, New Malden, Surrey.
Showroom: list of stockists supplied on request. All operate a kitchen planning service. All custom built units.
GOWER Gower Furniture plc, Holmfield Industrial Estate, Halifax, W Yorks.
Showroom: at above address. List of stockists available from firm. (SA)
GREENCRAFT Tom Green Products Ltd, Ingatestone, Essex.
Showroom: at Ingatestone and The Building Centre at Store St, London WC1. Contact firm for local distributor. Units made to measure. Planning service. Installation service in certain areas. (SA)
GREENFIELD SYSTEMS Greenfield Systems Ltd, Porsham Close, Belliver Industrial Estate, Roborough, Plymouth.
Showroom: at above address. Replacement doors, drawer fronts and worktops for existing kitchen units. Made to measure. Mail order. Send a first-class stamp for brochure, price list and all details.
GROVEWOOD Grovewood Products Ltd, Tipton, W Midlands.
Showroom: at Tipton. List of stockists from firm. Many offer a planning service. (SA)
GRUCO KITCHENS Gruco Kitchens (Milton Keynes) Ltd, Unit 5, Grove Ash, Dawson Rd, Mount Farm, Bletchley, Milton Keynes, Bucks.
Showroom: at Dawson Rd. Contact firm for address of nearest Gruco Studio. Each offers full planning and installation services.
HATHAWAY COUNTRY KITCHENS Hathaway Pine Furniture Ltd, Clifford Mill, Clifford Chambers, Stratford-upon-Avon.
Showroom: as above. Solid wood-fronted units in a choice of timbers, made to order. Contact firm for list of other showrooms. Manufacturer offers planning and complete installation service. (SD, D)
HAUENSCHILD Hauenschild Kitchens, 2-4 Circus Rd, London NW8.
Showroom: at above address from where list of dealers is also available. Planning and installation services at each.
HYGENA & SYSTEMATIC KITCHENS MFI Furniture Centres Ltd, Northend Rd, Wembley, Middx.
Showroom: at Wembley and more than 120 stores in UK and Republic of Ireland. Branch list from head office. Showrooms offer planning assistance. (SA)
HYPHEN Hyphen Fitted Furniture Ltd, Deeside Industrial Park, Sealand, Deeside, N Wales.
Showroom: 14-16 Grosvenor St, Chester and 12 William St, Edinburgh. List of appointed dealers from firm. Design and installation facilities available from showrooms and dealers.
JONELLE John Lewis Partnership, Oxford St, London W1.
Showroom: John Lewis Partnership stores except Caleys of Windsor and Bonds of Norwich. Planning service at all branches. Some do installation.
KINGSWOOD KITCHEN SYSTEMS Allied Manufacturing Co (London) Ltd, Sarena House, Grove Park, Colindale, London NW9.
Showroom: as above. Contact the same for nearest showroom/depot which also displays taps, tiles and appliances and can give the address of a local dealer. Many offer a planning service. (SA)
LADYLOVE Preston & Rowland Ltd, Century House, Knowles St, Widnes, Cheshire.
Showroom: at Widnes. Addresses of stockists from firm. Planning service at each. (SA, SD)
LÄGER KITCHENS Heinrich Läger (UK) Ltd, Läger House, Swan Mews, Lichfield, Staffs.
Showroom: as above. Address of nearest dealer showroom supplied on request. All operate design and installation services.
LEGEND Landywood Cabinet Co Ltd, Holly Lane, Great Wyrley. Nr Walsall, W Midlands.
Showroom: List of dealers available from firm. Most operate a planning and fitting service. (SA)
LEICHT Leicht Furniture Ltd, Leicht House, Lagoon Rd, Orpington, Kent.
Showroom: at Orpington. List of Leicht Studios from firm. Planning service available through these.
LYNLEY KITCHENS Simmons & Eldridge Ltd, 3 Beehive Rd, Bexhill-on-Sea, E Sussex.
Showroom: Write to above for a list of dealers. Mini-kitchen with appliances also available.
MAGNET & SOUTHERNS Magnet Joinery Ltd, Royd Ings Ave, Keighley, W Yorks.
Showroom: 250 branches/ showrooms. Details from firm.
MAGNUM KITCHENS Magnum Kitchens (London) Ltd, Mercy Terrace, Lewisham, London SE13.
Showroom: at above address, also at 83 Copers Cope Rd, Beckenham, Kent and 45A St George's Walk, Croydon, Surrey. Units made to measure and supplied direct from factory. Planning and installation service. (SA)
MANHATTAN Dennis & Robinson Ltd, Churchill Industrial Estate, Lancing, W Sussex.
Showroom: at Lancing, Croydon and Guildford. Planning service available. Addresses and further details can be obtained from Dennis & Robinson. (SA)
MEISTER KITCHEN SUITES John Knowles (London) Ltd, incorporating JKL (Meister) Ltd, Brickfields. Wallage Lane, Rowfant, Crawley, W Sussex.
Showroom: as above. Contact firm for address of nearest dealer. Individual dealers offer a planning service. (SA)
MIELE Miele Co Ltd, Fairacres, Marcham Rd, Abingdon, Oxon.
Showroom: at Abingdon and 19 Liverpool St, Salford, Manchester. List of Miele Studios from the firm. All offer planning and installation services.
MOBALPA KITCHENS Mobalpa UK Ltd, Unit E, Griffin Industrial Estate, Stephenson Rd, Totton, Southampton.
Showroom: at above address. List of dealers available from the firm. All offer a complete service of planning, fitting and arranging finance.
MOBEN CONTINENTAL KITCHENS Moben Continental Kitchens Ltd, Alberton House, St Mary's Parsonage, Manchester 3.
Showroom: Moben fitted kitchens can be found at a number of House of Fraser stores. Contact head office for free brochure. Moben operates a planning and complete installation service. All kitchens tailor-made.
MONZIE JOINERY Monzie Joinery Ltd, Crieff, Perthshire.
Showroom: at above address. Custom-built furniture, design and installation services supplied direct by Monzie Joinery. Sales restricted to Scotland.
MOORES S A AND ELYSEE Moores International Ltd, Durham Way South, Aycliffe Industrial Estate, Newton Aycliffe, Co Durham.
Showroom: write to above address for list of dealers. All are equipped to provide customers with a planning service (SA).
NEW WORLD KITCHENS New World Kitchens, Schoolfield Rd, West Thurrock, Essex.
Showroom: 641 London Rd, West Thurrock; also at 36 Gabriels Hill, Maidstone, Kent and 154-156 Hutton Rd, Shenfield, Essex. List of other dealers from firm. Planning and fitting services by manufacturer and dealers.
NICHOLLS & CLARKE Nicholls & Clarke Ltd, Niclar House, 3-10 Shoreditch High St, London E1.
Showroom: at above address. All sales enquiries dealt with from head office. Planning and installation service. (SD, D)
NIXON'S KITCHEN FURNITURE Nixon's Kitchens, Gt North Rd, Seaton Burn, Newcastle upon Tyne.
Showroom: at above address, also 47 King St, Manchester and 41 Drury Lane, Solihull, Birmingham. All furniture built to requirements of the individual and supplied direct. Planning service. Installation, including electrical and plumbing work.
NOBILIA B W Spear, 68 Broad Lane, Hampton, Middx.
Showroom: write or telephone for addresses of dealers. All offer planning service.
PAULA ROSA KITCHENS Kingfisher Wood Products Ltd, Water Lane Industrial Estate, Storrington, Sussex.
Showroom: at Water Lane, also North St, Brighton, and Friary St, Guildford. Furniture supplied direct from firm. Planning and installation services from Sussex, Surrey, Hampshire and S London.
PINE UNLIMITED COUNTRY KITCHENS Pine Unlimited, 13A Greenwich South St, London SE10.
Showroom: at above address. Phone to make an appointment. Tailor-made solid pine traditional kitchen furniture. Design service and installation available.
POGGENPOHL Poggenpohl (UK) Ltd, Thames House, 63 Kingston Rd, New Malden, Surrey.
Showroom: list of dealers from firm; all offer planning and installation services.
QUALCAST Qualcast (Fleetway) Ltd, Charlton Rd, Edmonton, London N9.
Showroom: addresses of local stockists available from the firm. Some offer a planning service. (SA)
RANGER KITCHENS Barget Kitchens and Interiors Ltd, 2-4 Circus Rd, London NW8.
Showroom: contact the firm for address of your nearest dealer. Planning and installation services at each.
RATIONAL W F Rational (UK) Ltd, 18, Queen Square, Bristol.
Showroom: Rational Marketing Ltd, 171 Scudamore Rd, Leicester and 16/40 Cherrywood Rd, Bordesley Green, Birmingham. Contact firm for stockists. Planning service at each.
REGINA Becher Kitchens Ltd, Scotia House, Goldsworth Rd, Woking, Surrey.
Showroom: at Goldsworth Rd. Units available direct from firm. Contact them for address of your nearest dealer. Planning service at dealers. (SA)
SCHIFFINI Robert McCreanor Ltd, 147 Sloane St, London SW1.
Showrooms: at Sloane St, where address of nearest dealer is available. Design and planning services operated by main agent and dealers.
SCHREIBER Schreiber Furniture Ltd, East Rd, Harlow, Essex.
Showroom: at 9 Baker St, London W1 and stockists. List available from firm. All Schreiber Centres offer planning and installation services.
SENIOR CITIZEN Senior Citizen Cumbria Furniture, Cumbria

House, Blackdyke Rd, Kingstown Industrial Estate, Carlisle.
Showroom: on view at Disabled Centres and hospitals throughout UK. Write to Carlisle for list of local disabled and rehabilitation centres. Planning service. (SD, D)
SHERBORNE & SHERWOOD
Showroom: units available only from British Gas showrooms and the British Gas Built-in Kitchen Centre in The Building Centre, Store St, London WC1. Compute-a-Kitchen planning service at the Kitchen Centre; advice on basic kitchen layout from British Gas showrooms. Installation service available. (SA, D)
SIEMATIC SieMatic (UK) Ltd, 11-17 Fowler Rd, Hainault Industrial Estate, Ilford, Essex.
Showroom: Information Centre with 18 kitchens on show at Hainault. List of SieMatic centres and studios from firm. All SieMatic dealers offer a planning service and will arrange and supervise installation.
SMALLBONE Smallbone & Co (Devizes) Ltd, Unit 3, Garden Trading Estate, London Rd, Devizes, Wilts.
Showroom: Harrods, Knightsbridge, London SW1; 72 Gloucester Rd, London SW7; Unit 4, 91 Wimpole St, London W1; 21 London Rd, Tunbridge Wells; 19 Holywell Hill, St Albans; 46 King St, Knutsford; 12 Waterloo St, Clifton, Bristol; Unit 10-11 Nimrod Way, Elgar Rd, Reading, Berks. Contact head office at Reading address for brochures. Planning, installation and maintenance service.
SOLARBO Solarbo Fitments Ltd, PO Box 5, Commerce Way, Lancing, W Sussex.
Showroom: at Lancing, also 61 Ebury St, London SW1; 5 Ridgefield (off John Dalton St) Manchester; 32 Cheltenham Parade, Harrogate and at Casa Fina, 97 Regent St, Leamington Spa and 3 Broad St, Bath.
Planning and installation service. (SA)
SOLENT FURNITURE Solent Furniture Ltd, Pymore Mills, Bridport, Dorset.
Showroom: at Pymore Mills. Contact firm for a list of dealers. All offer planning service (SA).
STONEHAM DESIGNED KITCHENS Stoneham & Son (Deptford) Ltd, Powerscroft Rd, Footscray, Sidcup, Kent.
Showroom: at Sidcup and kitchen specialist retailers. List available from firm. All have planning and installation facilities.
SUPER MINI KITCHEN S.K.C. Ltd, 5 Fox Lane, Palmers Green, London N3.
Showroom: at above address where planning advice is also available. Kitchen supplied direct. The kitchen is in a cupboard and can be extended. Particularly suited to senior citizens' accommodation.
SYSTEM FLEX F. Llewellyn & Co Ltd, Carlton Works, Carlton St, Liverpool.
Showroom: apply to firm for literature on this range designed for disabled people. Planning advisory service. Furniture supplied direct to one's home. Easily fitted by a local handyman. Variable height units to suit different degrees of disability (D).
TIELSA Tielsa Kitchens Ltd, Wakefield Rd, Gildersome, Leeds.
Showroom: at retail outlets – list available from above address. Planning and installation services at each.
UBM UBM Building Supplies Ltd, Avon Works, Winterstoke Rd, Bristol.
Showroom: at 72 UBM outlets. Most operate a planning service. (SA)
UNITED KITCHENS United Kitchens Ltd, Crown Industrial Estate, Priorswood, Taunton, Somerset.
Showroom: at above address. List of stockists from firm. Planning service 40 miles radius, also in London.
WELLMANN Wellmann Ltd, Wakefield Rd, Gildersome, Leeds.
Showroom: Kitchens available through Intoto stores and Wellman specialists. Contact firm for address of nearest stockist. Design and planning service available via the dealer.
WINCHMORE FURNITURE Winchmore Furniture Ltd, Mildenhall, Suffolk.
Showroom: at Mildenhall and Taunton. Dealers nationwide: list from firm. All operate planning and installation services.
WOODSTOCK Woodstock Furniture Ltd, Pakenham St, Mount Pleasant, London WC1.
Showroom workshop: as above. All solid maple or cherry units made to order and supplied direct. Matching tables and other furniture. Design and installation service.
WRIGHTON F. Wrighton & Sons Ltd, Nazeing Rd, Nazeing, Essex.
Showroom: 3 Portman Sq. London W1. Dealers' list and brochures from firm. Most offer a planning service.
XEY Xey (UK) Ltd, 8 High St, Worthing, W Sussex.
Showroom: contact firm for dealer list. All maintain full displays and offer a design, planning and installation service.

The Sitting Room

WALLPAPERS AND FABRICS

Many of the wallpaper and fabric ranges below are also stocked by good stores and decorating shops throughout the country.
Laura Ashley, Carno, Powys, and branches throughout the country. Cheap wallpapers, often with small-scale, Victorian-inspired designs. Also cheap matching fabrics and inexpensive paints.
Coles of Mortimer Street, 18 Mortimer Street, London W1. Expensive but top-quality hand-printed wallpapers and related borders. Many 18th and 19th century designs, printed from the original wood blocks.
Coloroll. Attractive range of inexpensive machine-printed wallpapers, some with matching or co-ordinated fabrics. For nearest stockist, write to Riverside Mills, Crawford Street, Nelson, Lancs.
Crown Wallcoverings. Inexpensive wallpapers and wallcoverings, some with co-ordinating fabrics. Also bright primary-coloured collections of kitchen and bathroom vinyls.
Designers' Guild, 277 King's Road, London SW3. Expensive but stylish machine-printed wallpapers and vinyl wallcoverings, usually with matching or co-ordinated fabrics.
Habitat branches throughout the country. Good modern wallpaper and fabric designs, at reasonable prices.
House of MayFair. Make the MayFair ranges of inexpensive wallpapers and vinyl wallcoverings. Write for stockist to: House of MayFair, Cramlington New Town, Northumberland.
ICI make medium-priced Vymura vinyl wallcoverings. For nearest stockist write to: ICI, Wexham Road, Slough.
David Ison, 75 Newman Street, London W1. Importers of very exclusive and very expensive wallpapers and fabrics from America and France.
Marks and Spencer p.l.c., Baker Street, London W1. Branches throughout the country. Popular range of attractive wallpapers.
Osborne & Little, 304 Kings Road, London SW3. Beautiful range of wallpapers and matching or related fabrics. Very good on textural designs: i.e. dragged, stippled, marbelised effects.
Paper Moon, 12 Kingswell, 58-62 Heath Street, London NW3. Importers of exciting Scandinavian collections of papers and fabrics – lots of bright, clear colours and sharp designs. Tend to be expensive.
Arthur Sanderson & Sons, 52 Berners Street, London W1. Make a wide range of machine-printed and hand-printed wallpapers, many with matching or co-ordinated fabrics.
Storeys. Make inexpensive wallpapers and vinyl wallcoverings, some with matching or co-ordinated fabrics. For nearest stockist write to: Storeys, Whitecross, Lancaster.
Brian Yates Interiors, 3 Riverside Park, Caton Road, Lancaster. Importers of designer collections of papers and co-ordinating fabrics at all prices – strong geometrics, exotic colourways and subtle stripes.

TRADITIONAL FABRICS

G.P. & J. Baker, 18 Berners Street, London W1. (Showroom only; write for nearest stockist.) Marvellous range of printed cottons and glazed chintzes, based on 18th and 19th century designs; some with matching plain fabrics, and matching wallpapers.
Colefax & Fowler Chintz Shop, 149 Ebury Street, London SW1. All kinds of traditionally-designed fabrics; emphasis on glazed cottons.
Fischbacher, Threeways House, 42 Clipstone Street, London W1. (Showroom only: write for nearest stockist.) Make the much-acclaimed Collier Campbell furnishing collections, of modern abstract designs.
Charles Hammond, 165 Sloane Street, London SW1. Superior interior decorator's shop. Superb but highly expensive imported fabrics: their own-label fabrics are as good and much cheaper.
Margo International make cotton lace in Victorian and Edwardian designs. Available from stores, or mail order from: Anna's Choice, Bedford Mills, Kilmarnock, Ayrshire.
Marvic Textiles, 12 Mortimer Street, London W1. (Showroom only: write for nearest stockist.) Importers of beautiful but expensive upholstery fabrics. A wide range of moiré (i.e. watered silk) effects and good colour range of glazed cottons.
Monkwell Fabrics, Monkwell House, 10-12 Wharfdale Road, Bournemouth. (Showroom only: write for nearest stockist.) Excellent range of upholstery fabrics: tapestry weave and heavy cottons in geometric, stylised flowers and plains.
Moygashel, 17 Bedford Row, London WC1. (Showroom only: write for nearest stockist.) Well-known for dress fabrics, Moygashel have recently launched an exciting furnishing collection, based on paisleys, ikats and old designs. Realistic prices.
Parkertex, 18 Berners Street, London W1. (Showroom only: write for nearest stockist.) Good, traditional woven fabrics. A wide range of cotton and synthetic velvets, as well as linen unions, and textured weaves.
Sekers, 15-19 Cavendish Place, London W1. (Showroom only: write for nearest stockist.) Extensive colour range of plain dupions, silks and chintzes; also subtle seersuckers and printed cottons.
Warner & Sons, 7-11 Noel Street, London W1. (Showroom only: write for nearest stockist.) Make mainly printed fabrics, many of them glazed cottons. Also make cotton laces.

BUDGET FABRICS

Felt & Hessian Shop, 34 Greville Street, London EC1. Sells cheap muslims, jutes, calicos etc, plus inexpensive felts and hessians in a vast range of colours. Mail order available.
Sue Foster Fabrics, PO Box 26, Portsmouth, Hants. A mail order service supplying a wide range of well-known manufacturers' fabrics at discounts. If you know the fabric you want, write for a quotation.
John Lewis, Oxford Street, W1, and Lewis Partnership stores throughout the country. Sell most manufacturers' fabrics at competitive prices, but their own Jonelle ranges are especially good value – particularly the dupions and linen unions.
Limerick Linens, 117 Victoria Avenue, Southend on Sea, Essex. Mail order only. Sell white and coloured sheeting, cotton damask, cambric and black and white ticking by the metre – all good for making up cheap curtains.

Nice Irma's Floating Carpet, 46 Goodge Street, London W1. A wide range of imported Indian fabrics, including plain and printed cottons, colourful ikats and patterned velvets. Direct and mail order.
Russell & Chapple, 23 Monmouth Street, London WC2. Sells hessians, jutes, cotton duck, etc, direct and mail order.

MODERN FURNITURE

To see the best in London, visit:
Coexistence, 17 Canonbury Lane, London N1; 13 Whitcomb Street, London WC2; and 10 Argyll Street, Bath, Avon. The best of old and new furniture (mostly new, cool and purist), plus wallpapers, fabrics, lighting, etc. All hand-picked with an overall look in mind.
The Conran Shop, 77 Fulham Road, London SW3. Modern classic furniture, English and Continental antiques, and whatever catches the discriminating eyes of the directors as they travel the world.
General Trading Company, 144 Sloane Street, London SW3. Best-known as an up-market gift shop, their Modern Living department is an excellent source of modern furniture and furnishings with co-ordinated accessories.
Harrods, Knightsbridge, London SW1. Literally acres of modern and traditional furniture showrooms. Useful if you want to know what's on the market, but gives no guidance in matters of taste.
Heal & Sons, 196 Tottenham Court Road, London W1. Recently re-launched by Terence Conran, this store is now the Mecca for people seeking top quality and design-conscious modern furniture. As it's big enough to offer quantity too, if you can only visit one place, make it Heal's.
Homeworks, Dove Walk, 107a Pimlico Road, London SW1. Import superb modern Italian furniture, and Interlübke storage from Germany, for which full planning and installation service is provided.
Liberty's, Regent Street, London W1. Their Modern Furniture department has a wide but highly discriminating range, often with designs exclusive to them.
Oscar Woollens Interiors International, 421 Finchley Road, London NW3. Exclusive, expensive and uncompromising modern furniture. The very best in starkly purist international design.
Charles Page, 61 Fairfax Road, Swiss Cottage, London NW6. Classic modern furniture that's easy-to-live-with rather than stark. Also lots of exclusive rattan furniture.

MODERN UNIT SEATING

Caspa Furniture, Lysander Road, Bower Hill, Melksham, Wilts.
Collins & Hayes, Ponswood, Hastings, Sussex.
Hitch Mylius, Spender House, Brettenham Road, London N18.
HK Furniture, Omega Works, Hermitage Road, London N4.
Michael Tyler Furniture, Castleham Road, Castleham Industrial Estate, St Leonards on Sea, East Sussex.

SOFAS AND ARMCHAIRS

Derwent Upholstery, Greenhill Industrial Estate, Greenhill Lane, Riddings, Derbyshire. Make a wide range of upholstery sold through most department stores.
Duresta Upholstery, Leopold Street, Long Eaton, Nottingham. Make classical upholstery by traditional methods, and use designer-fabrics. Sold through good quality furnishing stores.
Sinclair Melson, Unit 5, Hampton Farm Industrial Estate, Bolney Way, Hampton Road West, Feltham, Middx. Make a wide range of upholstery from traditional sofas to unit seating. Ordered through local decorator shops.
The following manufacturers sell direct to the public through their own shops, and should therefore be able to offer extra-good value.
Delcor Upholstery, Delcor House, Double Row, Seaton Delaval, Northumberland. Other branches at: 18 Park Walk, off Fulham Road, London SW10; 12 The Downs, Altrincham, Cheshire; 46-48 New Bridge Street, Newcastle-upon-Tyne; and 19 Yarm Lane, Stockton-on-Tees.
Kingcome, 304 Fulham Road, London SW10. The Rolls-Royce of upholstery manufacturers. Very expensive, custom-made sofas, etc, intended to last a lifetime.
Tulley's, 289-297 Fulham Road, London SW10 and 1 Ward Street, off North Street, Guildford. Make a wide selection of calico-covered sofas which can be covered in customers' own fabric. Medium price-range.
Wesley-Barrell, 86 Tottenham Court Road; 86 Bull Street, Birmingham; Queens Avenue, Clifton, Bristol; 105-107 Deansgate, Manchester; 3 Bridge Street, Witney, Oxon. Also available mail order from: Park Street, Charlbury, Oxford.

MIRROR

The Glass and Glazing Federation (see general addresses) will supply a list of local glass merchants – and answer specialist queries on mirror. Most good glass merchants will stock clear, tinted and antiqued float glass mirror.
Chelsea Artisans, Unit 2, Ferry Works, Summer Road, Thames Ditton, Surrey make Diamond Mirror. This is clear or tinted float glass mirror that has been backed by foam and insulation board. Should it get broken, it stays safely in place.
Garfield Glass, West Road, London N17 make clear and tinted float glass Mirrorwall tiles. They are self-adhesive and come in various sizes.
T & W Ide, Glasshouse Fields, London E1, make Bronzide Quartz, where acid, applied to the back of clear or tinted float glass mirror, creates dramatic swirls of colour.
Opals (Mirror-Flex) Company, Herbert Road, Clacton-on-Sea, Essex, make Mirror-Flex. This consists of tiny tiles of clear or tinted mirror on a fabric backing, for glueing to surfaces. It can be cut to shape between tiles and will bend round curves.
Rohm & Haas (UK), Plastics Department, Lennig House, 2 Mason's Avenue, Croydon, manufacture clear or tinted Oraglass Mirror. This is made from shatterproof sheets of silvered acrylic, which is much lighter than float glass, warm-surfaced, and can be sawn to shape – but it will scratch if badly mistreated.

LIGHTING

British Home Stores throughout the country. Cheap but good lighting. Outdoor lighting and spotlights are particularly good value.
John Cullen Lighting Design, 1 Woodfall Court, Smith Street, London SW3. Modern lighting – and a showroom where you can experiment with different lighting effects in a room-setting.
Habitat branches throughout the country. Excellent range of well-designed and reasonably priced lighting.
John Lewis, Oxford Street, London W1. Good for traditional table lamps. They offer a vast selection of ceramic bases.
London Lighting Company, 133-135 Fulham Road, London SW3. Very sophisticated lighting, much of it Italian.
Mr. Light, 275 Fulham Road, London SW10 and 279 King's Road, London SW3. A wide range of fittings to suit most tastes and pockets.
Christopher Wray's Lighting Emporium, 600 King's Road, London SW6. Marvellous range of reproduction and antique Victorian and Edwardian light fittings and shades. Emporiums also at Bristol and Leeds.

ANTIQUE FURNITURE

The following warehouse-style shops offer good selections:
Austin's of Peckham, 11-23 Peckham Rye, London SE15 and 39-41 Brayards Road, London SE15.
The Furniture Cave, 533 King's Road, London SW10.

AUCTION ROOMS

For expensive antiques:
Bonham's, Montpelier Street, London SW7.
Christie's, 8 King Street, London SW1.
Phillips, Blenstock House, 7 Blenheim Street, London W1.
Sotheby's, 34 and 35 New Bond Street, London W1.

For medium-priced antiques:
Christie's South Kensington, 85 Old Brompton Road, London SW7.
Harvey's Auctions, 22-23 Long Acre, London WC2.
Phillips West, 2 Salem Road, London W2.
Sotheby's Belgravia, 19 Motcomb Street, London SW1.

For cheaper antiques, and 20th century furniture, furnishings and equipment:
Bonham's New Chelsea Galleries, 65-69 Lots Road, London SW10.
Lots Road Galleries, 71 Lots Road, London SW10.
Phillips Marylebone, Hayes Place, Lissom Grove, London NW1.

STORAGE:

Acmetrack, Holland Road, Hurst Green, Oxted, Surrey. Floor and ceiling tracks with sliding doors, to provide alcove or wall-to-wall storage.
Behr, 148 Regent's Park Road, London NW1. (Showroom and stockist information only.) Beautiful but expensive imported storage, in many ranges.
Bruynzeel Monta International, Stocklake, Aylesbury, Buckinghamshire. (Stockist information only.) Industrial-inspired storage in natural, unsealed pine.
Cubestore, 58 Pembroke Road, London W8. Shop and showroom; mail order available. Modular system based on a cube-shape.
Gratnell's, 256 Church Road, London E10. Shop and showroom; mail order available. Interior fittings for built-in storage, consisting of clear perspex drawers and nylon-coated mesh baskets, with nylon-coated metal uprights from which to hang them.
Hulsta, 22 Bruton Street, London W1. (Showroom and stockist information only.) More beautiful but expensive imported storage.
Interlübke, 239 High Road, Greenwich, London SE10. Highly design-conscious German storage in many ranges and finishes.
McIntosh, Mitchelson Drive, Kirkaldy, Scotland. Unusual and stylish traditional free-standing storage – bookcases and display cases, etc.
Meredew, Dunhams Lane, Letchworth Garden City, Herts. Traditional dining and living room storage; modern bedroom storage: in a wide range of wood veneers and a tinted wood.
MFI Centres throughout the country. Cheap free-standing wardrobe units that can be made to look built-in with fascia boards. Also Panel Glide, a very cheap system of floor and ceiling tracks with sliding doors.
Practical Styling, 16-18 St Giles High Street, Centre Point, London WC2. Good source of shiny metal high-tech storage, and free-standing garment rails in bright colours.
Queensway Discount Warehouses throughout the country. Cheap free-standing wardrobe units that can be made to look built-in with fascia boards.
Shelfstore, 59 New King's Road,

London SW6. Direct and mail order. Industrial-inspired storage in natural but sealed pine.
Solarbo Fitments, PO Box 5, Commerce Way, Lancing, West Sussex. Make Spacemaker Storobe, a sliding door wardrobe system for alcoves and wall-to-wall. Also panelled wardrobe doors and a choice of interior fittings.
Strachan, Grastyn Works, Cross Green Way, Leeds. Traditional and modern fitted bedroom furniture in wood veneers and plastic laminates.
Ulferts, St George's House, 12b St George Street, London W1. (Showroom and stockist information only.) Beautiful but expensive imported storage.
Younger Furniture, Monier Road, Bow, London E3. Living and dining room storage, including a large range of dressers and bookcases.

The Dining Room

For curtains and furniture, see the relevant sections in The Sitting Room.

BLINDS

Blind Alley, 27 Chalk Farm Road, London NW1. Will screen-print, air-brush or hand-paint roller blinds. Can match designs – say a blind to a tile.
Dean's Blinds (Putney), Unit 4, Haslemere Industrial Estate, Ravensbury Terrace, London SW18. Make all types of blinds and awnings. Also sell wooden roller kits for DIY blinds.
Eaton Bag Company, 16 Manette Street, London W1. Make split-bamboo blinds to measure.
Faber Blinds, Viking House, Kangley Bridge Road, Sydenham, London SE26. Supply vertical louvre, venetian and roller blinds; also awnings.
Habitat, with branches throughout the country, sell wooden roller kits for DIY blinds. Also sell Pleatex paper blinds and split-bamboo blinds.
John Lewis, Oxford Street, London W1. Sell wooden roller kits for DIY blinds, as well as spray-on fabric stiffener. Stock a wide range of conventional roller and venetian blinds, but also sell screen-printed roller blinds with crisp, graphic designs.
Luxaflex, Hunter Douglas, The Industrial Estate, Larkhall, Lanarkshire. Make roller blinds, and venetian blinds (with extra-fine slats), in a wide variety of designer-colours.
Sander-Shade, 220 Queenstown Road, London SW8; also Sander-Shade Shop at Harrods. Will make up roller blinds in your own fabric, laminating it (even cotton lace) for a practical surface.
Silent Gliss, Star Lane, Margate, Kent. Make all kinds of curtain tracks, etc, but also make Roman blind and Austrian blind kits.
Tidmarsh & Sons, Transenna Works, Laycock Street, London N1. Make venetian blinds with natural or stained cedarwood slats. Also Pinoleum woven-reed roll-up blinds, and wooden roller-shutters.

The Bedroom

And So To Bed, 7 New King's Road and 640 King's Road, London SW6, 96b Camden High Street, London NW1. Antique and reproduction beds, mostly in brass.
Dunlopillo: make top quality foam mattresses. For leaflet on how to make a slatted wood bed base, send SAE to 'Foam', Dunlop Press Office, Dunlop House, Ryder Street, London SW1.
Futon Company, 267 Archway Road, London N6 and 654a Fulham Road, SW6. Futons, or slatted wood base and bedroll kit for making up your own futon.
Gold Plan Ltd, 13 Golden Square, London W1. All kinds of space-saving beds. Mail order available.
Heal's, 196 Tottenham Court Road, London W1. Produce handmade beds to order.
London Bedding Centre, 26-27 Sloane Street, London SW1. Good selection of beds.
London Sofa Bed Centre, 185 Tottenham Court Road, London W1. Good selection of sofa-beds: deliver nationally.
The National Bedding Federation, 251 Brompton Road, London SW3. A trade association to which most top manufacturers belong. Send SAE for their free advisory leaflets about beds.
Simply Sofa Beds, 130 Notting Hill Gate, London W11. Good selection of sofa-beds: deliver nationally.
Wesley Barrel, 86 Tottenham Court Road, London W1 and branches around the country. Manufacturers of sofa-beds sold direct to the public.

The Bathroom

Albion Hardware, Simon House, Sunderland Road, Sandy, Beds. Make matching porcelain WCs, basins and bidets (no baths) in choice of three pretty patterns.
Aqualisa, Flyer Way, London Road, Westerham, Kent. Make shower fittings.
Armitage Shanks, Armitage, Rugeley, Staffs. Make wide range of bathroom suites and matching accessories. London showroom at **The Better Bathroom Centre**, 303 High Holborn, WC1.
B & Q warehouse/superstores throughout the country. Sell cut-price package deals of bath, basin and loo.
The Bath Studio, 332 Uxbridge Road, Hatch End, Middx. Sole importers of the superb Arne Jacobsen Vola tap.
The Bathroom & Shower Centre, 204 Great Portland Street, London W1. Showroom displaying Twyfords bathroom suites and Walker Crossweller shower fittings. (See under Twyfords and Walker Crossweller.)
Bonsack Baths, Town Wharf, Town Wharf Lane, Rickmansworth. Make fibreglass baths in exclusive shapes, colours and patterns. Sell at Godfrey Bonsack, 14 Mount Street, London W1 or the Bonsack Shop at Harrods, Knightsbridge, London SW1. Very expensive.
British Bathroom Centre, 602-604 Seven Sisters Road, London N15. Sell wide range of British and imported bathrooms. Can apply choice of nine patterns to baths, basins or tiles in their nearby kilns.
The Building Centre, 26 Store Street, London W1. Displays a wide range of bathroom suites and bathroom equipment. Supplies information on manufacturers as well as bathroom planning.
Chloride Shires, Park Road, Guiseley, Leeds. Make bathroom suites.
Czech & Speake, 39c Jermyn Street, London SW1. Sell their own Edwardian range of reproduction baths, basins and accessories; also modern imported fitttings.
Dolphin Showers, Worcester. Make shower fittings.
C P Hart, Newnham Terrace, Hercules Road, London SE1. Sells vast range of bathroom suites and accessories, both domestic and imported, in 58,000 square feet of showroom space.
Heatons Bathrooms, Derby Way, Euroway Industrial Estate, Hellaby, Rotheram. Make bathroom suites.
Ideal Standard, PO Box 60, National Avenue, Hull, North Humberside. Make bathroom suites in sleek and stylish modern designs. All baths are acrylic.
Jacuzzi Whirlpool Bath & Spa Centre, 157-158 Sloane Street, London SW1. Sell Jacuzzi systems only.
Majestic Shower Company, The Square, Sawbridgeworth, Herts. Make handsome ranges of shower enclosures.
Royal Doulton Bathrooms, Whieldon Road, Stoke-on-Trent, Staffs. Make wide range of bathroom suites; also vanity units with tops post-formed to take their basins; shower surrounds and shower trays.
St Marcos, 45 Sloane Street, London SW1. Sell the best in Italian bathroom design; co-ordination a strong point.
Texas Homecare Warehouse/superstores throughout the country. Sell cut-price package deals of bath, basin and loo.
Twyfords Bathrooms, PO Box 23, Stoke-on-Trent. Make bathroom suites.
Vogue Bathrooms, Bilston Works, Batsman's Hill Road, Bilston, W. Midlands. Make cast iron baths. Vogue supply a free Bathroom Ideas booklet, available from the Bathroom Ideas Bureau, 11a West Halkin Street, London SW1.
Walker Crossweller, Wheddon Works, Cheltenham, Glos. Make shower fittings.

TILES

H & R Johnson, Highgate Tile Works, Tunstall, Stoke-on-Trent, Staffs. Britain's largest manufacturer of ceramic floor and wall tiles. An enormous selection of plains and patterns, all at very reasonable prices.
Minton Hollins, part of H & R Johnson at the above address. Make the Gladstone Range of reproduction Victorian ceramic wall tiles. Enchantingly pretty, and very reasonably priced.
Rye Tiles, 12 Connaught Street, London W2 and the Old Brewery, Wishward, Rye, Sussex. Ceramic tiles made to order in a choice of 50-odd designs in 100-odd colours. Hand-painted tiles are available, either for use singly, or for combining to create a mural – and you can supply your own design reference.
World's End Tiles, 9 Langton Street, London SW10. Wonderful collection of modern and traditional ceramic wall tiles, mostly available with co-ordinating border tiles. Each design can be screened in any one of 35 colours. To see the complete range of possibilities, visit the showroom at: British Rail Yard, Silverthorne Road, Battersea, London SW8.

Paint and Wallpaper Information Chart

GENERAL COVERAGE GUIDE FOR COMMERCIAL PAINTS

1 LITRE OF PRODUCT	...COVERAGE TO GIVEN NO. OF SQ METRES
PRIMER	
WOOD	12
METAL	13
PLASTER	15
UNDERCOATING	15
GLOSS PAINT	15
EGGSHELL AND FLAT PAINT	15
EMULSION PAINT	11–15
THIXOTROPIC PAINT (GEL)	12–14
EXTERIOR WALL PAINT	6

WALLPAPER CODE: SYMBOLS AND INSTRUCTIONS

- SPONGEABLE; WIPE DOWN GENTLY
- WASHABLE; WASH DOWN WITH A CLOTH AND WARM SOAPY WATER
- SUPERWASHABLE; CAN WITHSTAND VIGOROUS WASHING
- SCRUBBABLE; YOU CAN USE A CREAM CLEANSER FOR STUBBORN MARKS
- REASONABLE LIGHT FASTNESS
- GOOD LIGHT FASTNESS
- DRY STRIPPABLE
- PEELABLE; LEAVES A BACKING PAPER WHEN YOU STRIP IT OFF THE WALL
- READY PASTED
- PASTE THE WALL, NOT THE PAPER
- CO-ORDINATED FABRIC IS AVAILABLE
- DIRECTION OF PATTERN FOR HANGING
- REVERSE ALTERNATE LENGTHS TO MATCH PATTERN

THE RIGHT PAINTS FOR THE RIGHT SURFACE

SURFACE	LOCATION	RECOMMENDED PAINT ETC.
NEW WOODWORK	INDOORS	TREAT KNOTS WITH KNOTTING. APPLY WOOD PRIMER, UNDERCOAT AND GLOSS OR EGGSHELL PAINT.
	OUTDOORS	TREAT KNOTS, APPLY WOOD PRIMER AND TWO COATS OF UNDERCOAT. FINISH WITH GLOSS PAINT.
PREVIOUSLY PAINTED WOODWORK	INDOORS	UNDERCOAT IF DOING EXTREME COLOUR CHANGE, THEN GLOSS PAINT.
	OUTDOORS	PATCH PRIME BARE PARTS, TWO UNDERCOATS, GLOSS PAINT.
CEILINGS AND WALLS (NEW AND UNTREATED)	ANY ROOM	USE EMULSION PAINT UNTIL THE PLASTER HAS DRIED OUT. THEN GLOSS OR EGGSHELL IF PREFERRED.
CEILINGS AND WALLS (EMULSION PAINT)	ANY ROOM	EMULSION PAINT, GLOSS OR EGGSHELL.
CEILINGS AND WALLS (GLOSS PAINT)	ANY ROOM	UNDERCOAT, THEN EGGSHELL, GLOSS OR EMULSION PAINT.
CEILINGS AND WALLS (WALLPAPER)	ANY ROOM	EMULSION PAINT, MATT OR GREEN.
METAL WINDOW FRAMES	ANY	ONE COAT OF METAL PRIMER, UNDERCOAT, GLOSS PAINT.
METAL GUTTERING AND PIPES	OUTDOOR	PRIME WITH METAL PRIMER, UNDERCOAT, THEN GLOSS PAINT. TWO COATS OF BLACK BITUMINOUS PAINT INSIDE THE GUTTERS GIVE EXTRA WATER RESISTANCE.
RADIATORS	INDOORS	EMULSION PAINT, GLOSS OR SPECIAL RADIATOR PAINT.

WALLPAPER QUANTITY GUIDE

HEIGHT IN METRES FROM SKIRTING (columns); MEASUREMENT IN METRES ROUND WALLS INCLUDING DOORS AND WINDOWS (rows); NUMBER OF ROLLS REQUIRED

MEASUREMENT IN METRES ROUND WALLS INCLUDING DOORS AND WINDOWS	2·0 to 2·25	2·25 to 2·50	2·50 to 2·75	2·75 to 3·0	3·0 to 3·25	3·25 to 3·50	3·50 to 3·75	3·75 to 4·0
11·0	5	5	6	6	7	7	8	8
11·0	5	6	7	7	8	8	9	9
12·0	6	6	7	8	8	9	9	10
13·0	6	7	8	8	9	10	10	10
14·0	7	7	8	9	10	10	11	11
15·0	7	8	9	9	£0	11	12	12
16·0	8	8	9	10	11	11	12	13
17·0	8	9	10	10	11	12	13	14
18·0	9	9	10	11	12	13	14	15
19·0	9	10	11	12	13	14	15	16
20·0	9	10	11	12	13	14	15	16
21·0	10	11	12	13	14	15	16	17
22·0	10	11	13	14	15	16	17	18
23·0	11	12	13	14	15	17	18	19
24·0	11	12	14	15	16	17	18	20
25·0	12	13	14	15	17	18	19	20
26·0	12	13	15	16	17	19	20	21
27·0	13	14	15	17	18	19	21	22
28·0	13	14	16	17	19	20	21	23
29·0	13	15	16	18	19	21	22	24
30·0	14	15	17	18	20	21	23	24

INDEX

ACKNOWLEDGEMENTS

Designers: Bob Hook and Ivor Claydon
Artists: Ray and Corrine Burrows,
Grundy and Northedge Designers
Artwork of batterie de cuisine, pages 125-127 courtesy of David Mellor Ltd

Photographic credits
Key: GH – Good Housekeeping: EWA – Elizabeth Whiting Associates
Title page: Jan Baldwin/GH; *pages 6/7* Julian Nieman, Richard Davies, Jon Cook/GH; *8/9* Richard Davies/GH, Di Lewis/GH, Karl Dietrich Buhler; *10/11* Michael Nicholson/EWA; *12* Ann Kelley/EWA; *13* John Cook/GH; *14* Ann Kelley/EWA; *15* David Shapely, David Shapely; *16* Ann Kelley/EWA, Spike-Powell/EWA; *17* David Brittain/GH; *18* David Brittain/GH; *19* David Brittain/GH; *20* Spike Powell/GH; *21* Spike Powell/GH; *22* John Cook/GH; *23* Tim Street Porter/EWA, Richard Davies; *24/25* David Brittain/GH; *25* David Brittain; *27* Jan Baldwin; *28/29* Dennis Stone/GH; *34/35* John Cook/GH; *36* Dennis Stone/GH, David Brittain/GH; *37* David Brittain; *40* John Cook/GH; *41* John Cook/GH; *42* Robert Golden/GH; *43* David Brittain/GH; *52/53* David Brittain/GH; *54* Michael Nicholson/EWA; *55* John Cook/GH; *56* Michael Dunne; *57* David Brittain/GH, Spike Powell/GH; *58* Spike Powell, Richard Davies/GH; *59* David Brittain/GH; *60* Spike Powell/GH; *61* Dennis Stone/GH; *62* Dennis Stone; *63* Geoffrey Frosh/GH; *64/65* Dennis Stone; *66* David Brittain, David Brittain; *67* David Brittain, David Brittain, *68* John Cook/GH; *69* Jan Baldwin/GH, Michael Dunne; *70* Dennis Stone/GH; *71* David Brittain; *72* John Cook/GH, David Brittain/GH; *73* Richard Davies; *74* Dennis Stone/GH; *75* David Brittain/GH; *76* David Brittain/GH; *77* David Brittain/GH, Dennis Stone/GH; *78* David Brittain/GH; *78/79* David Brittain/GH; *80* David Brittain/GH; *81* Dennis Stone/GH; *82* Michael Nicholson/EWA; *83* Michael Nicholson/EWA; *84/85* Jan Baldwin/GH; *86* David Brittain/GH, David Brittain/GH; *87* David Brittain/GH; *88* Dennis Stone/GH; *89* Dennis Stone/GH; *90/91* David Brittain/GH; *92* David Brittain/GH; *93* David Brittain/GH; *94* David Brittain/GH; *95* John Cook; *96* David Brittain/GH; *97* John Cook/GH, John Cook/GH; *98* John Cook/GH; *99* Dennis Stone/GH, Jan Baldwin/GH, John Cook/GH; *100/101* David Brittain/GH, Di Lewis/GH; *103* Clive Helm/EWA, *104* Dennis Stone/GH, David Brittain/GH; *105* Michael Nicholson/EWA; *106* Spike Powell/EWA; *107* Michael Nicholson/EWA, Dennis Stone; *108* Dennis Stone/GH; *109* Dennis Stone/GH; *110* David Brittain/GH; *111* Dennis Stone/GH; *112* Richard Davies/GH, Spike Powell/GH; *113* David Brittain/GH; *114* John Cook/GH, John Cook/GH; *115* David Brittain; *116/117* John Cook/GH; *118* John Cook/GH, David Brittain/GH; *119* David Brittain/GH, Geoffrey Frosh/GH; *120* Robert Golden/GH; *121* Spike Powell/GH; *123* Brian Morris/GH; *128/129* Spike Powell/GH; *131* John Cook/GH; *132* John Cook/GH; *133* John Cook/GH; *134* John Cook/GH; *135* John Cook/GH; *137* Peter Giles/GH; *138* John Cook/GH; *139* Michael Nicholson/GH; *140/141* Slavin/GH; *142* Michael Nicholson/EWA; *143* Geoffrey Frosh/Gh; *146* Anthony Blake/GH, Dennis Stone/GH; *147* Spike Powell/GH; *149* Frederick Mancini/GH, Anthony Blake/GH, Paul Williams/GH, Graham Henderson/EWA, Dennis Stone/GH; *150* Paul Kemp/Ebury Press, Bill Richmond/GH; *151* Dennis Stone/GH; *153* Melvin Grey/GH, Philip Dowell/GH, Spike Powell/GH; *154* Ebury Press, Bill Richmond; *155* Spike Powell; *157* Bryce Attwell/GH, Ebury Press, Robert Golden/GH; *158* John Cook/GH; *159* David Shapely/GH; *160* Ebury Press; *160/161* Paul Kemp/GH; *161* Dennis Stone/GH, Anthony Blake/GH; *162* Di Lewis/GH; *163* Dennis Stone/GH; *164* Paul Kemp/Ebury Press; *165* John Cook/GH, Philip Pace/GH; *166* Melvin Grey/GH, Dennis Stone/GH; *167* Dennis Stone/GH; *168* Michael Nicholson, Ebury Press; *169* Bryce Attwell/GH; *170/171* Robert Golden/GH; *172* John Cook/GH; *173* Di Lewis/GH, Dennis Stone/GH; *176* Michael Nicholson; *177* David Lloyd; *179* Peter Rauter/GH, Clive Helm; *180/181* Spike Powell; *183* Di Lewis/GH; *184* John Cook/GH, David Brittain/GH; *185* Di Lewis/GH; *186* Di Lewis/GH; *189* Di Lewis/GH; *191* Jan Baldwin/GH; *192/193* Jan Baldwin/GH; *193* Jan Baldwin/GH, Jan Baldwin/GH; *194/195* Octopus Books; *196/197* Michael Dunne; *198* Michael Nicholson/EWA; *199* David Brittain/GH; *200* Michael Dunne, Michael Nicholson/EWA; *201* Michael Nicholson/EWA; *202* Camera Press; *203* Geoffrey Frosh/EWA; *204/205* Octopus Books; *206* Spike Powell/EWA, Dennis Stone/GH; *208* Octopus Books; *209* Michael Dunne; *210* Octopus Books; *211* Michael Nicholson/EWA, Ann Kelley/EWA; *213* Karl Dietrich Buhler/EWA, Michael Nicholson/EWA.